Teaching
Holocaust Literature

To Elie Wiesel, with admiration and appreciation

Related Title

Teaching and Studying the Holocaust
Samuel Totten and Stephen Feinberg, Editors
0-205-18495-2

Teaching Holocaust Literature

Edited by

Samuel Totten

University of Arkansas, Fayetteville

Foreword by

Israel W. Charny

Director, Institute on the Holocaust and Genocide, Jerusalum

Allyn and Bacon

Boston ▪ London ▪ Toronto ▪ Sydney ▪ Tokyo ▪ Singapore

Series editor: *Traci Mueller*
Series editorial assistant: *Bridget Keane*
Marketing manager: *Stephen Smith*

Library of Congress Cataloging-in-Publication Data

Teaching Holocaust literature / edited by Samuel Totten.

     p. cm.

  Includes bibliographical references and index.

  ISBN 0-205-27402-1

  1. Holocaust, Jewish (1939–1945), in literature—Study and teaching. I. Totten, Samuel.

PN56.H55 T43 2001

940.53'18'071—dc21   00-061856

Cover photo: Shraga Wainer. Courtesy of the United States Holocaust Memorial Museum.

Acknowledgments

    Chart on p. 90 adapted by permission of Sundance Publishing.

    Uri Orlev, *Island on Bird Street.* Excerpts shown on pp. 108, 111–114, and 116–119 reprinted by permission of Houghton Mifflin Company.

    Dan Pagis, "Written in Pencil in the Sealed Railway-Car," p. 147. From *Points of Departure,* Jewish Publication Society, 1982. Used by permission.

    Yevgeny Yevtushenko, "Babi Yar." Extracts shown on pp. 167–168 reprinted by permission of Yevgeny Yevtushenko.

    Moses Shulstein, "I Saw a Mountain," pp. 182–184. Mindele Wajsman and Bea Stadtler (trans.), in Michael Berenbaum (ed.), *The World Must Know: The History of the Holocaust as Told in the United States Holocaust Memorial Museum* (Boston: Little, Brown, 1993). Reprinted by permission of the United States Holocaust Memorial Museum.

    Charlotte Delbo, "This Black Dot," pp. 187–188. From *Auschwitz and After* (1995). Reprinted by permission of Yale University Press.

    Hannah Senesh, "Blessed Is the Match," p. 189. Quoted in Linda Atkinson, *In Kindling Flame: The Story of Hanna Senesh.* Copyright © 1985 by Linda Atkinson. Reprinted by permission of HarperCollins Publishing.

Printed in the United States of America

10   9   8   7   6   5   4   3   2   1   04   03   02   01   00

CONTENTS

FOREWORD

DR. ISRAEL W. CHARNY

Director, Institute on the Holocaust and Genocide
Jerusalem, Israel

Teaching Holocaust Literature is a wonderfully helpful book for the tens of thousands of teachers in the English-speaking world who are teaching about the Holocaust in their classrooms. The book presents a wide range of suggestions, illustrations, and reports of teaching methods that offer practical guidance to educators who design and organize curricular units and lesson plans in their everyday work. Many of the chapters are beautifully written; and in many, one also encounters the artfulness and skill of the authors as teachers working with their students.

The multiple goals the authors set for the teacher to assist students include (1) confronting the extent of the injustices and murderous actions of the Nazis; (2) recognizing the different roles of victim, oppressor, bystander, and rescuer—which were assumed or thrust upon people during the Holocaust—and their choices or lack of choices; (3) making important and unique distinctions regarding the various nuances and shades of gray concerning the actions of individuals and groups; (4) analyzing the corruption of language cultivated by the Nazis; (5) recognizing the deeds of resistance and heroism in ghettos and concentration camps; and (6) exploring spiritual resistance which portrays the dignity of an individual or a people whose spirits transcended the evil of their murderers.

The editor/compiler/author, Samuel Totten, is a kind, caring man. The reports of his own teaching experiences, along with the reports of the other educators whose works he has chosen, express a deep respect and caring for human life, which is, in fact, the essential meaning of the Holocaust. As one of the contributors, Rebecca Aupperle, aptly puts it: "I teach [the Holocaust] because I see it as a perfect case study of a terrible event done by one group of human beings to another that could have been stopped at any point along the way if the majority of citizens witnessing it had mounted a challenge against the perpetrators."

The book also provides a rich array of reports of student responses. Beyond being inherently interesting, these also illustrate and comment upon the high frequency of misconceptions and misunderstanding of the Holocaust by students in our contemporary world who translate reports of the Holocaust into the framework of their daily experiences and do not fathom the agony, or the courage, or the evil that was evident in the Holocaust. Many of the responses show us too clearly students busy at their tasks of surviving as students and trying to get good grades for getting into a college of their choice rather than being really available to the Holocaust experience as something that could happen to any one of us human beings. But aren't these also the hazards that are built into our basic human machinery for experiencing?

Virtually any choice a teacher makes with respect to contents of the Holocaust to be taught, or the methods of communication to students and the kinds of experiences one seeks to generate in their minds and hearts, is subject to legitimate criticism of distorting the reality of the Holocaust. The more so is it incumbent on teachers to develop carefully and thoughtfully their rationales for teaching the history/literature of this grave topic, and to teach it in as historically accurate and sensitive a manner as possible.

Thus, should one choose to facilitate a caring, loving identification with a child victim in the Holocaust? The resulting experience of feeling for and identification with the victim may turn into a sweet experience for the contemporary student of feeling clean and good and lovingly connected to a fellow human being, but hardly assists him/her to make contact with the rotten gore and profound suffering that characterized the Holocaust day in and night out.

If, on the other hand, one chooses to focus on ethnic and religious prejudices such as antisemitism, Nazi ideology, and stupid, slavish conformity to orders from above, another aspect of human nature, such as the disgusting, blind, and ferocious capacity of thousands of us human beings to kill victims with unbelievable indifference, just because it's the thing to do, may be missed. Yet again, try to teach the truth of man's readiness to be destructive and evil for no meaning or purpose other than triumph over others, and you miss important truths about prejudice and dehumanization in ideologies of hatred, and you certainly miss evoking compassion for the victims.

No matter which way one turns in the kaleidoscope of the Holocaust, no form of teaching and no direction of experience can possibly capture simultaneously the many levels of reality and truths about human nature that the Holocaust, as an archetypal transformative event in the history of civilization, screams at us to understand.

For my part, I would try, in teaching the Holocaust, to organize for the student an experience and connection with each of at least three major roles in the Holocaust: the victim, the bystander, and the perpetrator.

- Regarding the victims, I would be careful not to stay only in sympathy with the victims' heartfelt suffering, and often magnificently courageous spiritual transcendence, and thereby miss other truths, such as the bitter realities of how many of the victims were shattered, their spirits broken, their minds demented—for the Holocaust, and all genocides, are killers in every sense of the gift of life.
- Regarding bystanders, I would teach the cowardliness, self-serving opportunism, and selfish indifference of the bystanders—again our fellow human beings—and look with my students for examples of these qualities in our own behaviors every day, in the small events of our lives in our families and communities, let alone in response to the persecution and genocide of human beings around our contemporary world.

- Finally, regarding the perpetrators, I would teach the truths that the perpetrators are from all walks of life, including powerful military and political leaders who delight in their assumption of Godlike powers to destroy other living creatures, but also including hundreds of thousands of "ordinary people" who join in unquestioningly and willingly with the strange pleasure of wiping out fellow people.

As noted, I would try in my teaching to move back and forth between these different sides of us human beings until, finally, our hearts and minds burst with the truths of these terrible contradictions of the human spirit: that we who study the Holocaust are one with those who died in the Holocaust; and we are also one with those who stood by and allowed the Holocaust to take place; and are also one with those who perpetrated the Holocaust: We are sensitive, suffering souls; we are kind, helpful, courageous, and heroic; we are vulnerable, breakable nothings; we are selfish, self-interested grabbers and exploiters of others; we are stupid, slavish conformists who obey the most rotten orders; we are ugly killers.

In the just published first-ever encyclopedia on the subject of genocide, I wrote:

> Can it be that our species cannot be otherwise, by our very "nature," in our genetic reality?
>
> How can genocide be stopped?
>
> By legal means? By political and social evolution? Through moral and spiritual development? With the aid of better educational programs, or with the creative contribution of mass media that, at long last, perhaps in response to public pressures or new legislation against the pornography of violence, would adopt a policy of promoting life and opposing violence against all unprotected people. (Charny, 1999, p. lxii)

This book about teaching Holocaust literature provides teachers with a rich array of resources for teaching all of the above. It inspires deeper caring, sensitivity and integrity, even as it does not provide the answers for which our species is still looking 50 years after the Holocaust about how we humans can overcome and put aside the terrible parts of us that are given to us in the original "factory" where we are created. Perhaps that is the penultimate task awaiting the creativity and leadership of highly gifted teachers.

REFERENCE

Charny, Israel W. (Ed.). (1999). *Encyclopedia of Genocide.* Santa Barbara, CA, Denver, CO, and Oxford, UK: ABC-CLIO (2 vols.). Forewords by Archbishop Desmond M. Tutu and Simon Wiesenthal. Associate Editors: Rouben Paul Adalian, Steven L. Jacobs, Eric Markusen, Samuel Totten; Bibliographic Editor: Marc I. Sherman.

ABOUT THE CONTRIBUTORS

Rebecca G. Aupperle has been teaching about the Holocaust to her eighth graders at the Mary E. Volz School in Runnemede, New Jersey for the past 26 years. She is a graduate of the Teachers' Summer Seminar on the Holocaust and Jewish Resistance in Poland and Israel, led by survivor and former resistance member Vladka Meed. In 1995 Aupperle was the recipient of a grant from the New Jersey Commission on Holocaust Education, designating her school a Holocaust Demonstration Site—a model for other New Jersey educators vis-à-vis the implementation of the state mandate for Holocaust and Genocide Education. As director of this site, Aupperle hosts yearly workshops for teachers and administrators that support the mandate by including historians, authors, survivors, second generation, liberators, and veteran practitioners of Holocaust education from the U.S. and Israel.

Aupperle is also a consultant to the New Jersey Commission on Holocaust Education, and a member of a Consortium of Yad Vashem Graduates, which works in conjunction with the Yad Vashem Pedagogical Department in Jerusalem, Israel. In 1996 she was awarded the Anti-Defamation League's "Honey and Maurice Axelrod Pedagogical Award for Holocaust Education." In 1996, she was also a recipient of a fellowship from the National Endowment for the Humanities that enabled her to study Holocaust pedagogy with Professor Lawrence L. Langer. In 1998 she was named a Mandel Fellow for 1998–1999 by the United States Holocaust Memorial Museum in Washington, D.C. She is currently enrolled in the nation's first master of arts degree program in Holocaust and Genocide Studies at the Richard Stockton College of New Jersey.

Elaine Culbertson is currently the principal of Philadelphia Regional High School. She has been involved in Holocaust education since the writing of the first public school curriculum in Philadelphia in 1976. Culbertson now serves as the chair of the Pennsylvania Holocaust Education Task Force, and in that capacity she is working on a revision of the *Pennsylvania Guide for Teaching the Holocaust* with Jack Fischel of Millersville University.

Since 1995 she has been the curriculum coordinator of the Seminar on Holocaust and Jewish Resistance in Poland and Israel, which is sponsored by the Jewish Labor Committee, the American Gathering of Holocaust Survivors, and the American Federation of Teachers. She is also a Mandel Fellow with the United States Holocaust Memorial Museum and a Facing History and Ourselves National Teaching Faculty Fellow.

In 1999 she was the recipient of the B'nai B'rith Educator of the Year award for service to the community in Philadelphia, and a recipient of the Mordechai Anieliewicz Award of the Association of Jewish Holocaust Survivors in Philadelphia.

Culbertson's publications include "The Difference That It Makes: Holocaust Education in the Public Schools," in *Teaching Thinking and Problem Solving,* 1994, 16(2) (a publication of Research for Better Schools in Philadelphia, Pennsylvania); and, with Richard Libowitz, "Teaching the Teachers: Asking Questions," in Douglas F. Tobler (Ed.), *Remembrance, Repentance, Reconciliation: The 25th Anniversary Volume of the Annual Scholars' Conference on the Holocaust and the Churches* (Lanham, MD: University Press of America, 1998).

Carol Danks, a secondary-level teacher for over 20 years, teaches English and journalism at Roosevelt High School in Kent, Ohio. At Roosevelt High, she created and co-implemented a ninth-grade unit on literature of the Holocaust, which is part of the high school's curriculum.

Active in Holocaust education for many years, Danks is the author of numerous articles in both English and social studies journals, and has participated both locally and nationally in workshops on teaching about the Holocaust. She is a board member of the Ohio Council on Holocaust Education and has coedited the state's Holocaust curriculum, *The Holocaust: Prejudice Unleashed.* In 1987 she participated in a 3-week seminar on the Holocaust and Jewish Resistance, which took place in Israel. In 1997–1998 she was named a Mandel Fellow with the United States Holocaust Memorial Museum.

Danks also served as chairperson of the National Council of Teachers of English Committee on Teaching about Genocide and Intolerance from 1993 through 1998, and coedited its *Teaching for a Tolerant World, Grades 9–12: Essays and Resources* (Urbana, IL: National Council of Teachers of English, 1999).

Margaret A. Drew is a retired librarian, with over 30 years of service in the Brookline, Massachusetts, public schools. She has studied Holocaust literature for more than 20 years, and has worked with the Facing History and Ourselves National Foundation and the United States Holocaust Memorial Museum. She has compiled and edited two major bibliographies on the Holocaust for educators: *Holocaust and Human Behavior: An Annotated Bibliography* (New York: Walker and Company, 1988) and *Annotated Bibliography* [on the Holocaust] (Washington, DC: United States Holocaust Memorial Museum, 1993). She has also contributed essays and articles on teaching Holocaust literature to *Social Education,* the official journal of the National Council for the Social Studies, and the *Facing History and Ourselves Newsletter,* among other publications.

Beth Dutton teaches secondary social sciences and English at Windsor High School in Windsor, Vermont. Each semester at Windsor, she also teaches a 10-week Holocaust unit.

Dutton is a Mandel Teaching Fellow at the United States Holocaust Memorial Museum in Washington, D.C., and a Holocaust and Resistance Fellow, under the auspices of the American Gathering of Jewish Survivors of the Holocaust, the Jewish Labor Committee, and the American Federation of Teachers. As a Holocaust Resistance Fellow, she has traveled and studied in Poland and Israel.

She is chair of the board of directors of the Vermont-based Parents, Teachers, and Students for Social Responsibility, which sponsors the annual International Holocaust Institute for Youth. At the annual Holocaust Institute, Dutton teaches a course on the history of antisemitism and Holocaust history.

Dutton is the author of *Night People, a Story of the Holocaust*, the narrative biography of Harry Bialor, a survivor of the Holocaust from Poland, who now resides in Brooklyn, New York. She is presently working on another biography of a Holocaust survivor, Stephan Lewy, a German Jew.

William R. Fernekes is supervisor of social studies at Hunterdon Central Regional High School in Flemington, New Jersey. He serves as a consultant to the Education Department of the United States Holocaust Memorial Museum and has published widely in professional journals on issues-based education, global education, Holocaust and genocide studies, human rights education, and children's rights. Among his publications are *Children's Rights: A Reference Handbook* (with Beverly C. Edmonds), and "Theory and Practice of Issues-Centered Education" in Ronald W. Evans and David Warren Saxe (Ed.), *Handbook on Teaching Social Issues* (Washington, D.C.: National Council for the Social Studies, 1996). He has also served on the writing team for *Expectations of Excellence: Curriculum Standards for the Social Studies* (Washington, D.C.: National Council for the Social Studies, 1994).

Karen Shawn, Ph.D., formerly a teacher of English in Lawrence, Long Island, is an assistant principal at Moriah School of Englewood, a Hebrew Day School in New Jersey. She is the regional director of Educational Outreach for the American Society of Yad Vashem, and teaches the pedagogical component of the Yad Vashem Summer Institute for Educators from Abroad in Jerusalem, Israel. She is also a consultant to the Ghetto Fighters House (GFH) in D.N. Western Galilee, Israel, and coauthor of the teacher's guide for the GFH International Reading Project. She is the author of *The End of Innocence: Anne Frank and the Holocaust* (New York: Anti-Defamation League, 1994), and editor of *In the Aftermath of the Holocaust: Three Generations Speak* (Englewood, NJ: Moriah School, 1995).

Samuel Totten is currently a professor in the Department of Curriculum and Instruction at the University of Arkansas at Fayetteville. Before entering academia, he taught English and social studies at the secondary level in Australia, Israel, California, and Washington, D.C. He also served as a K–8 principal in northern California.

Prior to, and several years into, its operation, Totten served as an educational consultant to the United States Holocaust Memorial Museum. In this capacity, he co-authored (with William S. Parsons) *Guidelines for Teaching About the Holocaust* (Washington, D.C.: United States Holocaust Memorial Museum, 1993).

His essays on Holocaust education have appeared in such journals as the *British Journal of Holocaust Education; Canadian Social Studies;* the *Journal of Holocaust Education;* the *Journal of Curriculum and Supervision; Social Education,* and *The Social Studies.* He also served as coeditor (with Stephen Feinberg) of the 1995 special issue "Teaching About the Holocaust" of *Social Education,* the official journal of the National Council for the Social Studies.

Currently he is editing two books on the Holocaust —*Teaching and Studying the Holocaust* (Boston, MA: Allyn and Bacon) and *Remembering the Past, Educating for the Future: Educators Encounter the Holocaust* (Westport, CT: Greenwood)—and writing another entitled *Genocide Education: Issues and Approaches.*

INTRODUCTION

SAMUEL TOTTEN

All Holocaust art, whether memoir, biography, or fiction, is built on a mountain of corpses, so that it can never be an act of celebration, a triumph of form over the chaos of experience.

—Langer, 1998, p. 127

Genesis of the Project

The genesis of *Teaching Holocaust Literature* is the result of my interest in and efforts to teach Holocaust literature as an English teacher throughout the 1980s and 1990s as well as my experience as an educational consultant to the United States Holocaust Memorial Museum (USHMM) in the early 1990s. More specifically, early in my teaching career I discovered that it was nearly impossible to locate more than a minuscule number of historically accurate and pedagogically sound Holocaust literature lessons and units that had been published anywhere to serve as a guide for developing such lessons for my own students. Prior to the opening of the USHMM, I conducted another search for such materials and discovered, once again, that the situation had not changed dramatically from the early 1980s.

The pedagogical pieces I did locate in the 1980s mainly dealt with *The Diary of Anne Frank* and, to a lesser extent, Elie Wiesel's *Night*. Many of the lessons on Anne Frank's diary treated it as if it were the only piece of Holocaust literature available. Over and above that, the vast majority of the authors rarely acknowledged the fact that, as Elaine Culbertson notes in her essay in the present volume, the diary is more of a "coming of age" story than a piece that explores the Nazis' vicious exterminatory policies. Furthermore, most of the pedagogical pieces dealing with the *Diary* neglected to situate Anne's story within its historical context, thus leaving students bereft of key insights into why the Nazis committed genocide against the Jews.

As for Wiesel's *Night*, I discovered that many teachers taught it as a novel. The fact is, as Wiesel (1995), himself, notes: "*Night* is not a novel" (p. 271). On the other hand, the lessons and units that were designed to teach *Night* as a memoir rarely suggested the need to provide a historical context for the work. Even more disturbing, some of the lessons included gimmicky activities (e.g., absurd simulations) that were more likely to result in a fun-and-games-type situation than a pedagogical situation in which the students gained a deeper understanding of the historical period and/or a greater appreciation of what the victims faced.

This is not to say that all of the lessons and units being taught in the 1980s and 1990s were weak or poor. Indeed, I knew from my contact with friends and colleagues across the country that many outstanding and conscientious teachers were and are teaching strong units on Holocaust literature, but unfortunately many of these lessons had never been published and were unavailable to a wider audience. Also, once the United States Holocaust Memorial Museum opened in 1993, I had the benefit, during talks I gave to teachers on how to incorporate literature into a study of the Holocaust, of meeting many fine teachers who were teaching Holocaust literature in a very powerful manner. It was during the latter period that I decided to bring together some of these educators for the purpose of developing a book comprised of essays that describe lessons and units of study that were historically accurate and pedagogically sound.

The Problem Posed by the Proliferation of Holocaust Lessons/Units

Over the past decade there has been an explosion of pedagogical activity vis-à-vis the teaching of the Holocaust, a fact that has been both positive and negative. The positive is that more students are being introduced to this dark and significant period of history and are, hopefully, being encouraged and assisted to consider the ramifications that this history has for their own lived lives and the world in which they live. The drawback is that with the proliferation of materials there is much that is being produced, disseminated, and taught that is ahistorical, inaccurate, and pedagogically unsound. In 1979, Holocaust survivor and scholar Henry Friedlander perspicaciously asserted that "the problem with too much being taught by too many without focus is that this poses the danger of destroying the subject through dilettantism. It is not enough for well-meaning teachers to feel a commitment to teach about genocide; they must also know the subject" (pp. 520–521). That statement is as true today as in the year Friedlander made it—*if only teachers would heed Friedlander's admonition.* Ultimately, it is incumbent upon all teachers who teach anything related to this history to ask themselves: What is the point of even teaching about the Holocaust or a piece of Holocaust literature if that which students learn is inaccurate and verges on the puerile?

Preparing Oneself to Teach Holocaust Literature

Teaching about the Holocaust is a daunting task. Not only are there innumerable and complex issues to deal with, but much of the subject matter is of a horrific nature. Concomitantly, many, if not most, find it extraordinarily difficult—which is a gross understatement—to fathom how one group of people could target another for total annihilation. Whether one solely teaches the history of the Holocaust or combines the history and literature, it is a task that must be approached with great care and great accuracy. Put another way, to teach about this subject in a haphazard manner—a situation in which one is careless about the facts of the history, romanticizes the facts in any way whatsoever, or uses gimmicks to catch the students' attention—is inimical to sound teaching practices. It is also unconscionable.

Educators planning to design and conduct a study of Holocaust literature would be wise to examine carefully the United States Holocaust Memorial Museum's *Guidelines for Teaching about the Holocaust* (Parsons and Totten, 1993). Doing so will provide them with insights into what to consider and what to avoid when teaching this complex history. Only 15 pages in length, it addresses a host of critical issues, as indicated by the following headings: Why Teach Holocaust History?; Questions of Rationale; Methodological Considerations; Avoid Comparisons of Pain; Avoid Simple Answers to Complex History; Just Because It Happened, Does Not Mean It Was Inevitable; Strive for Precision of Language; Make Careful Distinctions about Sources of Information; Try to Avoid Stereotypical Descriptions; Do Not Romanticize History to Engage Students' Interest; Contextualize the History; Translate Statistics into People; Be Sensitive to Appropriate Written and Audio-Video Content; Strive for Balance in Establishing Whose Perspective Informs Your Study of the Holocaust; Select Appropriate Learning Activities; and Reinforce the Objectives of Your Lesson Plan.

Because so many teachers new to teaching the Holocaust and Holocaust literature have a propensity to include various types of simulations, role-playing, and games in their lessons, it is worthwhile to note the *Guidelines* authors' advice in regard to this issue:

> Just because students favor a certain learning activity does not necessarily mean that it should be used. For example, such activities as word scrambles, crossword puzzles, and other gimmicky exercises tend not to encourage critical analysis, but lead instead to low level types of thinking and, in the case of Holocaust curricula, trivialize the importance of studying this history. When the effects of a particular activity run counter to the rationale for studying the history, then that activity should not be used.
>
> Similarly, activities that encourage students to construct models of killing camps should also be reconsidered since any assignment along this line will almost inevitably end up being simplistic, time-consuming, and tangential to the educational objectives for studying the history of the Holocaust.
>
> Thought-provoking learning activities are preferred, but even here, there are pitfalls to avoid. In studying complex human behavior, many teachers rely upon simulation exercises meant to help students "experience" unfamiliar situations. Even when teachers take great care to prepare a class for such an activity, simulating experiences from the Holocaust remains pedagogically unsound. The activity may engage students, but they often forget the purpose of the lesson, and even worse, they are left with the impression at the conclusion of the activity that they now know what it was like during the Holocaust. (Parsons and Totten, 1993, p. 7)

Those teachers who are intent on teaching a piece of Holocaust literature and/or incorporating Holocaust literature into a study of the Holocaust would also be wise to consult one or more of the many fine books on Holocaust literature by Lawrence Langer. Margaret Drew, a contributor to the present volume and a long-time associate of the noted Holocaust education organization Facing History and Ourselves (FHAO), goes even further in her assertion that "anyone preparing to teach Holocaust literature ought to be required to read Langer's (1998) *Preempting the Holocaust*," a collection of hard-hitting essays in which Langer takes to task certain intellectuals, artists, clerics, and educators in regard to how they have addressed the Holocaust over the years (personal correspondence, May 1999).

Besides being an astute critic, Langer is also adept at raising critical issues regarding the reading, and, ultimately, the teaching of this literature. Some of the many issues he addresses that are worthy of consideration by educators who plan to teach Holocaust literature are: the difference between natural death and death faced by the victims of the Holocaust (Langer, 1995a, pp. 19–20); the "language of atrocity" (1995a, pp. 6, 129–130, 132), or the fact that "normal" words of the everyday world are totally inadequate to describe the situation within the "concentrationary world"; how the Holocaust constituted a "kind of physical and spiritual amputation" (1995a, p. 30); the moral chaos of the Holocaust (1995a, p. 94); the deprivation of dignity (1995a, p. 27, 146, 158, and 164); the "naive notion of heroism" and resistance during the Holocaust (1995a, p. 28); the humiliation inflicted by the Nazis on their victims (1995a, pp. 104, 168); and the euphemistic nature of the language used by the Nazis.

A particularly thought-provoking issue that Langer addresses—and one that is extremely useful to have students examine as they read and discuss Holocaust literature—is that of the many excruciating "choiceless choices" that were faced by the victims. Langer (1982) defines *choiceless choices* as those situations "where crucial decisions did not reflect options between life and death, but between one form of abnormal response and another, both imposed by a situation that was in no way of the victim's own choosing" (p. 72). The examination of such an issue by students will likely provide them with a greater appreciation of the extraordinarily difficult and horrific circumstances into which the victims of the Nazis were plunged between 1933 and 1945.

Finally, Langer's discussion of the distinctions between fiction and nonfiction as it relates to Holocaust literature is also something that all teachers of Holocaust literature should read as they prepare to teach such works to their students. The following discussion by Langer (1995a) on "writing and reading Holocaust literature" provides one with a good sense as to the thought-provoking nature of his ideas and insights:

Anne Frank . . . was a very talented young writer, but she has been ill-served by fervent admirers who have refurbished her work with their own sentimental provocations. Those who would convert death in Auschwitz or Bergen-Belsen into a triumph of love over hate feed deep and obscure needs in themselves having little to do with the truth. In addition, they pander to a hungry popular clamor for reassurance that mass murder had its redeeming features. The best Holocaust literature gazes into the depths without flinching. If its pages are seared with the heat of a nether world where, unlike Dante's, pain has no link to sin and hope no bond with virtue, this is only to confirm the dismissal of safe props that such an encounter requires.

... Western civilization has always prided itself on achieving the thinkable: When Hitler and his cohorts corrupted this vision by making the morally and physically *unthinkable* thinkable, and then practical, possible, and finally, *real,* they not only stained the idea of civilization, but infected the vaunted sources of its pride. Holocaust literature plays a vital role in raising questions about the integrity of language and identity and the dominion of history itself that if left unchallenged would plunge us back into the moral innocence that legend ascribes to the Garden of Eden.

... The dubious feat of wresting meaning from the murder of 5 to 6 million innocent men, women, and children I leave to more hopeful souls. (p. 7)

Of particular value for teachers who plan to develop and teach lessons or units on Holocaust literature are the following works by Langer: *Admitting the Holocaust: Collected Essays;* both the extremely thought-provoking general introduction to *Art from the Ashes: A Holocaust Anthology* as well as the introductions to the various sections of the volume, the authors, and works represented therein; *Versions of Survival: The Holocaust and the Human Spirit;* and *Preempting the Holocaust.*

I strongly believe that it is incumbent upon any teacher who is going to teach about any aspect of the Holocaust and/or a piece of Holocaust literature to become conversant with the history of the period prior to entering the classroom. In order to do so, it is wise to read one or more historical accounts by the most noted Holocaust scholars. Among the works that one might consider are: Yehuda Bauer's *A History of the Holocaust* (1982), Michael Berenbaum's *The World Must Know: The History of the Holocaust as Told in the United States Holocaust Memorial Museum* (1993), Lucy Dawidowicz's *The War Against the Jews, 1933–1945* (1986), the student edition of Raul Hilberg's *The Destruction of the European Jews* (1985), and Leni Yahil's *The Holocaust: The Fate of European Jewry, 1932–1945* (1993). It should be noted that Berenbaum's *The World Must Know: The History of the Holocaust as Told in the United States Holocaust Memorial Museum* (1993) is ideal for use with secondary-level students in that it is highly readable, thorough in its presentation of the history of the Holocaust, and includes scores and scores of fascinating and informative photographs that complement the text.

An essay that is of great value and use in the secondary classroom is Donald L. Niewyk's (1997) "Holocaust: The Jews." The essay is relatively short and clearly delineates the many historical trends that combined to make the Holocaust possible.

Incorporating literature into a study of the Holocaust and/or solely teaching a piece of Holocaust literature to students in an effective manner requires a fair amount of knowledge and skill on the teachers' part. When teachers and curriculum developers are not willing to put the requisite time, thought, and energy into such an effort, the students, the history of the period, *and* the memory of the victims are shortchanged.

Teaching Holocaust Literature

As readers will readily ascertain, the contributors to *Teaching Holocaust Literature* care deeply about the history of the Holocaust, and teach the literature in a way that assists students in placing the literature in a historical context. Further, all of the authors strive to develop and implement engaging and thought-provoking strategies to enable students to examine the literature in a good amount of depth. All also aim to leave their students with a deep appreciation of the myriad travails to which the victims were subjected. Finally, many—some directly, some indirectly—nurture in their students the sense that it behooves them to consider the profound ramifications that this history and literature have for their own lives.

Teaching Holocaust Literature is comprised of three parts: I. Rationales, Issues, Caveats, and Suggestions; II. Lessons/Units of Study (Novels, Short Stories, Poetry, Drama, and Memoirs); and III. Resources. There are a total of 11 essays and a detailed annotated bibliography.

The titles of the individual essays under each section reflect the eclectic nature of the collection of essays: **I. Rationales, Issues, Caveats, and Suggestions:** "Teaching Holocaust Literature: Issues, Caveats, and Suggestions," by Margaret A. Drew; "Incorporating Fiction and Poetry into a Study of the Holocaust" (including a select annotated bibliography of Holocaust literature), by Samuel Totten, and *"The Diary of Anne Frank:* Why I Don't Teach It," by Elaine Culbertson. **II. Lessons/Units of Study: Novels:** "Face to Face: The Study of *Friedrich*, A Novel about the Holocaust," by Rebecca G. Aupperle; "Virtual Community, Real-Life Connections: A Study of *The Island on Bird Street* via an International Reading Project," by Karen Shawn; **Short Stories:** "Analyzing Short Stories about the Holocaust via a Multiple Intelligences and Reader Response Approach" by Samuel Totten; **Poetry:** "'Written in Pencil in the Sealed Railway-Car': Incorporating Poetry into a Study of the Holocaust via a Reader Response Theory," by Samuel Totten; "The Babi Yar Massacre: Seeking Understanding Using a Multimedia Approach," by William Fernekes; "Tapping the Sensibilities of Teens," by Beth Dutton; **Drama:** "Choiceless Choices and Illusions of Power: A Study of *Throne of Straw in the Lodz Ghetto* in an Advanced Placement English Class," by Carol Danks; and **Memoirs/First-Person Accounts:** "Encountering the 'Night' of the Holocaust: Studying Elie Wiesel's *Night*," by Samuel Totten; and an appendix entitled "Diminishing the Complexity and Horror of the Holocaust: Using Simulations in an Attempt to Convey Historical Experiences," by Samuel Totten.

Bringing these authors' ideas, insights, and pedagogical suggestions under one cover was an interesting task. Indeed, the aforementioned discussion in regard to what has been and is now available regarding the teaching of Holocaust literature was borne out as I solicited and accepted proposals for inclusion in this volume. More specifically, in 1994, I placed scores of authors' calls in state and national social studies, English journals, and Holocaust journals, both in the United States and abroad. I also solicited the names of teachers who teach about the Holocaust from friends and colleagues, and sent each of the former an author's call. In addition, I sent authors' calls to scores of Holocaust resource centers in the United States, Canada, Australia, and various locations in Europe. Finally, I posted authors' calls on several Internet listserves and at various educational conferences, including but not limited to the annual conventions of the National Council for the Social Studies and the National Council of Teachers of English, the first International Educators Conference on the Holocaust (Yad Vashem, Israel), and the 1998 and 1999 Annual Churches and Scholars Conference on the Holocaust. Over a period of 4 years, I received 67 proposals, and during that time I accepted 15 of those proposals. Upon completion of the manuscript, seven of the latter authors had their essays accepted as book chapters. The low acceptance rate for proposals submitted is rather telling. It is only fair to note that some of the proposals were quite good and would likely have been accepted had certain authors been willing to revise and resubmit them for consideration. On a different note, several authors submitted strong proposals which were accepted but neglected to submit their final projects. Further, several authors submitted essays and were asked several times to revise them, but upon the request to revise a third or fourth time, they declined to do so and thus dropped out of the project. The point is that not all proposals submitted were rejected. That said, a vast majority of the 67 proposals were bereft of a strong historical context, while others were pedagogically unsound.

It is hoped that the essays and teaching suggestions delineated herein are helpful to teachers as they prepare to incorporate Holocaust literature into their curricular programs. At the same time, while it is understood that many teachers—indeed, most—may adapt the lessons and ideas they find herein to their own teaching situations, it is imperative that all closely note how carefully the contributors to this volume attend to incorporating the historical context of the period into their lessons, to avoiding using gimmicky ways to "engage" student interest, and to teaching the literature in ways that deepen and extend the students' thinking and understanding about the Holocaust.

REFERENCES

Bauer, Yehuda. (1982). *A History of the Holocaust.* Danbury, CT: Franklin Watts.

Berenbaum, Michael. (1993). *The World Must Know: The History of the Holocaust as Told in the United States Holocaust Memorial Museum.* Boston, MA: Little, Brown and Company.

Dawidowicz, Lucy S. (1986). *The War against the Jews, 1933–1945.* New York: Bantam Books.

Friedlander, Henry. (1979, February). "Toward a Methodology of Teaching About the Holocaust." *Teachers College Record,* 80(3): 519–542.

Hilberg, Raul. (1985). *The Destruction of the European Jews. Student Edition.* New York: Holmes and Meier.

Langer, Lawrence L. (1982). *Versions of Survival: The Holocaust and the Human Spirit.* Albany, NY: State University of New York Press.

Langer, Lawrence L. (1995a). *Admitting the Holocaust: Collected Essays.* New York: Oxford University Press.

Langer, Lawrence L. (Ed.). (1995b). *Art from the Ashes: A Holocaust Anthology.* New York: Oxford University Press.

Langer, Lawrence L. (1998). *Preempting the Holocaust.* New Haven, CT: Yale University Press.

Niewyk, Donald L. (1997). "Holocaust: The Jews." In Samuel Totten, William S. Parsons, and Israel W. Charny (Eds.), *Century of Genocide: Eyewitness Accounts and Critical Views* (pp. 136–170). New York: Garland Publishing.

Parsons, William S., and Totten, Samuel. (1993). *Guidelines for Teaching About the Holocaust.* Washington, DC: United States Holocaust Memorial Museum. (This booklet is now available in a larger format entitled *Teaching about the Holocaust: A Resource Book for Educators.* Washington, DC: United States Holocaust Memorial Museum, n.d. The latter includes the *Guidelines,* an annotated bibliography of key works, an annotated videography, a timeline, and many useful articles and essays on various facets of the Holocaust.)

Wiesel, Elie. (1995). *All Rivers Run to the Sea: Memoirs.* New York: Schocken Books.

Yahil, Leni. (1993). *The Holocaust: The Fate of European Jewry. 1932–1945.* New York: Oxford University Press.

PART ONE

Rationales, Issues, Caveats, and Suggestions

1 Teaching Holocaust Literature

Issues, Caveats, and Suggestions

MARGARET A. DREW

Teachers who incorporate Holocaust literature into their study of the Holocaust and/or teach the literature independent of a historical study must address at least two major areas of concern. The first involves the importance of looking at works on the Holocaust in regard to their literary and historical value; the second is the necessity of setting parameters between books that either avoid confronting the horrors of the Holocaust or that overwhelm the reader with accounts of atrocity.

First, any historical literature needs to be evaluated both as history and as literature. A book cannot be fully recommended unless it is good history as well as good literature.

Historical accuracy is not the only test of good history, which lies as much in what is left out as in what is included. Young people generally do not have a great knowledge of history, so that what they know about a period or an event is often limited to what they learn in the specific book they are reading. Nowhere is this more apparent than in Holocaust literature, and nowhere is it more difficult to find a work of literature that can come close to conveying the enormous scope and magnitude of this event.

The cataclysmic historical event that has become known as the Holocaust is something that many, if not most, adults have difficulty confronting. We even have difficulty finding a language that can fully describe the horrors that took place. For these reasons, teachers need to consider their own personal reactions to this literature, and history of the Holocaust, and then try to imagine, or perhaps remember, what it is like to be a young person confronting these events for the first time. Lawrence L. Langer's (1998) most recent collection of essays, *Preempting the Holocaust*, concludes with an essay entitled "Opening Locked Doors: Reflections of Teaching the Holocaust," which should be required reading for anyone teaching about the Holocaust. Langer emphasizes the need for providing both a context for Holocaust literature and direction and support for students reading it for the first time, because "the bleak landscape of Holocaust literature requires a guide" (Langer,

1998, p. 188). He goes on to say, "The average student of Holocaust literature is unequipped by his or her background to venture into those dark corners of the concealed self . . ." (Langer p. 189). Langer 's teaching experience was at the college level; the average middle school or high school student would be even more "unequipped" to deal with these concepts.

This is why it is imperative that, in addition to being both good history and good literature, books about the Holocaust must find a balance between those that fail to confront the true horror of the Holocaust and those that become "catalogues of atrocity" (Langer, 1978, p. 2). Books at the latter end of the spectrum tend to numb the senses, and, ultimately, desensitize the reader. Thus, teachers need to be careful how they use them in the classroom.

However, at the opposite end of the spectrum are books that fail to confront the true horror of the Holocaust; the best-known and most widely read of these is *Anne Frank: The Diary of a Young Girl*. Looking at it as literature, few could doubt the book's value. Looking closely at the book from a historical perspective, however, one finds that there is relatively little history here, and almost nothing about the wide scope of the Holocaust. The most traumatic parts of Anne's experience are just beginning when the diary ends; the diary, then, is essentially the story of an adolescent girl trying to deal with all the normal trials of growing up under extremely abnormal conditions, but it includes little information about those conditions from a historical point of view. The reader knows from early entries that the family is Jewish, originally came from Germany, and emigrated to Holland to escape the German persecution of the Jews. When Germany invaded Holland, the family was forced into hiding. Occasionally Anne reports on events she heard on the radio or events that were reported by those who are helping them, but basically her diary is about her personal struggles: living in hiding in cramped quarters with little or no privacy, sharing these quarters with strangers as well as other family members, and above all, the turmoil of the adolescent feelings growing within her. As Langer (1978) says of the diary, "It circumspectly skirts the horror implicit in the theme, but leaves the reader with the mournful if psychologically unburdened feeling that he has had a genuine encounter with inappropriate death" (p. 18).

This failure to confront the full horror of the Holocaust or examine the historical facts of the period occurs in Anne's diary because it is primarily about her personal life. That is, Anne is writing about what she knows, which is the impact of events on her own life; not the events themselves. Much Holocaust literature for young people, both autobiographical and fictional, is written from a child's point of view. These children neither knew nor understood what was going on around them; they knew only what was happening to their own lives. Unless readers bring with them some historical knowledge of the events surrounding these children, they know no more than the persons or characters in the book; they have no historical context into which to place what they have read.

Teachers who recommend or assign the Diary *should do so only after some basic Holocaust history has been taught.* For English teachers, here is an extraordinary opportunity to plan an interdisciplinary curriculum with a social studies teacher.

Social studies teachers, of course, could use the diary in conjunction with a Holocaust curriculum. In either case, some discussion of the Holocaust should take place before students start reading the diary. Students should begin their reading with at least a general knowledge of what the Holocaust was and should understand what was happening in Germany at the time the Franks fled. The history lessons should keep pace with the book, so that by the time students have finished the diary they are aware of the forced evacuations of Jews and the existence of extermination and death camps. The diary becomes Holocaust literature only when readers are able to put it into historical perspective with knowledge that they have brought to the book. For better or more interested readers who wish to know more about both Anne Frank and the historical period, Miep Gies's (1987) *Anne Frank Remembered* provides excellent supplemental reading. Gies, one of those who helped the Frank family survive in hiding, adds to the diary the essential story of what was happening in the outside world while the family was in hiding. More recently, Melissa Muller (1998) has written an adult biography entitled *Anne Frank: The Biography,* which not only adds perspective by describing the world outside as well as inside the attic, but chronicles what is known of Anne's life after she left the attic. Good readers who are caught up in Anne's story could fill in many of the blanks left by the diary by reading this work.

Holocaust Literature: What It Is and What It Is Not

It may be useful at this point to try to define exactly what constitutes "Holocaust literature." There are hundreds of books about the Holocaust—history, biography, memoirs, short stories, and fiction. There are also books about World War II that take place at the same time and place, but these are war stories rather than Holocaust stories. And there are hundreds of books that fall somewhere in between. I have read book reviews that describe a novel as "being set against the backdrop of the Holocaust." At first, that description made me angry; to consider the Holocaust as merely a "backdrop" *for anything* was to trivialize it; but it is a term that has been used frequently in recent years. I began to wonder whether that was a true description of the book or merely the rhetoric of the reviewer. If a book is described as being a coming-of-age story set against the backdrop of the Holocaust, this does not mean that it was intended to be a Holocaust novel.

Because the Holocaust was such a cataclysmic event, does it nullify or invalidate other events occurring during the same time and place? Does it mean that people whose lives were not impacted, or only slightly impacted, by the Holocaust do not have a story to tell and the right to tell it? Of course not. Obviously, anyone who has a story to tell also has the right to tell it. The point is that a story set in Germany in the thirties or France in the forties does not have to be a Holocaust story, any more than a story set in the United States in the sixties has to be about the Civil Rights movement or the assassination of President Kennedy. A coming-of-age story set in Holland during the forties is just as valid as one set in Australia in the

1870s or China during the 1920s, but it may not necessarily be about the Holocaust. It is imperative that teachers discriminate, and teach students to discriminate, between war stories, Holocaust stories, and stories that just happen to be set in the same time period and geographic locations as the Holocaust.

Key Works That Highlight Various Aspects of the Holocaust Experience

Among those works than can legitimately be called Holocaust literature, there is still a wide range of books. There are those that involve the early years of the Nazis' rise to power and what that meant to the Jews and Germany and elsewhere. There are those that involve the years of the ghetto, people in hiding, and those involved in rescue and resistance. Finally, there are those that go to the very center of the Holocaust, the death camps (where the sole purpose was to mass murder people) and the concentration camps (holding camps where many perished, but where the sole purpose was not the manufacture of death). There are also different types of literature, from novels and short stories to memoirs and biographies.

Hans Richter has given us one of the most powerful pictures of the early years of the Third Reich in his novel *Friedrich*. The story begins before the rise of Hitler and Nazism and describes the friendship between the narrator, an Aryan boy, and Friedrich, his Jewish neighbor. They grow up together and are good friends; by 1933, however, the narrator's father has joined the Nazi Party, the persecution of the Jews has begun and the impact on the friendship as well as on Friedrich and his family is devastating.

The novel is short and highly readable; it is easy enough to be accessible to younger readers, and at the same time compelling enough to satisfy high school students. It draws a credible picture of what life was like in urban Germany during the early years of Nazism, as seen through the eyes of an Aryan child. The author was born in Germany in 1925, as are both the boys in this story. In his second book, *I Was There*, Richter confirms that his novels are autobiographical when he states in the preface, "I am reporting how I lived through that time and what I saw—no more" (n.p.).

There is an authenticity in *Friedrich* that does not reflect the experiences of all German children who lived during these years, but certainly expresses the experiences of many. It is critical, however, that teachers discuss this book with students, and not simply assign it as outside reading. When students have preconceived ideas about Jews, especially about their economic status, this book can reinforce stereotypes. This is particularly true in light of the fact that in the story, Friedrich's family is better off economically than is the Aryan narrator's family, which is poor. Some students read *Friedrich* and conclude, "You see? It's true. The Jews had the money and the jobs." Teachers need to be aware of this aspect of the novel and be prepared to address it; otherwise a book with the potential to enlighten this phase of history could instead distort it. The prerequisite that teachers of Holocaust literature must also be familiar with Holocaust history is clearly illustrated here.

Specifically, teachers need to provide information about the economic depression in Germany during the twenties, and the fact that preexistent antisemitism made the Jews a convenient target to blame for the economic situation. In spite of German claims to the contrary, Jews controlled only a small percentage of the jobs in important areas like banking and commerce, and Jewish unemployment rates were high. Friedrich's family situation was realistic, but not typical; the depression in Germany, like that in the United States, did not exclude any ethnic or economic group.

A novel that presents a unique perspective on another phase of the Holocaust is Uri Orlev's *The Man from the Other Side*. It is set in the Warsaw Ghetto and is based on real events and real people. The main character is a teenaged boy named Marek, who lives just outside the walls of the Warsaw Ghetto. Marek's stepfather smuggles food, and occasionally weapons, to the Jews in the Ghetto, not because he is a "righteous Gentile," but to supplement his income: in other words, he sells the food to the Jews. He is motivated by profit, not humanitarianism. Marek works with his stepfather, smuggling in food and occasionally smuggling out babies to hide with the nuns; he is also antisemitic, until told by his mother that his biological father was Jewish. Orlev is an accomplished Israeli writer who was himself a child of the ghetto. Many years after the war, Orlev met the man known in the book as Marek, a Polish journalist, now residing in Israel. They discovered they had both been boys in Warsaw during the war, and shared stories of their personal experiences. The journalist becomes the character of Marek in the book. Marek had never revealed his resistance activities to anyone, even his family, and made Orlev promise never to write about them as long as he was alive. Shortly after, in 1987, the journalist was killed in a plane crash, and Orlev began writing his story. Combining "Marek's" story with knowledge based on the author's own experiences, Orlev is able to give readers a unique look into the Warsaw Ghetto and the city outside it. Marek's ability to move into and out of the Ghetto gives us insight into life on both sides of the wall, including a dramatic description of the Warsaw Ghetto Uprising and the destruction of the Ghetto. This powerful novel presents complex issues and characters in a simple and vivid way that is dynamic, but never melodramatic.

One of the few books that can meet the criteria in both history and literature is Elie Wiesel's *Night*. It succeeds in confronting the horrors of the Holocaust without overwhelming the reader with graphic details, at least for high school readers. It may be too strong for students younger than this, however, especially if it is read without the context of a Holocaust curriculum or the close guidance of perceptive teachers. Even readers who turned to this book with no prior knowledge of Holocaust history would understand a great deal about the event when they finished it. Here there is no glossing over the horrors, no failure to confront "inappropriate death." But it is also a story of survival that keeps the reader from being overwhelmed by the horror and left without hope.

Night is also an important work for high school students who may have been overwhelmed by the scope of the horrors of the Holocaust. Statistics can numb the sensibilities; 6 million dead is a statistic that the mind cannot comprehend in human terms. Reading this memoir turns the 6 million from a statistic to a personal experience that can be multiplied by 6 million; or, as Andre Schwarz-Bart (1960) expresses it in his novel *The Last of the Just,* the story of one individual "dead six million times" (p. 422). It is strongly recommended that *Night* be assigned toward the end of a Holocaust unit, simply because it translates all the overwhelming statistics back into human terms. The study of the Holocaust is, or should be, a search for humanity through the study of inhumanity; no one has contributed more to that search than Elie Wiesel.

For middle school students who may not be ready for *Night,* the best work for younger readers that goes to the heart of the Holocaust is James Forman's (1976) *The Survivor.* Published in 1976, this was the first Holocaust novel written for young people that confronted the true horror of the Holocaust, and it has not been surpassed to this day. Unfortunately, it is out of print; it should, however, be available in most libraries. When the story opens in the summer of 1939, David is 14, with a twin brother, two sisters—one 7 and the other 19—parents, and grandparents. They are Dutch Jews; David's father is a physician in Amsterdam. The family has already been affected by the rise of Hitler; David's Uncle Daniel, his father's brother, lost his wife when their home in Berlin was burned down during the "Night of Broken Glass." When the Nazis invade Holland, the family goes into hiding, but are eventually captured. The next stop is Westerbork Detention Camp, which turns out to be only a waystation on the road to Auschwitz. Between death, disappearance, and capture, the rest of the family is gradually reduced until the death of David's twin brother during the death march from Auschwitz in 1945 leaves David as the only survivor. The story does not end with the liberation, however. Indeed, one of the most painful parts of this novel is David's return to his former home, where he learns that discrimination and antisemitism still exist.

A close second to *The Survivor* in terms of content, if not literary value, is *The Cage,* by Ruth Minsky Sender, published 10 years later, in 1986. It is still in print. *The Cage* has been criticized by some reviewers as not being very well written; many of the same reviewers, however, got so caught up in the story that they recommended the book in spite of its flaws. It is the autobiographical account of a 16-year-old girl and her younger brothers, beginning shortly after the invasion of Poland and tracing their journey first to the Lodz Ghetto and from there to Auschwitz. It is a gripping story, hard to put down; it depicts the terrible ordeals of this young woman without overwhelming the reader with horror. While it may not be a literary masterpiece, a number of young people have referred to it as the best book they ever read, and its continued popularity attests to its value in conveying the story of the Holocaust to young readers.

High school students who have already read *Night* can select from a number of other excellent works, both fiction and nonfiction. One of the best is Isabella Leitner's *Fragments of Isabella: A Memoir of Auschwitz.* As the subtitle indicates, this is the author's personal experience as she, with her mother and siblings, were transported from Hungary to Auschwitz. Unfortunately, this is another work that is out of print, but it is available in libraries.

The Death Train by Luba K. Gurdus is another personal memoir. Her account begins in Warsaw in 1938, with the birth of her son, but quickly moves to the invasion of Poland a year later, and their escape from the city. At one point in their travels they find refuge near the railroad tracks that carry the transport trains. Her son becomes obsessed with the "death train." Just before his fourth birthday, he draws a picture of the death train, which is included in the book. A short time after his birthday, he dies of diphtheria. Both before and after his death, the death train is like a leitmotif running throughout the memoir. There are numerous descriptions of and stories about the death trains. Ironically, however, the author is never actually on a transport train. She travels by foot and several times by commercial passenger train, with false papers. When she is finally arrested and taken to Majdanek concentration camp, it is by truck. This book was not written specifically for young people, but it is a very readable first-person narrative, made more compelling by the author's drawings throughout.

In *Dry Tears: The Story of a Lost Childhood,* Nechama Tec describes her family's experiences as Polish Jews surviving on the Aryan side of the ghetto; she adds a different perspective on the Holocaust by looking at events through the eyes of a child, but with the perception of an adult.

In his unique two volumes called *Maus I* and *Maus II,* Art Spiegelman turns his family's story into a cartoon. It may be difficult for those who have not read these books to take their use in the classroom seriously. Indeed, the Holocaust in cartoons would seem, if not to trivialize the subject, at least to treat it lightly; when you add the fact that the Jews are depicted as mice and the Nazis as cats, it sounds offensive as well as trivial. Spiegelman, however, succeeds in raising this genre to an art form, and his sarcastic irony adds sufficient depth to the work to make it appeal to all readers, from the most reluctant to the most sophisticated.

One novel that has achieved great popularity in recent years with teachers of middle school students is Lois Lowry's *Number the Stars.* It deals with the rescue of Danish Jews. The fact that the American Library Association chose this as the recipient of its Newbery Award, a prize given to the best children's book of the year, establishes its literary quality. It is also accurate historically.

Another excellent novel, also about the Danish resistance, is Carol Matas's *Lisa's War.* In Matas's novel, some of the members of the resistance are Jewish—an important element, because so much Holocaust history and literature portrays the Jews as victims. The novel is very well written, especially in its ability to convey the emotions of a 12-year-old girl who lives in a country that has just been invaded by Hitler's troops, and who becomes involved in the resistance. It is difficult to portray the excitement combined with fear, the sense of triumph when acts of resistance are carried out practically in front of the enemy, without having the story deteriorate into a romantic adventure story. Matas avoids such pitfalls, and at the same times provides the reader with an authentic description of events.

The rescue of the Danish Jews is one of the most remarkable events in the history of the Holocaust, and one that should be part of any Holocaust curriculum. In view of the overwhelming statistics regarding the loss of human life in the Holocaust, and particularly the number of Jews exterminated, the fact that 98.5 percent of the Danish Jews survived is a remarkable statistic. In *Rescue in Denmark,* Flender (1964), though, makes a point of the fact that "the Danes were not alone in acting heroically and effectively in saving their Jewish population. In every country under Nazi control, including Germany, there were individual acts of courage and humanity . . . but it was only in Denmark that virtually the entire Jewish population of the country was saved" (p. 205). Flender's description of the return of Jewish families to their homes after the war, whereupon they found their pets fed, their plants watered, their houses cleaned, and their businesses running cannot fail to move the reader and restore a little of the faith in humanity that the atrocities of the Holocaust may have brought into question.

It should be borne in mind, however, that if stories of rescue and resistance are all that children know about the Holocaust, they will have an extremely distorted view of history. *Essentially, the Holocaust is not about courage and heroism, but about persecution and extermination.* A Holocaust curriculum should neither begin nor end with stories of rescue and resistance; they should be seen in perspective, as a few candles lit amidst the darkness of this part of history.

At one and the same time, it is important that some discussion of rescue and resistance, particularly Jewish resistance, be included in a Holocaust curriculum. In the first place, children always ask, "Why didn't the Jews fight back?" and "Why didn't somebody help them?" They need to know that there were those who resisted and those who rescued; they also need to know how difficult it was and how great the risks were. A more imperative reason, however, is that young people can quickly become overwhelmed by the brutality and inhumanity implicit in the study of the Holocaust. The story of the Danes can alleviate a little of the horror, and can leave room for hope. Indeed, it is an important part of any Holocaust curriculum, and it would be a disservice both to the students and to the Danes to omit it. *However, taking it out of the context of the Holocaust, failing to present it within the context of the surrounding horror, would be an even greater mistake.*

One appropriate place to introduce the resistance into a Holocaust curriculum would be with the study of the Warsaw Ghetto; in particular, the Warsaw Ghetto uprising. This could then lead to a discussion of other resistance movements, including the one in Denmark. In discussing the resistance, mention could also be made of the White Rose movement, and the fact that there was resistance even within Germany itself. Most novels of resistance written for young people, especially older books such as Marie McSwigan's classic *Snow Treasure*, are little more than adventure stories, describing events in terms that romanticize war and distort history. Although it is a story of resistance, this is really a war story, not a Holocaust novel. One novel that can be recommended is James Forman's *Ceremony of Innocence*, a fictional account of Hans and Sophie Scholl and the White Rose movement. The White Rose was a student resistance movement in Munich, Germany; Hans and Sophie Scholl were the brother and sister who led the movement until they were executed for treason in 1943. Forman tells their story without romanticism or sensationalism, but in a way that brings both the people and the history to life.

The best book for middle school students on the Jewish resistance is probably the biography, *In Kindling Flame: The Story of Hannah Senesh, 1921–1944.* Senesh was a Hungarian Jew who migrated to Palestine in 1939, but returned during the war to join the Resistance; she was caught and executed in 1944. The account of her brief life includes excerpts from her diary and her poems, as well as relevant historical background; it is the skillful way the author merges these elements that makes this such an outstanding book. In spite of the numerous excellent books available on the subject of rescue and resistance, *the amount of time devoted to this aspect of the Holocaust should not be out of proportion to its place in history.*

Short stories can also be very effective for classroom use, and one of the best collections of short stories about the Holocaust is Ida Fink's *A Scrap of Time* (1989). Most of the stories in this collection are very brief. Two of the most powerful, "The Key Game" and "Crazy," are each only three or four pages long. "The Key Game" is a game that a married couple "play" each night with their three-year-old son. The woman works during the day, and both parents live in fear that the SS will come looking for the father. They are training the child to delay answering the doorbell until the father has time to hide. Every night the woman pretends to ring the doorbell, and, as the man struggles to get into his hiding place, the little boy runs around the apartment, stamping his feet, dragging chairs, yelling that he is looking for the keys. The frantic desperation of the situation is eloquently stated in the final phrase, describing the man as one "who was already long dead to the people who would really ring the bell" (p. 38).

"Crazy" is a more abstract story, and better suited to high school readers. It opens with the narrator trying to convince a doctor that he is not crazy, that his illness is in his heart, not his head. As his story unfolds, we learn that he is a hunchbacked dwarf with a wife and three children. Everyone expects that because of his disability, he will be taken in the first roundup, or "action." He is still working as a garbageman, however, when the third "action" takes place; the trucks pull in just as he is going to work, and he hides between two buildings with his broom in front of him. As the trucks are being loaded, someone runs by him and knocks the broom away; on the truck, he sees his three children. In a half-page of text, Fink creates an unforgettable image of a single moment of time that will remain engraved forever on a man's soul.

Caveats about Certain Pieces of Holocaust Literature

Of the numerous other books written for middle school readers about the Holocaust, one that I cannot recommend is Jane Yolen's *The Devil's Arithmetic*. The novel won the National Jewish Book Award, so obviously there are many who do not agree with me. There is certainly no question of the book's literary merit; here, as in her other works, Jane Yolen demonstrates that she is one of today's finest authors of books for children and young adults. In addition, she presents in this work some of the most graphic and powerful concentration camp scenes that can be found anywhere in literature for young people. The book is written as fantasy, but even though the Holocaust as fantasy may seem a little bizarre, this in itself is not the problem. The problem comes later in the book, in a story and fantasy of a young Jewish girl named Hannah. Hannah has listened to her relatives tell stories of the Holocaust for years, and she is tired of dwelling on the past. Suddenly she opens a door and finds herself in a Polish town in the 1940s. In this story-within-a-story, she lives through the Holocaust, from her Polish home to the death camp. Because this is a fantasy, however, as she walks through the door leading to extermination, she finds herself back home. It is here that I have a problem with the book. Personally, I found this offensive, reminiscent of the Wizard of Oz, where you only have to click your heels three times and say, "I wish I were home" and all your troubles are over. If anything can be said to trivialize the Holocaust, it is this simplistic ending. It is a disservice to the millions who walked through the doors into the gas chambers and found neither home nor hope, but only smoke and ashes.

This is not to say that fantasy can never have a place in Holocaust literature. *The Shadow Children,* by Steven Schnur, takes place in France after the war. In it a boy visits his grandfather and becomes aware of the fact that there seem to be no young people living in the town, but many refugee children begging along the road and living in the woods. He seems to be the only one who sees them, however, and his grandfather tells him he is imagining things. Eventually he learns the truth from his grandparents. During the war, thousands of Jewish children were sent to the village to be hidden from the Nazis, and one night the Nazis came and demanded that all the children be turned over to them. If they were not, both the children and their protectors would be shot. Trying to believe the Nazis' story that the children would be cared for until they could be returned to their parents, the villagers delivered the children to the bridge below town and watched in horror as they were loaded into cattle cars. Now no one in the village will cross that bridge. They all live with the guilt of their cowardice in not defending and protecting the children, and they know that they can never forget, for the shadow children will be there to remind them. This is a powerful and moving story that presents a unique perspective of the Holocaust.

In Holocaust literature the main characters are usually either victims or rescuers. We see very little of perpetrators or bystanders, at least in literature written for young people. Perhaps the stepfather in *The Man from the Other Side* and the villagers in *The Shadow Children* defy categorization. The stepfather was certainly not a rescuer, although he did provide life-sustaining aid to the Jews in the ghetto, and by the end of the book he is more generous than money-grubbing in his rescue attempts. The French villagers were more than bystanders and less than perpetrators—they were weak and they were human, but they were not evil and they were not indifferent.

I mentioned above that there is little literature for readers below high school level about the perpetrators of the Holocaust. There is much adult literature on the subject, however, including numerous studies about Hitler, and biographies or autobiographies of other well-known Nazis, such as Goebbels, Höss, Speer, and Stangl. Many of these books could be read by high school students, but I would caution against encouraging students to focus on this aspect of the Holocaust. While there is a legitimate place for the study of evil and evildoers by scholars, historians, and others with a serious interest in understanding how people can be capable of such inhumanity, there is a tendency among some young people to find a fascination with evil, and with Hitler in particular. When they immerse themselves in this type of reading, they frequently end up getting completely off the subject of the Holocaust and becoming absorbed in violence, sensationalism, and a dehumanization of the victims. Like the kind of graphic violence young people often are attracted to in video games, movies, and television, Hitler and the Nazis become merely an addition to a list ranging from *Mortal Kombat* to *Natural Born Killers* and the Jerry Springer show. One of the most frightening thoughts that can occur to teachers of the Holocaust is that in any given classroom, there could be not only victims, witnesses, and heroes of future atrocities, but also potential perpetrators. Evil exists in our society, in the forms of white supremacy, neo-Nazism, antisemitism and a variety of other hate groups; every member of the KKK or Aryan Nation was once a student in somebody's classroom. Genocide still exists in the world, although today it is more apt to be called "ethnic cleansing"; but sanitizing the language does not minimize the atrocity. Teachers need to help students confront humans' inhumanity, both in history and in the contemporary world around them, while at the same time enabling them to embrace the concept of humanity.

Although I have tried to indicate whether each book mentioned above is fiction or nonfiction, it would be misleading not to mention that making that distinction is not as simple as it sounds. This is especially true of the books that are published for younger readers, but it also applies to books for older students and adults. *Night* is clearly Wiesel's account of his personal experiences, and yet in some libraries it will be found in the fiction section. A number of works published as children's books and aimed at middle school readers are found in the fiction section in some libraries, and in others in the biography or history section. For example, I have seen *The Upstairs Room,* Joanna Reiss's autobiographical account of being hidden by a Dutch family in the upstairs room of a farmhouse, classified as fiction, as autobiography, and in the history section under World War II. Now that almost all books are classified by the Library of Congress, rather than by each library individually, there will be fewer examples of one title showing up in several classifications. However, the decision made by the Library of Congress may itself be arbitrary, and will not necessarily indicate whether the book is fact, fiction, or a combination of both. Some of these books bring us into an area that Langer (1995) describes in an essay in *Admitting the Holocaust,* as "fictional facts and factual fictions" (p. 75); the line between fact and fiction is not always clearly drawn. Much of the fiction is based at least in part on actual people and events. For example, while James Forman's novel *The Survivor* is a work of the imagination, Art Spiegelman's two *Maus* volumes, although depicting animal cartoon characters and obviously showing a great deal of imagination, are based on the story of his own parents. The full title page of Volume I reads, *Maus: A Survivor's Tale, I: My Father Bleeds History*; Volume II is *Maus: A Survivor's Tale, II: And Here My Troubles Began.* The opening sentence of the description of the book on the inside flap of the dust jacket (vol. I) is "Maus is the story of Vladek Spiegelman, a Jewish survivor of Hitler's Europe, and his son, a cartoonist who tries to come to terms with his father, his father's terrifying story, and History itself" (Spiegelman, 1986). It is even classified by the Library of Congress in the nonfiction section under World War II.

Another, almost opposite, example of "fictional facts and factual fictions" occurs because much Holocaust nonfiction is in the form of personal memoirs, which sometimes contain factual errors. Memoirs are by definition based on memory, and memory is frequently imperfect, particularly when the events remembered are so traumatic. Even under ordinary circumstances, there will be almost as many versions of an event as there are witnesses to it; people who suffered through the atrocities of a concentration or death camp, particularly as children, are going to have distorted memories or gaps in their memory. This does not invalidate their stories, but it does illustrate the distinctions between personal narratives of the Holocaust and historical accounts of the places and events described in those narratives.

Teachers who have been teaching and reading Holocaust literature for a number of years may sometimes need to be reminded that the audience for these books is constantly changing. They may feel that they have read it all, and a new Holocaust novel or memoir may give them the sense that they are reading the same book for the hundredth time. While adults may have been desensitized to some of this material through years of overexposure, it is all new to the young people. Parents and teachers of young children may groan when asked to read *Madeline* or *Where the Wild Things Are* one more time, but each generation of children rediscovers these classics as new delights. In the same way, the horrors of the Holocaust are new to each generation of young people, and whether the book is as old as *Night* or as new as the most recent publication, it is all new to the students.

Conclusion

In conclusion, it must be kept in mind that no individual book, not even *Night,* can truly convey the full story of the Holocaust. Every survivor has a story, each one unique. Beyond them, there are the 6 million who did not survive, whose stories can never be fully told, if told at all. There are thousands of books about the Holocaust—personal accounts, general historical overviews, histories of specific events, and those with specific themes or perspectives. Each represents only a piece of the whole picture. Reading 10 books about the Holocaust gives the reader a bigger piece of that picture; reading 100, an even bigger piece. In the previously mentioned essay from Langer's (1998) most recent collection, *Preempting the Holocaust,* Langer states, "Only by multiplying voices can we begin to present the moral complexity of the Holocaust experience to individuals accustomed to basing their conduct on stable value systems" (p. 190). The picture, however, is never completed; each additional book only makes the reader aware of how much of the picture still has not been seen. What teachers can do is try to present as balanced a piece of the picture as possible, conveying the facts, demonstrating the scope and magnitude of the event, and not losing sight of the human aspect. This is where the role of literature comes in. History records the events and compiles the statistics, and literature translates the events and statistics into real things happening to real people. Each without the other is inadequate; together, they provide a window into the truth.

Note: Portions of this essay were previously published in the October 1995 special issue (on the Holocaust) of *Social Education,* the official journal of the National Council for the Social Studies.

REFERENCES

Atkinson, Linda. (1985). *In Kindling Flame: The Story of Hannah Senesh, 1921–1944.* New York: Lothrop, Lee & Shepard.

Fink, Ida. (1989). *A Scrap of Time and Other Stories.* New York: Schocken.

Flender, Harold. (1964). *Rescue in Denmark.* New York: Manor Books, Inc.

Forman, James D. (1970). *Ceremony of Innocence.* New York: Hawthorn Books.

Forman, James D. (1976). *The Survivor.* New York: Farrar, Strauss & Giroux.

Frank, Anne. (1952). *Anne Frank: Diary of a Young Girl.* New York: Doubleday.

Gies, Miep. (1987). *Anne Frank Remembered: The Story of the Woman Who Helped to Hide the Frank Family.* New York: Simon and Schuster.

Gurdus, Luba K. (1987). *The Death Train: A Personal Account of a Holocaust Survivor.* Washington, DC: United States Holocaust Memorial.

Langer, Lawrence L. (1978). *The Age of Atrocity: Death in Modern Literature.* Boston: Beacon Press.

Langer, Lawrence L. (1995). *Admitting the Holocaust: Collected Essays.* New York: Oxford University Press.

Langer, Lawrence L. (1998). *Preempting the Holocaust.* New Haven, CT: Yale University Press.

Leitner, Isabella. (1978). *Fragments of Isabella: A Memoir of Auschwitz.* New York: Crowell.

Lowry, Lois. (1989). *Number the Stars.* Boston, MA: Houghton Mifflin.

Matas, Carol. (1987). *Lisa's War.* New York: Scribner's.

McSwigan, Marie. (1942). *Snow Treasure.* New York: Dutton.

Muller, Melissa. (1998). *Anne Frank: The Biography.* New York: Henry Holt.

Orlev, Uri. (1991). *The Man from the Other Side.* Boston, MA: Houghton Mifflin.

Reiss, Johanna. (1972). *The Upstairs Room.* New York: Crowell.

Richter, Hans. (1972). *I Was There.* New York: Holt, Rinehart & Winston.

Richter, Hans P. (1987). *Friedrich.* New York: Puffin Books.

Schnur, Steven. (1994). *The Shadow Children.* New York: Morrow.

Schwarz-Bart, Andre. (1960). *The Last of the Just.* New York: Bantam Books.

Sender, Ruth Minsky. (1986). *The Cage.* New York: Macmillan.

Spiegelman, Art. (1986). *Maus: A Survivor's Tale, I: My Father Bleeds History.* New York: Pantheon.

Spiegelman, Art. (1991). *Maus: A Survivor's Tale, II: And Here My Troubles Began.* New York: Pantheon.

Tec, Nechama. (1984). *Dry Tears: The Story of a Lost Childhood.* New York: Oxford University Press.

Wiesel, Elie. (1960). *Night.* New York: Hill & Wang.

Yolen, Jane. (1988). *The Devil's Arithmetic.* New York: Viking.

2
Incorporating Fiction and Poetry into a Study of the Holocaust

SAMUEL TOTTEN

Most people have a difficult time comprehending a million of anything, let alone the murder of millions of people. Those who wish to attempt to understand what happened during the Holocaust period, and why, are faced with an enormous and complex task, one which leads into a tangle of historical, political, social, religious, and moral issues and conundrums. Compounding this is our increasing distance from the events; and added to this is the fact that for many, if not most young people today, all history seems like "ancient history." In light of these factors, incorporating literature into a study of the Holocaust may be one of the most powerful and effective entry points into this complex history.

It is through stories that human beings come to ponder myriad facets of the human condition—the beauty and the horror, the hope and the despair, the thoughtfulness and thoughtlessness, and the kindness and cruelty of which humans are capable. Fortunately, a great quantity of outstanding Holocaust literature—including novels, short stories, poetry, and plays—exists that is ideal for use by teachers and students who choose to wrestle with this unique—and often overwhelming—aspect of history.

The Value of the Incorporation of Literature into a Study of the Holocaust

Literature has the power of affecting people in ways that many other pieces of writing often do not. In addition to impacting one's thoughts, it has the ability to impact one's beliefs and feelings. In other words, it is capable of affecting both the cognitive *and* affective levels of one's being. Outstanding literature is also capable of "personalizing" this history, placing a "face" on the horrendous facts and events. In a real sense, the incorporation of high-quality literature into a study of the Holocaust is often capable of "moving the study from a welter of statistics, remote places and events, to one that is immersed in the 'personal' and the 'particular'" (Totten, 1987, p. 63). By combining the study of literature with the study of history, students are often more apt to contemplate and reflect on the significance of the history of the Holocaust.

Teichman (1976) argues that, "The Holocaust cannot remain an abstraction to those who read the literature. It becomes infinitely more than historical facts, theories, speculations—important as these may be. It becomes the experience of individuals—of victims, perpetrators, bystanders. It becomes a crushing personal event in individual lives. . . . One *feels* the tragedy; one is moved to anger, indignation, compassion. And one is often led to confront one's own values and to reflect on the meaning the Holocaust offers for one's own life" (p. 615). He concludes by stating that Holocaust literature "is a literature which shows how precarious our being human is, how easily humans can forfeit their humanity . . . In short, it is a literature with a massive human weight and generates intense self-questioning and self-searching. It can touch students on deeply personal levels . . . [Indeed,] it give[s] students unique opportunities for self-confrontation, self-understanding, and the enlargement of sensibility" (Teichman, 1976, p. 613). If students are going to benefit from reading this literature, then they will need the guidance of an instructor who encourages the raising and examining of penetrating questions. Likewise, it will require a teacher who embraces a pedagogy that is not satisfied with simple answers to complex questions.

In *The Call of Stories: Teaching and the Moral Imagination*, Robert Coles (1989) delineates the power that stories (both fiction and people's personal stories) can have on the reader/listener. At one point, he says, "We all remember in our own lives times when a book has become for us a signpost, a continuing presence in our lives. Novels [as well as other types of literature] lend themselves to such purposes; their plots offer a psychological or moral journey, with impasses and breakthroughs, with decisions made and destinations achieved" (Coles, 1989, p. 10). Indeed, not only do certain works of literature induce one to become "involved" with the stories of others, but they also provide a means to journey into one's self—one's own mind, heart, and soul. By reading, studying, and discussing literature, one can begin to make connections between one's lived life and those of others. That is not to say that one will even come close to completely understanding what a person experienced during something so overwhelming as the Holocaust, but it is a powerful entry point for attempting to appreciate another's experiences, insights, sorrows, pain, and hope. In that sense, literature provides a unique and powerful lens with which to view and examine the world.

The eminent poet William Carlos Williams suggested to Coles that while "novels or short stories aren't meant to save the world, [a] story *can* engage a reader—not every reader, and some readers only somewhat, but plenty of readers a lot, a whole lot. I mean, art reaches the mind and the heart, and in a way that it doesn't easily get shaken off" (Coles, 1989, p. 120). Isn't this exactly what most educators would hope would happen during a study of the Holocaust—that is, that the students experience such an awakening to this soul-shattering event that its import and ramifications would *never leave them?*

The best literature about the Holocaust is also capable of assisting students to come to an understanding of "deep truths" (Drew, 1991, p. 128). Such truths may include truths about the motivations of the perpetrators, the cataclysmic impact of the daily incidents upon victims during the Holocaust years, the varied reactions of the victims, the motivations of the bystanders and rescuers, and the shattering ramifications that the world should have experienced due to the Holocaust's occurrence.

Directly related to the above point, Holocaust survivor and scholar Henry Friedlander (1979) suggests that "a study of the literature of the Holocaust could serve as a springboard for analysis" [of the whys, hows, whens, and whats of the Holocaust] (p. 541). He goes on to state, "Using various readings—memoirs, novels, plays, essays—students can engage in a semistructured discussion of the issues raised by the Holocaust" (Friedlander, 1979, p. 541).

Ultimately, studying literary responses to the Holocaust can assist students to:

1. confront the extent of the injustices and murderous actions of the Nazis;
2. recognize the deeds of resistance and heroism in ghettos and concentration camps;
3. explore the spiritual resistance manifested by the various responses—including the literary—that portray the dignity of an individual or a people whose spirits transcended the evil of their murderers;
4. recognize the different roles—such as victim, oppressor, bystander, and rescuer—which were assumed or thrust upon people during the Holocaust and the choices or lack of choices that evolved;
5. analyze the corruption of language cultivated by the Nazis; for example, the use of the terms *emigration* for expulsion, *evacuation* for deportation, *deportation* for transportation to a place that often resulted in death, *aktions* for roundups that usually led to mass murder, and *Final Solution* for the systematically planned annihilation of every single Jew; and
6. make important and unique distinctions regarding the various nuances and shades of gray concerning the actions of individuals and groups.

High-quality literature avoids stereotyping individual and group personalities, beliefs, and actions; and in doing so, "complicates," in the most positive sense of the word, people and situations so that they are portrayed in a way that is "true to life."

Carefully selected literature also provides the older and more mature students with a glimmer of insight into the devastating reality of the Holocaust; that is, "life lived in extremity." Examples include the unbearable and horrific injustice, cruelty, and hatred meted out by the perpetrators; the overwhelming fear, anxiety, and loss experienced by the victims; and the degradation and abject horror that permeated all aspects of life and death under the Nazi reign of terror. That said, while it is essential to study the devastation of the Holocaust in order to understand that the Holocaust was not simply another human rights infraction but rather something cataclysmic in the annals of humanity, teachers should not bombard their students with one horror after another to the point where the students descend into a state of hopelessness and abject anger directed at all of humanity.

The best literature on the Holocaust allows students to examine their own lives and to ponder what it means to be "just," to be prejudiced, to discriminate and hate, and to be a bystander, a perpetrator, or a victim. Literature is also capable of assisting students to ponder how some are ill-treated or made to feel like the "other." It also assists them in considering serious ethical and moral questions and dilemmas that place them in the shoes of the characters in order to gain a sense of the characters' predicaments. Literature highlights the complexities and ambiguities inherent in behavior, which far too many prefer to think of in strict terms of black and white.

In regard to the latter point, Farnham (1983) asserts that:

> The teaching and learning opportunities inherent in the Holocaust are immense . . . it can be taught from many points of view, those of literary analysis, history, and psychology to name but three, but it has been my experience that dealing with the ethical dimensions of the literature of the Holocaust is a strong invitation to students to confront the values of life in general. . . .
>
> Few bodies of literature are so pregnant a source of problematic issues as the literature of the Holocaust. . . . That this thinking is stimulated is, I think, most vital. Teaching students the historical and sociological facts of the Holocaust is of little value unless the ethical implications of the facts are raised. (p. 67)

Be that as it may, in order for students to come to a *clear understanding* of the Holocaust, they must understand the history of the Holocaust. In light of that, it is imperative that teachers undergird their use of literature on the Holocaust with a substantial amount of history. This can be accomplished in a number of ways, and it doesn't matter how it is done; what does matter, however, is that students have a solid sense of the whos, whens, hows, and whys of the Holocaust. Peggy Drew (1989) has argued that:

> The magnitude of the Holocaust is so great that any individual story, if read in isolation, is going to reflect only one aspect of historical truth. Some [literature] deals more directly with the atrocities themselves, but even these, without the historical perspective, only tell one person's [or family or group's] story. They do not differ to any great degree from any story of personal tragedy, because they do not, indeed they cannot, reflect the "disruption of a familiar moral universe." Only when read within an historical context, with some knowledge of the scope and magnitude of the Holocaust, is the reader able to put the individual story into a more universal perspective. (p. 21)

Drew (1991) has also astutely observed that:

> Young people have little sense of time, in historical terms. Unless they have studied the history of the period about which they are reading, they have no framework within which to put it. Rarely do they make the connections between what they have read and actual historical events unless they have had some formal study of the historical period in question. They have read an exciting, perhaps moving, story that may leave a lasting impression on them, but adds nothing to their understanding of history, as they do not have the knowledge necessary to put it into historical context. (p. 128)

Drew (1991) concludes by asserting that "unless [the history and situations within that history] are made real, there is little point in studying these events. If the study of genocide is not also the study of humanity and inhumanity, if it does not add to our understanding of human behavior, then what is its purpose in the curriculum?" (p. 128). This point suggests the critical need for teachers to establish clear and strong rationales for teaching a piece of Holocaust literature.

Finally—and this is germane to the aforementioned point—what should *never* be forgotten as teachers go about preparing and implementing lessons about this history is the profound fact that *millions upon millions of innocent people*—mothers, fathers, children, grandmothers, grandfathers, uncles ,and aunts—were subjected to horrendous discrimination, cruelty, and horrific deaths at the hands of the Nazis, not because of what they did but because of who they were. Teaching this material should not *ever* simply result in another English or history lesson, where stories are typically selected simply because they are "exciting" (as the author heard one teacher say) or a poem simply for the purpose of examining its prosody and structure.

Availability of Literature on the Holocaust

There is a huge amount of literature (novels, novellas, short stories, children's and early adolescent literature, young adult literature, and poetry) that addresses various facets of the Holocaust. It is eclectic in style, and includes, but is not limited to, that which is documentary-like, realistic, surrealistic, and lamentative. The story lines address a wide array of situations, incidences, and events, including the ever-increasing prejudice and discrimination against the Jews in Nazi Germany, the roundups and deportations, the abject hardships and death in the ghettos, resistance efforts, the deportations to the concentration and death camps, the selections and killings, the horrific "medical experiments" conducted in some of the camps, the liberation, and life in the post-Holocaust years.

Much of the finest literature was written by those who experienced the Holocaust firsthand. Some of this literature, including a great deal of poetry, was written during the period 1933–1945, in ghettos and camps and by partisans in the woods, but most was written after the conclusion of World War II. Many who did not experience the Holocaust firsthand have also written plays, poetry, novels, short stories, and young adolescent literature about the Holocaust.

Like most bodies of literature, the quality of works that portray some aspect of the Holocaust ranges from the mediocre to the superb. As this author has argued elsewhere:

> The mediocre is that which trivializes the magnitude of the Holocaust or turns it into melodrama. It is also that writing that treats the Holocaust as simply another event in history or another story to be told, without fully acknowledging its specialness. Finally, it is also that writing that uses the tragedy of the Holocaust as a background event or metaphor in order to either heighten the interest of the primary story or to draw historical or personal but flawed analogies between one event and another. (Totten, 1988, p. 211)

The weakest literature also has a tendency to portray the history inaccurately; to stereotype the appearance, ideas, behaviors and beliefs of people; and to create wooden or unbelievable characters. Two examples of such works are Elisabeth Reuter's *Best Friends*, and Carol Matas's *Daniel's Story.*

The strongest pieces of literature about the Holocaust for young adolescents are those that are well written, engaging, developmentally appropriate, and historically accurate. (For a listing and description of many of the best literary works available for children and young adolescents, see the U.S. Holocaust Memorial Museum's *Annotated Bibliography* and the *Facing History and Ourselves Holocaust and Human Behavior Annotated Bibliography.* Complete citations of these bibliographies are included in the annotated bibliography at the end of this chapter.)

The strongest literary works for older students meet basically the same criteria, except that they contain a more complex story line and/or involve more sophisticated character development. (For a listing and description of these works, readers should consult one or more of the annotated bibliographies included in the bibliography at the end of this chapter.)

Selection of Holocaust Literature for Use in the Classroom

When selecting any resource or curricular material for classroom use, teachers need to reflect continuously on their curricular rationale. Ascertaining the *why* will influence the selection of genre (e.g., novel, short story, poetry, drama) as well as the focus of the story line (e.g., the particular aspect of the Holocaust such as the pre-Holocaust period and beyond; life in the ghettos; the roundups; deportations to the concentration and death camps; the resistance; or a combination of these). Selection of the genre and specific works will also be contingent upon student interest as well as on the amount of time that can be allocated for such a study. Early on, teachers also need to decide how they are going to use the literature (e.g., what sort of teaching strategies and learning activities will be most effective in assisting the students to study and learn the literature).

Prior to using a work, teachers must ascertain whether a piece is developmentally appropriate for use with their students. The most effective way to accomplish this is by reading the material prior to using it. For the most part, the most conscientious teachers do this. In those situations where teachers have neglected to read a work prior to using it with their students, the results have often been less than positive—and, in certain cases, disastrous. This is due to three main reasons: (1) the work proved too difficult for students to understand; (2) the work included profanity unsuitable for classroom use; and/or (3) the carnage described and depicted was excessively graphic and thus unsuitable for use with certain students.

Teachers need to take into consideration a number of other key issues prior to selecting a piece of Holocaust literature for classroom use:

■ *First, the work should be historically accurate, and not convey misconceptions about the history or the people involved.*

On a simple, but important level, one needs to ascertain the following: Are the dates of actual events correct? Are the names of actual people correct? Is the chronology of actual events correct? On a more complex level, one must ask: Does the literary work delineate the incidents and events in their varied complexity versus providing a simplistic portrayal that is bereft of the intricacies involved (including the torturously difficult no-win decisions many of the victims faced)?

Furthermore, even though the events are fictionalized, teachers should ask themselves such questions as: Could the events have happened in the manner described or are they outlandish? Is the work set in a historical context that conveys the significance of the historical period, events, incidents? Does the literature address or complement those issues that we are examining in the larger study? If a teacher answers "No" to any of these questions, then another piece of literature needs to be selected.

Drew (1991) also suggests that:

> If the literature is to add to the understanding of history . . . teachers should select books that represent the broad events of that history rather than uncommon or unique occurrences. For example, books on the Polish resistance during the Holocaust may be historically accurate; the fact that 85 percent of the Polish Jews died in the Holocaust, however, makes it obvious that this is far from typical of Holocaust experiences in Poland. A story of resistance, like . . . [the] Newbery Award winner, *Number the Stars,* by Lois Lowry, represents a larger movement, as 98 percent of the Danish Jews were saved, but even so, the Holocaust is essentially a story, not of resistance, but of atrocity. Used in conjunction with other books, works like this can add to the understanding of the Holocaust, used in isolation, they distort the history. (p. 128)

■ *Second, teachers need to evaluate the readability of the piece.* Is the piece at the right reading level (not too easy, not overly difficult) for their particular students? Is the reading level at the right level of sophistication (e.g., not simplistic or too erudite)?

Shawn (1994) suggests that in order to provide students with the best learning experience possible, teachers need to consider the "flexibility" of the piece (p. G4). That is, (1) Is the piece "relatively easy for students to read, and for teachers to discuss with students, individually or in groups"?; (2) Would the piece be useful in "laying the groundwork for the teaching of Holocaust history"?; and (3) Do the pieces "offer opportunities to explore a variety of important issues and themes"? (Shawn, 1994, p. G4).

■ *Third, the work must be engaging and thought-provoking to the students.* There is little justification in using a work that students are likely to find boring or bereft of the power to move them to deeper thought. This is not to say that a difficult work or one that challenges their abilities should not be used. It is to say that there are an ample number of works to choose from and teachers should attempt to select a work that will most likely engage their students. When feasible, it is wise to provide the students with an opportunity to select those works that they find most engaging, thus capitalizing on the students' natural curiosity and interests.

■ *Fourth, literary works should be selected that are not so long or so complex that they almost automatically result in there not being adequate time for ample discussion of the work.* A study of the Holocaust demands that there be ample time for the students to wrestle with and discuss the complex and horrific material to which they are being introduced, to raise questions and issues that they are likely to have, and to be allowed to vent their concerns and, in many cases, their horror. Thus, works (either due to their size or complexity) that almost automatically leave no time for such discussion should be avoided for classroom use and replaced by other works. Students should be encouraged to read the longer or more complex works on their own outside of class.

■ *Fifth, literary pieces that romanticize the history of the Holocaust should be avoided.* Some authors use the Holocaust as a "setting" in order to develop a maudlin story or one of unrequited love. Such works need to be totally avoided, because they distort the history and draw the reader away from the significance that the Holocaust period has for humanity. On another note, which is related to the above point by Drew, some authors have a tendency to overemphasize the aspect of rescue, thus distorting the history. Teachers need to keep in mind that "at best, less than one-half of one percent of the total population [of non-Jews] under Nazi occupation helped to rescue Jews" (Oliner & Oliner, 1991, p. 363).

■ *Sixth, the literary work should present "true-to-life" characters, as opposed to caricatures or stereotypes.* In this regard, the works should "offer recognizable human experiences, and foster involvement and identification with the victims of the Holocaust" (Shawn, 1994, p. G4).

Corroborating Shawn's points, Rudman and Rosenberg (1991) sensibly suggest that: "Jewish characters should be portrayed as functioning human beings who have decisions to make, and who, rightly or wrongly, make them. Protagonists should be three-dimensional, neither wholly sweet-natured and generous nor constantly strong and heroic" (p. 163). They go on to argue that the most "[e]ffective stories of the Holocaust refrain from elevating their characters to mythic proportions. Instead, they underscore the common humanity of all the victims as well as the survivors and rescuers" (Rudman & Rosenberg, 1991, p. 170).

■ *Seventh, in light of the fact that many of the literary works on the Holocaust include ghastly and horrifying images, scenes, incidents, and events, a teacher must use the soundest judgment possible when selecting and employing such works in class.* Teachers must absolutely avoid bombarding their students with one horrific image after another. Unfortunately, some teachers believe that only by bombarding students with the most horrific images and stories will they (the teachers) "get through" to their students; that is, drive home the horror of the Holocaust. However, instead of capturing the students' attention or inducing learning, such actions may, paradoxically, achieve the opposite effect. While some students may simply turn away from the history, others may become so numb that they cannot focus on it.

It is best to use those "texts that do not exploit . . . the students' emotional vulnerability" (Parsons & Totten, 1993, p. 6). More specifically, "[g]raphic material should be used in a judicious manner and only to the extent necessary to achieve the objective of the lesson" (Parsons & Totten, 1993, p. 6).

■ *Eighth, literature of the Holocaust should "offer sufficient stimulus for readers to draw their own conclusions and avoid didactic sermonizing"* (Rudman & Rosenberg, 1991, p. 163). Literature that presents powerful and historically accurate story lines with believable characters do not need to "preach" about the horrors of the Holocaust; it will be evident throughout.

■ *Ninth, the literature selected should be capable of challenging students to examine their own lived lives and world.* Ideally, a study of such literature will prod students to examine their own prejudices, including why and how they interact with and treat people whom they may perceive as different from themselves. Hopefully it will also make students more conscious and concerned about civil and human rights infractions in their own communities, state, nation, and around the world.

■ *Tenth, works should be chosen that "enlighten students [and] encourage further study of the Holocaust, thus helping to ensure remembrance"* (Shawn, 1994, p. G4). Teachers need to select works that will "plant a seed" of concern in their students' minds vis-à-vis the significance that the Holocaust has for humanity as well as for their own lives.

When selecting pieces for children and young adolescents (10- to 15-year-olds), stories that use particularly offensive profanity are better left unused. There are enough outstanding works for use in the classroom that teachers do not need to select pieces the language of which will either offend certain students and/or incense parents.

Finally, it is worth noting that both early adolescents and older students often are intrigued with stories and novels whose protagonists are approximately the same age as themselves. Works such as these are likely to engage the students even more than other Holocaust literature due to the fact that many young readers will more readily identify with the characters in the story.

Holocaust Poetry

The most finely wrought poetry has the power to penetrate as deeply as anything language has to offer into the mysteries of being and the multifaceted aspects of life. Just as the brutality of the genocide of the Jews, the Gypsies, and others causes one to ponder long and hard over the "face" of humanity, the most powerful poetry about the Holocaust also causes one to ponder long and hard about the fact of genocide, including the human and inhuman proportions of it. Furthermore, "poetry encourages us to view the human and natural scene with a fresh eye, uncontaminated by the clichés of customary speech" (Langer, 1995, p. 558). This is particularly important when examining such a devastating event as the Holocaust.

As far as using poetry in the classroom, one of its many advantages over long short stories, novels, and plays is its brevity. Its succinctness is ideal for those facing a packed curriculum and/or serious time constraints.

The subject matter addressed in the poetry of the Holocaust is as rich as that found in fiction. There are poems by those who wrote poetry in the forest, the ghettos, the concentration camps and even in the death camps; by survivors of the Holocaust who wrote in the aftermath of that tragedy; and by Jews and non-Jews who either did not live in Europe during that period and/or were not even alive. Regarding the first group, Nobel laureate and Holocaust survivor Elie Wiesel (1970) has written the following:

> Poems, litanies, plays: to write them Jews went without sleep, bartered their food for pencils and papers. They gambled with their fate. They risked their lives. No matter. They went on fitting together words and symbols. An instant before perishing in Auschwitz, Bialistok, in Buna, dying men described their agony . . . There was then a veritable passion to testify for the future, against death and oblivion, a passion conveyed by every possible means of expression. (p. 39)

In the same vein, Aaron (1983) has noted that

> Astonishing as it may be, literary activity was vital and widespread in the ghettos, in hiding, among the partisans, on the "Aryan" side, and even in some of the concentration camps. Indeed, after waves of mass deportations to death centers, those who temporarily hugged life in the various places feverishly turned to writing. Spontaneous literary activity not only continued but actually increased when one would expect language to evaporate, to turn to ashes in the conflagration of gas chambers and crematoria.
>
>   . . . Although the writers availed themselves of the entire spectrum of literary genres, the most popular one was poetry. That this poetry is probably the richest of the Holocaust literature should not be surprising. For poetry—perhaps because it provides, more often than any other literary genre, the most precise correlatives for states of consciousness—was the first vehicle of reaction against Nazi barbarism. Moreover, the poets, writing from "the heart of darkness," reflect an immediacy of experience that is untainted by the remembering process of memory. Nothing but total recall could unveil the truth articulated in this body of literature. (pp. 120, 121)

There are poems that are easy to understand, as well as a huge body of poetry that is difficult and complex. Many of these poems are interwoven with erudite allusions and symbols. The latter need not be avoided, but prior to introducing them into the classroom, teachers need to make sure that their students have the cognitive abilities, reading skills, and knowledge bases to analyze and ultimately understand such poetry. (For a list of poems appropriate for various students at the secondary level, see the Appendix to this chapter, page 52.)

On a different note, those poems and songs that use the Holocaust as a metaphor for one's personal ills and pains, and draw false and simplistic analogies between the Holocaust and certain other human rights infractions or other injustices should be avoided. Such pieces as Sylvia Plath's "Lady Lazarus" and "Daddy," Aaron Kurtz' "Behold the Sea," the Boomtown Rats' "I Never Loved Eva Braun," and Lenny Bruce's "My Name is Adolf Eichmann," all of which have found their way into various Holocaust curricula, do little or nothing to further student understanding of the Holocaust. Indeed, most of them are more likely to provide students with a skewed view of the Holocaust and pass the Holocaust off as simply another "ailment" among many found in society. Over and above that, their wording (e.g., "cute" rhymes, mocking voices, and flippant tone) can seduce students into thinking that the Holocaust was no more serious than the issues their favorite musicians and bands sing about in their songs today. In light of that, a simple rule of thumb is to avoid them; instead, teachers should use those poems that are truly thought provoking, well wrought, and most important, deal with significant aspects of the Holocaust.

Methods for Incorporating Literature into the Classroom

There are, of course, innumerable ways in which teachers can incorporate literature into their study of the Holocaust. Provided here are selected instructional strategies appropriate for use in grades 7–12. They are based on the author's personal teaching experiences as well as those of other successful educators.

1. **Anticipatory Sets.** At the beginning of a study, it is always worthwhile to obtain a sense of the students' existing knowledge base of the Holocaust. One way of doing so is for teachers to have their students write down everything they know about the Holocaust—basic facts such as dates, countries involved, people involved; concepts such as totalitarianism, fascism, antisemitism; focus; and so on. Next, the students should work individually to develop a "cluster" or "mind-map" reflecting their knowledge. Once that is completed the class as a whole could develop a single "cluster" on the board. Such a preassessment allows teachers to ascertain their students' knowledge base regarding the breadth, depth, and accuracy of their students' knowledge. (For information on using clusters, mind-maps, or webbing in the classroom, see Carol Booth Olson (Ed.), *Practical Ideas for Teaching Writing as a Process at the Elementary School and Middle School Levels.* Sacramento, CA: California State Department of Education, 1996.)

2. **Establishing a Basic Understanding of Holocaust History.** When studying a piece of Holocaust literature it is vital that students gain an understanding *about the history* of the Holocaust. Grace Caporino, an English teacher at Carmel High School in Carmel, New York, helps her students gain key insights into the history of the Holocaust prior to reading literary works by doing the following:

> I begin with a brief chronology of the immediate events in Europe which preceded the Holocaust and then I assign Chapter One ("Precedents") in the student edition

of Raul Hilberg's *The Destruction of the European Jews* (New York: Holmes and Meier, 1985). That chapter illuminates both the historical and religious policies that paved the way for the events of the Holocaust. [More specifically,] Hilberg discusses the cyclical 'trend in the three successive goals of anti-Jewish administrators' (e.g., the conversion, expulsion and exclusion policy from the fourth century through the middle ages laid the groundwork for Hitler's final solution of annihilation). My students raise questions such as "Why the Jews?" They do not understand why the Jews have been a target group for persecution throughout history and they know nothing of Christian complicity in this matter. Students examining Holocaust literature for the first time are often confused about the apparent ease with which Hitler implemented the Final Solution. Hilberg's historical perspective explains the present by shedding light on the past. Hilberg notes that in the past, "The missionaries of Christianity had said in effect: You have no right to live among us as Jews. The secular rulers who followed had proclaimed: You have no right to live among us. The Nazis at last decreed: You have no right to live" (p. 8). Another feature of this chapter is Hilberg's illustration of a side-by-side comparison of the Church Canonical Law and the Nazi anti-Jewish measures. For students seeking a better understanding of the dynamics of both perpetrator and victim in the Holocaust, as well as an understanding of the forerunners of Hitler's policies, Hilberg's "Precedents" provides satisfactory answers. (Written statement provided to the author by Caporino, 1991.)

Another excellent work for assisting students in gaining an understanding of the history of the Holocaust is Michael Berenbaum's *The World Must Know: The History of the Holocaust as Told in the United States Holocaust Memorial Museum* (Boston, MA: Little, Brown, 1993). This volume was written for use by high school students and not only is it reader-friendly, but it includes numerous and invaluable photographs and excerpts from first-person accounts.

The same sort of historical preparation can be done for specific pieces of poetry about various aspects of the Holocaust. For example, if students read poems in *". . . I Never Saw Another Butterfly": Children's Drawings and Poems from Terezin Concentration Camp, 1942–1944* (New York: Schocken Books, 1993), they could first read, study, and discuss the chapter entitled "A 'Model' Concentration Camp: Theresienstadt" in Bea Stadtler's *The Holocaust: A History of Courage and Resistance* (West Orange, NJ: Behrman House, 1994).

3. Reader Response Theory. An extremely powerful way to engage students in a study of literature is through the use of reader response theory. Commenting on the basic difference between a traditional approach to literary study and the reader response process, Louise Rosenblatt, a pioneer in the field of reader response theory, argues persuasively that the reader should not be perceived as "a blank tape registering a ready-made message. [Rather, he or she should be] actively involved in [coming to an understanding of a work] out of his/her responses to the text" (quoted in Sheridan, 1991, p. 804). Unlike many traditional methods of literary study, reader response is a process that honors the students' backgrounds, diverse experiences, unique insights, and perspectives as an integral component in the study of literature. Thus, instead of relying on the omniscient thoughts of a critic or the privileged knowledge of the teacher, it recognizes and highly values each individual student's response to a piece of literature.

In an essay entitled "Rewriting the Book on Literature: Changes Sought in How Literature is Taught, What Students Read," O'Neill (1994) has written that:

> Basically, reader response theory differs most radically from previous theories about teaching literature in the degree of emphasis placed on the reader's response to an interpretation of the text . . . In reader response theory, the text's meaning is considered to reside in the 'transaction' between the reader and the text, not from the text alone.
>
> . . . In practice, reader response theory considers very carefully how students respond intellectually and emotionally to the text . . . By validating students' responses, teachers can spark a lively discussion from which a careful literary analysis will flow. . . . Rather than beginning with a discussion of symbolism or metaphor, for example, teachers should allow an exploration of these aspects to develop from students' own observations about the work.
>
> . . . *The emphasis on getting students to respond to the literature doesn't mean that any response is as good as another. Students are continuously urged to return to the text to find validation for their views.* [italics added] (pp. 7, 8)

The key is to provide the students with an opportunity to begin to examine literature from their own unique perspective, without imposing anyone else's interpretation on them. This is a method that avoids that stultifying situation where students feel compelled to come up with the so-called "single correct answer." For a thorough and enlightening discussion of reader-response theory methodology, see Alan C. Purves, Theresa Rogers, and Anna O. Soter, *How Porcupines Make Love III: Readers, Texts, Cultures in the Response-Based Literature Classroom* (White Plains, NY: Longman, 1995). For a discussion of a pedagogical strategy that uses reader response theory to assist students to examine a Holocaust-related poem, see Chapter 7, Samuel Totten, " 'Written in Pencil in a Sealed Railway-Car': Incorporating Poetry into a Study of the Holocaust via a Reader Response Theory Activity."

4. Reflective Journals. Having students keep reflective journals throughout the study is a good method for accomplishing all of the following: assisting students in examining their newfound knowledge of the Holocaust; raising questions or concerns they have about what they're reading; enabling them to ponder the meaning the literature has for their own lives; and providing the teacher with critical information in regard to the level of the students' understanding or misunderstanding of key facts, concepts, and issues.

Specific journal assignments could require students to reflect on the meaning that a story or poem has for them; comment on new insights they have gleaned about the Holocaust from a story or poem; discuss whether a literary work is one they will likely remember or not remember and why; examine and comment on a novelist's or poet's use of inverted symbolism or biblical allusions; or record a line or image in a poem that particularly stood out for them and provide an explanation as to why that was the case. There are unlimited ways to use such a journal; indeed, teachers and students are limited only by their imagination.

The journals can also serve as a means of two-way communication for the teacher and student. While reading a student's journal, the teacher could pose questions for the student to address in the next set of entries. Likewise, a student could raise questions and/or issues for the teacher to address. Writing in the journals could be done both in class and at home.

It is imperative that clear and well-structured guidelines be provided to the students (e.g., how they should go about writing a reflective journal, the need for depth over superficial coverage, the need to avoid simply reiterating what one has read versus the need to comment on one's new insights/perspectives). If the latter is not done, then more often than not the journals will become not much more than a recapitulation of the content and/or what the teacher has said about a work.

5. Writing Assignments for Reflective Purposes. Any type of writing assignment that requires students to reflect on what they've read and to analyze and synthesize is an ideal exercise. One worthwhile assignment is to have the students write a letter to a character in a literary work in which they comment on the most important new ideas, concepts, and insights gleaned, what they may never forget after reading the work, what they wish *always* to remember, and what they want to share with someone else about the work. Students need not address all of the questions, but rather may choose the one or two that really catch their individual interest. Students should be encouraged to let their "own voices" and feelings shine through. They should be reminded (and required) to include a salutation and a closing, just as they would in any letter they write.

Such writing becomes much more personal, powerful, and meaningful than many staid assignments where students are required to write a typical essay. By writing about something they deeply care about and by connecting the affective and cognitive domains, the assignment becomes less of a school assignment and instead something that has personal relevance for the student. (Note: This is not to say that essays do not have a place in such a study. They do!)

6. Using Individual Poems as an Introduction to a Lesson. Individual poems can be used as an introduction to a lesson on a particular topic (e.g., life in the ghettos, deportations, the mass murder of the Jews), theme (e.g., bystanders, loss, remembrance), or unit of study. For example, when focusing on the issue of remembrance and the ramifications that the Holocaust has for those living today, a teacher might introduce Yuri Shul's "The Permanent Delegate." Or, if teachers wish to focus on the issue of culpability or denial, they might introduce William Heyen's "Riddle." Yet if teachers wish to drive home the point that individuals were behind the statistics (e.g., the six million who perished), they may design a learning activity around Herman Taube's "A Single Hair." Discussion of a poem can raise a host of issues that the students can pursue and revisit during their study of the actual history of the Holocaust period.

7. Outside Reading Assignments. To both conserve classroom time and to provide a worthwhile homework assignment, Stephen Feinberg, a former middle school teacher in Wayland, Massachusetts who now works at the United States Holocaust Memorial Museum, assigned his students an outside reading assignment in which each student was asked to select a book from the following list: *Friedrich, Devil in Vienna, Night, The Diary of Anne Frank, Upon the Head of the Goat,* and *The Upstairs Room.* Students were allowed to select any other novel or memoir that deals with the Holocaust, as long as it constituted quality literature. The directions he gave his students were as follows: "Two weeks after you begin reading the book, you will be asked to write me a letter in which you will describe what you have read so far. The description should include mention of the main characters in the book and a brief description of the plot and/or theme of the book." This part of the assignment constitutes a check on whether the students are making progress or not on their reading; and as such, it is not graded.

The rest of the directions are as follows: "After you have finished reading the book, you will be asked to write me another letter. This second letter should indicate how the book increased your understanding and knowledge of the Holocaust or Nazis. This letter should include specific references to the action in your book. This second letter will receive a grade."

8. Comparing and Contrasting a Fictional Work and a First-Person Account. Having students read a fictional work and a first-person account by a victim of the Holocaust, a survivor, a liberator, or other eyewitness about a similar event, and then comparing and contrasting (during a classroom discussion, a small group discussion, or in writing) the information and insights gleaned from the two genres provides them with a rich lens to examine the events of the Holocaust. For other ideas on how to incorporate first-person accounts into a study of the Holocaust, see Samuel Totten's "The Use of First-Person Accounts in Teaching about the Holocaust," *The British Journal of Holocaust Education,* Winter 1994, 3(2): 160–183 and/or the chapter on first-person accounts in Totten and Feinberg's *Teaching and Studying the Holocaust* (Boston: Allyn and Bacon, 2001).

9. An In-depth Study of an Author-Survivor's Life and Works. For those teachers who wish to have their students engage in an in-depth literary study, a powerful assignment is to have the students examine how an author's life influenced the plots, themes, motifs, and symbolic structure of his or her works. Prior to assigning this project (which is most appropriate for 10th, 11th, and 12th graders), the teacher needs to ascertain whether enough biographical or autobiographical materials (biographies, autobiographies, oral histories, interviews, biographical essays, etc.) are available on particular authors. Without ample materials available on an author, this project is nearly impossible to undertake. Next, the teacher should develop a list of 20 to 30 authors (novelists, playwrights, short-story writers, poets), and then provide his or her students with a quick and concise overview of the author's life, works, and so on. In this way, hopefully, the students will discover an author they wish to learn more about. The basic assignment for each student is as follows: Read at least one major biography or autobiography about or by the author; if the author selected is a novelist or playwright, then read at least three major works by the author; if the author selected is a short-story writer or poet, then read approximately 10 short stories and 20 poems, respectively (the teacher could require that certain stories and poems be read but also allow the student to select a number on his or her own); and read at least three critical essays about the author's work. Finally, in a major paper, analyze how the author's life (formative years, various experiences, beliefs, friendships, religious and political affiliations, etc.) had an impact on his or her plots, symbolic structure, imagery, motifs, and themes. (For a more detailed description of such a project, see Samuel Totten's "Examining the Holocaust through the Lives and Literary Works of Victims and Survivors" in Robert Hauptman and Susan Hubbs Motin [Eds.], *The Holocaust: Memories, Research, Reference,* pp. 165–188. New York: The Haworth Press.)

10. Highlighting Certain Topics and/or Themes. Select pieces of literature that address certain topics and/or themes that can be used to complement a historical study of the Holocaust. Some of the many themes one might focus on are the ever-increasing discrimination faced by the Jews from 1933 onward; the bystander syndrome; life and death in the ghettos; the death camps; resistance; the "choiceless choices" people were forced to make; resistance; the "other victims" of the Holocaust (Gypsies, the mentally handicapped, the physically handicapped); hope against hope; abject fear; loss; mourning; the aftermath of the Holocaust. For example, Ida Fink's short story entitled "The Key Game" could be used to illuminate such issues as the abject fear Jews experienced at the hands of the Nazis, the plight of children during the Holocaust years, the problems of attempting to go into hiding, and the fate of the Jews.

The literature can serve as entry points into an examination and discussion of key issues as well as a "springboard for analysis" (Friedlander, 1979, p. 541). Ideally, the literary works and their themes could be interwoven throughout the study in order to assist the students at becoming more reflective about what they are reading, studying, and discussing.

11. Comparing and Contrasting Literary Works on the Same Subject and/or Theme. Select two or more literary pieces (novels, novellas, short stories, poems) on the same or a similar incident or event, and have the students compare and contrast the various perspectives, experiences, and actions of the characters; the similarities and differences of the portrayal of events; the similarities and differences evident in the perspectives of the authors; and the differences in the style of the works.

12. Using Literature to Introduce Students to a Study of the Holocaust. Stephen Feinberg, a former middle school teacher in Wayland, Massachusetts and now a museum educator at the United States Holocaust Memorial Museum, found that "novels such as Lois Lowry's *Number the Stars,* and Esther Hautzig's *The Endless Steppe* are good to introduce middle school students (grades six through eight) to the study of the Holocaust. Questions that can be addressed in a three to five day study of any these works are: 'What was the Holocaust?' (*Number the Stars*); 'Who were the Nazis?' (*Number the Stars*); 'What are some of the consequences of war and the mistreatment of people?' (*Endless Steppe, Number the Stars*); and

'Where did this activity take place?' (*Number the Stars* and *Endless Steppe*)." (Written statement provided to the author by Feinberg).

Feinberg also found that such novels as Doris Orgel's *The Devil in Vienna* and Hans P. Richter's *Friedrich* appeal to upper middle level/junior high school students (grades seven through nine), "for they all deal with the emotional and social issues that teenagers grapple with." He adds that "the videotape entitled *Friendship in Vienna,* based on Orgel's novel, deals with issues of courage, survival, friendship, and family dynamics. All of these issues strike a responsive chord in middle school and junior high school students, and serve as the entry way to a fuller examination of the Holocaust as a historical reality. [It should be noted that] with a limited amount of time available, these works can raise meaningful and pertinent questions, moral and philosophical in nature, about the Holocaust. Students can address the issue of personal versus collective responsibility for the actions of nation states or the sort of power an individual has in dealing with social issues. Encouraging a comparison with our own time, they can wrestle with the possibility of a Holocaust-like tragedy happening in our own society." (Personal communication, July 1992)

13. Examining "Choiceless Choices." During a study of Holocaust literature, the students could focus on what literary critic and Holocaust specialist Lawrence Langer (1982) refers to as the "choiceless choices" that the Nazis' victims were forced to make on a daily basis. For example, the people "were plunged into a crisis . . . where crucial decisions did not reflect options between life and death, but between one form of abnormal response and another, both imposed by a situation that was in no way of the victim's own choosing" (p. 72). Langer (1982) cites several examples of such choiceless choices. In one situation, in a barrack at Auschwitz, "there was a single limited source of water for washing and for draining excrement from the latrine. If the women took the water for washing, the primitive sewage system would be blocked, creating an intolerably offensive (and unhealthy) situation" (p. 74). In another case, a non-Jewish physician/prisoner at Auschwitz "was able to save one woman selected for gassing by reporting to the Political Division that an SS man needed her particular skill in his work. But her success was tainted by the response from that department: 'We'll have to take another in her place'" (Langer, 1982, p. 75). Holocaust literature is rife with such situations. By examining such "choiceless choices," the students can begin to gain unique insights into the tortuously difficult situations faced by the victims of the Nazis. Likewise, through an examination and discussion of such situations the students may be more likely to empathize with the horribly difficult dilemmas that confronted the victims.

As students come across such situations in their readings, they could be required to record and comment on them in their learning logs/journals. Or, a large piece of butcher paper could be taped to the class wall during the study, and each time a student or the class as a whole comes across such a situation, it could be noted on the butcher paper. Periodically, the teacher could draw the class's attention to the list and conduct a class discussion or learning activity around it.

14. Responding to One's Newfound Knowledge about the Holocaust via Poetry. Following an in-depth study of the history of the Holocaust (in which students read primary and secondary documents, study various types of literary responses, view films, listen to guest speakers and/or view tapes of survivors), students could create poetry to express their thoughts, feelings, and new insights.

15. Using Poetry as an Alternative Means of Reflection and/or Assessment. Instead of having students keep journals on a daily basis, allow those students who wish to do so to create a poem in regard to their newfound insights and/or feelings concerning the Holocaust. This activity serves to provide powerful and unique closure to lessons and/or sections of a unit.

16. Using the Poem "Hangman" in Conjunction with the "Hangman" Video to Examine Key Issues Relevant to the Holocaust. Many Holocaust curricula include Maurice Ogden's poem, "Hangman." As a result, numerous activities have been designed by teachers and others to use with the poem. For example, the Facing History and Ourselves Foundation (1994) has designed the following questions and activities for use with it:

1. What choices were open to the townspeople when the Hangman arrived? By the time he had finished his work in the town? Was there a way to stop the Hangman? If so, how? If not, why not?
2. How does the poem relate to Germany in the 1930s? To society today?"
3. In 1933, Martin Niemöller, a leader of the Confessing Church, voted for the Nazi party. By 1938, he was in a concentration camp. After the war, he is believed to have said, "They came for the communists, and I did not speak up because I was not a communist. They came for the socialists, and I did not speak up because I was not a socialist. They came for the union leaders, and I did not speak up because I wasn't a union leader. Then they came for the Jews, and I did not speak up because I wasn't a Jew. Then they came for me, and there was no one left to speak up for me." How is the point Niemöller makes similar to the one Maurice Ogden makes in "The Hangman"?
4. "The Hangman" is also available on video from the Facing History Resource Center (16 Hurd Road, Brookline, MA 02146). Teachers who have used the film have stated a need to show it several times to allow their students time to identify the various symbols and reflect on their meaning. After seeing it, think about why the filmmaker turned the animated people into paper dolls. Why did the shadow grow on the courthouse wall? Why did the gallows-tree take root? (pp. 206–207).

For a different and much more detailed approach to using the "Hangman," see *South Carolina Voices: Lessons from the Holocaust,* which is available from the South Carolina Department of Education, South Carolina Council on the Holocaust (1429 Senate St., Room 801, Columbia, South Carolina 29201). What is particularly interesting about the South Carolina approach is that it uses excerpts from actual newspaper articles published in the mid- to late-1930s about Nazi activities.

17. Critiquing Holocaust Poems Written by Those Who Did Not Personally Experience the Holocaust through the Lens of History. Students who have engaged in *a fairly thorough study* of the Holocaust can use their newfound knowledge of the history to critically examine the themes, content, and style of the poems written by those who did not personally experience the Holocaust. For example, students could be asked to critique the strengths and weaknesses of a poem like "Yellow Starred" by Sister Mary Philip deCamara, included in Charles Fishman (Ed.), *Blood to Remember: American Poets on the Holocaust* (Lubbock, TX: Texas Tech University Press, 1991). Among the issues that might be raised are:

> What is the author trying to convey through her use of the literary device of synecdoche?
>
> Is this an effective device or not? Explain.
>
> What are the strengths and the weaknesses of using synecdoche to "get at" the heart of the Holocaust? Select illustrative lines from the poem, and provide an explanation for each of your points.
>
> Why does the author use Anne Frank's name as opposed to that of another victim?
>
> In light of the focus of Anne Frank's diary and the point at which it ends, is there anything problematic in using Anne Frank's name in this poem?
>
> What is the danger and incorrectness of claiming Hitler is the single perpetrator of the Holocaust? Explain your answer.

All of these questions should simply be used as "starter" questions in order to examine key issues surrounding the significance of the history of the Holocaust and the ramifications it has for contemporary society.

18. Examining the Concept of the Shrinking World of the Jews. In order to explore the idea of the "shrinking universe" of the Jews as the Nazis perpetrated their crimes, teachers could—during a study of the history—use Wladyslaw Szlengel's powerful poem "Things" (which is included in Frieda W. Aaron's *Bearing the Unbearable: Yiddish and Polish Poetry in the Ghettos and Concentration Camps* [Albany, NY: State University of New York Press, 1990], and is a poem that focuses on the "contraction of the history of the Warsaw ghetto") in conjunction with the following statement by Elie Wiesel (1984): "The Nazis' aim was to make the Jewish universe shrink—from town to neighborhood, from neighborhood to street, from street to house, from house to room, from room to garret, from garret to cattle car, from cattle car to gas chamber. And they did the same to the individual—separated from his or her community, then from his or her family, then from his or her identity, eventually becoming a work permit, then a number, until the number itself was turned into ashes" (p. 1). If used with care, the use of the history, Szlengel's poem, and Wiesel's statement are capable of providing students with a powerful view of what the Jews faced. Another poem that would be ideal for use with this activity is Abraham Sutzkever's " Teacher Mira," which is a poem about the ever-shrinking number of surviving children in the Vilna Ghetto school.

19. Focusing on the Fate of Children via Poetry Written by Children during the Holocaust. During a study of the Holocaust that draws particular attention to the fate of the approximately one and a half million child victims of the Nazis, the students could study poems that children wrote while incarcerated in Theresienstadt. Many are included in Hana Volavkova's (1993) "*. . . I Never Saw Another Butterfly*": *Children's Drawings and Poems from Terezin Concentration Camp, 1942–1944* (New York: Schocken Books, 1993). The poems could be used in conjunction with diary excerpts written by children during the period and/or other types of first-person accounts in which individuals relate what they experienced as children during the Holocaust period.

20. Studying Poems by Victims and/or Survivors. A special study could be conducted of the poetry that was written about various facets of the Holocaust *by those who actually experienced the events.* More specifically, the students could be introduced to poetry that was actually written during the Holocaust years as well as that which was written in the aftermath of the Holocaust by survivors. As Henryk Grynberg has written, "the quickest reaction" to the genocide "came in poetry; first of all from the Polish-Jewish poets who wrote while locked in the ghettos and isolated in their hideouts before the annihilation of the ghettos and the so-called final solution" (quoted in Aaron, 1990, p. 1). Information about the poets' lives could be introduced by the teacher or researched by the students in order to gain a greater understanding of the poets and their poetry. An excellent place to begin a search for biographical information on various poets' lives is Lawrence Langer's *Art from the Ashes: A Holocaust Anthology* (New York: Oxford University Press, 1995). Other useful sources are introductions to a poet's collected works and critical essays on a poet's poetry. The poets that might be considered for such a study include Jozef Bau, Paul Celan, Yitzhak Katzenelson, Abba Kovner, Nelly Sachs, Hanna Senesh, Abraham Sutzkever, and Wladyslaw Szlengel.

21. Exploring and Reacting to Gripping Images and Phrases. An engaging way to help students understand how different poets have attempted to illustrate and convey the "reality" of the Holocaust as well as how they, paradoxically, have attempted to address its ineffability is to have students focus on the gripping images and extraordinary phrases that poets have used—many of which are likely to "stick in the mind" long after the study is over.

A thought-provoking activity along these lines is to have the students either individually or as a class, keep a running chart (preferably on large sheets of butcher paper which can be taped to a wall in the classroom) of the various lines, phrases, and images that they come across that stand out for them and make them see the Holocaust with different eyes. Across from the listing, they can briefly comment on their perception of the image or phrase and how it has assisted them to begin to see the Holocaust in a new and unique way. Class discussion could revolve around the delineation of such information.

22. Ascertaining Why People Wrote Poetry during the Holocaust. People wrote poetry for different reasons during the Holocaust period—to produce art as a form of resistance, to break out of their forced isolation and assert their humanity, to commemorate the victims, to serve as a form of remembrance, or to constitute a unique form of testimony. As Holocaust survivor and noted author Elie Wiesel (1977) has asserted, "If the Greeks invented tragedy, the Romans the epistle, and the Renaissance the sonnet, our generation invented a new literature, that of testimony. We have all been witnesses and we all feel we have to bear testimony for the future. And that became an obsession, the single most powerful obsession that permeated all the lies, all the dreams, all the work of those people. One minute before they died they thought that was what they had to do" (p. 9).

Students could read biographical and critical essays about poets who have written about the Holocaust, and select quotes by these poets in regard to their reasons for writing. Students could then design posters or other media such as murals or poems to post around the classroom that include the quotes and their sources. These quotes could be used during the study of the Holocaust to revisit issues such as resistance, remembrance, lamentation, and for other poetic purposes (e.g., an affirmation of life, a cry for help, testimony, "moral and cultural sustenance" [Aaron, 1983, p. 129], etc.) as well as to delve into why and how people attempted to respond to such an overwhelming catastrophe as the Holocaust.

23. Combining a Study of a Poem with the Study of a Poster of a Museum Artifact. A way for students to begin to understand both the depersonalization and the personal nature of the Holocaust is to combine a reading of Abraham Sutzkever's "A Cartload of Shoes" with a photograph or poster of the piles of shoes left behind by the victims of the Nazis. For a powerful translation of Sutzkever's poem, see Frieda W. Aaron's *Bearing the Unbearable: Yiddish and Polish Poetry in the Ghettos and Concentration Camps*. (Albany: State University of New York Press, 1990, pp. 55–56.)

The United States Holocaust Memorial Museum's Education Department has designed a set of posters based on artifacts included in the museum's permanent exhibit. Among these is a poster of victims' shoes. A teaching guide with ideas on how to incorporate the posters into a study of the Holocaust accompanies the poster series. The poster on the shoes and the suggested teaching activities complement the above exercise. For additional information on the Poster Set, write to: Museum Shop, U.S. Holocaust Memorial Museum, 100 Raoul Wallenberg Place, S.W., Washington, D.C. 20024.

24. Combining a Photograph and Poetry on the Same Holocaust Situation. After locating the famous photograph of a young boy with his hands up as the Nazis round up the people imprisoned in the Warsaw Ghetto, the photograph should be photocopied and made into an overhead. While viewing the overhead, the students should be given the following directions (which could be typed on a handout and given to each student so he or she can proceed at his or her own pace): (1) Describe in as much detail as you can what you see in the photograph by jotting down phrases or sentences; and, (2) Once you have described the photograph in as much detail as possible, in a sentence or two explain in writing what you think is taking place in the photograph. Once all of the students have completed task number two, a small group and/or a class discussion could be conducted. Sources that include the aforementioned photograph are Barbara Rogasky's *Smoke and Ashes: The Story of the Holocaust* (New York: Holiday House, 1988, p. 188) and Seymour Rossel's *The Holocaust: The World and the Jews, 1933–1945* (West Orange, New Jersey: Behrman House, 1992, pp. 13 and 15).

After discussing the photograph, each student should be given a copy of a poem entitled "The Little Boy with His Hands Up" by Yala Korwin. The poem is available, among other places, in Charles Fishman (Ed.), *Blood to Remember: American Poets on the Holocaust* (Lubbock, TX: Texas Tech University Press, 1991, pp. 54–55). The teacher or a student should read the poem. Upon completion of the reading, the students should engage in a reader response activity; in doing so, students can refer back to their initial reaction to the photograph.

Finally, the teacher could give a minilecture on the situation that was captured in the photograph, providing the students with details from historical and first-person accounts that would add to the students' greater understanding of the situation.

25. Addressing the Issue of Reparations via "Draft of a Reparations Agreement" by Dan Pagis. Following a reader response theory activity on Dan Pagis's poem, "Draft of a Reparations Agreement," the class could research and/or examine first, the purpose reparations generally serve, and second, the arguments that have ensued in Israel over accepting reparations from Germany for the crimes against humanity it committed during the Holocaust years. A discussion could then ensue over the students' own positions in regard to reparations vis-à-vis the Holocaust and the reasoning behind such positions, as well as over the attitude reflected in the poem in regard to the issue of reparations. (For a thought-provoking discussion of the issue of reparations, as well as of Pagis's poem, see the chapter entitled "Israel" in Albert H. Friedlander's *Riders Towards the Dawn: From Holocaust to Hope*. [New York: Continuum, 1994, pp. 223–253].)

26. A Chronological Overview of the History via a Combination of Essays, First-Person Accounts, and Fiction/Poetry. Select a number of literary works that provide a chronological overview of the Holocaust (from pre-Holocaust days through the concentration and death camps to liberation and beyond), and interweave them with a set of essays and first-person accounts that address the same events in the same order.

27. Incorporating Art into a Literary Study. After studying about the Holocaust or reading a literary work (novel, poem, short story, or play) that particularly moved him or her, a student could create a piece of art (watercolor, oil painting, pen-and-ink drawing, pastel drawing, charcoal drawing, photographs, collage, sculpture, mobile, etc.) that expresses his or her feelings and new insights.

Alternately, after handing out a particularly powerful poem to each of the students, either the teacher or a student could read the poem aloud. Then, without further discussion (though students could refer to the poem and reread it as many times as they wish), each student could create a piece of art (e.g., a drawing, painting, collage, piece of sculpture, mobile, etc.) in response to the poem. Upon completion of the artwork, students could write a short response as to why they created what they did; in doing so, they should include statements as to the meaning the poem has for them. Students could also address how their work elucidates the poem. Finally, the teacher could conduct a class discussion about the poem and, when appropriate, have the students introduce and discuss their individual pieces of art. As a final activity, the students could create a new piece of artwork based on their new insights. Again, they could write a short response to what they have created, and add an extended response as to how their initial creation differs from their second and why.

Ruth Ann Cooper, a curriculum coordinator for the Tulsa (Oklahoma) Public Schools, has students develop murals that depict their response to the Holocaust literature they have read and studied: "Murals made of individual Holocaust drawings [by each student] and then glued to butcher paper," she suggests, "[can be hung] on a back wall" (Cooper, 1994, p. 16). Alternatively, students could develop a large mural (on butcher paper) around key topics and/or information they have studied in the literature. The mural should reflect key characters, time periods, events and history.

Another engaging and thought-provoking activity is to provide the students with small (5" × 5") tiles, have them paint their responses to their study of the Holocaust literature on the tiles, glaze and fire the tiles in a kiln, and display them in an area such as a wall space or countertop where the tiles can be viewed by other students and the general public. Generally, both the artistic and the heartfelt responses are indicative of the impact that the study of the Holocaust has had on the hearts *and* minds of the students.

All of these activities are ways to engage students in the use of various multiple intelligences (Armstrong, 1994; Gardner, 1983).

28. Developing an Anthology of Literary Works on the Holocaust. Different groups of students could develop their own anthology of literary readings by copying off key works they wish to include, creating their own artwork to accompany the volume (or using copies of the art created during and/or following the Holocaust years), and writing up connecting information (such as introductions) between the pieces. The students, along with the teacher, could develop a set of criteria for selecting those works to be included in the anthology. The anthology could be bound and included in a class or school library for use by other students.

29. Book Reviews. Students could write book reviews of novels, novellas, plays, short-story collections, and poetry collections that are about the Holocaust, and publish them in the school newspaper or in publications that solicit and publish student work. Prior to having students attempt such a project, they should be informed of what constitutes a quality book review and be provided with exemplary examples.

30. Studying Inverted Symbolism. A thought-provoking way to assist students in coming to an understanding and appreciation of how various authors have attempted to come to grips with an event that has often been deemed unbelievable, unspeakable, ineffable, incomprehensible, inexpressible, and beyond imagination is to have them study the use of inverted symbolism. Drawing the students' attention to the use of inverted symbolism may also assist them to begin to understand how the Holocaust "turned the world upside down." A useful activity in this regard is to have the students, as a class, keep a running chart (preferably on large sheets of butcher paper that can be taped to a wall in the classroom) of the various instances of inverted symbolism that they discover. Across from the listing of the symbol, they can comment on: (1) the traditional or typical use of the symbol; (2) the way in which the author used the symbol; and (3) the purpose for the author's use of the inverted symbol. As the list grows, the students will begin to gain a more holistic view of the use of such literary devices. Periodically, class discussions could focus on the information on the list.

An example of the use of an inverted symbol is Elie Wiesel's use of the word *night.* He has stated:

> [W]henever I say "night" I mean the Holocaust, that period. "Night" has become a symbol for the Holocaust for obvious reasons. As we have said, a night has descended upon mankind, not only in Europe, but everywhere. . . . Night enveloped human destiny and human history. . . .
>
> It is strange but night, before that, would have meant different things: dreams, poetry, waiting for the Messiah. . . . Night is a poetic image, a romantic one at that. Night had become the opposite of whatever we call creativity and creation. After all, night preceded day, night induces people to love each other, to give birth and life. Ironically, it has become the opposing symbol, anti-life, anti-man, anti-Messiah. (Cargas, 1976, p. 54)

31. Studying Parody. When used effectively, parody can be illustrative of how "normality" and/or the accepted view of life and beliefs are turned upside down. A classic case in point is Elie Wiesel's (1960) parody of Psalm 150 in his work, *Night.* As Simon P. Sibelman (1992) notes in his essay, "Chaos into Art: The Holocaust and Literature":

> The ultimate psalm of the Psalter positively enjoins Man to exalt in God's presence, each verse possessing a driving spirit of joy. Wiesel's lugubrious eight-lined parody negates the psalmist's message while openly accusing God of complicity in the creation of the *anus mundi* and in the callous murder of His "Chosen People." The result of this anti-psalm is to press the reader to question the Divine message and the one by which Wiesel negates it. We are uncomfortably compelled to construct an inventory of our beliefs and perceptions of reality and of God. Wiesel's art engages us in a dialogue of re-evaluation of traditional Western moral and religious values. (p. 179)

Students could locate an example of a situation, person, group, idea, etc. that is being parodied and write the passage out on a large sheet of butcher paper.

Next, small groups of students could select one parody and then discuss it in relation to the following: (1) how the parody and original idea differ (and list the differences point by point); (2) the meaning of the parody; (3) whether the parody works for them, and why or why not; and (4) how the parody enhances, neglects to enhance, or detracts from the meaning of the story and why that is the case. Class discussion could serve as a follow-up to this activity.

32. Examining the Use of Language. When undertaking a study of the Holocaust, it is useful for students to focus on the issue of language, particularly the need to "strive for precision of language" (Parsons and Totten, 1993, p. 3). An important lesson is how people's use and understanding of language today (including the use of such common terms as *train* or *hunger*, for example) does not parallel the reality of what the victims of the Nazis experienced.

For example, when young people think of the term *train*, they generally think of a line of coaches with comfortable seats, large windows, a dining car, etc. However, during the Holocaust period, the trains used to transport the Jews to the concentration and death camps were boxcars without seats, toilets, air-conditioning, or heating, and into which people were stuffed and left until they arrived at their destination (many of whom may have perished due to suffocation, heart attacks, and other physical crises). In speaking of her unit on Jane Yolen's *The Devil's Arithmetic*, Vicki Zack (1991) comments on her young (fifth grade) students' reaction to the Jews being deported: "They [the students] asked why the people did not look out the windows and how people could suffocate in a train. For the children the word train evoked common, everyday images; indeed, who would believe that humans would be transported in cattle cars and later branded" (p. 45).

On a related note, Parsons and Totten (1993) point out that

> [w]ords that describe human behavior often have multiple meanings. Resistance, for example, usually refers to a physical act of armed revolt. During the Holocaust, it also meant partisan activism that ranged from smuggling messages, food, and weapons to actual military engagement. But, resistance also embraced willful disobedience: continuing to practice religious and cultural traditions in defiance of the rules; crafting fine art, music and poetry inside ghettos and concentration camps. For many, simply maintaining the will to remain alive in the face of abject brutality was the surest act of spiritual resistance. (p. 4)

Students should be provided with the opportunity to compare and contrast their use of common terms (e.g., *starvation, trains, resistance, camps, resettlement*) with the way the Nazis used them. An easy and effective way to do this is to have the students, at the outset of the lesson or during the course of the lesson, each define in his or her own words and in writing such terms as *hunger, starvation, evacuation,* and *resistance*. As the class moves through the unit, a chart (made of butcher paper) could be kept and posted at the front of the room that delineates the vast and radical differences of such usage.

This is also the ideal place to introduce the concept of euphemism (e.g., using the word *resettlement* instead of *deportation; emigration* instead of *expulsion; evacua-*

tion instead of *deportation; special treatment* for the gassing of people, and *Final Solution* for the annihilation of every Jew on the face of the earth), and the distinction between figurative and literal language.

33. Concluding Activities. As a concluding activity to a lesson or unit, students could examine various peoples' perception of the term *Holocaust literature* (see examples below). Students could select one of the following quotes and then write a short piece in which they agree or disagree with the statement; and in doing so, provide solid rationales for their answers.

> *It would seem that a "Holocaust literature" is an impossibility—that, indeed, the phrase itself is a contradiction in terms. The reasons are at least threefold: first, there is no way to link a life-affirming enterprise such as literature with a death-bound phenomenon of such magnitude; second, no gift for literary description, no matter how blessed that gift, could possibly encompass the horror of the Holocaust experience itself; third, since any writing involves some degree of distance, such "detachment" would violate the sanctity of the actual suffering and death undergone by the victims.*
> —Gila Ramras-Rauch (1985), "Introduction." p. 3. In Gila Ramras-Rauch and Joseph Michman-Melkman (Eds.), *Facing the Holocaust: Selected Israeli Fiction.* Philadelphia: The Jewish Publication Society, 1985

> *Through aesthetic principles or stylization and even through the solemn prayer of the chorus the unimaginable ordeal still appears as if it had some ulterior purpose. It is transfigured and stripped of some of its horror and with this, injustice is already done to the victims.*
> —Words of German refugee philosopher T.W. Adorno, quoted in Ezrachi, 1980, p. 52. In Sidra Dekoven Ezrachi's *By Words Alone: The Holocaust in Literature.* Chicago: University of Chicago Press, 1980.

> *There is no such thing as Holocaust literature—there cannot be. Auschwitz negates all theories and doctrines, to lock it into a philosophy is to restrict it. To substitute words, any words, for it is to distort it. A Holocaust literature? The term is a contradiction.*
> —Elie Wiesel. In Elie Wiesel's *A Jew Today.* New York: Random House, 1978, p. 234.

> *The opposite of art is not ugliness but indifference.*
> —Elie Wiesel, 1986, EY 21. "Welcoming 1986." *The New York Times,* January 5.

Another useful concluding activity is to provide students with thought-provoking quotes to respond to in writing with the charge to analyze the meaning of the quote through the prism of the literary works and historical pieces that they have read and studied. One such quote might be Albert Einstein's "The world is too dangerous to live in—not because of the people who do evil, but because of the people who stand by and let them." Another thought-provoking quote that could be used is the following one by literary critic and Holocaust scholar Lawrence Langer (1978): "With the disruption of a familiar moral universe, the individual must find 'new' reasons for living and 'new' ways of confronting the prospect of death introduced into reality by atrocity. Such disruption mars not only an ordered universe, but the identity of one's self, one's conception of where he fits and how (and why) he is to act as a human being in a dehumanized world" (p. 10). These are just two of the scores of quotes by victims and survivors of the Holocaust, literary artists, and others that could be used.

Conclusion

Powerful stories and images found in Holocaust literature and poetry often adhere to the minds and hearts of those who have read and studied them. Hopefully, this in turn will cause some readers to become more reflective about what they have studied, the world they live in, how they treat people, and how they react to civil and human rights infractions committed in their communities and beyond. If educators seek to assist students in gaining deeper insight into the Holocaust, to become more reflective and thoughtful human beings, to ponder and care about man's inhumanity to man, and to examine one's lived life in regard to personal and social responsibility, then the thoughtful use of Holocaust literature is a valuable vehicle for reaching toward those goals.

REFERENCES

Aaron, Frieda W. (1983). "Poetry in the Holocaust Dominion," pp. 119–131. In Randolph L. Braham (Ed.), *Perspectives on the Holocaust.* Boston and London: Kluwer-Nishoff Publishing.

Aaron, Frieda W. (1990). *Bearing the Unbearable: Yiddish and Polish Poetry in the Ghettos and Concentration Camps.* Albany, NY: State University of New York Press.

Armstrong, Thomas. (1994). *Multiple Intelligences in the Classroom.* Alexandria, VA: Association for Supervision and Curriculum Development.

Cargas, Harry James. (1976). *Harry James Cargas in Conversation with Elie Wiesel.* New York: Paulist Press.

Coles, Robert. (1989). *The Call of Stories: Teaching and the Moral Imagination.* Boston: Houghton Mifflin.

Cooper, Ruth Ann. (March 1994). "From Holocaust to Hope: Teaching the Holocaust in Middle School." *Middle School Journal, 25*(3): 15–17.

Darsa, Jan. (1991). "Educating about the Holocaust," pp. 175–193. In Israel W. Charny (Ed.), *Genocide: A Critical Bibliographic Review. Volume Two.* London and New York: Mansell Publishers and Facts on File, respectively.

Drew, Margaret A. (February 1991). "Merging History and Literature in Teaching About Genocide." *Social Education, 55*(2): 128–129.

Drew, Peg. (Fall 1989). "Holocaust Literature and Young People: Another Look." *Facing History and Ourselves News,* pp. 20–21.

Ezrachi, Sidra Dekoven. (1980). *By Words Alone: The Holocaust in Literature.* Chicago: University of Chicago Press.

Farnham, James. (April 1983). "Ethical Ambiguity and the Teaching of the Holocaust." *English Journal, 72*(4): 63–68.

Felstiner, John. (1986). "Paul Celan's *Todesfuge.*" *Holocaust and Genocide Studies: An International Journal, 1*(2): 249–264.

Friedlander, Henry. (February 1979). "Toward a Methodology of Teaching about the Holocaust." *Teachers College Record, 80*(3): 520–542.

Gardner, Howard. (1983). *Frames of Mind: The Theory of Multiple Intelligences.* New York: Basic Books.

Langer, Lawrence L. (1978). *The Age of Atrocity: Death in Modern Literature.* Boston: Beacon Press.

Langer, Lawrence L. (1982). *Versions of Survival: The Holocaust and the Human Spirit.* Albany: State University of New York Press.

Langer, Lawrence. (Ed.). (1995). *Art from the Ashes: A Holocaust Anthology.* New York: Oxford University Press.

O'Neill, John. (June 1994). "Rewriting the Book on Literature: Changes Sought in How Literature Is Taught, What Students Read." *ASCD Curriculum Update,* 1–4, 6–8.

Oliner, Pearl M., & Oliner, Samuel. (1991). "Righteous People in the Holocaust," pp. 363–385. In Israel W. Charny (Ed.), *Genocide: A Critical Bibliographic Review.* London: Mansell Publishing.

Parsons, William S., & Totten, Samuel. (1993). *Guidelines for Teaching about the Holocaust.* Washington, DC: United States Holocaust Memorial Museum.

Ramras-Rauch, Gila. (1985). "Introduction." In Gila Ramras-Rauch and Joseph Michman-Melkman (Eds.), *Facing the Holocaust: Selected Israeli Fiction.* Philadelphia: The Jewish Publication Society.

Rudman, Masha Kabakow, & Rosenberg, Susan P. (Summer 1991). "Confronting History: Holocaust Books for Children." *The New Advocate, 4*(3): 163–176.

Rushforth, Peter. (1994). "'I Even Did a Theme Once on That Anne Frank Who Kept the Diary,' and Got an A Plus on It': Reflections on Some Holocaust Books for Young People." *Dimensions: A Journal of Holocaust Studies, 8*(2): 23–35.

Shawn, Karen. (1994). "'What Should They Read and When Should They Read It?': A Selective Review of Holocaust Literature for Students in Grades Two through Twelve." *Dimensions: A Journal of Holocaust Studies, 8*(2): G1–G16.

Sheridan, Daniel. (November 1991). "Changing Business as Usual: Reader Response Theory in the Classroom." *College English, 53*(7): 804–814.

Sibelman, Simon P. (1992) "Chaos into Art: The Holocaust and Literature." The *British Journal of Holocaust Education, 1*(2):171–184.

Teichman, Milton. (February 1976). "Literature of Agony and Triumph: An Encounter with the Holocaust." *College English, 37*(6): 613–618.

Totten, Samuel. (1987). "The Personal Face of Genocide: Words of Witnesses in the Classroom." *Social Science Record: The Journal of the New York State Council for the Social Studies, 24*(2): 63–67.

Totten, Samuel. (1988). "The Literature, Art, and Film of the Holocaust, pp. 209–240. In Israel W. Charny (Ed.), *Genocide: A Critical Bibliographic Review.* London and New York: Mansell Publishing and Facts on File, respectively.

Totten, Samuel. (1998). "Examining the Holocaust through the Lives and Literary Works of Victims and Survivors." In Robert Hauptman & Susan Hubbs Motin (Eds.) *The Holocaust Memories, Research, Reference* (pp. 165–188). New York: The Haworth Press.

Volavkova, Hana. (Ed.). (1993). *". . . I Never Saw Another Butterfly": Children's Drawings and Poems from Terezin Concentration Camp, 1942–1944.* New York: Schocken Books.

Wiesel, Elie. (1960). *Night.* New York: Hill and Wang.

Wiesel, Elie. (1970). *One Generation After.* New York: Random House.

Wiesel, Elie. (1977). "The Holocaust as Literary Inspiration." Speech.

Wiesel, Elie. (1978a). *A Jew Today.* New York: Random House.

Wiesel, Elie. (1978b). "Then and Now: The Experiences of a Teacher." *Social Education, 42*(4): 266–271.

Wiesel, Elie. (August 19, 1984). "All Was Lost, Yet Something Was Preserved." *The New York Times Book Review,* p. 1.

Wiesel, Elie. (January 5, 1986). "Welcoming 1986." *The New York Times*, p. EY 21.

Young, Gloria. (1993). "The Poetry of the Holocaust." In Saul S. Friedman (Ed.), *Holocaust Literature: A Handbook of Critical, Historical, and Literary Writings* (pp. 547–574). Westport, CT:
Greenwood Press.

Zack, Vicki. (January 1991). "'It Was the Worst of Times': Learning about the Holocaust through
Literature." *Language Arts, 68*: 42–48.

APPENDIX

With so much poetry available, only those pieces that this author has found particularly
useful for classrooms at the secondary level will be highlighted. Each poem selected has
been chosen for one or more of the following reasons: it is extremely thought provoking, it
highlights a theme that teachers are likely to explore with their students, its focus is such
that it is capable of capturing a student's mind and heart, and it is, for one or more reasons
(e.g., its language, images, theme), likely to stay with one long after its has been read. Many
of the poems contain fairly simple language, allusions that are not arcane, and readily
accessible ideas and points. They also contain imagery that is, for the most part, bereft of
horrific images and scenes. What follows, of course, is a mere sampling of what is available. There are sure to be dozens, if not scores, of other poems that teachers would find
interesting and worthwhile to include in their lessons or units on the Holocaust.

The poems that the author has found to be readily accessible and of greatest interest
to most students in grades 9–12 are: "Riddle," by William Heyen; "The Little Boy with
His Hands Up," by Yala Korwin; "There Were Those," by Susan Dambroff; "Written in
Pencil in the Sealed Railway-Car," by Dan Pagis; and some of the many poems included
in ". . . I Never Saw Another Butterfly": Children's Drawings and Poems from Terezin Concentration Camp, 1942–1944,* edited by Hana Volavkova. Particularly powerful among the
poems in the latter volume are "Terezin," by Mif, "The Butterfly," "Fear," "Untitled,"
"The Garden," and "Homesick."

Prior to reading and studying the Terezin poems in ". . . I Never Saw Another Butterfly": Children's Drawings and Poems from Terezin Concentration Camp, 1942–1944,* students
need to study the facts of life and death in Terezin. Then and only then can they begin
fully to appreciate the sense of anxiety, longing, want, sadness, hope against hope, loss,
and unintended irony that come through so clearly in these poems. They need to know,
for example, that

> [W]hile at the camp [the children] were forced to work from eighty to one hundred
> hours per week, with those over fourteen years of age working the same hours and
> type of work as the adults. From Terezin they were shipped further east to the death
> camps, usually Auschwitz. Of the fifteen thousand children under the age of fifteen
> who were sent to the camp, only one hundred survived. (Young, 1993, p. 553)

Without such knowledge, many of the poems may sound like they are about poverty-
stricken areas found in many cities throughout the world (e.g., New York, Detroit, Los
Angeles, Lahore, Delhi, Bangkok, and Mexico City).

As mentioned earlier, a particularly popular poem with educators who teach the
Holocaust is Maurice Ogden's "The Hangman." While not about the Holocaust per se, it
is an interesting resource for examining certain issues (e.g., bystanders, choices people do

and do not make, individual responsibility, social responsibility) that get to the heart of many concerns vis-à-vis the Holocaust.

The following poems may find an appreciative readership among the more advanced students: "Draft of a Reparations Agreement," by Dan Pagis; "Testimony," by Dan Pagis; "Europe, Late," by Dan Pagis; "Autobiography," by Dan Pagis; "There Were Those,"* by Susan Dambroff; "1945,"* by Bernard S. Mikofsky; "Babi Yar," by Yevgeny Yevtushenko; "For Our Dead,"* by Marilynn Talal; "The Survivor," by Tadeusz Rozewicz; "Pigtail," by Tadeusz Rózewicz; "Why I Write About the Holocaust,"* by Gary Pacernick; "Survivors,"* by Mary Sarton; "Burnt Pearls" and "Smoke of Jewish Children," by Abraham Sutzkever; "The Permanent Delegate," by Yuri Shul; "A Dead Child Speaks" and "O the Night of the Weeping Children!," by Nelly Sachs; "I Have Never Been Here Before," by Jacob Glatstein; "A Single Hair," by Herman Taube; "Terezin," by Hanus Hachenberg; "Say This City Has Ten Million Souls," by W. H. Auden; "Digging,"* by Frank Finale; "AD,"* by Kenneth Fearing; "Memories of December,"* by Gizela Spunberg; "Shema," by Primo Levi; "Yellow Starred,"* by Sister Mary Philip de Camara; "A Few More Things About the Holocaust,"* by Leatrice H. Lifshitz; "Yahrzeit,"* by Miriam Kessler; "Tattoo,"* by Gregg Shapiro; "Roses and the Grave,"* by Vera Weislitz; "It's High Time,"** by Wladyslaw Szlengel; "Hospital,"** by Jozef Bau; "A Cartload of Shoes,"** by Abraham Sutzkever; "The Teacher Mire,"** by Abraham Sutzkever; and "Things,"** by Wladyslaw Szlengel.

Teachers who teach advanced placement students may also wish to consider Paul Celan's "Todesfuge." While extremely complex, Celan's poem is powerful and thought provoking. Other poems that advanced placement students may find interesting and/or challenging are: "XXXVIII,"* by Derek Walcott; "The Hindenburg,"* by Van K. Brock; "There is One Synagogue Extant in Kiev,"* by Yaacov Luria; "Miserere,"* by William Pillin; and "The Tailor,"* by Patricia Garfinkel.

Note: While most of the poems marked with a single asterisk (*) have appeared in separate collections and/or journals, all are contained in Charles Fishman (Ed.). (1991), *Blood to Remember: American Poets on the Holocaust.* Lubbock, TX: Texas Tech University Press. Those poems marked with a double asterisk (**) all appear in Frieda W. Aaron's (1990) *Bearing the Unbearable: Yiddish and Polish Poetry in the Ghettos and Concentration Camps.* Albany, NY: State University Press of New York.

SELECT ANNOTATED BIBLIOGRAPHY

In light of the vast number of poems, short stories, and novels available on the Holocaust, individual literary works have not been included here. Readers should consult the bibliographies listed below for information regarding individual works.

Bibliographies

Cargas, Harry. (1985). *The Holocaust: An Annotated Bibliography.* Chicago, IL: American Library Association. 196 pp. Includes a large number of annotations of key literary works, including a brief but useful section on poetry (pp. 148–150).

Drew, Margaret. (1988). *Facing History and Ourselves: Holocaust and Human Behavior Annotated Bibliography.* New York: Walker and Company. 124 pp. Especially developed for use by educators who are interested in teaching about the Holocaust, this bibliography is divided into five key parts (I. Children's Books; II. Adult Books; III. German Culture; IV. Genocide of the Armenian People; and V. Choosing to Participate). It also includes five useful appendices (A. Basic Reading Lists; B. Literature as History; C. Legacy of the Holocaust: A Supplementary Reading List; D. Human Behavior: A Supplementary Reading List; and E. Genocide of the Cambodian People).

Edelheit, Abraham J., & Edelheit, Hershel, (Eds.) (1986). *Bibliography of Holocaust Literature.* Boulder, CO: Westview Press. 842 pp. This massive bibliography contains a section entitled "The Holocaust and the Literary Imagination."

Shawn, Karen. (1994). "'What Should They Read and When Should They Read It?': A Selective Review of Holocaust Literature for Students in Grades Two Through Twelve." *Dimensions: A Journal of Holocaust Studies, 8* (2): G1–G16. Provides an overview of 47 works. It also includes a short but thought-provoking introduction that suggests possible criteria to use when selecting Holocaust literature for classroom study. A must read for educators.

Szonyi, David. M. (Ed.) (1985).*The Holocaust: Annotated Bibliography and Resource Guide.* New York: KTAV Publishing House. 396 pp. Includes annotated works of fiction and imaginative literature (novels, short stories, drama, poetry).

Totten, Samuel. (1988). "The Literature, Art, and Film of the Holocaust," pp. 209–231. In Israel Charny (Ed.), *Genocide: A Critical Bibliographic Review.* London and New York: Mansell Publishers and Facts on File, respectively. Includes an essay and an accompanying annotated bibliography of novels, short story collections, drama, and collections and volumes of poetry.

United States Holocaust Memorial Museum. (1993). *Annotated Bibliography.* Washington, D.C.: Author. This bibliography includes sections that highlight fiction ideal for use with middle level and junior high school students, high school students, and adults. It also includes a section for adults entitled "Poetry, Drama and Art" and another entitled "Literary Criticism."

General Anthologies

Brown, Jean E., Stephens, Elaine, C., & Rubin, Janet E. (1997). *Images from the Holocaust: A Literature Anthology.* Lincolnwood, IL: NTC Publishing Group. This anthology is ideal for use in the secondary level classroom in that it includes a rich and valuable array of short historical pieces, first-person accounts, short stories, poetry and drama on a wide range of key issues vis-à-vis the Holocaust. The titles of the 10 chapters are "Rumblings of Danger," "In Hiding," "Fleeing for Their Lives," "Surrounded by Ghetto Walls," "Imprisoned in the Camps," "Resisting Evil," "Liberation," "The Days After," "A Mosaic of Courage," and "Echoing Reflections."

Langer, Lawrence. (Ed.) (1995). *Art from the Ashes: A Holocaust Anthology.* New York: Oxford University Press. A massive and superb anthology that includes essays; excerpts from journals, diaries, and first-person accounts; drama and poetry; and examples and a discussion of art in the piece called "Painters of Terezin."

Teichman, Milton, & Leder, Sharon. (1994). *Truth and Lamentation: Stories and Poems on the Holocaust.* Urbana and Illinois: University of Illinois Press. This anthology is divided into two sections ("Transmitting Truths" and "Lamentations"), each of which includes a rich collection of short stories and poetry. Among the many authors whose works are included herein are Tadeusz Borowski, Sara Nomberg-Przytyk, Cynthia Ozick, Elie Wiesel, Aharon Appelfeld, Pierre Gascar, Jakov Lind, Charlotte Delbo, Paul Celan, Dan Pagis, William Heyen, Abraham Sutzkever, Abba Kovner, Nelly Sachs, Ida Fink, Primo Levi, and many others.

Literary Criticism/Commentary

Ezrahi, Sidra DeKoven, (1980). *By Words Alone: The Holocaust in Literature.* Chicago: University of Chicago. 262 pp. This volume is comprised of eight chapters: "Introduction"; "Documentation as Art"; "Concentrationary Realism and the Landscape of Death"; "Literature of Survival"; "The Holocaust as a Jewish Tragedy A: The Legacy of Lamentations"; "The Holocaust as a Jewish Tragedy B: The Covenantal Context"; "The Holocaust Mythologized"; and, "History Imagined: The Holocaust in American Literature."

Langer, Lawrence. (1978). *The Age of Atrocity: Death in Modern Literature.* Boston: Beacon Press. 256 pp. In one of the initial chapters ("Dying Voices"), Langer provides a perspicacious examination of various issues germane to the Holocaust as they are depicted in modern literature. The book concludes with a chapter entitled "Charlotte Delbo and a Heart of Ashes."

Langer, Lawrence. (1982). *Versions of Survival: The Holocaust and Human Spirit.* Albany: State University of New York Press. 267 pp. A penetrating examination of how various researchers and survivors/authors/poets view what it means to be human in the aftermath of the Holocaust. A large section of Chapter 2 is dedicated to an examination of Tadeusz Borowski's work; Chapter 3 focuses on the work of Elie Wiesel, and Chapter 5 analyzes the work of Gertrud Kolmar and Nelly Sachs.

Langer, Lawrence. (Spring 1987). "Cultural Resistance to Genocide." *Witness,* 1(1): 82–96. A thought-provoking essay that questions the common assumption that art created during the Holocaust by Jews constituted "cultural resistance."

Langer, Lawrence L. (1995). *Admitting the Holocaust: Collected Essays.* New York and Oxford: Oxford University Press. 202 pp. This well-written and highly readable collection of essays addresses a wide array of issues vis-à-vis the Holocaust, including but not limited to its portrayal in literature. Among the many fine essays in the book are "Cultural Resistance to Genocide"; "Fictional Facts and Factual Fictions: History in Holocaust Literature"; "The Literature of Auschwitz"; "Aharon Appelfeld and the Language of Sinister Silence"; "Myth and Truth in Cynthia Ozick's 'The Shawl' and 'Rosa'"; and "Malamud's Jews and the Holocaust Experience."

Rosen, Norma. (Spring 1987). "The Second Life of Holocaust Imagery." *Witness* [Special issue on the Holocaust], 1(1): 10–15. An examination of "the way in which certain images from [Holocaust] literature reverberate . . . at intense moments."

Rosenfeld, Alvin H. (1988). "Holocaust Fictions and the Transformation of Historical Memory." *Holocaust and Genocide Studies: An International Journal,* 3(3): 323–336. Rosenfeld examines how "[t]he trend in popular Holocaust fiction [that] appeals to the cravings of the tabloid imagination points to a progressive erosion of historical memory of the Nazi crimes against the Jews."

Stadtler, Bea. (1993). "Juvenile and Youth Books about the Holocaust," pp. 575–581. In Saul S. Friedman (Ed.), *Holocaust Literature: A Handbook of Critical, Historical, and Literary*

Writings. Westport, CT: Greenwood Press. Stadtler's piece should be of particular use to middle-level and junior high teachers.

Essays/Criticism on Poetry

Aaron, Frieda W. (1983). "Poetry in the Holocaust Dominion," pp. 119–131. In Randolph L. Braham (Ed.), *Perspectives on the Holocaust.* Boston and London: Kluwer-Nijhoff Publishing. An insightful essay on various aspects of Holocaust poetry. The titles of some of the many sections of the essay provide a sense as to the breadth of the essay: "Role of the Poet in the Landscape of Death"; "Poetics of Confrontation with the Anus Mundi"; "Constriction of Language and Image"; "Crisis of Faith in the Trauma of History"; and "Poetics of Testimony."

Aaron, Frieda W. (1990). *Bearing the Unbearable: Yiddish and Polish Poetry in the Ghettos and Concentration Camps.* Albany: State University of New York Press. 242 pp. A highly praised pioneering study of Yiddish and Polish-Jewish concentration camp and ghetto poetry. It includes numerous poems in Yiddish and Polish as well as their English translations.

Alexander, Edward. (1979). *The Resonance of Dust: Essays on Holocaust Literature and Jewish Fate.* Columbus: Ohio State University Press. 256 pp. This volume includes a chapter on the poetry of Nelly Sachs and Abba Kovner ("Holocaust and Rebirth: Moshe Flinker, Nelly Sachs, and Abba Kovner"), and a section on Yiddish Holocaust poetry (which primarily focuses on the poetry of Jacob Glatstein and Aaron Zeitlin) in a chapter entitled "The Holocaust and the God of Israel."

Cargas, Harry James. (1993). "The Holocaust in Fiction," pp. 533–546. In Saul S. Friedman (Ed.), *Holocaust Literature: A Handbook of Critical, Historical, and Literary Writings.* Westport, CT: Greenwood Press. This essay includes a brief commentary on the works of Emily Borenstein (*Night of the Broken Glass*), Albrecht Haushofer (*Moabit Sonnets*), William Heyen (*Erika: Poems of the Holocaust*), Charles Reznikoff (*Holocaust*), W.D. Snodgrass (*The Führer Bunker*), and Elie Wiesel (*Ani Maamin*), among others who have produced works on the Holocaust.

Ezrahi, Sidra DeKoven. (1982). *By Words Alone: The Holocaust in Literature.* Chicago: The University of Chicago Press. 262 pp. While this volume (which basically constitutes a literary history of the Holocaust) primarily focuses on prose works, Ezrahi also addresses the poetry of an eclectic group of poets (Paul Celan, Irving Feldman, Uri Zvi Greenberg, Itzhak Katzenelson, Randall Jarrell, Denise Levertov, Abba Kovner, Dan Pagis, Sylvia Plath, Tadeusz Rozewicz, Nelly Sachs, and Abraham Sutzkever).

Ezrahi, Sidra DeKoven. (1992). "'The Grave in the Air': Unbound Metaphors in Post-Holocaust Poetry," pp. 259–276. In Saul Friedlander (Ed.), *Probing the Limits of Representation: Nazism and the "Final Solution."* Cambridge: Harvard University Press. A fascinating essay that primarily addresses various facets of Celan's "Todesfuge." Ezrahi also briefly discusses Pagis's "Written in Pencil in the Sealed Railway-Car."

Ezrahi, Sidra DeKoven. (1994). "Conversation in the Cemetery: Dan Pagis and the Prosaics of Memory," pp. 121–133. In Geoffrey H. Hartman (Ed.), *Holocaust Remembrance: The Shapes of Memory.* Oxford, England, and Cambridge, MA: Blackwell Publishers. A fascinating and instructive essay in which Ezrahi discusses, analyzes, and wrestles with the question, "How are we to read the poet of undeciphered riddles and uncharted mazes, who in his last writing provides maps and compasses, a whole new syntax to restructure the inscriptions of memory?"

Felstiner, John. (1986). "Paul Celan's Todesfuge." *Holocaust and Genocide Studies: An International Journal,* 1(2): 249-264. A critical and thought-provoking essay about one of the most powerful poems on the Holocaust.

Felstiner, John. (1992). "Translating Paul Celan's 'Todesfuge': Rhythm and Repetition as Metaphor," pp. 240–258. In Saul Friedlander (Ed.), *Probing the Limits of Representation: Nazism and the "Final Solution."* Cambridge: Harvard University Press. An insightful and informative essay that discusses how Celan's language was a valiant attempt to convey the "rupture" that the Holocaust constituted in the history of humanity, the brouhaha that erupted over his poem when another poet charged Celan with plagiarism, and an analysis of the poem in which Felstiner examines how and why Celan wrote the poem as he did. The essay concludes with the full text of "Todesfuge" in German and English.

Friedlander, Albert H. (1993). *Riders Towards the Dawn: From Holocaust to Hope.* New York: Continuum. 328 pp. In addition to briefly addressing the poetry of Primo Levi, Dan Pagis, Uri Greenberg, Else Lasker-Schueler, Yehuda Amichai, and Abba Kovner, this volume includes a thought-provoking chapter entitled "A Different Language: The World of the Poets," which provides an examination of the poetry of Paul Celan, Nelly Sachs, and Erich Fried.

Langer, Lawrence L. (1975). *The Holocaust and the Literary Imagination.* New Haven and London: Yale University Press. 300 pp. A pioneering and valuable work on the aesthetics of Holocaust literature. Among the poets Langer discusses in this volume are Paul Celan and Nelly Sachs.

Langer, Lawrence. (1982). *Versions of Survival: The Holocaust and Human Spirit.* Albany: State University of New York Press. 267 pp. Chapter 4 focuses, in part, on the work of poet Nelly Sachs.

Rosenfeld, Alvin H. (1980). *A Double Dying: Reflections on Holocaust Literature.* Bloomington and London: Indiana University Press. 210 pp. A valuable work on Holocaust literature, it includes insightful commentary on the works of such poets as Paul Celan, Jacob Glatstein, Uri Zvi Greenberg, Yitzhak Katznelson, Dan Pagis, Nelly Sachs, and Sylvia Plath.

Roskies, David G. (1984). *Against the Apocalypse: Responses to Catastrophe in Modern Jewish Culture.* Cambridge: Harvard University Press. 374 pp. This volume includes an informative essay on the life and poetry of Abraham Sutzkever.

Young, Gloria. (1993). "The Poetry of the Holocaust," pp. 547–574. In Saul S. Friedman (Ed.), *Holocaust Literature: A Handbook of Critical, Historical, and Literary Writings.* Westport, CT: Greenwood Press. An insightful bibliographic essay that is divided into three major sections: "Poets Who Did Not Survive," "Poets Who Survived," and "Others."

Drama

Skloot, Robert. (1983). *The Theater of the Holocaust.* Madison: University of Wisconsin Press. 416 pp. This anthology comprises several plays that deal with various aspects of the Holocaust. Among the plays are Charlotte Delbo's *Who Will Carry the Word?,* George Tabori's *The Cannibals,* and Simon Wincelberg's *Resort 76.*

Steinhorn, Harriet. (1983). *Shadows of the Holocaust.* Rockville, MD: Kar-Ben, 1983. This volume, by a survivor of Bergen-Belsen, contains five short plays. In an essay entitled "Juvenile and Youth Books About the Holocaust," Bea Stadtler states that "while some of the dialogue is a bit forced, the book is a very worthwhile classroom tool."

Poetry Collections

Ausubel, Nathan, & Ausubel, Maryann. (Eds.) (1957). *A Treasury of Jewish Poetry.* New York: Crown. 471 pp. This anthology includes a number of powerful poems on the Holocaust, including those by Ephim Fogel ("Shipment to Maidanek") and Hirsh Glik ("We Survive!").

Borenstein, Emily. (1981). *Night of the Broken Glass: Poems of the Holocaust.* Mason, TX: Timberline Press. 83 pp. Written by a woman whose relatives were murdered in the Holocaust, the poems in this book are categorized under three main headings: I Must Tell the Story; May It Never Be Forgotten; and Psalm of Hope.

Celan, Paul. (1972). *Selected Poems.* Middlesex, U.K.: Penguin Books. 108 pp. This volume includes Celan's "Todesfuge."

Fishman, Charles. (Ed.) (1991). *Blood to Remember: American Poets on the Holocaust.* Lubbock, TX: Texas Tech University Press. 426 pp. This volume contains 256 poems by 191 poets, some of whom are survivors of the Holocaust.

Fishman, Charles. (Ed.) (in progress). *On Broken Branches: World Poets on the Holocaust.* Fishman also edited *Blood to Remember: American Poets on the Holocaust.* This book promises to be a valuable addition to the field.

Heyen, William. (1984). *Erika: Poems of the Holocaust.* New York: The Vanguard Press. 128 pp. This collection, which includes Heyen's "The Swastika Poems," contains a number of haunting poems that would be ideal for use with upper middle school/junior high and secondary level students. Earlier editions of this volume were published under the title *Swastika Poems.* Heyen's father emigrated to the United States from Germany in 1928, but his two brothers remained in Germany where they fought and died for Nazi Germany in World War II. In addition to addressing the horrific nature of the Holocaust, many of the poems also reflect the anguish that the latter situation caused both Heyen's father and himself.

Howe, Irving, & Eliezer Greenberg. (Eds.) (1969). *A Treasury of Yiddish Poetry.* New York: Holt, Rinehart, and Winston. 370 pp. This volume of modern Yiddish poetry contains numerous important poems on the Holocaust.

Katzenelson, Yitzhak. (1980). *The Song of the Murdered Jewish People.* Haifa, Israel: Ghetto Fighters' House. 133 pp. A major poem by a man who was murdered at Auschwitz in 1944, this epic chronicle comprises 15 cantos that were composed in an internment camp in France. The poem, which serves as a lament for the murder of the Warsaw Jews, delineates, canto by canto, the ever-increasing terror and brutality (the German invasion of Poland, the *aktions,* the deportations, the agonizing decisions made by the Judenräte, the fate of the children, the revolt of the Warsaw Ghetto) to which the Jews in Poland were subjected. The events described in the poems were well known by Katzenelson, a member of the Warsaw Ghetto.

Kovner, Abba. (1973). *A Canopy in the Desert: Selected Poems.* Pittsburgh, PA: University of Pittsburgh Press. 222 pp. This volume includes such poems as "My Little Sister,"

"A Parting from the South," and "A Canopy in the Desert." All, in various ways and to different degrees, address the tragedy of the Holocaust by a poet/survivor who was the leader of the Vilna Ghetto resistance group, the United Partisan Organization. The introductory essay by poet/translator Shirley Kaufman is both interesting and informative.

Kovner, Abba. (1986). *My Little Sister and Selected Poems 1965–1985.* Oberlin, Ohio: Oberlin College. 159 pp. This volume contains Kovner's major poem sequence on the Holocaust, "My Little Sister," as well as other pieces that address various aspects of the Holocaust. The short introductory essay by poet/translator Shirley Kaufmann is very informative.

Lefwich, Joseph. (Ed.) (1961). *The Golden Peacock: A Worldwide Treasury of Yiddish Poetry.* New York: Thomas Yoseloff. 722 pp. This collection contains much of the best Yiddish poetry about the Holocaust. It includes poems by Itzik Feffer, Mordecai Gebirtig, Hirsh Glick, Binem Heller, Leib Olitzky, and Simcha Shayevicth.

Levi, Primo. (1976). *Shema: Collected Poems of Primo Levi.* London: The Menard Press. 56 pp. These poems by the noted Jewish Italian author, who fought with a band of partisans until he was captured by the Nazis, present vivid images of life and death in Nazi-occupied Europe. The title, "Shema," means "Hear!" in Hebrew, which is the first word of prayer affirming God's oneness.

Ogden, Maurice (n.d.). "The Hangman." This poem is included in a number of Holocaust curricula and curriculum guides, including Facing History and Ourselves National Foundation's (1994) *Facing History and Ourselves: Holocaust and Human Behavior.* Brookline, MA: Author.

Pagis, Dan. (1989). *Variable Directions: The Selected Poetry of Dan Pagis.* San Francisco: North Point Press. 153 pp. This volume includes a number of powerful poems (including "Written in Pencil in the Sealed Railway Car," "Europe, Late," "Testimony," and "Draft of a Reparations Agreement") about different aspects of the Holocaust.

Rózewicz, Tadeusz. (1991). *They Came to See a Poet.* London: Anvil Press Poetry. This collection contains such poems as "The Survivor," "Pigtail," and others that are either about certain aspects of the Holocaust or informed by it. The volume includes an informative introductory essay about Rósewicz and his poetry.

Sachs, Nelly. (1967). *O The Chimneys.* New York: Farrar, Straus, and Giroux. 387 pp. This collection, by a German Jewish survivor of the Holocaust (who fled to Sweden in 1940) and a Nobel Prize recipient for literature, includes a wealth of poetry the focus and themes of which are the Holocaust.

Sachs, Nelly. (1970). *The Seeker and Other Poems.* New York: Farrar, Straus, and Giroux. 399 pp. These poems by Nelly Sachs, who fled Germany in 1940 and was later the recipient of the Nobel Prize for Literature, are about various aspects of the Holocaust.

Schiff, Hilda. (Ed.) (1995). *Holocaust Poetry.* New York: St. Martin's Press. This collection includes a wide selection of Holocaust poetry by authors from around the world (including those who perished under Nazi rule, survivors, and those born after the Holocaust). It is divided into eight sections: Alienation; Persecution; Destruction; Rescuers, Bystanders, Perpetrators; Afterwards; Second Generation; Lessons; and God. Among the poets whose work is represented here are Dan Pagis, Abraham

Sutzkever, Paul Celan, Nelly Sachs, Mikos Radnoti, William Heyen, Tadeusz Rozewicz, Abba Kovner, Primo Levi, and Jacob Glatstein. Curiously, some of the works included are actually statements by noted figures (e.g., Niemöller and Wiesel, for example) rather than poetry per se.

Sutzkever, A. (1991). *Selected Poetry and Prose*. Berkeley and Los Angeles. University of California Press. 433 pp. This volume, written by a survivor of the Holocaust and a poet who has been referred to as Israel's foremost Yiddish poet, includes numerous powerful and haunting poems about various aspects of the Holocaust.

Volavkova, Hana. (1993) *"...I Never Saw Another Butterfly": Children's Drawings and Poems from Terezin Concentration Camp, 1942–1944*. New York: Schocken Books. 106 pp. The poems and drawings in this volume were created by children incarcerated at Theresienstadt. A note at the end of the volume reports that of the 15,000 children under the age of 15 who passed through Terezin, "only 100 came back." As mentioned in the body of the above essay, prior to reading these poems, students need to have learned about the facts of life and death in Terezin; then and only then will they be able to begin to fully appreciate the sense of anxiety, longing, want, sadness, hope against hope, loss, and unintended irony that clearly come through in these poems.

Whitman, Ruth. (1986). *The Testing of Hannah Senesh*. Detroit: Wayne State University Press. 115 pp. In this book of poetry, Whitman "explores the last nine months of Hanna's dramatic mission as a British emissary behind enemy lines in Nazi Europe" (p. 13) (from the essay, "Historical Background," by Livia Rothkirchen, which serves as the preface to the volume).

Short-Story Collections

Borowski, Tadeusz. (1967). *This Way to the Gas, Ladies and Gentlemen*. New York: Viking Press. 180 pp. The haunting short stories in the collection are based on Borowski's experiences in Auschwitz. Each story presents life and death in the concentration camp in all of its "brutal and naked reality."

Fink, Ida. (1996). *A Scrap of Time and Other Stories*. Evanston, IL: Northwestern University Press. A remarkable collection of stories about life and death in Poland during the Holocaust years. The stories are short, powerful, and thought provoking, and thus ideal for the classroom.

Lind, Jakov. (1964). *Soul of Wood and Other Stories*. New York: Grove Press. 190 pp. This collection of short stories portrays the evil that was prevalent while the Nazis carried out their atrocities. Many of the stories are surrealistic in tone, while others constitute allegories of sadism.

Lustig, Arnost. (1976). *Night and Home*. New York: Avon. This book of powerful short stories "explores the nightmarish interaction between Jews and the meticulous efficiency of the Nazis' program for extermination."

Ramras-Rauch, Gila, & Michman-Melkman, Joseph. (1985). *Facing the Holocaust: Selected Israeli Fiction*. Philadelphia: The Jewish Publication Society. 292 pp. "The [12] stories [some of which are excerpts from novels] contained in this volume represent attempts by contemporary Israeli writers to come to terms" with the Holocaust (eds.). The authors represented in this volume include Uri Orlev, Aharon

Appelfeld, and Yehuda Amichai. The volume also includes an excellent introduction to Holocaust literature by Israeli authors and an outstanding afterword, which addresses the relationship of Hebrew literature to the Holocaust.

Pedagogical Pieces

Danks, Carol. (October 1995). "Using Holocaust Short Stories and Poetry in the Social Studies Classroom." *Social Education, 59*(6): 358–361. In this article, Danks succinctly discusses certain caveats and guidelines that need to be taken into consideration when using short stories and poetry in a study of the Holocaust. She specifically discusses ways to teach the short stories in Borowski's *This Way to the Gas, Ladies and Gentlemen,* Ozick's *The Shawl,* and various pieces of poetry.

Drew, Margaret A. (October 1995). "Incorporating Literature into a Study of the Holocaust." *Social Education, 59*(6): 354–356. Among the issues Drew discusses in this piece are criteria teachers ought to use in selecting literature for use in the upper elementary and secondary school classrooms, key issues that should be addressed in the study of the Holocaust, and various first-person accounts and novels that can be incorporated into such a study.

Drew, Peg. (Fall 1989). "Holocaust Literature and Young People: Another Look." *Facing History and Ourselves News,* pp. 20–21. Drew argues that in addition to reading literature, students need a solid grounding vis-à-vis the history of the Holocaust. Only in that way, she argues, will they be able to make sense of the events that led up to and resulted in the Holocaust.

Farnham, James. (April 1983). "Ethical Ambiguity and the Teaching of the Holocaust." *English Journal, 72*(4): 63–68. A thought-provoking piece that discusses the clash between the value systems of students and actions of victims in the camps, the complexities of ethical behavior, and "ethical problems from the [Holocaust] literature."

Greeley, Kathy. (1997). "Making Plays, Making Meaning, Making Change," pp. 80–103. In Samuel Totten & Jon E. Pedersen (Eds.), *Social Issues and Service at the Middle Level.* Boston: Allyn and Bacon. In this fascinating essay, Greeley discusses and explains how she involved her students in the writing and production of a play that dealt, in part, with key issues germane to the Holocaust.

Kimmel, E. A. (February 1977). "Confronting the Ovens: The Holocaust and Juvenile Fiction." *The Horn Book Magazine,* 84–91. In his examination of juvenile fiction about the Holocaust, Kimmel notes that as of the late 1970s no Holocaust fiction written for children had been written about the death camps. After predicting that a novel about the death camps would eventually be written, he raises the issue as to "whether or not that novel [would] come any closer to the question at the core of all this blood and pain" (p. 91).

Meisel, Esther. (September 1982). "'I Don't Want to be a Bystander': Literature and the Holocaust." *English Journal, 71*(5): 40–44. Very briefly discusses the use of two poems: Nelly Sach's "The Chorus of the Rescued," and Ka-Tzetnik's "Wiedergutmahung."

Rudman, Masha Kabakow, & Rosenberg, Susan P. (Summer 1991). "Confronting History: Holocaust Books for Children." *The New Advocate, 4*(3): 163–176. This article presents and discusses numerous rationales for including literature in a study of the

Holocaust, issues several caveats in regard to selecting and using Holocaust litera-ture in the classroom, and then provides a critique of various types of Holocaust lit-erature on various subjects.

Rushforth, Peter. (1994). "'I Even Did a Theme Once on That Anne Frank Who Kept the Diary, And Got an A Plus on It': Reflections on Some Holocaust Books for Young People." *Dimensions: A Journal of Holocaust Studies*, 8(2): 23–35. Provides a solid overview of ten key books appropriate for use by teachers whose students are in the upper middle level to junior high levels.

Shimoni, Gideon. (Ed.). (1991). *The Holocaust in University Teaching*. New York: Pergamon Press. 278 pp. This volume includes selected syllabi of Holocaust courses, four of which focus on literature about the Holocaust: The Holocaust and Canadian Jewish Literature; Literature and Historical Memory: Holocaust Literature; Literature of the Holocaust; and Analysis of Literature for Children and Young Adults: Books About the Holocaust. Many of the other syllabi also include the use of key literary works.

Totten, Samuel. (1998). "Examining the Holocaust through the Lives and Literary Works of Victims and Survivors." In Robert Hauptman & Susan Hubbs Motin (Eds.), *The Holocaust: Memories, Research, Reference* (pp. 165–188). New York: Haworth Press.

Yolen, Jane (March 1989). "An Experiential Act." *Language Arts, 66*(3): 246–251. Discusses the value of the literary device of "time travel," especially as it relates to her novel about the Holocaust, *The Devil's Arithmetic.*

Zack, Vicki (January 1991). "'It Was the Worst of Times': Learning About the Holocaust Through Literature." *Language Arts, 68*: 42–48. Zack, a fifth-grade teacher in Canada, discusses a study of the Holocaust that she and several of her students conducted using Jane Yolen's *The Devil's Arithmetic.*

Films

The Hangman. (12 minutes, color. Available from Contemporary Films/McGraw Hill, Princeton Road, Highstown, New Jersey 08520; and Facing History and Ourselves Foundation, 16 Hurd Road, Brookline, Massachusetts 02146). This film, which is based on a poem written by Maurice Ogden, relates a parable in which the citizens of a town are hanged, one by one, by a stranger who has built a gallows in the town square. Hanging after hanging is met by one rationalization after another by the townspeople. The film can be used in conjunction with the poem of the same title. Librarian Margaret Drew (1982) has noted that "The [film's] theme is complex and rich in symbolism; [and in light of that] it should probably be shown more than once to be effective with students but it can be an excellent film for discussion with good teacher preparation" (p. 78).

3 The Diary of Anne Frank: Why I Don't Teach It

ELAINE CULBERTSON

For the past 20 years I have not taught *The Diary of Anne Frank*, although I have been actively engaged in teaching about the Holocaust to my own students and in preparing teachers to do the same with their students. Anne Frank's diary is the most anthologized piece of material for adolescents in the United States. It appears in one form or another, as the full diary, as an excerpt, as a stage play, even as poetry, in every major publisher's middle school anthology series, and is available in numerous languages, in abridged and unabridged versions. One will find Anne Frank's diary, in one form or another, in most book rooms in middle, junior high and high schools across the nation. Excerpts from her diary are available as posters for decorating the classroom, as frontispieces for blank journals that children are encouraged to keep, as Christmas and Chanukah cards, on stationery, etc. There are at least two film versions available, and in recent years several documentaries have been made about Anne, her family and friends, her righteous rescuers and their story, and what happened after the diary ended.

Anne is Hitler's most famous victim, an immediately recognizable face. Her fame is so great that in a *New York Times* op-ed piece on what women are looking for in a man, Maureen Dowd (1999) quoted a woman as saying that she did not know if she could justify a relationship with a particular man to whom she was attracted because, when questioned, he admitted he had never read Anne Frank. His ignorance of the diary was equated with ignorance of the Holocaust, and therefore an indication of his obvious insensitivity. So Anne Frank's cachet extends beyond the classrooms of schools and universities and into the fern bars of downtown Manhattan.

And yet . . . I find that with all its availability and with its enduring role as a cultural icon, it is the most inaccessible of texts because it purports to do something that it cannot do. Let me explain: Those of us who used Anne Frank when it was one of the few pieces we could find related to the Holocaust did so with the belief that our students possessed enough general knowledge about the Holocaust that they would be able to piece together the events prior to the attic, and those after it. Within that context, the story of Anne Frank, her girlish yearnings, her struggles with her mother, and her love for Peter were all perfectly acceptable adolescent fare. Interspersed with these things was a smattering of philosophy about the world, about our inability as humans to live together in peace and harmony, and about our heroine's desire to see the world be a better place.

Anne Frank was noble in the face of adversity, and that is what we liked about her. What many liked even more was that the real adversity, the terror of the Nazis, was, for the most part, if not entirely, absent from the book. In most editions, there was very little before and no after. This is precisely why the book is—in certain cases—so popular, why it is easily fit into anthologies, why it is used with children as young as nine years old. The book skirts the real issues of the Holocaust because the story takes place apart from them. Teachers could explain to their classes why Anne was hiding in the attic, but did not really have to in order for students to read and even like the book. Indeed, most of my colleagues who taught the book did not offer much explication. The abrupt ending of the book, with the sudden departure of the family, signaled the end of any real explanation; some would say things like "then the Nazis came to get them," or "it seems that they were informed upon and they were taken away." That was usually enough to satisfy students who were more intrigued with Anne's teen troubles than they were with her reason for being in the attic in the first place.

So, after teaching the text several times, and finding that the discussions were not about the Holocaust, or not about the goodness of those who risked their lives to help, or not about the bigotry and hatred that brought about these events, I began to examine what it was I had hoped the text might provide and where it was failing me. My motives in teaching about the Holocaust were that I hoped students might find therein lessons about the nature of humans, about the possibility for good and evil in each of us, about the necessity of caring about others, and about the importance of standing up for what one believes in. As sweet and caring as Anne Frank was, and as optimistic her view of the nature of man and of the world, she wrote from a sheltered place, where others were making the sacrifice to save her, and where she was able to exist in relative comfort for two years, while millions around her were murdered.

One day one of my students asked me why Anne was in the attic; when I replied that we had studied about that at the beginning of the book in order to set the context, she said that she was not sure that those events of World War II were in any way related to Anne's story. She did not really see Anne as suffering very much; she had her family with her, they were not really starving, and there was a nice boy there for her to fall in love with. Suddenly something that my father— who, along with my mother, is a Holocaust survivor and was incarcerated in concentration camps—had said to me years before came back to haunt me. They experienced great deprivation, and my mother was the sole survivor of her family (my father survived with his brother). When my father saw the Anne Frank film made in the 1950s, he told me that anyone who could save a cat was not really suffering, because most people could not even save their children! My student was telling me the same thing in a different way. It did not seem that bad. Anne had a roof over her head and her family around her. Sure, she had to be quiet during the day, but was that such a terrible price to pay, when most people were paying with their lives?

What I realized on that day was that the story of Anne Frank does not depict the life of the average victim of the Holocaust. If it did, many more people would be alive today, and there would be vast forests planted for the righteous instead of tiny groves of trees. Anne Frank was lucky for two years longer than most others, who eventually suffered and perished, or who survived with only a remnant of their lives and their culture. To have students read her story as the one piece of Holocaust literature that they will most likely encounter in their school careers, is almost as inappropriate as not studying about it at all. What would be more elucidating would be to read the story of her rescuers, to understand why they risked their lives to help the Frank family, and to hope that students would emulate those people in their daily lives. Yet it is only in recent years that any attention has been given to people like Miep Gies, even though her heroism is much more evident than Anne's.

I want to make my point very strongly: since most teachers are limited in the time they have to teach about the Holocaust, using a book like *The Diary of Anne Frank* provides a very skewed view of that world, and does not really accomplish what I believe should be the goals of Holocaust educators: to provide a glimpse of the world that was lost, to show how actions by responsible individuals can make a difference, and to empower students to believe that they do make decisions in their lives that will affect them and those around them. I do not believe that Anne Frank's diary can accomplish these goals. What it can do is to provide a very sentimental picture of one girl's experiences. However, students must be given more powerful examples of what life was like for the "average" Jew in order to be able to draw conclusions about what happened to whom and why. Holocaust education should not be about establishing the virtue of the victim and then lamenting her fate; it must be about educating students into a moral paradigm that values and demands action in the face of immoral behavior. To portray the Jew only as victim is to perpetuate the same stereotypes that were prevalent in Europe and which led to the Holocaust.

Perhaps the most powerful way to illustrate my point is to offer alternative materials that I feel accomplish the goals I have stated. Most of these materials have become available in the past few years because so much emphasis has been placed on Holocaust education, but some of them have been around for a very long time and were ignored because survivor or rescuer or bystander testimony or memoir was not particularly fashionable or valued or easy to read or—in the estimation of certain historians—historically accurate. The materials I will be quoting from are examples of real events in which individuals exhibited both spiritual and physical resistance against insurmountable odds. In addition, I will use an excerpt from a fictional piece that was written by a survivor's daughter and which I think represents an artistic view not far removed from the survivor's own story.

Let me also state that some of the materials I will suggest might not be acceptable for young students—which brings me to another of my beliefs about teaching the lessons of the Holocaust. Teachers who bring the Holocaust into classrooms where students are under the age of 12 or 13 are often worried about the graphic representations in some of the resources available; they do not want students to see the "piles of bodies" or the "walking skeletons" or to have access to the photos of naked women. They do not want students to dwell on the methods of annihilation because the descriptions as well as the statistics are disturbing. One of my colleagues told me that she takes her fourth graders "up to the gates of the concentration camps and not inside"—and she calls this Holocaust education! If one's students are too young to hear about or see the camps, then they are too young to learn about the Holocaust. Teachers may want to teach them about prejudice or discrimination or brotherhood, but one is not teaching about the Holocaust if little or no mention is made about what really happened. Do not misinterpret what I am saying here. I am in no way endorsing an intense study of the death camps, nor am I asking teachers to feed into that kind of morbid fascination that preadolescents often have for blood and gore. What I am saying is that unless the realities can be addressed, students cannot understand how the Holocaust differs from any other prejudice-motivated mass action.

Perhaps a concrete example will illustrate my point. In 1944, the Hungarian Jews were brought to Auschwitz. They had been shielded from much of the news about the war and were relatively ignorant of what they might expect upon their deportation. Their lives in Hungary during the war years had been unpleasant, but had retained a semblance of normal daily activities, enough so that a woman gynecologist who tells of her experiences in the camps writes about her attempts to help an infertile woman conceive a baby during the time when many of Europe's Jews were being gassed in the camps. As the Hungarians began to experience the peculiarities of life and death in Auschwitz, Dr. Gisella Perl (1997) describes the contrasts and moral dilemmas that she suddenly confronted:

> One of the SS chiefs would address the women, encouraging the pregnant ones to step forward, because they would be taken to another camp where living conditions were better. He also promised them double bread rations so as to be strong and healthy when the hour of delivery came. Group after group of pregnant women left Camp C. Even I was naive enough at that time to believe the Germans until one day I happened to have an errand near the crematories and saw with my own eyes what was done to these women.
>
> They were surrounded by a group of SS men and women, who amused themselves by giving these helpless creatures a taste of hell, after which death was a welcome friend. They were beaten with clubs and whips, torn by dogs, dragged around by their hair and kicked in the stomach with heavy German boots. Then, when they collapsed, they were thrown into the crematory—alive. I stood rooted to the ground, unable to move, to scream, to run away. But gradually the horror turned into revolt and this revolt shook me out of my lethargy and gave me a new incentive to live. I had to remain alive. It was up to me to save the lives of the mothers, if there was no other way than by destroying the life of their unborn children. I ran back to camp and going from block to block told the women what I had seen. Never again was anyone to betray their condition. It was to be denied to our last breath, hidden from the SS, the guards and even the Blockova, on whose good will our life depended.
>
> On dark nights when everyone else was sleeping—in dark corners of the camp, in the toilet, on the floor, without a drop of water, I delivered their babies. . . .
>
> No one will ever know what it meant to me to destroy these babies. After years and years of medical practice, childbirth was still to me the most beautiful,

the greatest miracle of nature. I loved those newborn babies not as a doctor, but as a mother and it was again and again my own child whom I killed to save the life of a woman . . . I prayed to God to help me save the mother or I would never touch a pregnant woman again. And if I had not done it, both mother and child would have been cruelly murdered. (quoted in Berenbaum, 1997, p. 207)

I have omitted the descriptions of the actual abortions as they are not central to my purpose here, nor should they be the focus of the discussion with students. What I would want my students to discuss are the questions posed by this passage: How can one justify killing one person to save another? Was Dr. Perl right or wrong? Are moral decisions situational or is there a higher morality that prevails here? What would they have done in a similar situation? How could a civilized people like the Germans behave in such a way? And the most important question of all: How does this relate to what goes on in our world today? These questions do not have right or wrong answers and cannot be filled in on a multiple choice scan sheet; they will not be provided in the teacher's edition of the book that so often accompanies a text such as *The Diary of Anne Frank.* One's students will not make crossword puzzles of the vocabulary words or design their own hiding place, as I have seen suggested. But they will be forced to confront the realities of the Holocaust and to debate choice and responsibility, which, I feel, is the ultimate reason for even bringing up the topic. If the passage seems too graphic for one's students or too controversial, is there one that allows students to write about and debate these issues in the text one is using? If not, is one really teaching about the Holocaust?

The following excerpt is from Mary Berg's *Warsaw Ghetto: A Diary:*

Dr. Janusz Korczak's children's home is empty now. A few days ago we all stood at the window and watched the Germans surround the houses. Rows of children, holding each other by their little hands, began to walk out of the doorway. There were tiny tots of two or three years among them, while the older ones were perhaps thirteen. Each child carried a little bundle in his hand. All of them wore white aprons. They walked in ranks of two, calm, and even smiling. They had not the slightest foreboding of their fate. At the end of the procession marched Dr. Korczak, who saw to it that the children did not walk on the sidewalk. Now and then, with fatherly solicitude, he stroked a child on the head or arm, and straightened out the ranks. He wore high boots, with his trousers stuck in them, an alpaca coat, and a navy blue cap. . . . He walked with a firm step, and was accompanied by one of the doctors of the children's home, who wore his white smock. This sad procession vanished at the corner. . . .

Thus died one of the purest and noblest men who ever lived. He was the pride of the ghetto. His children's home gave us courage, and all of us gladly gave part of our own scanty means to support the model home organized by this great idealist. He devoted all his life, all his creative work as an educator and writer, to the poor children of Warsaw. Even at the last moment he refused to be separated from them.

The house is empty now, except for the guards who are still cleaning up the rooms of the murdered children (Berg, 1995, pp. 238–239)

Mary Berg, herself a victim of the Holocaust, but in this instance a bystander to Korczak's last day, gives us an account of a true hero of the Holocaust, someone who purposefully resisted his enemies by attempting to maintain and sustain the lives of his orphans in the Warsaw Ghetto. Even at the end of his life Korczak refused to be saved, preferring to accompany the children in his orphanage to their deaths. Spiritual resistance is often more purposeful and usually requires greater fortitude than physical resistance.

Why not allow students to read about this kind of hero, rather than constantly to reiterate the story of the Jews who were able to save themselves by buying their safety? To portray the Jew as instrumental in saving himself and others is important; to portray the Jew as coping as best he could under the particular set of circumstances presented by the Holocaust is essential; and this must be done without an undue emphasis on the use of money and influence, lest we again go down that same path where Jews are viewed as dealing with all problems on a cash-and-carry basis. I have found that students react negatively and with the expected stereotypes to that kind of activity. They will tell me that the Jews always solve things through money, and that none of them has the heart to respond with courage to situations that require physical or moral courage. It becomes incumbent upon those of us who are teaching the lessons of the Holocaust to incorporate a kind of subliminal awareness about what message the medium might be sending.

An additional concern to me is the kind of saccharine pop psychology that Anne Frank has come to represent. Her most quoted line, the one about still believing in the goodness of people, tends to diminish the true suffering of and consequences for those who were victims. What right have we to quote such lines and use them as proof that, in the best of all possible worlds, the victim forgives the perpetrator, and that everything returns to normal. Anne Frank can only forgive those who did wrong to her; yet she is incapable of doing that, because her forgiveness comes before the fact. Her real horror was yet to come after she wrote the diary, when she traveled from detention at Westerbork to her eventual death at Bergen-Belsen in 1945. I wonder what epilogue she would have written to her diary had she survived the camps. What pieces might have been edited or amended if Anne had been the one to rescue the diary? Would she have been so worried about the sexual content, or the parts that showed her relationship with her mother in a bad light, or would she have found it necessary to dismiss some of what she had written as the idealistic musings of an untried soul?

In a book titled *Nightfather,* Carl Friedman (1991) fictionalizes the experiences of her survivor father and the impact his life had on their family:

> Camp is not so much a place as a condition. "I've had camp," he says. That makes him different from us. We've had chicken pox and measles. And after Simon fell out of a tree, he got a concussion and had to stay in bed for weeks. But we've never had camp.
>
> Most of the time he drops the past participle for convenience. Then he says "I have camp," as if the situation hadn't changed. And it's true, it hasn't. He still has camp, especially in his face. Not so much in his nose or ears, although they're big enough, but in his eyes.

I saw a wolf in the zoo once, with eyes like that. He was pacing back and forth in his cage, up and down and up and down, to the front and back again. I spent a long time staring at him through the bars.

Full of worry, I went to look for Max and Simon. They were hanging over the railings around the monkey rock, laughing at a baboon throwing pebbles.

"Please come and look at the wolf," I said, but they weren't interested. Only when I started to cry did Max reluctantly turn away and follow me.

"Well?" he said in a bored voice when we were standing in front of the wolf's cage, "what's the matter with him?"

"He has camp!" I sobbed. Max glanced through the bars.

"Impossible," he said. "Wolves do not get camp."

Then he pulled me by the hand. I had to go back to the monkeys with him.

When we got home and my mother saw my tear-stained cheeks, she asked what had made me so unhappy. Max shrugged. "She isn't big enough yet for the zoo." (pp. 1–3)

It is an insult to survivors and to their families to believe that what happened to them can be forgiven; it is infantile to believe that there is no bitterness attached or that survivors live absolutely normal lives after what they experienced. How can they? Do we expect survivors of auto accidents not to fear riding in automobiles? Do we think that having been burned in a fire, the victim will not harbor some latent fear of fire? Those of us who have witnessed violent incidents may have flashbacks of the event for years afterwards. Yet survivors of such horrific inhumanity are expected to forge on with their lives unscathed, to raise families and to forgive and forget. Let me rephrase that. We do not care if they do not forget; what we are looking for is that "higher moral example" of the sufferer who is big enough to rise above his tormentors. Anne Frank is a prime example of this kind of morality—she sees the good in people. I do not expect that of my students. I want them to see the real in people, in themselves and in others. I want them to confront that and deal with it. There is more courage in knowing that you have the capacity to do evil and in choosing not to, than in believing that evil does not exist.

REFERENCES

Berg, Mary (pseudonym). (1995). "Warsaw Ghetto: A Diary." In Laurel Holliday (Ed.), *Children in the Holocaust and World War II*, pp. 209–248. New York: Pocket Books.

Dowd, Maureen. (April 11, 1999). "Liberties: Cowboy Feminism." *New York Times*, n.p.

Frank, A.O.H., & Pressler, M. (Eds.) (1997). *The Diary of a Young Girl: The Definitive Edition.* New York: Doubleday.

Friedman, Carl. (1991). *Nightfather.* New York: Persea Books.

Perl, Gisella. (1997). "I Was a Doctor in Auschwitz." In Michael Berenbaum (Ed.), *Witness to the Holocaust*, pp. 204–209. New York: HarperCollins.

PART TWO

Lessons/Units of Study

Novels

Short Stories

Poetry

Drama

Memoirs/First-Person Accounts

CHAPTER

4

"Face to Face"

The Study of *Friedrich*, a Novel about the Holocast

REBECCA G. AUPPERLE

How do we enable young adolescents (12 to 15 years old) to comprehend that six million Jews were murdered in the Holocaust? How do we take the unfathomable nature of that number and make it resonate? How do we assist the students in gaining some sense of the injustice, prejudice, discrimination, and anguish that each individual must have experienced?

As important as the study of history is, history alone cannot do this for our young people—especially if it is taught in a traditional and staid manner. Unfortunately, it is accepted pedagogy by many to have students solely memorize names and dates, battles won and lost. I will remember 1066—the Battle of Hastings—until the day I die (if I am ever a contestant on *Jeopardy,* I will be ready!). But what did I learn about the people whose lives were affected by that event? Not much!

The presentation of dates and dry facts, however, falls far short of making flesh-and-blood connections with the events about which they speak, especially in the case of a complex occurrence like the Holocaust. In addition to providing a sound approach to history, teachers need to help students personalize the mind-boggling number of six million. Read within historical context, literature can personalize events otherwise inaccessible in human terms. It is capable of presenting the Jews of Europe and others not only as a category of people who became victims, but as a viable, productive, dynamic group that lived rich and varied lives and who were confronted with a myriad of unjust and horrific situations.

As I approached the subject of the Holocaust by providing a chronology and short historical overview (key vocabulary terms, timelines, a historical overview of antisemitism), three things became obvious: (1) my students had very little understanding about what I was teaching: they vaguely knew, courtesy of some war movie they had seen on TV, that the Nazis were the perpetrators of this heinous event, but they had no knowledge of the victims, much less the rescuers or bystanders; (2) when asked to name one prominent Jew in history, the majority of students could name no one but Anne Frank: they had no idea that Albert Einstein, Sigmund Freud, Marc Chagall, and Jonas Salk were Jews; and (3) each year, without fail, at least one of my students felt compelled to ask: "Ms. Aupperle, are you Jewish? You're not? Then why are you on such a crusade about the Holocaust?"

It was clear that, with few exceptions, my students had absolutely no idea who the Jews of Europe were, what they were like before the war, and what kinds of lives they lived before they were victims. How could I possibly teach the results of hatred and racial antisemitism without teaching what preceded it? How could I possibly show a group of kids—kids who could not fathom why a gentile found it necessary to teach about this topic—that one does not have to be a member of a group targeted *for* state-sponsored annihilation to decry such inhumanity?

Endeavoring to reach my classes in the most effective manner, I chose to proceed on a "continuum from information to knowledge to understanding," as my colleague and friend, Elaine Culbertson, a noted Holocaust educator, characterizes it. Yet, I have found that the use of primary source material (archival photographs, documents, diaries, memoirs), items that students can see and touch, in conjunction with a powerful piece of fiction, helps young adolescent students relate to a subject on a concrete basis. Indeed, they provide the tangible, one-on-one connection with information that captivates the students' interest, facilitates the processing of knowledge, and ultimately results in understanding.

I start with Susan D. Bachrach's (1994) *Tell Them We Remember*, which combines brief, thematic segments illustrated by artifacts and photographs with the personal stories of more than 20 young people of various social, religious, and national backgrounds who were affected by the Holocaust. The photographs, many of which are formal portraits, illustrate the importance and diversity of Jewish family life *before* the Holocaust. This is imperative, because most extant photos and film footage of the Jews during the Holocaust years were the product of the Germans, portraying their derogatory and unflattering perception of the Jews. This archival information provides an intimate connection to the more than one million children and teenagers murdered by the Nazis. It reveals that before the Holocaust, these young people enjoyed a world that revolved, not unlike my students' worlds, around family, friends, school, and social activities—until their worlds were turned upside down and annihilated under Nazi rule.

Next, we watch and discuss *The Camera of My Family: Four Generations in Germany, 1845–1945* (Anti-Defamation League), an 18-minute film made by American Catherine Hanf Noren about her German Jewish roots and heritage, which had been totally unknown to her throughout her childhood. As Noren states: "One day while visiting my grandmother, she showed me a picture from her past and I discovered it was *my* past, for the face of this stranger was so like my own at the same age. It was my great Aunt Elsa." This is an intriguing vehicle for introducing teenagers to the Holocaust: it combines a clear visual and textual foundation for the experience of the Jews in Germany in the prewar period and also delves into the issue of protecting children from unpleasant "family secrets," a practice that many Jewish immigrants and survivors have followed. Because of her relatives' reluctance to talk about their lives in Germany before World War II it was not until she was a grown woman that Catherine "met" her family through the "face" in the picture her grandmother showed her, the face so much like her own, the face so powerful that it compelled her to seek out the information about her family members' lives that culminated in the film. By getting to know them, she could know herself better.

Subsequent to this preparatory activity, I announce that we are "going to meet and get to know" some of my students' Jewish counterparts from 50 years ago. After the kids gawk at me as if I am a crazy woman (a look I become accustomed to as the year progresses), I ceremoniously present each student with a copy of an actual photograph of a Holocaust victim which I have fashioned, in an attempt to provide them with a sense of familiarity and comfort through a common object, into a faux frame. These pictures have been culled from a variety of sources, including the aforementioned Bachrach book, Michael Berenbaum's (1993) *The World Must Know,* and Dobroszycki and Kirshenblatt-Gimblett's (1977) *Image Before My Eyes.* The individual nature of each photograph is meant to elicit an aura of personal connectedness with their subjects. I place a short blurb on the back of each, offering a name, location, and year, if available. As these unique images make their way down the aisles, typical eighth-grade pandemonium erupts. Before even looking at her own, Ashley is leaning to the girl sitting across from her, demanding, "Who'dja get? Let me see!" Carlee exclaims, "Where in the world is Titiance?" Sarah is more reflective: "I have a bunch of kids having fun in a boat." Mike yells, "Check it out! I have an entire family at a wedding in Belgium in 1939. Belgium?" "Look," says Amy, "Here's a little Gypsy girl from Hungary before the war. Are Gypsies Jewish?" "Mine's some old lady," grouses John, none too happily, "and she's dressed all in black." The potential motivation for personal investigation of each singular face by my students is infinitely higher than had I decreed, "Look up what was happening to the Jews in Holland in 1938." They are captivated by the reality that the likeness they are holding is the face of a *person who once lived;* the limited information on the back whets their curiosity; they want more.

While perusal of the photos continues, I distribute a variety of maps from Martin Gilbert's (1988) *Atlas of the Holocaust* and *The United States Holocaust Memorial Museum's Historical Atlas of the Holocaust* (1996). By starting with the maps and then accessing other sources as necessary, a treasure trove of information is unearthed about pre-Holocaust life in the different Jewish communities of Europe, including the names of countries, cities, and towns where their "faces" resided, the contributions of Jewish culture made to society by Jews in that geographical area, and 2,000 years of Jewish life in general prior to the onslaught. Sarah discovers that the teens frolicking in the boat in Holland are most likely adrift on a canal, one of the many waterways on which Dutch streets are built. She has also discerned that no one even dreamed that Holland, traditionally neutral, would eventually be invaded. She reports that Holland's neutrality and its reputation as a haven for religious minorities were the prime factors in Anne Frank's family emigrating there from Germany in 1933. Mike determines that during the post-World War I years things were bad economically, so it was not unusual for weddings to be simple, just as in any country experiencing the deprivations of a depression. "That's probably why this bride is wearing a suit, not a gown," he explains. Amy becomes our resident expert on the Gypsies, revealing that the two main non-Jewish nomadic clans were the Sinti and Roma, considered to be subhuman in the ideology of the National Socialist People's Party. Dana is stunned by the knowledge that some prescient Jews, fearing the worst from an antisemitic government and possessing the necessary resources, made the heart-wrenching choice to send their children out of the country to relatives or strangers elsewhere. According to the information on the back of her portrait, Dana discovers that Dora, a German girl near her own age, is preparing to leave for Palestine. "Isn't Palestine in the Bible?" she asks. "She's going there by herself?" John's "old lady in black," he discovers, is probably the much-respected grandmother of an Orthodox Jewish family in a Russian border town of Lithuania, sitting, as was the custom in early twentieth century Europe, for a formal, somber portrait. The minutiae of facts about their "faces" flows as if from a wellspring; the kids have uncovered the mere tip of the iceberg. I encourage them to continue their quest.

The next day I introduce to the class a thinking/writing exercise utilizing their newfound information: each of my students will author an essay or short story delineating his/her concept of a day in the life of his personal "face" prior to the Holocaust. A torrent of questions assails me, and *I reiterate in detail that I am looking for a written portrait based on their research*, one that reflects what they have come to understand about the life of this individual prior to the upheaval caused by Hitler. Certain assumptions will be considered a given—such as that children between the ages of six and eighteen went to school—but character development will need to be augmented by imagination, *based on historical accuracy. This is a vital component, not to be confused with a creative writing assignment,* even though I encourage the kids, many of whom are classified as "gifted and talented" and therefore enrolled in the school's Special Program for Individual Enrichment, to employ their facility for language while at the same time maintaining high standards of composition and infusing previously studied vocabulary into their written pieces. The goal is for students to utilize all available resources (books, atlases, primary documents, CDs) to glean the information necessary to achieve a working understanding of Jewish life in that time and place; *only then can they begin to appreciate what was lost.* The subsequent task—to "flesh out" the character in this specific setting, to give life to the "face"—is couched within the primary objective of achieving historical accuracy. I move up and down the aisles, hanging over shoulders, giving encouragement, making suggestions; I have faith. A few seem stumped, but those who have availed themselves of the succinct and incisive material offered by the maps and other references are not tuned out or bored, those twin adolescent curses; they are researching and writing. They are leaning over the tops of their desks, frowning with concentration as they transfer their ideas into words on paper. The first to share their written reports the next day are shy. I call on Kim, who writes of Clara, her "face," going to secondary school and working afterwards in her parents' bakery shop in Poland. She will probably not go on to gymnasium, the European equivalent of college, because her family can't afford it. Most likely she will look for a husband, marry early, and start a family; that's what girls do in her small town.

According to Sarah, the kids' "faces" she writes about belong to teenage students in Holland, who are on vacation from school. They have just finished exams, she says, and have rented a boat to celebrate. At this moment they are carefree, with not a thought of impending doom. They know they are Jews, but they are also Dutch; what harm could possibly come to them?

Dana raises her hand and continues telling her story of a day in the life of Dora, who lives in Mainz, Germany, and is a high school student. "She belongs to an Orthodox Jewish family," explains Dana, "which means they are very religious and follow strict rules."

"Oh, you mean they go to mass every Sunday?" asks one of her classmates. I help her explain that the day of worship for Jews, the Sabbath, is Saturday, not Sunday, as it is for Christians, and that Jews attend a synagogue, or temple, not a church. This is a major news flash to most of my students, who are members of an extremely homogeneous community of white Christians. Dana continues, "The Jewish people begin their Sabbath at sundown on Friday by lighting candles and reciting a special prayer. If they are extremely observant, they do no work and observe explicit dietary laws, eating what is called kosher food. The celebration of the Sabbath is a family affair, beginning with the dinner on Friday evening and continuing on Saturday when Dora goes with her family to the local synagogue for services where she sits in the balcony with her mother and her sisters; the men sit downstairs. See the little skullcaps on the men's heads? They are *yarmulkes*, or *kipot*, the traditional head covering of Jewish men for religious occasions. And that cloak with the strings hanging from it that her father is wearing is a *tallit*, or prayer shawl."

"Can I go next?" clamors Mike. "Mine's a group, so I have more than one 'face'!" Mike reports that this is the wedding of two Belgian residents. They are standing on the steps of an Antwerp synagogue after the ceremony with a large group of family members, both young and old. The date had to be sometime after 1941, because both bride and groom and many others in the photo are wearing a six-pointed yellow star on the left-chest side of their clothing, and the edict of the Nazis demanding that Jews be marked as targets for persecution in this manner did not go into effect until that date. This symbol, called the Star of David, is representative of Judaism, just as the cross is the symbol of Christianity. Nazi law required that Jews wear the yellow star at all times, and penalties for refusal to do so were harsh.

In the inquisitive and ingenuous hands of my students, the "faces" in their portraits have come to life. We now know something of the prewar geography of many of the European countries that would be squeezed in the Nazi grasp, and we have a glimpse of the encroaching antisemitic restrictions that would affect everyday lives. We also know something about where and how the Jews lived, as well as something of their culture and religious beliefs. I tell my class that they have done a terrific job, but there is more work to be done. We must take this foundation, this personal relationship they have developed through historical research and primary documents, and expand and develop it as we continue the study of the Holocaust and its effects on every victim's "face."

Friedrich is the fictional story (actually a novel) of the friendship between Friedrich Schneider, a Jewish boy, and the narrator, a non-Jewish boy, as they grow up in Nazi Germany just before and during World War II. Through this terrible time, which brings restrictions, hardships, and finally, persecution to the Schneiders, Friedrich's friend rejects the prejudice and hatred that ruins Friedrich's young life, but he is also forced to see the limits of his friendship and loyalty to a Jewish person in Hitler-run Germany. This dilemma involving peer pressure represents possibly the defining value judgment of adolescent life, and its appeal is what makes *Friedrich* a powerful tool in teaching young people about the Holocaust. *In making the transition from nonfiction to fiction, it is important for students to be cognizant that this book, although considered a novel, is based on autobiographical information.*

As a prereading strategy, I ask students to imagine a situation in their own lives in which they experience peer pressure when they wish to remain loyal to a friend, and to address their feelings about supporting an unpopular friend which might affect their acceptance by their peers.

Amber pipes up, "I'd just tell them that he's my friend, and if they don't like it, tough!"

"But what happens if he is very unpopular," I prod, "and nobody else wants anything else to do with him?"

"If they're really my friends, they won't care," Lisa responds.

"Okay, but what if they do all drop you," I press, "and it ends up that he is the only friend you have left?"

"My friends would never do that; they like me too much!" the never-shy Amber asserts with all the assurance of an egocentric 14-year-old. It is obvious that today's teens have difficulty imagining a situation that they cannot control, one that challenges their "rights." Perhaps this should not be startling, since they have been raised in a democracy where the rights and liberties of the individual are valued above all else.

"What if the pressure is the result of a government law?" I press. The answer to this is easy to predict.

Jason declares, "Nobody can tell me whom I'm allowed to be friends with; that's *my* business!"

The next day I build on Jason's declaration by distributing a handout that delineates "Anti-Jewish Laws in Nazi Germany" and serves as a catalyst for precipitating a discussion of current laws and how they affect people. The students read the laws imposed on Jews by the Nazi government from April 1933 to September 1941.

Matt reacts, appalled, "They could control everything like that?" "Yes," I reply, and then point out that the Nuremberg Laws, promulgated in 1935, were particularly virulent because they stripped the Jews of their citizenship.

"Do we have laws like this today?" I inquire.

Silence greets my question until Amber makes it perfectly clear that she believes no one in the United States would tolerate that kind of government oppression.

"Did laws like this ever exist in this country?" I press.

Most of my students seem surprised at that mere suggestion, but Justin, a history buff, volunteers, "Remember hearing about segregation in the South? There were laws that said blacks couldn't vote in elections up until the 1960s."

"But that was only thirty-some years ago! Is that possible?" Gina voices her shock.

"Not only was it possible, it happened right here in America; besides not being able to vote, blacks were restricted from using 'white' water fountains and 'white' bathrooms or attending 'white' schools," I amplify. "They couldn't get a sandwich at a deli counter with whites, and if they rode a bus, they had to sit in a back seat."

This gives my ethnically homogeneous class, which boasts a grand total of two or three children of color yearly, something to ponder. I explain that this sad period in America's history, a result of institutionalized prejudice and bigotry, ultimately caused a major upheaval in American society, a society created on the proposition that all men are created equal. I am careful to note that despite the repressive, inhumane and awful nature of these laws, *they did not culminate in the genocide of a particular group.* "So what happened to these laws?" I prompt Justin. "Did blacks have any recourse against segregation and persecution?"

He continues to explain, telling the story of the civil rights movement and the method of nonviolent resistance that slowly, painfully led to legislation that permitted blacks the freedom of exercising their constitutional rights in a country based on the thesis that "All men are endowed by their creator with certain inalienable rights." The difference between this situation and the one in Nazi Germany is clear: the Jews could not seek redress through the government because all of their rights were inexorably stripped away.

"But," I caution, "there are still many American citizens today who believe that African Americans, Hispanics, Asians, and other minorities are genetically inferior, just as Hitler believed the Jews were." To illustrate these issues more graphically, I show the class excerpts from the 40-minute 1995 video *The Shadow of Hate: A History of Intolerance in America* (Teaching Tolerance), which uses real events to examine the persecution and discrimination that existed in the United States, aimed against certain individuals and groups simply because of who they were. I select the segment entitled "The Ballad of Leo Frank," because it addresses three elements important to our study: prejudice and bigotry in general; anti-semitism in America in particular; and the dangers of scapegoating. We watch this vignette set in Georgia in 1913, which relates the tale of the "Jewish conspiracy myth," finding its focus in the murder of Mary Phagan, a 13-year-old girl who worked for a Jewish factory superintendent named Leo Frank. The bell rings, and my eighth graders depart with the story of Mary Phagan and public hangings of innocent people in Georgia in 1913 fresh in their minds.

The next day, having had time to digest the video, the kids enter the class exploding with questions. "How could the people in that town have allowed that lynching to happen?" demands Amber. "How could they have watched and acted like they were at a party?"

"Why didn't somebody do something to stop it?" adds Mike.

Amy says, "The more I thought about it, the sicker I felt. God, if something like this could happen in America, no wonder the Nazis could get away with what they did in Germany!"

This is the exact response I had hoped for. I try to direct their outrage by asking, "What conditions contributed to a general mood of intolerance toward Jews in Atlanta at the time of Leo Frank's arrest?" I lead them through an examination of the effects that drought and blight were wreaking on Georgia's main crop, cotton, causing depressed economic conditions. Low wages and the high cost of urban living made it necessary for women and children to work long, hard hours in dangerous factories, with many families living in overcrowded and unsanitary slums. Jews were resented as wealthy "outsiders" who were believed to control the economy. Most of my kids had overlooked the effects that a wage earner's inability to place food on the table could have on a populace's mind-set; I endeavor to help them see the parallels and the differences between this situation and the one Friedrich faces in Nazi Germany.

I conclude by noting that, "The Nazis' scapegoating of Jews was the first step to greater persecution, isolation, and finally, murder. Of course, this didn't all happen overnight. It was aided by hundreds of years of Christian antisemitism. Also at play was an extreme form of nationalism and the desire on the Nazis' part to create a "pure race," all of which the class will examine later.

"Now let us take a look at the story of two 'faces' who lived through this very kind of situation. Hopefully, it will make things clearer for us," I add.

At this point, I assign the class the reading of the first 7 chapters of the novel *Friedrich* by Hans Peter Richter (1970). Since we have done a great deal of preparation as a class, I ask them to read these 30 pages on their own over the next two class periods and after school. At the same time, I provide them with a handout entitled "The Nature of Nazi Thought," which I ask them to examine after they finish their reading. This document is a composite of quotes from prominent National Socialists including Adolf Hitler, and it unequivocally states the nature of Nazi ideology in regard to the leadership of the "volkish" state, education, religion, living space, and racial theories of "German science." I inform them that their preparation includes not only reading the assigned chapters, but also documenting in their journals how and by whom the "Nazi thought" theories were illustrated.

Upon their completion of the assignment, I ask, "Why would/should an educated citizenry have balked at or challenged the ideas that you read about in 'The Nature of Nazi Thought'?"

"Because they're not fair—they're inhuman!" blurts Amber. "They treat some people like they don't count and can be done away with, and others like they don't have to answer to the law at all."

"Why didn't they do something then?" I probe.

This is the perfect juncture at which to discuss the difference between a totalitarian and a democratic state. I use this activity to help introduce the difficulties Friedrich and his friend encounter because of the rules and attitudes at the time of the story.

I ask, "What distinguishes a democratic government from a nondemocratic one?" Students who have learned their civics will quickly tell you that a democratic government is one in which the citizenry elects its leaders by public vote and employs checks and balances to prohibit one branch of government from getting too powerful and taking over the others.

"Was Germany ever a democracy?" I pursue.

This one slows them down, so we access our history books and encyclopedias online and discover that following their defeat in World War I (1914–1918), the German people created the Weimar Republic, their nation's first experience in democracy. Overwhelmed by problems the government could not control, such as postwar inflation so severe it wiped out the middle class and fostered Communist-led demonstrations and strikes that created the fear of a repeat of the Russian Revolution in Germany, the republic lasted only 15 years. This was the situation that Hitler manipulated to establish a totalitarian state. He promised to tear up the peace treaty, wipe out the Communists, restore German greatness and pride, and build an empire that would "last 1,000 years." He fed on the existing antisemitism, blaming the Jews for everything, including inflation and the economic depression that followed, claiming that they were responsible for Germany's loss of the war, the Treaty of Versailles, which he felt "crippled" Germany, and the weak Weimar Republic. While promising to "rid Europe of Jews," Hitler legally gained the office of chancellor in 1932 but soon discarded the fledging democracy, and took the title *Der Fuhrer* (the Leader). Through his National Socialist Party (the Nazis), the passage of the Enabling Law, and his feared special police (the Gestapo), he came to control *every* aspect of German life as he waged his campaign against the Jews. This was the societal milieu in which Friedrich and his friend were born and raised.

"So, in a government like this," I ask, "would there have been any restrictions at all on Hitler's power?"

Dennis answers seriously, "No way. Nazi Germany was a dictatorship, and that means it was a nation in which Hitler had absolute power and authority."

We begin tying this material into the chapter of *Friedrich* entitled "Grandfather" by generally agreeing that the narrator's father cannot find a job because of the poor economic conditions in Germany, and the only way he can support his family is with Grandfather's subsidy each month. Lisa asserts that this is so humiliating to him that she believes he would have pledged allegiance to any government that promised to restore his self-respect. Dana thoughtfully muses, "Any man wants what is best for his family, and if the Nazi Party gave it to them, they went along."

"But is it fair," I interject, "if it comes at the expense of others? I think we need to examine what kind of people in those societies would permit situations that involved fellow citizens turning their backs on a persecuted minority." This presents the opportunity to correlate the data they have been gathering in their journals with the content of the chapters they have read so far. I ask my students: "What were the feelings of Herr Resch, Friedrich's landlord, toward the Jews?"

"That's obvious," Danny replies, checking the notes in his journal. "Herr Resch was willing to put up with a Jew under his roof because he got something out of it—rent money! In the chapter 'Snow,' he reveals how he really feels when he calls Friedrich a 'dirty Jewboy.' When he was asked why he had permitted the Schneiders to live in his building for ten years and now wanted them out, he replied, 'Times have changed.' The minute it became a disadvantage to him politically because the Nazi Party did not approve, he wanted nothing to do with them."

"It is a perfect example of the theories of living space and the race element of Nazi thought," I add. "Now how about the narrator's grandfather?"

"I've got that one," volunteers Brian. "Despite the fact that history tells us the Romans were responsible for Jesus' murder, the narrator's grandfather comes right out and says he does not want his grandson playing with a Jew because the Jews killed Jesus. That's definitely the 'religious views' of 'Nazi Thought.'"

"Were their feelings common among Germans of that age?" I probe further. "Oh yes, they were very common," Danielle calls out. "According to the Nazis' ideas about 'Educating the Young and Old' in last night's homework, many people of that generation had been raised with antisemitism, as the vicious comments Friedrich's grandfather makes about his former Jewish foreman illustrate. It was easy for them to buy into the scapegoating of Jews if they thought it would pave the way to their own security."

Most of my students agree that the narrator is a good friend to Friedrich, so the next question I ask is why they think he assumes the role of a *bystander* during the incident at the stationery shop in Chapter 7, "On the Way to School."

"He was afraid to do anything," Christina replies slowly.

"Does this mean he's a bad person?" I challenge.

When I get no response, I produce the first of some 40 "display boards" in my classroom, each devoted to a separate aspect of the Holocaust, each composed of photos, text, historical data, and contemporary print news, each a compact "miniarchive" which I have assembled over my 25-year tenure as a teacher of the Holocaust. This one tells the story of Kitty Genovese, relating how in 1965, 38 people in New York City listened as she was attacked and repeatedly stabbed outside her apartment building, and how not one person even did as much as call the police until after she was dead and her attacker had fled. "Were those bystanders bad people?" I reiterate.

"I don't think so," Christina allows tentatively.

"Why not, then? What was their reasoning? How could they listen to someone being murdered and do nothing?"

The kids compete to get their answers out first:

"Number one—fear. Maybe they thought the guy would come after them."

"Lack of caring for others."

"Selfishness."

"Indifference."

"Maybe they were in shock and didn't know what to do."

"By not doing anything to help," I stress, "they most definitely allowed the attacker to continue murdering Kitty; now, I want you to do some really heavy thinking about that." I pass out copies of an interview with a police lieutenant who was on the scene at the investigation of this tragedy; in it he quotes the killer and several of the "bystanders" [Wainwright, 1964, pp. 7–8]. I tell the kids that our purpose is to determine what indifference does, regardless of the context, and how *we* might be indifferent. We read this piece as a class, and I inquire if anybody thinks the circumstances of Kitty's murder reveal anything about human nature.

There is unanimous agreement that the witnesses' prime motivation was not wanting to get involved.

"But all they had to do was call the police!" screeches Amber. "They didn't have to give their name or anything—and they didn't have to get physically involved!"

I tell the class that Amber has hit upon an important issue. "While the refusal of the 38 'bystanders' to come to Kitty's aid is not directly analogous to Nazi domination in that there was no fear of retribution by the U.S. government for doing so, we have to acknowledge that they were afraid of involvement—being questioned or going to court or being found out by the attacker—all elements of being more concerned about themselves than the victims."

"Maybe if one person had done something, others would have joined in," offers Justin.

"Safety in numbers, huh?" I muse. "How about the converse? Does thinking that everybody would act as did these thirty-eight people make it easier for the rest of us to be indifferent to pain and danger experienced by others?"

"Now we must consider the issue of the bystanders." As a prompt, I bring out a poster of the famous Niemöeller quote for display on the front board:

> They came for the communists and I did not speak up because I was not a communist. They came for the socialists, and I did not speak up because I was not a socialist. They came for the union leaders, and I did not speak up because I was not a union leader. Then they came for the Jews, and I did not speak up because I wasn't a Jew. Then they came for me, and there was no one left to speak up for me.

I tell them that Martin Niemöeller was a pastor of a Protestant congregation in Dalem, a suburb of Berlin, who ended up being imprisoned for 7 years, from 1938 to 1945, for openly criticizing the Nazi regime.

We consider his words about indifference; then I instruct the class to close their eyes and inject themselves into the following scenario: Imagine that you are a Gentile in Nazi Germany during World War II. You know how the Nazis *think* and you know about their anti-Jewish laws. How would you feel if your best friend were Jewish and had such horrible restrictions placed upon him?

Again, I am making a direct connection to a major source of tension in *Friedrich*, the novel the students are reading. The students write their answers on slips of paper (later to be copied into their journals) and then share. The replies are brutally honest:

> As a gentile I would feel safe. On the other hand, I would pity my friend's family because they are Jewish. Still our friendship will not change, even if Hitler had a law saying that non-Jewish children could not play with Jewish children.

I feel I would probably not hang out with him. If the Nazis caught me hanging with him, they would hurt me, maybe even kill my family.

I really don't know how I'd feel. I'd probably have mixed feelings like, I think, Friedrich's friend must have had. I'd be happy because things were getting better for German people such as we wouldn't be so poor we'd have to decide between going to the amusement park or eating lunch like we saw in the Chapter "School Begins," but I'd also be sad because my best friend is getting his life taken away. I'd also be confused about why this is happening to the Jewish people. I'm sure that the Schneiders, and certainly Friedrich, never did anything to hurt Germans.

I would feel sorry for the Jews; they couldn't even walk the streets without being hassled. I think somebody should have done something about Hitler and his evil ways.

I certainly would not turn against my friend, and I would not join Hitler clubs and organizations. I know I wouldn't want people to treat me as though I had the plague.

As the kids read their responses, I have them come up and pin what they have written on the bulletin board. When they finish, I direct Amber to collate them in columns according to those which offered direct assistance to a Jewish friend as opposed to those who expressed concern but did nothing. The size of the "do nothing" column is troubling and advances the discussion in a new direction.

While considering this question, students must be made aware of the terror under which normal citizens lived in the Nazi regime as they were constantly threatened with the horrific ramifications of disobeying Nazi laws. I inform them that as early as 1933, there were numerous concentration camps operating in Germany. Even though these were not killing centers, the intent of the threat of incarceration and abuse in these camps was to instill terror in the German people and to force them to obey Hitler's dictates. Even Friedrich's teacher, Herr Neudorf, who is sympathetic to Friedrich's plight in the chapter "The Teacher," feels compelled to protect himself by giving the Nazi salute after explaining to his students that Friedrich must leave their class because he is a Jew. Similarly, I reveal that in an upcoming chapter in *Friedrich* called "The Festival," we will witness the narrator's consternation about attending Friedrich's bar mitzvah when he confesses, "I had gone with him, even though I had to keep thinking of my father. Only a week ago he had begged me, 'Don't show yourself so often with the Schneiders; otherwise I'll have difficulties.'"

Another example can be made by referencing the risks and the stress that Miep Gies and others endured while helping the Franks and the VanDaans to hide in Amsterdam for over two years. In her book *Anne Frank Remembered*, (1987) Gies explains how extremely dangerous it was to go outside of the city to secure food for the inhabitants of the Secret Annex with black-market ration books. She reports that righteous people caught in these actions disappeared and were never seen again. We acknowledge that every break-in of the factory above which they hid created paralyzing fear that the "righteous Gentiles" would be denounced for harboring Jews. In fact, Mr. Kraler and Mr. Koophuis were ultimately arrested and imprisoned by the Nazis.

A major moment in our study of the Holocaust occurs when survivor Clara Isaacman visits my class and relates an incident from her memoir, *Clara's Story,* (1984) about watching from her hiding place in a basement and seeing a young boy, one of her brother's classmates, mortally shot in the back by a Nazi soldier when the child refused to obey the command to halt as he walked fearfully down an Antwerp street. Clara goes on to say in her testimony that seeing the child murdered in cold blood was horrible enough, but her horror grew as she continued to watch the street before her, peopled with hundreds of regular Belgian citizens on their way to work, walking north and south, up and back—people afraid to stop and give aid to this Jewish child, people too terrified even to remove his corpse from the street, people who just passed him where he lay. Despite her tender years, she knew all too well the reason for their lack of action: their overwhelming fear not only of the uniforms of the German soldiers, but that the guns in their holsters would be turned on them as well if they intervened.

I integrate this material into our study because I feel it is important for my students to understand that the apathy demonstrated by most of the crowd gathered outside the Jewish stationery store in the chapter "The Way to School" contains the seeds of the behavior Clara witnessed on the streets of Belgium, and likely constitutes the first roots of total indifference. I want them to know that it is precisely at times like these, when the crowd hangs back or even responds with laughter, that a person makes the decision whether he or she will be a "bystander" who does nothing or a "rescuer" of his or her fellow humans. Friedrich and the old woman who wants to buy book covers are the only ones who take a stand against the boycott of Jewish businesses, and even though they face broomsticks instead of guns, the narrator's inability to say anything more than a weak hello to the shop owner, Herr Rosenthal, indicates his fear of getting involved.

I stress that the risk varied according to country and circumstances. Gentile rescuer Irene Opdyke recalls posters on every street corner in Poland during the war saying, "This is a Jew-free town, and if any one should help an escaped Jew, the sentence is death." She relates, "There were Polish families being hung with Jewish families that they had helped. We were forced to watch them die, as a warning of what would happen if we befriended a Jew" (Rittner and Meyers, 1986, pp. 48–49).

"And since the Nazis followed the principle of collective responsibility," Nechama Tec (1991) tells us, "the same punishment applied to the family members of those who defied this law. There are many cases on record where entire families of Poles were murdered, including infants, only because one of them had protected Jews" (pp. 211–212).

I remind the class that the ramifications of helping Jews in mid-1930s Germany had not yet escalated to this horrific level, but certainly fear of harsh reprisals kept the narrator's family from championing the Schneiders.

I ask my students if they were faced with this circumstance as Gentiles, would they seek help for their Jewish friend, or would they, too, remain a bystander like Friedrich's friend? With the altruism of the young, many are adamant that they would definitely try to enlist help for Jewish friends from their own families, but an equal number admit that even in an imagined setting it is difficult to step in to help someone if there is danger of physical harm. I also want to know if they think the penalties for civil disobedience would be a deterrent as they project their parents' response, and why they think people in this society would permit circumstances like this to continue. Among their responses were the following:

> Gentiles were afraid to stand up to the Nazis because they had nothing to protect them. They would be taking their life and their family's lives at risk.

> Gentiles wanted to follow Hitler because they were afraid if they didn't, they would lose their jobs and financial status or be physically harmed.

> They were eventually brainwashed into believing what Hitler said about the Jews.

"These are all viable answers, " I tell the class. "But what about the people who did help the Jews—the rescuers? What made them different from the bystanders?"

I display my many books about rescuers—among them *Schindler's List*, by Thomas Keneally (1982), *Anne Frank Remembered*, by Miep Gies (1987), *Assignment Rescue*, by Varian Fry (1992), *Lest Innocent Blood Be Shed: The Story of the Village of LeChambon and How Goodness Happened There*, by Philip Hallie (1979), and *Conscience and Courage: Rescuers of Jews during the Holocaust*, by Eva Fogelman (1994). I summarize the stories of Corrie tenBoom and her family, of Oskar Schindler, Magda and Andre' Trocme, Irene Opdyke and Raoul Wallenberg, and Marion Pritchard—just a few of the Gentile rescuers of Jews during the Holocaust.

I show clips of interviews with rescuers from the powerful film *The Courage to Care* (Social Studies School Service), in the hope that it will bring my students somewhat closer to an understanding of the altruistic personality and what made these people different from the vast majority who chose to do nothing.

I break the kids up into groups of four, and based on my summary of an individual righteous gentile's behavior, along with the books as a guide, each quartet chooses a "rescuer" and creates a Venn diagram in their journals illustrating the characteristics of this person's behavior and how they contrast and possibly intersect with the behavior of the novel's narrator, his family, and Herr Resch. This exercise clearly points out that even though the altruists share many similar qualities with the average person, they were unique because they were among the few who realized that all life was worthy; they had the "courage to care."

Over the following 2 days, my students read the next 7 chapters of *Friedrich*, which encompass the events of 1933; this provides a perfect entry for a discussion of the Hitler Youth as described in the chapter entitled "The Jungvolk." When they enter class, I tell them it *is* vital that they know that young people were singled out to play a major role in Hitler's drama; to further illustrate this, we view the video

Heil Hitler: Confessions of a Hitler Youth (Social Studies School Service). This short film fascinates my class and precipitates a comparison of information gleaned from the chapters we have just read in the novel. Two teams of 6 students each assemble at the front and side chalkboards respectively: Team 1 will chart responses to questions from Hitler Youth Alfons Heck's point of view and Team 2 from Friedrich's and his friend's. I first ask the kids to describe the Jungvolk and the types of things they preached. Team 2 replies that it was kind of like the Boy Scouts, listing things like wearing a uniform, going camping, and marching in parades. Team 1 agrees but adds that they were obsessed with duty to their country: "It was far more important than people. Hitler was all-powerful and all-wise; the Fuhrer was to be obeyed because he was creating a thousand-year rule that would restore Germany to its former greatness."

Next I ask them to list the things that made belonging to the Jungvolk attractive to kids of Alfons's and Friedrich's age. Team 1 ranks items like the feeling of importance gained by doing things to make your country powerful again, while Team 2 selected items such as precision marching, hiking, camping, war games, and sports, each documenting their choices with supporting details from the book and film.

I then request the class to contrast the two films that Alfons watched as part of his Jungvolk training: *The Eternal Jew* and *Hitler Youth Boy,* listing the images that stand out in each and how they might appeal to an adolescent. Teams 1 and 2 agree that the paraphernalia, such as uniforms and neck scarves, flags and banners; the symbols, such as flying eagles and a broken, twisted cross; the pomp and mysticism, such as parades and maneuvers, singing, slogans, and orchestrated marching in ethereal settings so similar to religious experience, were captivating to kids who wanted "to belong," to feel special and important.

At this point I inquire whether Alfons or Friedrich's friend harbored any personal animosity toward Jews. All agree that both boys seem curiously free of the bigotry and hate that we associate with Hitler's followers; how, then, could they be so caught up in a movement that advocated persecution and sequestration of those considered inferior? Team 2 responds simply, "Even Friedrich, a Jew, was intrigued enough by it to want to attend a meeting!" underlining once again the fierce power of the pageantry, indoctrination, propaganda, and peer pressure.

Kids are mystified when watching this film (*Heil Hitler: Confessions of a Hitler Youth*) to see "racial science" being taught in German classrooms as a subject, just like math and history. They are appalled at the combined efforts of science and politics to eliminate the "foreign" element of the population and to prevent the "defective" element from bearing children. Again, I display posters from the U.S. Holocaust Memorial Museum showing racial science techniques such as measuring skull and nose size with archaic-looking calipers and examining eye color to determine "inferiority." I follow this with a brief clip from the feature film *Europa, Europa* (Social Studies School Service) in which the Jewish boy masquerading as an Aryan fears discovery when these methods are employed by his teacher in his classroom. They are repulsed when they learn that certain non-Aryans were sterilized and the mentally ill and retarded were the objects of "mercy killing."

doesn't say "eugenics" or U.S.

I caution that although Hitler did not invent the racial theories he used in Nazi Germany, he was able to capitalize on them due to the entrenched traditional Christian antisemitism in existence.

I share with my students information disseminated by the Simon Wiesenthal Center in Los Angeles that delineates the difference between the Nazis' racial antisemitism and traditional antisemitism: "The explanation of the Nazis' implacable hatred of the Jews rests on their distorted worldview which saw history as a racial struggle. . . . There is no doubt that other factors contributed toward Nazi hatred of the Jews and their distorted image of the Jewish people. These included the centuries-old tradition of Christian antisemitism which propagated a negative stereotype of the Jew as a Christ-killer, agent of the devil, and practitioner of witchcraft." A description of kosher butchering in "The Jungvolk" presents Jewish dietary practices as evil, sadistic, and "otherworldly." Also significant was the political antisemitism of the latter half of the nineteenth and early part of the twentieth centuries, which singled out the Jew as a threat to the established order of society. The policeman called to the scene in the chapter "The Ball" instructs Friedrich's friend, "You can't trust them; they're sneaky and they cheat." This statement of "fact" is echoed in the words of the song the physical education teacher has the German boys chant when they are out marching and encounter the Jewish class in the chapter "The Encounter." Similarly, during "The Hearing," Herr Resch implores the judge, "This Jew will ruin my business. Every reader of our party newspaper, *Der Stürmer,* knows about the devastating effect of the Jews on our economy." This anti-Jewish ideology is succinctly crystallized for Friedrich in two incidents: when he attends the Jungvolk meeting with his friend and is subjected to the diatribe against the Jews by the Nazi hunchback, "The Jews are our affliction," and in the chapter "The Ball," when the woman whose window is accidentally broken rants, "You pack of Jews, they should get rid of you. First you ruin our business with your department stores, then you rob us on top of it. Just you wait, Hitler will show you yet." These, combined, point to the Jew as a target for persecution and ultimate destruction by the Nazis." (To obtain this material, write and request "The Holocaust, 1933-1945 Educational Resource Kit" from the Simon Wiesenthal Center, 9760 West Pico Blvd., Los Angeles, CA 90035-4792).

I decide to raise the level of the cognitive challenge. "As you read the chapter entitled "The Jungvolk," did you spot any similarities between the trappings of the Hitler Youth and organized religion, especially the belief in one religion?" A garden of hands waves in answer to this one; I pick Fran first.

"Well, the Hitler Youth had a uniform which they wore for all state functions, and in lots of religions you dress a certain way for special events."

"Good, Fran. Can you give some examples?"

"At First Communion the girls wear a white dress and veil and the boys wear a blue suit."

"And for weddings, the bride wears a gown and a veil."

"When we get to the chapter called 'The Festival,'" I add, "you will read that when Friedrich goes to synagogue he dons a *tallis,* a special prayer shawl boys and girls wear for their bar and bat mitzvahs, the ceremony when they publicly proclaim their commitment to their religion. What else, Fran?"

"The music; it seems like all religions have hymns, or chants, or special songs. You know how music gets you pumped up."

"And the idea of the one leader thing," adds Amber.

"And the special ceremonies with candlelight—very emotional and spiritual," acknowledges Megan.

"Excellent observations," I affirm. "He sucked these kids in to the point where they would do anything for the state—for him—and that is how he achieved the support to implement his ideas of Nazi philosophy which led to the Final Solution."

"Isn't it a little odd," questions Dan, "that Friedrich's friend joined the Jungvolk, even though he still chose to remain friends with a Jew?"

"Not really, Dan. In the film we've just seen, Alfons Heck, a Hitler Youth, says, "Far from being forced to enter the ranks of the Jungvolk, I could barely contain my impatience and was, in fact, accepted before I was quite ten. It seemed like an exciting life, free from parental supervision, filled with duties that seemed sheer pleasure."

"But the real question," I maintain, "is why did Friedrich go to the Jungvolk meeting? Come on, guys, help me out here."

"At first I couldn't figure that one out, but I decided he was just curious. He didn't want to be left out of anything; it all looked so neat," Amy postulates.

"He wanted to fit in," Max responds.

"What was its effect on him?" I inquire.

"In the beginning he is excited because he gets to wear the kerchief around his neck and he is a part of things, but then as he listens to all the lies they are preaching about Jews, Friedrich becomes pale, leans forward in his seat tensely, and finds it hard to breathe," Dave replies.

"How did he feel when the hunchback tells him to repeat, 'The Jews are our affliction'?"

"He freezes, and it takes a great effort for him to speak, but he finally does repeat the sentence."

"Do you recognize any indoctrination and brainwashing techniques?" I persist.

"It seems they repeated things a lot, like we did when we were learning our multiplication tables, and everything was very formal."

"Very sharp, Mindy," I affirm. I explain that the elements of Nazi philosophy were drilled into every German from childhood onward. Through special techniques that stirred the emotions, such as the use of symbols, drama and ritual, marching, patriotic music, and uniformity of dress, many *individual* Germans lost their sense of uniqueness and joined the *mass* of the select, "superior" community—the Volk—under the total domination of Hitler.

I ask the kids to recall the scene early in the film *Heil Hitler: Confessions of a Hitler Youth* when the boy at the Nazi rally said, "Hitler looked directly at *me*," and his friend replied, "No, he looked directly at *me*." One of the most seductive qualities of the Nazi campaign, I explain, was to captivate the young *personally*. Hitler had the rare ability to stand before thousands and to tailor his remarks to highly different audiences, to make each individual feel as if he were speaking solely, intimately with him or her; this was undoubtedly his greatest talent. Both of those boys felt as if they were getting a personal invitation from the Fuhrer himself.

Students read the next four chapters in class; these 15 brief pages, which contain some of the most vivid and telling material in the entire book, afford the opportunity for kids to examine the cause-and-effect relationship between the German-Nazi laws we have previously studied and the comfort and safety of Friedrich's family. I model this exercise by selecting and delineating one of the German-Nazi laws from our handouts. For example, *cause:* the 1933 Decrees, which dictated the forcible retirement of all non-Aryan civil servants (with the exception of soldiers) and the refusal to admit Jewish children to German schools and universities. Students are then charged to pinpoint the *effect* of such laws on one person, Friedrich, while remembering our previous discussions of laws aimed at marginalizing minority groups. Each chooses his own law and follows this process in his journal for homework.

We begin the next day's class by sharing the cause-and-effect breakdowns of the German-Nazi laws that the students arrived at for the previous night's assignment. By delineating the effect of these laws, the goal is for my students to become personally engaged in a vicarious exploration of the ramifications of changes in Jewish community life resulting from unjust laws. The following chart (from the *Friedrich Workbook* by Hans Peter Richter) enables us to organize our findings on the board:

Year	Cause (Law)	Effect
1933	All non-Aryan civil servants forced to retire; Fewer Jewish children are admitted to public schools	Friedrich's father loses his job; Friedrich has to leave school.
1935	Nuremberg Laws forbid Jews to hire Aryan servants under the age of 45.	The cleaning lady stops working for Friedrich's family.
1938	Jews must carry identification cards; Jews forbidden to attend movies, plays, concerts, etc.	Friedrich is humiliated after showing his I.D. at the swimming pool; he is run out of a movie.
1941	All Jews must wear a yellow Star of David on clothing.	Friedrich and his father endure public ridicule.

Reprinted by permission of Sundance Publishing

This exercise is perfect preparation for our discussion of the chapter entitled "The Cleaning Lady," in which we are made aware of an intriguing by-product to one of the Nazi laws.

"How would you feel if, in the midst of a depression you were told, like the Schneider's cleaning lady, that you had to relinquish a job of long standing because your employers were members of a group targeted for persecution?"

"Well, I'd get another job, that's all."

"But there were no jobs—it was a depression."

"Oh, well, then I would wait until things got better."

"What if you couldn't wait? What if you had kids to support? Kids can't wait to eat. Would you break the rules or let them starve?"

"I guess I'd have no choice. I'd have to follow the rules or get in trouble."

"And let the kids starve?" I nearly jump out of my seat.

"But how could anyone make that choice? If you broke the law and got taken away, then the kids would be worse off!"

"What we're saying here is that it was either you or the kids."

"Who could make that choice? It's a no-win situation."

I share with them Holocaust scholar Lawrence L. Langer's concept of the "choiceless choice"—the painful reality that the Jews had *no* choice in that either case, a "choice" involves catastrophic loss, that in the eyes of the Nazis they were vermin, not human beings with control of their own lives.

As I lead the kids through an evaluation of the chapter "Reasons," we search for insight into the motives of the two fathers as they attempt to survive this frustrating and unsettling time. Our first goal is to understand why Friedrich's friend's father joined the National Socialist German Workers Party (NSDAP), or Nazi Party, although he was not an outspoken anti-Semite or committed Nazi.

"What was his explanation for joining the Nazi Party?" I ask.

Joey tells us that he was now able to get a job, he had security for his family, and they were even able to take a vacation—which had been unheard of before he joined the party.

"What was Friedrich's father's reaction to this?"

"He was very sad and upset, but quietly," Mike contributes.

"It was almost as if he sort of understood the predicament of his neighbor."

Our investigation of the chapter "Herr Schneider" reveals Friedrich's father as a man debilitated by persecution. Losing his job and being told he must leave his apartment have left him a broken man; nevertheless, he rejects the suggestion of the narrator's father that he accept the "writing on the wall" and get his family and himself out of Germany. I initiate the inquiry, "If you were a Jew who was aware, like Friedrich's father, of the Nazi ideology and realized the danger of the Nazi laws, what do you think you might have done to protect your family?" This question produces an onslaught of response:

Paul says if he were in that situation, he might not be able to go into hiding because of a lack of money for sustenance or bribes, but he might take his family and move to another country if he could.

Desiree discounts his answer by telling him, "That would cost just as much or more as hiding, and what if you couldn't get the necessary papers and documents?"

"The only solution," Amber maintains peremptorily, "is to hide. But where? How would you know whom you could trust, and how would you get food, let alone pay for it? It seems to me that any route you take, the outcome would be death."

"If I were a Jew, I would definitely hide from the Germans and put my family in the attic of my house or an abandoned building," offers Kim.

Domenick states that he would also try to find a hiding place for himself and his family.

Beth rejects these theories caustically: "Did it ever occur to you geniuses that the first place the Gestapo would look would be attics and empty buildings? Besides, you don't think you're going to be able to survive in hiding without help, do you? Who is going to protect you and feed you and connect you to the outside world—the Germans who want to kill you in the first place?"

Fran, with a shot of bravado, retorts, "I would revolt against the Germans because we Jewish people are getting blamed for everything that's going wrong."

This is too much for Beth: "I suppose you plan to do this with the millions of guns and bullets you just happen to have hoarded in your basement?," she blasts back facetiously.

Timidly, thoughtfully, Lisa says, "I might try to convert to another religion to save my life, but that would be wrong because I was born Jewish. Besides, after this whole business is over, what am I going to do—convert back or stay this new religion?"

"My family and I would try to pretend that we are German. We would call others 'dirty Jews' and things like that."

"I'd rather die fighting than give in to the Germans."

I've entertained this discussion because it is essential that the kids understand the rationale which caused so many Jews to make no effort to emigrate or go into hiding when the opportunity existed, or what restricted them from doing so. I attempt to facilitate their understanding by offering an excerpt from the testimony of hidden child Clara Isaacman (1984), wherein she relates an impassioned plea in 1938 from her Uncle Emil to her father; he begs his brother-in-law to get out of Belgium because of his fear that Hitler will take over that country just as he did Romania, from which the family had originally fled in 1932. Clara's father responds by saying, "I feel you are too pessimistic. World opinion will stop Hitler. And we can't run again. Once is enough" (p. 2).

Possibly the most frequent question I am asked during discussions of the Holocaust is, Why didn't the Jews leave when they saw what was happening? I encourage students to empathize by writing a list in their journals of reasons accountable for the reluctance of many Jews to emigrate. They concluded that the traumas of abandoning family, especially older relatives who could not withstand travel; leaving the country of one's birth; lack of financial resources; resistance to "starting over" in a new country; quotas; inability to believe that a civilized country would treat its patriotic citizens in such a manner; and the paucity of information under which the average Jew was operating at the hands of the devious Nazis were the primary reasons for not pursuing an escape from Europe.

I further expand by sharing the opinion of renowned scholar Nora Levin (1990), who, in her book *The Holocaust Years*, attributes this situation in large part to the intense patriotism of the German Jews. She cautions us not to judge with the hindsight of history, and reminds us that, "Virtually all Jews at first believed—as did most observers in the West—that National Socialism was a transitory affair, something that would pass, but must not be aggravated by anti-Nazi actions. Passionately attached and long-rooted to the German Fatherland, most German Jews believed they could hold on and hold out, that they could count on long-time friends and allies to help them in their negotiations and bargaining with the regime. Culturally and economically assimilated to a high degree, German Jews had faced antisemitism during their long history in Germany and prevailed. They, at first, felt they could do the same in the face of Nazi antisemitism. . . . The fact that they were confronting a wholly new kind of antisemitism dawned slowly" (Levin, 1990, p. 20).

While giving her testimony to my students, Auschwitz survivor Leah Kalina also singles out this issue by stressing that to countless German Jews, having been honored by their country for patriotically defending it in World War I was considered a virtual guarantee of protection. They could not conceive of their "Fatherland" abandoning them.

The purpose of bringing up options for escape that the Jews might have had is to illustrate how impotent they were in the face of the ever-tightening restrictions closing in around them. Some Jews escaped the country only to be caught in the Nazi web elsewhere, such as the Franks' experience in Holland.

Friedrich's father, like many German Jews, chose not to leave Germany when he had the chance. I encourage the kids to explore this topic by seeking factual reasons for Friedrich's father's reluctance to leave; hopefully it will shed light on the larger reason.

"He said they were Germans; surely no one would want to hurt patriotic Germans," Dan replies.

Dana adds, "Friedrich's father said anywhere the Jews went they would be persecuted; they always had been, so why would it be better anywhere else?"

"He always believed that if they just stuck it out, things would get better," Joey adds.

"What would you do if similar things were happening in the U.S. today?" I inquire. The answers are fast and furious from a cross section of the class.

"I would leave immediately. I wouldn't wait around until they came to arrest me," Joey declares.

"I'd get out and go somewhere safe," asserts another of his classmates.

"Let's be realistic," I challenge. "Would you want to leave all your relatives and friends? Your school? Your job?"

"What if you were the only one in your family who could get out? Would you have the courage to start a new life somewhere all by yourself?" Dana muses.

"What if they hunted you?" I persist.

"Okay, but how could anybody risk their family's lives by staying?" demands Joey.

"What if you didn't have the money? You don't think you could get out for nothing, do you?" Dana ripostes.

"What if it was impossible to get out? After a while, didn't the Nazis block all emigration by Jews?" Nichelle thoughtfully adds.

"And don't forget," I interject, "that many nations, including the United States, refused Jews admittance based on a quota system that in many cases was a thinly disguised mask for antisemitism."

"Come on, you guys, get real!" As frequently happened, Amber had the last word. "Put yourselves in their places. It's easy to say you'd do this and you'd do that, but do you honestly think that you could believe that the government of a country to which you'd been a loyal citizen was out to torture or kill you just because you belonged to a certain group? It's too hard to imagine, so let's go easy on Herr Schneider."

"Imagine you are told you can't attend a basketball game because you are a Catholic," I begin the following day's discussion of the chapter, "In the Swimming Pool." "How would you feel, especially when you saw your other friends going?"

"I wouldn't be able to understand the unfairness of it," admits Michelle.

"What if someone didn't believe something you say you witnessed just because you are Baptist?"

"It's ridiculous. Why would someone's religion have anything to do with whether or not they were reliable?" Matt answers rhetorically.

We develop a list of the incidents of persecution and prejudice that Friedrich encountered in the swimming pool and on the way home: (1) the person at the counter acted like he was a piece of scum unfit to swim in the pool with Gentiles; (2) he was not considered a believable witness when he tried to give evidence about the stolen bike; and (3) he was also told that soon all of "his kind" would be gone from Germany.

"What feelings do you think he experienced as he was subjected to this denigration?" I ask.

"He felt like an outcast in a society he desperately wanted to be a part of," Lauren offers.

"I can't even begin to imagine how he must have felt always having to be on the lookout and being put down all of the time," Danielle responds sadly.

"He must have been mad as all get-out. Man, I wouldn't want to stand there dripping practically naked in front of everybody and be called a dirty Jew!" Kenny "tactfully" offers.

Nichelle has a different take on it: she feels that instead of being mad, he would be more frustrated and sad knowing that he can't even go swimming without being persecuted.

"Have you ever experienced a situation remotely close to this?" I ask them. "How did you feel and respond?"

I ask my students to write their experiences anonymously on index cards that I collect. Their responses are honest and poignant; when I read them I am deeply gratified that they feel enough safety within the boundaries of our class to share even upsetting pieces of their lives:

"When I couldn't do a forward roll in gym and the P.E. teacher said something about my hips being in the way, I thought I'd die. My face got *hot* and I knew everyone was staring at me. It was so hard not to cry."

Preston, a quiet boy who rarely volunteered, told us of his reticence to venture far from home after his family felt compelled to leave a vacation campground at the Jersey shore because the racist remarks and attitudes of the other campers were humiliating and uncomfortable to his African American family.

I tell them an anecdote of my own from high school. When I was a senior, I was going out with a guy who was Methodist. Even though I was a Catholic, I didn't consider it a big deal because we weren't exactly walking down the aisle. But his mother, I was told, used to say nasty things about Catholics whenever she got the chance. I was very hurt and couldn't figure out why she would be so prejudiced when she was always nice to my face.

I conclude by addressing my 14-year-olds: "Imagine how you all feel right now about your looks." A self-conscious murmur spreads throughout the class. "Come on, be honest. They are so important to you that if your hair isn't just right or your clothes are out of style, your day is ruined. If you don't like your body because it's too tall or too fat, you are miserable. Imagine also that the 'in crowd,' the group you want to be popular with, magnifies your limitations and humiliates you in public for it, while you stand practically *naked* in front of them!"

Understanding fills their adolescent faces. It is eminently clear that not one of our degrading experiences remotely approximates the situation that Friedrich was subjected to.

Students are assigned the reading of the next seven chapters of the novel, which is followed by an evaluation of how Friedrich and the narrator grow and change as the story progresses.

Amanda's opinion is that Friedrich's growth is the more obvious and dramatic of the two: "He starts off trying to hide being Jewish when he goes to the Jungvolk meeting, but he eventually comes to take great pride in his heritage and is willing to fight for survival."

I ask the class if they feel that in the midst of all this awful stuff Friedrich's concern is limited only to himself.

Steve volunteers an example from the chapter "Benches": "Not at all. Look how he protects Helga by not sitting with her on the 'Jewish' bench and by breaking off with her even though he obviously has a major crush on her. He knew she wasn't Jewish and that she would get in trouble if caught sitting on the 'Jewish' bench with him; a girlfriend was quite a thing to give up—probably the only nice thing in his life at the time."

"Good thinking, Steve. How would you feel if you couldn't even sit on a bench with your friend without getting arrested or worse?" I inquire.

Ashley doesn't have to consider long: "I would feel awful, like I was a nonperson, like I didn't deserve to exist. I mean, it's only a bench."

We return to the narrator and his motivations as David offers, "The narrator tries to help Friedrich and is brave, taking risks for him on several occasions."

"What book are you reading?" sneers Dan. "Look how many times he had the opportunity to help and didn't do anything but disappear. What a wimp!" Various class members haggle over David's and Dan's opinions. Jennifer maintains that during the incident in which Friedrich's ball accidentally broke the window, the narrator tries to stand up for his friend but is once again shouted down. Dan wants to know why he didn't go to his dad for help. Danielle is frustrated: "Don't you see? There was nothing that would change that woman's mind. Her hatred of Jews was too strong."

Finally Melissa says, "I'm not sure if we're supposed to be able to decide or judge. Obviously some of us think he was a courageous friend and others think he meant well but lacked the guts to act. I don't really know if the narrator is a specific person or a symbol." I can barely contain my pride in this student's reasoning as I acknowledge that perhaps Friedrich's friend is but an icon representing how the escalating German bigotry and the inaction of bystanders kept the spiral of hate going.

"Maybe that's why we never find out his name," Melissa conjectures.

We move ahead to the chapter entitled "The Pogrom." I explain that a pogrom is an organized destruction of helpless people, and I try to guide the class to see that this chapter can be used as an efficient basis for a discussion of character motivation.

I begin by asking what infamous event is discussed in this chapter. Brian responds, "They call it Kristallnacht, but what does that mean?" At my urging, he determines an answer to his question by using the information boards on that particular subject in my "visual library."

"In German it means the 'night of broken glass.' That was the night in 1938 when Jewish shops and homes were ransacked and destroyed by the Nazis in an act of mass terrorism orchestrated throughout Germany," he explains. "Synagogues were burned and over ninety Jews were killed. When it was over, the streets were filled with glass from smashed windows and storefronts; you can see it in the picture there." While praising his effort, I add that Kristallnacht took place over a 48-hour period, and that it was not spontaneous but rather planned and systematic. I further add that many historians feel that Kristallnacht was a turning point in the Holocaust, because an act of such an overt nature left little doubt about Germany's hate for its Jews.

Now I hit them with the biggie: "Would you agree that Friedrich's friend's actions in this chapter are out of character?"

Before the majority can respond affirmatively, I instruct them to put their thoughts about the narrator's motivation in the form of letters to Friedrich from his friend and vice versa, remembering that the action referred to took place over a two-day period across the territory that the Germans controlled.

Nichole reads from her first letter from Friedrich to his friend, saying, "I never expected you to do destructive things like you did in that Jewish building."

Nichelle writes that he also reprimands, "I always thought you were on my side; I can't believe you destroyed Jewish property and belongings and enjoyed it."

Lincoln's letter has the friend respond sarcastically to Friedrich, "I am a German; what do you expect?"

"No, no, no!" Kenny vigorously disagrees. "He wouldn't have said that. He would have said, 'I accidentally ran into this "mob" of fired-up Germans; all they wanted was to destroy anything Jewish. It wasn't something I was planning to do. At first I just went along because I was curious.'"

Choiceless choice

mob mentality

"Can you see the 'mob mentality' at work?" I interject. "Can people's actions be changed by other people and their surroundings?"

"Obviously," Kenny allows. "'Listen,' the friend tells Friedrich, 'in the beginning I was just curious, but it didn't take long before I got swept up in the wildness of the whole thing. I didn't consider what I was doing or why; all I knew was that I felt powerful—a part of the destruction.'"

"Amber," I refer to her question from our earlier discussion, "the narrator's actions here are not unlike those of the mob ripping off pieces of Leo Frank's clothing as souvenirs; they were caught up in a senseless frenzy."

"Is this why adults are always telling kids not to follow the crowd without thinking first?" Max asks coyly.

I answer by directing attention to the board where I solicit connotative responses as we compose a list of vocabulary the author uses in this scene: excited, exhilarating, enjoying, smashing, drunk with desire, lust for destruction, words that clearly conjure an image of how hard it is to be different and how difficult it would be to reject the actions of the crowd when they are moving forward with such certainty. I ask my kids what these words tell them.

Paul responds to Friedrich in a letter from the narrator that says, "It's like you're caught up in a tidal wave that just takes over your body and you have no control; it almost felt like a drug-induced high."

Dana brings this activity to a close by reading her final letter from the narrator to Friedrich, which says, "It wasn't until I looked in the mirror after joining in the pogrom that I saw myself as a person apart from the crowd. When I saw what I had become, I got scared and ran home." *chap 25-32*

As we complete this attempt to get a definitive handle on the narrator's reasoning, my students are assigned the reading of the final seven chapters of *Friedrich.*

Day 14 [next day]

The following class period, we evaluate the narrator's continuing dilemma by starting with the chapter "The Rabbi," wherein he is confronted with the knowledge that Friedrich and his father are hiding a rabbi who is being hunted by the Nazis. I ask the kids to write a list of decisions or choices that they would be called on to make in one regular day of their lives and then to make a similar list of the decisions Friedrich's friend must make in this chapter. By comparing their lists, we are able to consider the reasonableness or fairness of a boy their age being faced with the choice of informing on close friends, of being put in the position of making the excruciating decision of being a "good German" or possibly endangering his parents and himself for the sake of a stranger. We concur that these are decisions a fair and just world would not ask a 14-year-old to make. In a massive understatement, Friedrich's friend says, "I don't know what to do! I don't know." The kids agree: How does one make this "choiceless choice"?

Compare lists of decisions have to make they're normal vi. choices

In "Stars," the chapter that follows, there is some character movement as the narrator displays an unwillingness to denounce the Schneiders. When he discovers the rabbi sewing yellow cloth Stars of David on every piece of his clothing, he is treated to a history lesson on antisemitism dating back to the Middle Ages. We utilize this conversation as a catalyst for investigation of the trenchant antisemitism that existed in Europe at the time of our story. After providing a series of primary documents chronicling this issue (chronological broadsheets, the front

history antisemitism

page of an issue of *Der Stürmer*, a copy of the Reich Citizenship Law, maps charting antisemitic violence, newspaper articles, and photographs), I direct the kids to devise a "visual timeline" of antisemitism reflective of classical, religious, political, and social "Jew-hatred." For a listing of many primary documents on the Holocaust, request the Social Studies Service resource booklet, *Holocaust Resources and Materials,* (10200 Jefferson Blvd., Room J6, P.O. Box 802, Culver City, CA 90232-0802), and the *United States Holocaust Memorial Museum Teacher's Catalog* (c/o The USHHM, 100 Raoul Wallenberg Place SW, Washington, D.C. 20024-2126).

As they work on this collage of history, the walls of my room gradually become covered with copies of archival exhibits such as propaganda cartoons and posters depicting the German view of the Jews' role in the black plague during the Middle Ages; a copy of the cover of *The Merchant of Venice* by William Shakespeare in which the moneylender, Shylock, is depicted as a sly, greedy, Jew; an illustration from a 15th-century publication that shows Jews slaughtering Christian babies for "blood libel," the use of their blood in the making of matzoh, the unleavened bread eaten at Passover; a copy of a page from the children's book *The Poisonous Mushroom* by Ernst Heimer (1938), a propaganda "picture book" used to teach German students that the Jew was a poisonous fungus that must be eradicated; copies of religious documents assailing the Jews as killers of Christ; a front page from *Der Stürmer,* a radical antisemitic tabloid from 1938 boasting a caricature of a dark, swarthy, hook-nosed Jew sneakily spying on Aryan females; yet another cartoon showing the "wandering Jew" leaving town with bags of the Gentiles' money.

I explain that despite the historical fact that the Romans crucified Jesus, many Christian denominations falsely preached that the Jews were evil and to be despised because they had killed Christ, the Christian savior. Friedrich's friend's innate lack of hatred for Jews is touchingly displayed when he asks the rabbi why it is that they have been singled out for persecution in the past and now in 1941. The rabbi responds, "Because we are different, just because we are different, we are persecuted and killed."

As we approach the conclusion of the book, my students continue their "search" for character development, despite the fact that the primary source of growth continues to be exhibited by Friedrich. In the chapter "A Visit," they observe the rabbi and Friedrich's father being arrested. The narrator's father, who witnesses the delight of Herr Resch, the landlord, when this happens, experiences a gut reaction and calls him a "pig," but he still makes no attempt to intervene when they are taken away.

They watch in the chapter "Vultures" as Friedrich, now alone, stumbles upon Herr Resch looting his family's meager belongings. He snaps and angrily confronts the landlord, all signs of fear gone, like a trapped animal turning to fight. "Do you see any evidence of courage being displayed in this scene?" I inquire. Kenny rejoins, "I agree the landlord was a pig, and that was really cool how Friedrich was brave and finally stood up to him; it was like he didn't even think of the consequences. But once again the narrator wimped out and did nothing, even when Resch pretends he is being attacked by Friedrich. He is definitely a bystander."

The chapter "The Picture" poignantly paints a vivid portrait of Friedrich's life on the run. When he sneaks into the narrator's home, ever-cognizant of his danger to them, he pathetically announces that he won't stay long. The once-confident and well-groomed Friedrich has regressed to a jumpy, dirty, little animal. The narrator's mother feeds him and says they must shelter him, but the narrator's father says they'd be put in jail, so they do nothing. Friedrich displays courage by venturing out to visit them, but the narrator and his family fear the retaliation of the Nazis if they help. While there, he gets caught in an air raid.

"Well, I think it's awful that the so-called friends couldn't overcome their fear to help a child—and someone they obviously care about!" contributes Amber. "Friedrich is afraid, too, of concentration camps, the bombing, yet he still shows courage—when he seeks entry into the air-raid shelter reserved for 'Germans.'"

The kids are numbed by the wrenching scene from "In the Shelter," when Friedrich begs for admission and is refused by Resch, even after a Nazi sergeant and the other occupants plead on his behalf.

The point of view used in a book determines which events and opinions a reader learns about. *Friedrich* is told from the point of view of Friedrich's German friend; hence, the reader learns about the events in Friedrich's life from the friend's perspective. "Would the story be told differently if Friedrich were the narrator or Herr Resch?" I challenge.

To determine this, I assign my students the task of choosing one event from the novel and rewriting it in their journals from a different character's point of view. We decide that Friedrich's father, his mother, either of the narrator's parents, Herr Resch, Herr Neudorf, and Friedrich are suitable choices as narrator.

The next day the students share with me and their peers' many tales from various viewpoints. There are interesting stories narrated by Mrs. Schneider, telling how impotent she felt as a wife and mother powerless to help her demoralized husband and befuddled son; one story told by Friedrich's father details his bitter feelings of guilt as he scourges himself for subjecting his family to the indignities and danger of Hitler's rule by refusing to emigrate when he had the opportunity; and still another, told from Herr Resch's viewpoint, recounts the sadistic delight the landlord took in watching people he had housed for 10 years dehumanized and tortured by the Nazis. Most affecting, however, was the piece written by Dan, a new transfer student to our school. Dan chose to rewrite the final two chapters of the novel *Friedrich*—as told by Friedrich:

> *I slink through the streets, trying desperately to find a safe place. Everything is dark until a shell hits. Then the sky lit up a fiery red and the earth shook. This is what hell must be like, I thought. The smell of burning rubber is in the air, and Germans are running like crazy to their assigned air raid shelters. Will they let me in? Surely someone will let me in! They can't let me die out here! As I crawl along, trying to avoid being hit, I think of mother and father, of the picture from the amusement park, a memento of my parents, the last and only thing I have of them. . . . Another bomb explodes; the sound is deafening. It must be the end of the world. I reach the shelter. I don't even realize I'm on my hands and knees banging on the door and screaming hysterically for help until it opens and I look up. Herr Resch stares down at me with a face full of disgust, and then shrieks for me to leave. I*

get a glimpse of the inside of the shelter. It is damp and people are crowded close together, but they are safe. I think I see my friend and his family in one corner. Dear God, please, let them save me. Several people inside are coming forward, telling Herr Resch to let me stay, that I'm just a boy. But in his eyes I see his hate telling him that I'm a boy who will some-day be a grown-up Jew, and he cannot allow that to happen. I look to my friend's parents, and even though his mother is quite agitated and crying, they don't move. Totally con-sumed by fear, I feel the door slam in my face. The bombs and explosions are all around me. I am alone.

Somehow I make it back to our apartment. My fear is so great that I barely realize that buildings are on fire and there are dead bodies in the street. When I get to the house, I dumbly look at Herr Resch's prized rosebushes now littered with pieces of broken glass and jagged chunks of concrete. I stare at Polycarp who has lost the tip of his cap; Herr Resch will be angry. I am overcome with sadness. Why does the world hate the Jews so much? What has my father ever done but work hard to make a living for his family? Whom have we ever hurt? Why wouldn't my friend's family rescue me? Will we always be outcasts? I don't think I have the will or the energy to go on. I am too tired. If this is what it means to be a Jew, what's the point of running? As I sit on the step, I see a soldier in a brown shirt approach-ing. He is pointing a gun at my head.

People frequently ask me why I teach my students about the Holocaust. "Isn't it too gory for them? Isn't it too depressing for you?" they want to know. I tell them that I teach the Holocaust because I ardently believe that it is important for our young people to cultivate an appreciation for and an understanding of the human behaviors that led to this unique and defining event in history. I teach it because I see it as a perfect case study of a terrible event done by one group of human beings to another simply because of who those victims were—an event with a beginning, a middle, and an end—an event that could have been stopped at any point along the way if the majority of the citizenry witnessing it had mounted a concerted challenge against the perpetrators instead of giving tacit consent. I teach it because I want my students to be aware that this event set the stage for decisions to be made regarding personal involvement, apathy, resistance, and active rebellion; I want my students to use their thought processes to determine that life involves making choices and demands accountability for our actions. Do I want my students to believe that all Germans are evil and all Jews saints? Of course not. But they must be aware that crimes against humanity can be directed and perpetrated by a government, and that individuals have the power and responsibility to make a difference.

When I teach the Holocaust through literature, I do so in the hope that the "face" of a character will reach out from the page and captivate the imagination and interest of a 14-year-old. I do it with the firm belief that the "face" of a singular individual, fiction or nonfiction, can provide a lens through which adolescents may view with clarity the effects of intolerance and prejudice on its participants, whether they be victims, perpetrators, bystanders, or rescuers. I do it so my stu-dents will have no doubt that they, one person, one face, can make a difference in the future of the world. As a teacher of society's children, it is by far the most important thing that I do.

REFERENCES

Books

Bachrach, Susan D. (1994). *Tell Them We Remember: The Story of the Holocaust.* Boston, MA: Little, Brown.

Berenbaum, Michael. (1993). *The World Must Know: The History of the Holocaust as Told in the United States Holocaust Memorial Museum.* Boston, MA: Little, Brown.

Carnes, Jim. (1995). *Us and Them: A History of Intolerance in America.* Montgomery, AL: Teaching Tolerance, a Project of the Southern Poverty Law Center.

Dobroszycki, Lucjan, & Kirshenblatt-Gimblett, Barbara. (1977). *Image before My Eyes: A Photographic History of Jewish Life in Poland Before the Holocaust.* New York: Schocken Books.

Fogelman, Eva. (1994). *Conscience and Courage: Rescuers of Jews during the Holocaust.* New York: Anchor Books.

Fry, Varian. (1992). *Assignment: Rescue.* New York: Scholastic Inc.

Gies, Miep. (1987). *Anne Frank Remembered: The Story of the Woman Who Helped to Hide the Frank Family.* New York: Simon and Schuster.

Gilbert, Martin. (1988). *Atlas of the Holocaust.* New York: Pergamon Press.

Hallie, Philip. (1979). *Lest Innocent Blood Be Shed: The Story of the Village of LeChambon and How Goodness Happened There.* New York: Harper and Row.

Heimer, Ernst. (1938). *Der Giftpilz: Erzahlunger* [The Poisonous Mushroom]. Berlin, Germany: Der Stürmer.

Isaacman, Clara. (1984). *Clara's Story: As Told to Joan Adess Grossman.* Philadelphia, PA: The Jewish Publication Society of America.

Keneally, Thomas. (1982). *Schindler's List.* New York: Simon and Schuster.

Levin, Nora. (1990). *The Holocaust Years: The Nazi Destruction of European Jewry, 1933–1945.* Malabar, FL: Robert Kriefer Publishing.

Richter, Hans, Peter. (1970). *Friedrich.* New York: Holt, Rinehart and Winston.

Rittner, Carol, & Myers, Sondra. (1986). *The Courage to Care.* New York: New York University Press.

Tec, Nechama. (1991). "Helping Behavior and Rescue during the Holocaust." In Peter Hayes (Ed.), *Lessons and Legacies: The Meaning of the Holocaust in a Changing World* (pp. 210–224). Evanston, IL: Northwestern University Press.

United States Holocaust Memorial Museum. (1996). *Lest We Forget: A History of the Holocaust.* CD-Rom for Mac/Windows.

United States Holocaust Memorial Museum. (1996). *The United States Holocaust Memorial Museum's Historical Atlas of the Holocaust.* New York: Macmillan.

Wainwright, Loudon. (1964). "The Dying Girl Who No One Helped." Cited in Harry Furman & Richard Flaim. (Eds.) (1983). *The Holocaust and Genocide: A Search for Conscience*

(p. 78). Vineland, NJ and New York: Vineland Board of Education and the Anti-Defamation League of B'nai B'rith.

Zobrowski, Mark, and Herzog, Elizabeth (1962). *Life Is with People: The Story of the Shtetl.* New York: Schocken Books.

Films

The Camera of My Family: Four Generations in Germany, 1845–1945. 18 minutes. Available from the Anti-Defamation League, Materials Library, 22D Hollywood Ave., Dept. CA 98, Ho-Ho-Kus, NJ 07423.

The Courage to Care. 29 minutes. Available from Social Studies School Service, Holocaust Resources and Materials catalog, 1999. 10200 Jefferson Blvd., Room J6, P.O. Box 802, Culver City, CA 90232.

Europa, Europa. 120 minutes. Available from Social Studies School Services.

Heil Hitler: Confessions of a Hitler Youth. 30 minutes. Available from Social Studies School Service.

Image Before My Eyes. 90 minutes. Available from the Simon Wiesenthal Center, 9760 West Pico Blvd., Yeshiva University of Los Angeles, Los Angeles, CA 90035.

The Shadow of Hate: A History of Intolerance in America. 40 minutes. Available from Teaching Tolerance, 400 Washington Ave., Montgomery, AL 36104.

CHAPTER

5 Virtual Community, Real-Life Connections

A Study of *The Island on Bird Street* via an International Reading Project

KAREN SHAWN

Dear friends, hello! We are students from the Amit School in Karmiel [Israel], and we want to tell you about our seventh grade classes."

It sounds like a simple introduction to a letter from foreign pen pals, something that we teachers might have received when we were seventh graders. But this cheery greeting wasn't through "snail mail"; it was our students' first electronic mail (e-mail) correspondence from students in Israel, not pen pals but "key pals" who had committed themselves to the "International Book-Sharing Project": a literary and technology partnership between American and Israeli students. What follows is a description of the genesis and evolution of the idea, and the experience of seventh graders at the Moriah School of Englewood, a Jewish Day School in New Jersey, and their key pals at the Amit School in Karmiel, Israel.

This computer-based reading project, now in some 36 schools, is a cooperative effort between American and Israeli students to discuss what they have learned about the Holocaust after reading the same literature. Yad Layeled, the Children's Holocaust Museum of Beit Lohamei Haghetaot, the Ghetto Fighters' House Museum and Documentation Center in Israel's Western Galilee, is the sponsoring institution of this unique venture, designed for middle and high school students.

Teachers and students in two cooperating schools, one in the United States and one in Israel, read the same novel about the Holocaust. Then, using e-mail, students discuss the book, its significance, and its echoes in their lives as Americans, as Israelis, and as Jews. As they respond to the text and to one another, their shared inquiry enriches and enhances their oracy and literacy development, sense of self, and appreciation of one another's abilities, perceptions, and cultures. As a culminating project, students create journals that include the best of these dialogues, and add artwork and photographs.

The book selected for our project was Uri Orlev's (1984) *The Island on Bird Street* (Boston: Houghton Mifflin). It is a novel about a young boy's solitary struggle for survival in a destroyed Polish ghetto. Written by Israeli author Uri Orlev, himself a survivor, the story is in many ways autobiographical, told with immediacy and adventurousness from a child's point of view. Alex, the 11-year-old protagonist, creates a relatively secure hiding place on an "island," a lonely, bombed-out street in the unnamed ghetto surrounded by relentless Nazi pursuers, chaos, and murder. Accompanied only by his pet white mouse, Snow, Alex daily confronts questions of life and death, and must make decisions that will keep him alive and also true to his promise to remain in the ghetto until his father, separated from him during a roundup, returns. Alex is inventive, clever, exceedingly resourceful, and yet utterly vulnerable. Gripping and moving, *Island* is the winner of five awards, including the Association of Jewish Libraries Best Book Award and a Book List "Editor's Choice."

We chose this novel for a number of reasons. First, it is based on fact, presenting an authentic and accurate picture of a ghetto experience without traumatizing young readers. Second, it is the personal story of a child in the Holocaust, a boy the age of our students, fostering involvement and identification with a child survivor. Third, because it is well written, featuring a suspenseful plot and dynamic story, vividly described setting, finely drawn, strong characters, and age-appropriate themes of resistance and survival, it engages students and encourages further study of Holocaust history. Fourth, it is classroom-tested and appropriate for students with a wide range of reading abilities. Fifth, it appeals to parents. Finally and pragmatically, it is available in an inexpensive paperback edition in both English and Hebrew.

"We think the project is a good idea, because we like the opportunity to communicate with teenagers from the U.S.A. about a common subject. How did you think of such a project?" the collective e-mail from Karmiel continued.

The question amused me. The genesis of this undertaking began when our students were still in kindergarten! In the early nineties, as a teacher of seventh-grade English in a public middle school in Lawrence, New York, I fell in love with *The Island on Bird Street*. I presented it eagerly, wanting my classes to meet and befriend Alex, the sensitive but feisty main character; to learn about his experiences in the ghetto; and to reflect on the significance of such learning for them, children just three generations away from the event. My students were very receptive to the book, able to empathize with Alex's loneliness, isolation, and fear; appreciative of his need to play games to stave off despair; and eager to respond to his musings about fate, life, and other issues of paramount concern to youngsters approaching adolescence.

The Island on Bird Street could have remained simply a class novel, taught much in the manner of others, with a focus on narrative and literary aspects. That is, I could have assigned chapters to be read at home, and the class would have been filled with discussion about dynamic and static characters and their motivations, plot meanderings and climaxes, themes, and moral dilemmas. But the questions raised by this book took the class in directions that no ordinary novel could. Alex's father and Boruch, the father's best friend, argue about how best to save Alex's life during the next "selection." When the father is grabbed by Nazis, Boruch distracts a guard, and Alex, promising he will wait for his father, "even if it took a whole year" (p. 21), runs to a hideout, a ruined building at 78 Bird Street, and remains there until months later, when his father does, miraculously, return safely to Alex. Students wondered about every aspect of the story. Was it really possible to survive alone in the ghetto under such conditions? What were various ways Jews in the ghetto resisted the Nazis? What makes someone risk his life for another, as both Alex and a kind-hearted Polish doctor do for a wounded partisan? Why were the Nazis so utterly unrelenting in their pursuit of one little boy in the midst of a world war?

We struggled through these and many other questions, feeling a need to read, learn, reflect, and talk still more, realizing that formulating the right questions was the first step to learning about the watershed we call the Holocaust. But with only two weeks allotted to this unit of study, there was not enough time for every student to raise questions, ponder dilemmas, or share and process his or her beliefs with peers and with me. Students wrote essays, but in my traditional, teacher-directed English class, I was the sole reader and evaluator, and could not respond fully to all of their questions, misunderstandings, and misperceptions, which hung over us all year.

For example, in writing about Alex's father, who, before the war, "wouldn't hear of going to Palestine. He felt at home in Poland" (p. 13), Lisa, righteous in the way only a 12-year-old can be, decided, much to my horror, that "it was people like Father who really helped start or even cause the Holocaust because no matter what they were not going to leave their homeland. The Germans started to get jealous of the Jews and angry at them, too. They started to get back at the Jews by setting up propaganda and limiting their privileges, which then unfortunately led to the Holocaust."

There were purely factual errors as well that went uncontested except for my red-pencilled comments on their papers. For example, when asked to explain our response today to the Holocaust, Laura, gentle and earnest, wrote, "We should be sensitive to other nations and religions such as the Japanese who were also persecuted during the Holocaust."

Practitioners of English and Holocaust education suggest that the provision of a caring community of readers is a prerequisite to help students make information personally significant. In such a community, students have a secure environment in which they can explore their responses to even the most troubling texts, such as those about the Holocaust. Louise Rosenblatt (1976), author of the seminal *Literature as Exploration*, pioneered the concept of reader response theory and the notion that it is the transaction between a reader and a text that makes the "poem"--that is, the meaning. Without this interactive participation, the text remains simply "squiggles on the page."

Readers of Holocaust literature need to share their thoughts and impressions as they attempt to make meaning from what they have read. According to reader response theorist W. Iser (1980), all readers do this:

> When we have been particularly impressed by a book, we feel the need to talk about it; . . . we simply want to understand more clearly what it is in which we have been entangled. We have undergone an experience, and now we want to know consciously what we have experienced. (p. 64)

In 1982, Lytle coined the term *think-alouds* to describe "the complex thought processes involved in orally exploring meaning" (cited in Beach, 1990, p. 66). In think-alouds, students explore their responses to a text by "expressing their emotional reactions, sorting out and clarifying their conceptions, or coping with difficulties in understanding meanings" (Beach, 1990, p. 66).

In the very act of responding to literature through conversation, our perceptions about what we are reading begin to change. Nelms (1988) explains that "the minute we begin to articulate our feelings, ideas, and judgments about a piece of literature, it begins to take another shape. We see things we had not seen before" (p. 7). Concerning the role of discussion in learning, McMahon and Raphael (1997) assert that "individuals construct a sense of self as they participate in social contexts" (p. 18).

The next time I taught *The Island on Bird Street,* I used cooperative reading groups of 4 to 6 students to allow for an intimate, daily exchange of ideas, reflecting a transactional approach to learning. In the first week of the now 3-week unit, I presented a brief overview of the Holocaust from 1933 through 1939, and then discussed the ghetto experience in Warsaw from 1940 to 1943. I assigned the second and third weeks for the book to be read and discussed, both in class and at home.

As they read, students kept personal journals, in which they commented on unfolding events, and answered such journal prompts as: "What is the significance of this particular detail, conversation, situation, or event? How does this dialogue, description, or turn of events affect my understanding of what has gone before? How does it help me to predict events? What am I learning about the main character? Am I changing my feelings about him? What am I learning about the world described here? What pleases or troubles me about the story so far?" (See Appendix A.)

I asked students to note, by page and paragraph number, passages which they felt were worthy of discussion, which seemed to them particularly moving, beautiful, surprising, provocative, evocative, puzzling, profound, familiar, reminiscent, painful, ironic, illustrative of an important concept; or which portrayed a person, setting, or situation especially well. Each group was then required to meet with me for three 15-minute discussions of the passages and the journals.

The small-group forum allowed students to share and accept peers' ideas about literature as willingly as they did mine, something they rarely did in class, where they saw me as an evaluator. And it provided the opportunity for students' misperceptions to be aired, challenged, and corrected. For example, as we talked, Roger's anger spilled from his journal: "If I had the weapons, I would have killed every German in sight to retaliate against all the Jews they killed." But others in his group pointed out that that would have been impossible.

"First of all, where would a Jew get weapons?" Jennifer asked him earnestly. Her friend Michelle, speaking, as she wrote, in italics, pointed out, "Even *the whole Polish Army* surrendered to the Germans. Do you think *an unarmed Jewish kid* could fight them?"

"And besides," Rory reminded him, "what about collective punishment?" He skimmed the book to find the page he wanted to show Roger to support his point. "Remember that Alex's father told him that Germans killed lots of Jews if the Jews dared to kill even one German?"

The discussion continued until Roger, listening intently, relented. "Well, I know I couldn't have really done it. But it's what I feel I want to do!"

Students "who explain, explore, argue—whether with parents, teachers, or peers—are more likely to grow as writers and readers than children who do not use language in this way" (p. 122) according to research summarized by Daiute (1993).

As important as these small-group exchanges were, there were problems with finding the time for them; with keeping students on task at their seats when they were not with me; and with finding a suitable conclusion for these "seminars." The children loved the forum and wanted it to continue, but I felt the need to return to the curriculum, especially because many good writing topics had suggested themselves and we had not utilized the writing process for weeks!

The following year, at Moriah Jewish Day School, and in a new position, director of Holocaust Studies, I was eager to revise and expand the project. But now I was responsible for the Holocaust education of the entire school, close to 1,000 students. How would I find time to have ongoing discussion groups with middle school students? I turned to the method of traditional Jewish learning to seek an answer.

"Traditional Jews rarely speak about reading texts at all; rather, one talks about studying or learning. . . . [Jewish learning] is as much about talk as it is reading; in fact, the two activities of reading and discussing are virtually indistinguishable" (Holtz, 1984, pp. 18, 19).

Like much of the best learning in any setting, Jewish learning is social rather than solitary. It is active and interactive, taking place in study sessions, classrooms, community centers, synagogues, and at the dining room table. Thus, reading/learning is both "an act of self-reflection . . . [and] a way of communal identification and communication" (Holtz, 1984, p. 18). Furthermore, students often learn in pairs, each on a journey of discovery, teaching one another, learning through the articulation of a thesis, the defense of a text analysis, the explanation of a difficult passage. I began to wonder: Did every group meeting need an adult facilitator? Since children tend to focus on making meaning through personal connections with peers, with the text, and within the social context of the classroom, did they really need me in each discussion?

"If literacy is a social process," Daiute, Campbell, Griffen, Reddy, and Tivnan

(1993) write, "then social interaction may be an optimum context in which to develop and practice literacy" (p. 45). This is especially true among middle school adolescents, who focus strongly on their peers. Daiute and the others, who have explored the role of talk and activity in children's construction of literacy, believe that "active engagement with peers around written texts can be more important for certain aspects of literacy development than access to an expert" (p. 41). Moriah's seventh-grade English teachers, Jane Wallace and Carol Span, eagerly embraced this concept. If my project were lengthened and redesigned to engage students around written texts, we reasoned, we would solve the major problems previously encountered. More specifically, we would not rely formally on teachers as discussion leaders, so all groups could be engaged at the same time; and all readers would take part in the writing process as well as in oral communication. Their collective writings would constitute a final product, allowing a logical, satisfying conclusion.

Now, in addition to individuals' personal journals, each group of four students was given a blank 8½" × 11" hardcover book to design. We asked for an illustrated cover, title, and dedication pages; an introduction; 8 to 10 passages from the novel chosen by group consensus as worthy of shared deliberation; and personal responses by each group member to the passages and to one another's commentary. The content and form of each journal would vary, reflecting each group's particular vision and skills. But each would be an ongoing, written conversation among students reflecting their reactions and responses to one another's ideas.

Carol and Jane agreed to meet with each of their classes as a whole at the beginning of each period to review the reading done at home and help with any problems. Two days a week the students would continue to read silently in class while the teacher examined the journals, and three days a week the students would sit with their groups to discuss their journal entries and plan their design, with the teacher sitting with each group for five minutes or so during the period. Suggested completion time for the unit, including learning about the ghetto, reading the book, and making the journal, was four weeks of class and homework.

For the next two years our students proudly produced illustrated literary journals we all thought were remarkable for their thoughtful responses to issues confronted by those in the ghetto.

Many students, for example, focused on the setting of the ghetto, where Jews were imprisoned and hunted while, literally on the next street, non-Jewish Polish children lived relatively normal, albeit wartime, lives. One group responded to the following passage:

> The entire length of the street behind the house [78 Bird Street] was divided by a high brick wall that was topped by broken glass. Beyond it you could see the houses on the Polish side. They were so close you could almost reach out and touch them, but they belonged to a different world. It was a world that we too had once lived in without really appreciating it. (p. 27)

Mark, not interested in history until this unit, wrote, "The people living around him, the non-Jewish Poles, were as if they were living in a different world. . . . They didn't seem to care what happened to the Jews—their neighbors."

Andrea, who often spoke of her desire to be a psychologist, thought it was "very strange how people just ignored the fact that down the street Jews were being starved and killed. Maybe that's not true, though. They might have tried to hide their fear and anxiety by ignoring this issue. I still can't understand how one wall could separate two worlds and isolate Jews in one of them."

Mark agreed with Andrea, asking, "How could people not worry and not care about starving people just down the street? Do they hate Jews so much that they can't care and help the starving and suffering Jews? This is the terrible environment Jews lived in then."

Steven, an avid viewer of World War II news reels, wrote, "Even in the death camps, prisoners were only a mile away from civilization. The villagers knew very well what was going on and didn't seem to care."

The unit was successful, but by the third year we were ready for a new challenge. When our school upgraded our computer labs to include Internet access, and, simultaneously, forged a connection to Yad Layeled, the new children's museum built by the Ghetto Fighters' House, this project became the basis for the current International Book-Sharing Project.

We all had questions regarding modifications necessary to make this interclass project successful as a distance-learning adventure, a two-class, multiteacher, bicultural, binational project produced via e-mail.

The staff of Yad Layeled, including Monia Avrahami, Dr. Moshe Shner, Aliza Badmor, Beth Seldin-Dotan, Raya Kalisman, Varda Shiff, Tali Shner, and American representative Debbie Nahshon, number among them scholars, historians, classroom and museum educators, editors, and administrators. All are fluent in English, so we did not anticipate difficulty in formulating either the goals or a suitable program. But problems arose in other areas.

The Yad Layeled staff, for example, had long been devoted to the work of Uri Orlev and had been developing their own plans for sharing his books with Americans via e-mail. The exhibit in the main hall of their Holocaust museum is based on Orlev's autobiography, *The Sandgame,* so that book was their first choice for the shared text. We liked *The Sandgame,* which interweaves memories of Orlev's childhood with his reality as an adult forced to confront his painful losses, including his unresolved feelings of anger toward his father, from whom he was estranged for 15 years after the war. But we felt that, at 59 pages, the book was too short for this project. Furthermore, Jane and Carol taught the novel, not autobiography, as a genre in seventh grade, and thus considered *The Island on Bird Street* more appropriate.

There were other differences as well. The Israelis wanted to focus on Holocaust history; we, on literature. They wanted to begin with a few students; we wanted to involve all 90 of ours. Many of their students did not have advanced English skills; ours lacked advanced Hebrew. They wanted the book taught as a class novel; we felt students should read independently and keep daily journals. They wanted to begin in the fall; we, in the spring. They wanted a flexible timeline; we were locked into a computer lab schedule. Even our software wasn't compatible: they had IBMs with Microsoft Word; we had Macintoshes with Clarisworks. We met, e-mailed, faxed, and phoned each other with suggestions and countersuggestions. We wrote and rewrote discussion questions and teachers' guides. We wondered if this idea would ever come to fruition.

Moriah's seventh graders, meanwhile, were paired with those in an Israeli school, but nothing went as planned. Our technology was still in its infancy; neither staff established frequent communication; there were misunderstandings involving differing time and curricular constraints. Our students ended up producing an illustrated, computer-generated journal, but had held no substantive discussions with the Israelis. The final product did not reflect our shared vision.

After more than a year of goodwill, optimism, and compromise, the Yad Layeled staff and I produced a document to guide the project to its conclusion.

Together we identified the core elements of the project, and agreed to keep *The Island on Bird Street* and add *The Sandgame* (see Appendix B). The books would be read in the children's first language. E-mail discussion, when possible, would be in English, but if necessary, Israelis would send responses in Hebrew and our Hebrew teacher, Rachel Rubenshtein, would help our students with translations.

We set joint goals. For example, we wanted students to read and listen critically and empathetically; develop an understanding of the capacity for good and evil; and develop respect for, and confidence in, their intellectual and emotional responses to literature. We wanted teachers to promote the importance of being sensitive to the pain of others and recognizing the consequences of indifference; create awareness of the existence and extent of Jewish resistance during the *Shoah* (the Hebrew word often used in place of the term "Holocaust"); and help students realize that study of the Shoah leads to exploration and clarification of personal, communal, and national values.

We added an "About the Authors" section, requested photographs of the students, and included a variety of project options and enrichment activities, including the viewing of the 1997 feature film *The Island on Bird Street* (106 minutes), writing to the author, incorporating artwork, and using the Ghetto Fighters House archives for relevant research. To obtain information about the purchase or rental of *The Island on Bird Street,* contact: Ms. Debbie Nahshon, Director, The American Friends of the Ghetto Fighters' House (181 The Plaza, Teaneck, New Jersey 07666).

We stressed the importance of meetings for all administrators and staff involved, and of establishing regular e-mail contact throughout the project as well as a mutually acceptable timeline. We even included a sample of a typical day's work (see Appendix C to this chapter).

How did this activity of independent reading, cooperative learning, and technology work in the classroom? First, the limitations of second language skills and the subsequent need for far more translations than we had anticipated caused delays that prevented many of the students from responding directly to one another in a timely manner. We now recommend that participants must be fluent in the language of discussion, that only one book be used for the joint journal, and that only six to eight passages be chosen to discuss jointly.

Second, although our student numbers matched the Israeli school's numbers, only 20 or so of their students actually responded to our students. For us, it was a class requirement; for them, because of unexpected, long-term problems with technology, it became an optional, after-school, once-a-week activity, so their responses were limited and late, adding weeks to our time frame. As progress with technology continues, this difficulty, too, will be resolved.

Despite these limitations, the concept enabled readers to share their insights with an interested, like-minded "virtual" cohort group. They articulated and exchanged ideas about the personal connection they had made to Alex and his life in the ghetto, and about the varied lessons they had drawn from the event. Students' initial journal offerings, honest and forthright, encouraged, in turn, authentic and thoughtful responses that included opinions, fears, speculations, analyses, hypotheses, inferences, reminiscences, predictions, and satisfactions. At Moriah, responses were discussed within the small group, typed, and then sent to group mates as well as key pals in Karmiel. Group mates responded promptly and eagerly, so even when key pal responses were delayed a week or more, Moriah students were engaged in discussion with each other. Because students wrote about what was meaningful to them, they never asked what to say or how long a response should be. Because they had a real-world audience, whether a student sitting at the next computer terminal or in an Israeli classroom, their writing was fluent, organized, and specific.

For example, in response to the journal prompt "What did you learn about yourself from reading this book?" Boaz, a small, dark, bespectacled Moriah student, wrote, "I'm sad to say I guess I learned that deep down I really believe that Hitler won because he and the Nazis killed six million Jews and damaged the lives of all of the survivors. My grandparents have nightmares every night, even now."

His classmate Ruthie, whose brown eyes flash with indignation at any suggestion of injustice, responded, "I couldn't disagree with you more, Boaz. I've learned that I think we've won. We have Israel, and the Jews are still a people. And you and I are here, living Jewish lives!"

Alexandra, also a grandchild of survivors and always the peacemaker, addressed them both. "I've learned that you can't really talk about the Holocaust in terms of winning and losing. We lost people and communities and a whole culture, but the Germans lost the war and the respect of the entire world. Hitler didn't accomplish what he wanted, murdering every Jew. But he killed one and a half million children, so he 'accomplished' too much. Boaz, my grandparents still have nightmares, too, but at least they lived to see their grandchildren have very happy lives, in America and in Israel. It's not all one way or the other. So we can't use easy words like 'won' and 'lost'."

Themes of *The Island on Bird Street* reflect endemic adolescent concerns, such as fairness, equality, racism, identity, fear, loneliness, isolation, and especially loss (of control, supports, family, and childhood). Passages illustrating those concerns were consistently chosen by the groups at Moriah as worthy of discussion.

The issue of fairness and the loss of childhood, for instance, are reflected in the following paragraph, which describes the dilemma Jews faced because of the German policy of collective punishment, a concept that outraged Moriah students:

Father once said to me that you didn't have to fight fair against the Germans because they were the first to break the rules. Only father couldn't use his gun . . . because if anything ever happened to one single German in the factory or on the street, the Germans would kill lots of men, women, and children to make sure it didn't happen again. A retaliatory action, it was called. And so no one dared to do anything. How could you be responsible for so many lives just because you felt like killing a German? (p. 6)

Jessica, one of the youngest of Moriah's seventh graders, responded to the journal prompt that asked, "What was the most important fact about the Holocaust that you learned from this book?" She wrote, "I don't know if the idea of collective punishment was really the most important fact, but it was a fact I didn't know before. I felt really upset and angry at the Germans. They can walk into a street and kill a handful of Jews without thinking twice, and no one could do anything back to a German. I just don't understand how human beings can be so cruel to their fellow men!"

Yonatan, monosyllabic in class, wrote, "I agree with you, Jessica, but I also believe this idea of retaliatory action shows just how much thought went on in the mind of those who planned to kill the Jews!"

Lara, the niece of a well-known Holocaust historian, was the first to initiate the discussion of "choiceless choices." She noted that Alex's father has taught him how to use the gun he has smuggled into the ghetto despite the policy of collective punishment. She "was surprised that Father agreed to teach his son how to use his pistol, especially at such a young age. But," she wrote, "whatever decision he made might be the wrong decision. If Alex had no gun, he could be murdered. With a gun, he could be murdered. Really, the Holocaust gave the Jews no choices at all."

She also addressed the importance of refraining from using hindsight to judge the actions of Jews in the Shoah. "War can change your priorities," she explained. "How can we sit safe and sound in Englewood today and judge a father's decision to help his son protect himself during the Holocaust?"

Shani, a shy poet, wondered "if Alex knew what he was feeling at that moment. He probably felt scared and excited, but he probably also feels grown up and big because his father is treating him like a man."

Estee's comment seems to reflect a longing for order and rules in the chaotic world of the ghetto. Estee, a grandchild of four survivors, wrote, "Knowing how to shoot was important for Alex. I just think Father should have told him when it was necessary to shoot and when not to shoot."

Alex gets these rules much later, after he has killed a Nazi who was about to kill a partisan. A Polish doctor to whom Alex turns for help gives him the advice Estee requested:

People shouldn't kill each other, son. . . . People should help each other to live. . . . But if you're saving the life of a friend or someone in your family, or defending your country, or just trying to keep yourself alive, there's nothing to be ashamed of. It's no disgrace to kill a murderer like the soldier you told me about. On the contrary, I think you were very brave. (p. 116)

Moshe, a solemn boy bereft since the recent death of his mother, felt it was "very kind of the doctor to comfort Alex."

"I agree," wrote Uri, the star of Moriah's basketball team. "This little speech by the doctor gave Alex the necessary confidence to try to survive. Everyone should have a little speech in their life to help them reach an important goal."

Ariella's written response, like many of her opinions during class discussions, was measured. "It is okay to kill for self-defense, but only if it's your last resort and for a very good reason. This is clearly another example of a 'choiceless choice' forced on the Jews by the Holocaust. You should not be happy when you kill someone, and Alex was not. I do not judge Alex, but I feel very sad knowing that a boy so young has to learn to kill. The Holocaust made children into little adults."

Nazi collaborators, "rats," as Alex called them, provoked heated discussion among the Moriah students, many of whom responded to the following passages describing a round-up of Jews in the ghetto:

> Everyone began running around . . . Nobody knew what to do. Should we try to escape? . . . There was a secret passage that led to the roof, and from there, up the street through empty apartments and lofts. Before we could make up our minds . . . shots rang out. Someone had ratted and given the passage away. (pp. 15–16)

> Someone must have ratted. Maybe someone who thought it would save him. Rats were even worse than Germans. You knew the Germans couldn't be trusted. They didn't try to hide that they were murderers. They even wore skull patches on their uniforms. But a rat smiled and talked to you like a friend and then went and squealed behind your back. He thought he'd gain time for himself. (pp. 17–18)

Jay, quiet but eloquent, wrote, "Although the Germans murdered six million Jews, the rats played a very big part in the murders. With the Germans you would just be killed, but if you had a rat as a friend, you would be betrayed and then killed."

Abby, the daughter of a psychologist and granddaughter of survivors, wrote, "I'm not excusing them. But they did this because they were panicking and that was the only thing to do."

Ephie, who usually ignored girls, supported Abby's statement. "The war changed people. It made them mean and stubborn. They were angry and needy. The war even changed good friends to mean and untrustworthy ones."

"I agree with you, Ephie, even though I usually don't," Tova, a twin, commented. "The war changed everyone from good to bad. It was a sad time, but people tried to stay alive."

Anna, a lawyer's daughter, responded, "But, Tova, don't you think it's horrible that people would go to such horrible measures just to save themselves?"

Eliyahu, who always found his voice when he wrote, addressed three group mates when he responded. "Tova, Ephie, and Abby, you sound like you're defending them. The rats were worse than the Germans. They were willing to help the Germans kill Jews just to prolong *their* lives."

Allison saw more than one side of every argument; her response reflected this ability. "In the *Torah*," she wrote, "it says that when you don't stop a person from doing a sin, then it is as if you are doing it, too. Not only are the rats not stopping the Germans, they are helping them kill the Jews. So in a way it is true that the rats are worse than the Germans. On the other hand, they wouldn't be rats if the Germans hadn't made the situation so bad for everyone in the first place."

At least half of our students are grandchildren of survivors, and virtually every child in the seventh grade has visited or will soon visit Israel; many, upon high school graduation, will live in Israel for a year before college. We were all interested to see what, if any, differences in perspective the Israelis and American students would reveal, and eagerly read the first overseas responses. The importance of one's heritage and the issue of racism were important to students in both schools, but each responded to different passages. Moriah students chose the following:

> "[Boruch] told me that there were grey mice in the storeroom that would kill my mouse. . . ."
> "But why will they kill him?"
> "Because he's white."
> "Maybe they'll make friends with him."
> "Then you'll never see him again." (pp. 8–9)

Yonatan, whose knowledge was more freely expressed in his writing than it had been all year in class, wrote, "This paragraph shows great symbolism about racism geared for someone of Alex's age. The last two sentences illustrate the intermarriage and integration of Jews in Germany, where the Reform Movement started in the late 1800s."

Moshe, who seemed to use this project to distract him momentarily from his sadness, answered, "I'm not sure if you're right about the last two lines. Here we have an 11-year-old boy who can't comprehend racism. He is trying to understand why a gray mouse would want to kill a fellow mouse simply because it is white. This is symbolizing Alex's feelings of racism among people. He can't understand why one human would want to kill another simply because of his race, color, or religion."

"I think you're both right," concluded Dan, who is tall, dark, and scholarly. "Alex, in this paragraph, is asking a simple question which millions of people ask each day: 'Why? Why is there racism?' And then he tries to solve the problem of racism by suggesting that in order to end racism, the race that is being discriminated against should make friends and assimilate with the 'dominant' race. But that is not a good solution because then the entire race will be lost."

The Israeli students offered this passage to discuss:

> Father liked to say that we all were human beings. It didn't matter what color your skin was, how long your nose was, or by what name you called God . . . But mother would sigh and say, 'If only you were right . . . It may make no difference whether you were born a Chinese or an African or an Indian, but once you've been born, you can't deny your roots. When you dig up a tree's roots, it dies . . . People don't die when they deny their past, but they can't be themselves. They grow up sad and twisted, and so do their children. (pp. 13–14)

In her e-mail from Karmiel, Danielle mused, "That's why I don't understand why the Germans are angry at us for our roots."

"During the Holocaust the Germans hated us because we were Jewish, Danielle. They didn't have any reason!" Adena, at Moriah after living in Israel for several years, tried to explain.

"It's just like the black slaves, how they were treated cruelly just because they were black," Yaakov, the son of an Israeli teacher at Moriah, added. "Now, still, some people think they are better than people with different color skin or a different religion. But God didn't put us in this world to fight over who has the better color."

Ronit e-mailed from Karmiel, "This also shows that the Jews couldn't hide by converting. Once trouble started they couldn't turn their backs on their past and pretend to be something they weren't. Once they were Jewish, they were always Jewish."

"But Ronit," Adena reminded her by return e-mail, "some Jews, like Stashya in the book, had to deny their past and pretend they were somebody else, but after the Holocaust, it was sometimes hard to go back to what they were before. They ended up never knowing exactly who they are."

"This passage shows the importance of recognizing your past," Rachel, another Karmiel student, e-mailed. "It doesn't matter who you are but where you came from. You should learn about your heritage and teach it to your children so no one will forget where they came from."

The Moriah students also commented on the reality of racism in America. Jessica, articulate and self-confident, summed it up by saying, "Something that humanity has to realize is that everyone is equal no matter what they look like. The day we can all say 'I don't care what he or she looks like or what his or her religion is,' then that will be a true accomplishment."

As the teachers read the responses, we debated at length the necessity of taking the time to guide students toward a deeper understanding of the complex history of the Holocaust. But the seventh-grade American history curriculum in our school didn't allow for such a diversion, and to add it to the English curriculum would mean eliminating other required literature and writing. Furthermore, we concluded, a goal of this project was not to teach a definitive Holocaust unit, but was instead to help students feel comfortable making their own sense of what they had learned from the novel and from our brief introductory unit on the ghetto. The Holocaust is a subject for lifelong learning, and we knew from their interest in the subject that our students would continue their search for answers. The discussions continued, therefore, without further formal teaching about the Holocaust.

Whether from Karmiel or Englewood, students were sympathetic to Alex's fears, and empathized with his feelings, which they believed would mirror their own. In response to Alex's admission, "My greatest fear had always been that father would be caught somewhere and I would be left alone" (p. 16), Dahlia e-mailed from Karmiel, "I started to tear!"

Tamar, also from Israel, wrote, "I would also be worried that I would be left behind alone."

Moriah's Victoria, always composed and self-contained, told her key pals, "I think what I learned about myself is that if I were in his situation, I don't think I would survive, mentally or physically."

Other passages most commonly shared were those that evoked key questions for students of the Holocaust, such as the seminal "Why the Jews?" "How was the Holocaust possible?" "If there had been a State of Israel, would the Holocaust have happened?" Students from both cultures frequently focused on passages that dealt with life in the Jewish Diaspora, sharing similar concerns and conclusions:

> I took Mother's side when it came to Zionism. Father didn't agree with her there. Before the war he wouldn't hear of going to Palestine. He felt at home in Poland. Mother didn't. . . . [She] wanted to go to Palestine [because] Polish society denied her roots. (pp. 13–14)

Responding to this passage, Jessica noted that "some people were very comfortable and happy where they were, and then the Holocaust came. This is very scary because the Holocaust could happen again . . . to us."

"I agree with Jessica," affirmed Anna. "Most people never thought anything bad would happen to them, maybe to others, but never to them. I think the Holocaust could happen again, moreover, in America, 'the land of the free.' This thought is blood-chilling."

Hadar e-mailed promptly from Karmiel. "This was a very touchy issue among Jews in Germany as well. Many Jews' lives ended because they didn't want to leave what they thought was their homeland, Germany. If only they had gotten out and come to their REAL home in Israel! But, of course, how could they have known there would be such a thing as Holocaust? They can never be blamed for not being able to see into the future!"

"But we know now," Moshe answered. "This should be a lesson for all Jews who are 'visiting' in another country. They shouldn't get too comfortable. They shouldn't forget that Israel is their true homeland."

Moshe was born and raised in Englewood, New Jersey, but his response was indistinguishable from Hadar's, born and raised in Israel. His perspective and so many others like his answered our earlier question: There would be no discernable political differences between our students, Zionists all, and the Israelis.

Many students in both countries chose this passage as well:

> [Henryk, the partisan,] talked about the Jews, whose whole problem was that they had no country of their own. . . . He . . . talked on and on . . . as though he could actually see the Jewish state that we would have one day, with a flag and a President of its own. . . . It was strange to think of a whole city being Jewish. You'd walk down a street, for instance, and everyone would be a Jew. . . . No one would have to be afraid to go outside because he had a Jewish face and big, sad Jewish eyes. No one would make fun of him or pick on him. No one would laugh and say he had a Jewish nose. (p. 118)

Rachel, the soft-spoken daughter of a rabbi, believed this passage showed "how much Alex wants a place where he can be a real Jew, and how much he wants Jewish unity and acceptance. . . . It also shows how war has taken a toll on him. He feels strange when someone mentions a place that is totally Jewish because it has been a very long time since he has seen a Jew practicing his religion out in the open, without fear."

Danielle, who sent a photo of her three dogs along with her e-mail, reminded her group, "Today we don't see what a blessing it is to have a state where we can just walk down the street and be treated nicely even though we are Jewish."

Amy, with the poise of a high school senior, responded, "There is an old saying, 'What you don't have you don't miss.' That's not true! Although there were almost no Jews left in the ghetto, Alex desired to be with his people, where he could be himself, and where it is a privilege, not a danger, to be a Jew."

"Alex would have loved to see how it is in Israel today!" wrote Adena, her longing to be back in that country evident. "In Israel, Jews live all over, in every neighborhood. Nobody has to worry that they might get killed or taken away if they play outside. There is terrorism, but that is because Arabs and Israelis haven't found a peaceful solution yet. Where Alex was, you couldn't even walk out your door without fear if you were born a Jew."

"This teaches us that in the Holocaust every Jew dreamed for the time when they would be free, a time when a Jew could walk down the street and be proud of who he or she is. Here in Israel today, this is our feeling," e-mailed Hadar.

"If there had been a Jewish state, as Henryk said, there wouldn't have been a Holocaust," Josh, a Moriah student, summed up, perhaps simplistically, but illustrative of his particular understanding of the critical importance of Israel.

Students learning about the ghetto are always shocked by the proximity of the Polish and Jewish sections. Two passages detailing Alex's isolation within touching distance of the Polish world were discussed at length:

> I felt as though I were living on a desert island. Instead of an ocean all around me, there were people and buildings, but though they seemed close, they were really a world away. (p. 87)

> Sometimes I didn't feel like reading or playing . . . or even looking at the Polish side of the wall. All of a sudden I'd start thinking about father and mother. I never cried, but I'd lie in the larder thinking about all the terrible things that could happen, and about how lucky the Polish kids were for having homes and being able to play where they wanted. (p. 95)

Dani e-mailed his feelings that because "Alex has so much time on his hands, [he] starts thinking bad thoughts."

Elana e-mailed that these passages "show how hard it was for Alex to keep thinking positively" and show "how tough Alex had to be."

"Since these are very human thoughts," wrote Sara, yet another Moriah grandchild of four survivors, "they make Alex very human. Sitting in the larder and watching the Polish side must have been almost like watching television. The 'characters' were so far out of reach that they were almost fictional. Instead of a glass screen, there is a brick wall keeping him from communicating with them."

"Sara, I disagree," Rachel responded. "I think these paragraphs show that Alex thought he was lucky to be waiting for his father. After all, some children saw their parents killed in front of their eyes during the deportations!"

Some students concluded that no one can be trusted in times of danger, while others reached just the opposite conclusion, illustrating that there are no lessons to be pulled, fully formed, from history. Only one's current context and personal meanings can shape the lessons one may choose to draw from the Holocaust, if, in fact, there are any lessons. This is evident as students discussed the differing, and often contradictory, advice Alex remembered getting from his parents:

> I remembered Mother's advice: "Trust people and appeal to the good in their hearts, and they'll never do you any harm." And yet Father had said, "Trust only yourself." (p. 69)

Lisa, an avid journal writer, used many of the journal prompts to enrich her writing. In response to the question, "What passages most clearly challenged your ideas, beliefs, or attitudes about the Shoah?" Lisa wrote, "This passage is powerful because of the way father and mother disagree. . . . Father is always a pessimist, and Mother is always trying to bring up someone's confidence. It challenged my belief about survival. I always believed that the mother's advice was the way I would have gotten through the Holocaust, that somehow if I could just make friends with a Nazi, I could make him see that I was okay even though I am Jewish. But after reading this book, I see I was wrong, and the father is right. I know that if the Nazis wouldn't let a good, innocent boy like Alex live, I couldn't trust them to let any of us live, no matter how much I appealed to them."

Kivi, halting in his speech, was a fluent and gracious writer. He responded, "I do not think the father is a pessimist, [but] more of a realist. He knows that in this terrible time, you cannot trust anybody too much. Mother, I feel, is a bit too much of an optimist for this time of war."

"I agree with Kivi," wrote Aaron, level-headed and pragmatic. "However, his mother was also correct because you cannot go on forever without trusting anyone. The friendship Alex creates with people now may pay off in the future."

Yaron, responding to Aaron from Israel, noted that "in the Holocaust there were a lot of cases where a Jew was saved by a non-Jew because at an earlier time, the Jew had related to the non-Jew with trust and human kindness. Being kind and trusting to someone can be the difference between life and death."

Yaron's friend David e-mailed a terse "Father is right. His are words of power."

Orlev's book helps readers understand that during the Holocaust Jews hid in different ways. Alex's hiding was physical, while Stashya hid her Jewish identity, assuming the posture of a Polish girl and living just across from Alex on the Polish side of the ghetto wall. Desperate for companionship, Alex confides in Stashya. While most students appreciated their friendship, some thought it was too sentimentalized, and talked about Alex's feelings the day Stashya and her mother leave Warsaw to move to a safer place in the country. Such responses seemed to indicate that adolescent concerns transcend superficial cultural differences.

In the morning I watched the wagon come to take her and her mother with all their things. She knew that I was looking. When they started out, she waved to me. And then her mother waved too. That really bowled me over. Could they have been waving to someone else? No, they were looking straight at me. (p. 154)

Shiran, Yona, Elinore, and Tamar, best friends from Karmiel, e-mailed their responses as one. Shiran was touched "the moment when they separated."

Yona liked this part "because it is sad. Stashya and Alex shared a lot of experiences together. Stashya was the only thing that made Alex happy, so I was upset that, when she left, Alex may not be happy any more."

But Elinore was unsentimental. "I thought this passage was too dramatic. Alex and Stashya could have gone to Israel at the end of the war and reunited. If they really loved each other, they wouldn't have cried because they would have known that they would reunite in Israel."

Her partner Tamar agreed. "They're making it into too much of a big deal. If they were really meant for each other they would have planned to meet later on."

"Well, I agree with Yona," insisted Moriah's Alexandra. "When Stashya left, I felt Alex's pain. He was all alone and she was the only person that brought him happiness during this lonely and horrible time."

"I disagree with you, Elinore," Lisa, polite but never afraid to be direct, wrote from Moriah. "They couldn't make a plan to reunite because they couldn't be sure if they would both survive!"

Ultimately, the Holocaust did not offer any Jewish family, including Orlev's, a "happy ending." Yet Orlev's novel reunites Alex with his father. The powerful climax is analyzed in every journal.

> "Alex."
> He didn't shout it. He said it in a very strange voice. Maybe that's how a person talks to a ghost.
> "Father." (p. 160)
> "I had cried and hugged father as hard as I could. He had cried too. And I didn't know if I was crying for myself, because I was so happy and had waited so long for him to come without admitting that I never thought he would, or if I was only crying because he was. Crying can be catching. Just like laughter." (p. 162)

"At first the paragraph [p. 160] didn't have much impact on me," wrote Yoni. "But as I analyzed it, the word 'ghost' stood out. . . . that Alex was the ghost, because Alex's father had thought he was dead."

Moshe added, "Alex had been alone for such a long time and had seen so few people that in a way he had begun to doubt his own existence and thought of himself as a ghost."

"So what you're saying," Dan responded, "is that the word 'ghost' plays a dual role in this paragraph. On one hand it shows how his father pictured Alex—dead, because he had not seen him for such a long time and because conditions in the ghetto were horrible. On the other hand, Alex pictures himself as a ghost because he had been stranded on an 'island,' isolated from civilization for many months."

"Exactly!" added Lisa. "When Alex finally saw his father, he realized that he knew all along that he might never see him again but he hadn't allowed himself to admit it until he saw him. It was as though he was staring at a ghost. His father probably felt exactly the same way."

The Israelis were more interested in the "happy ending" debate. Hadar believed "the best way to end this book [is] with a good happy ending!" Na'ama e-mailed, "Really, after all the hard times Alex went through, he deserves to be happy." And Yoni, translating a difficult word, called it happy and exuberating. But Moriah's Sara took issue with their wording.

"I disagree with what Hadar and Yoni said about a happy ending. I think the ending was powerful and meaningful, but it wasn't a happy, jubilant ending. Maybe a better word would be 'nice.'"

David, considered the group's wordsmith, added, "Maybe 'relief' is even better than 'nice.'"

Ben had done much of this project from home, wheelchair-bound for months as a result of an accident on the basketball court. He wrote that he was relieved that the father returned, and wondered "how much longer he [Alex] could have gone without one of his parents. Although Alex has matured since the beginning of the book, he's only 11 and still needs a parent."

And Sara responded, "That's another reason the ending is not jubilant. He doesn't have his mother."

Elisheva e-mailed from Israel, "This is very emotional, exciting, but expected. What I don't like is that the book prepares the story so it's clear the father will live."

Talia, who spent most of her time illustrating the journal, dashed off a response to Elisheva: "It is expected that the father will live. Even so, it is nice to have a happy ending. Alex deserved to get his father back, because he was brave, strong . . . and helped people throughout the book."

Also Israeli, Yedida found the passage "very emotional," and asked, "So what if the ending is expected—people won't like it? It's better if the ending is good!"

Ariella responded: "Personally, I thought Alex's father would not return. I nearly gave up hope as Alex did."

Hilla agreed with her key pal Ariella, e-mailing from Karmiel: "It actually was a surprise to me too that he met his father. This paragraph affected me, this meeting between the father and his son. . . . I loved it and hope you did, too."

Israeli Dinit responded that "this paragraph found favor in my eyes," and her classmate Na'ama was "happy that it ended like this . . . All during the book I saw that because of the father's teaching and the promise that he'll return, Alex, although he was lonely, succeeded to survive [sic]."

Estee, writing from Moriah, enthused, "This paragraph was my favorite part of the book. [During] the entire book I had this one main question: Would Alex ever see his father again? I was so happy when I read this paragraph, and I felt like I was part of the book."

While there are differences in the quantity and quality of the writing, the length, variety, and sophistication of the sentences, the use of appropriate and correct vocabulary, the inclusion of literary allusion, and the depth of responses to characters, plot, and themes (excluding the differences due to second language difficulties), it was clear to all of us that all students had used this forum to process their reading, search for some personal meaning from the tragedy of Orlev's childhood, and identify individual lessons, truths that connect them to the world of their grandparents.

Jane Sullivan (1998), a professor of literacy education at Rowan University in New Jersey, notes that her students' "electronic journals" "reflected a conversation, albeit in cyberspace" (p. 92). Her students, "as communities of learners . . . explore their literary worlds and share the results with their peers" (p. 90). Such discussions, she says, are a "coup [that] has taken hold in language arts classrooms across the U.S." (p. 90). We think the coup is now an international one, with Israeli students full participants in the quiet revolution in learning about the Holocaust through literature.

"Dear Pupils and Teachers," our last collective e-mail message from Karmiel, read: "Thank you for your creative work and cooperation. We really enjoyed communicating with you on the topic that is so important for the Jewish people. Our students learned a lot, enriched their knowledge about the Holocaust, and learned how to share their feelings with those who care. Best wishes to you from your Israeli friends."

ACKNOWLEDGMENT

Excerpts from *The Island on Bird Street* by Uri Orlev. Copyright © 1981 by Keter Publishing House, Jerusalem, Ltd. Translation copyright © 1984 by Houghton Mifflin Company. Reprinted by permission of Houghton Mifflin Company. All rights reserved.

REFERENCES

Books

Beach, Richard. (1990). "New Directions in Research on Response to Literature." In Edmund J. Farrell & James R. Squire (Eds.), *Transactions with Literature: A Fifty-Year Perspective* (pp. 55–78). Urbana, IL: National Council of Teachers of English.

Daiute, Colette. (1993). "Synthesis." In Colette Daiute (Ed.), *The Development of Literacy through Social Interaction* (pp. 121–124). San Francisco, CA: Jossey-Bass Publishers.

Daiute, Colette, Campbell, Carolyn H., Griffin, Terri M., Reddy, Maureen, & Tivnan, Terrence. (1993). "Young Authors' Interactions with Peers and a Teacher: Toward a Developmentally Sensitive Sociocultural Literacy Theory." In Colette Daiute (Ed), *The Development of Literacy Through Social Interaction* (pp. 41–63). San Francisco: Jossey-Bass Publishers.

Holtz, Barry. (Ed.) (1984). *Back to the Sources: Reading the Classic Jewish Texts.* New York: Summit Books.

Iser, Wolfgang. (1980). "The Reading Process: A Phenomenological Approach." In Janet Tompkins (Ed.), *Reader Response Criticism: From Formalism to Post-Structuralism* (pp. 50–69). Baltimore, MD: The Johns Hopkins University Press.

McMahon, Susan I., & Taffy E. Raphael. (1997). "The Book Club Program: Theoretical and Research Foundations." In Susan I. McMahon, Taffy E. Raphael, Virginia J. Goatley, & Laura S. Pardo (Eds.), *The Book Club Connection* (pp. 3–25). New York: Teachers College Press.

Nelms, Ben F. (Ed.). (1988). *Literature in the Classroom: Readers, Texts, Contexts.* Urbana, IL: National Council of Teachers of English.

Orlev, Uri. (1989). *The Island on Bird Street.* Boston, MA: Houghton Mifflin. Translated from the Hebrew by Hillel Halkin.

Orlev, Uri. (1997). *The Sandgame.* D. N. Western Galilee, Israel: Ghetto Fighters' House. Kibbutz Lohamei Haghetaot.

Rosenblatt, Louise M. (1976). *Literature as Exploration* (3rd ed.) New York: Noble and Noble.

Shawn, Karen, Shner, Moshe, Badmor, Aliza, Seldin-Dotan, Beth, Kalisman, Raya, Shiff, Varda, & Shner, Tali. (1997). *International book-sharing project teacher's guide.* D. N. Western Galilee, Israel: Yad Layeled, The Ghetto Fighters' House. Kibbutz Lohamei Haghetaot.

Sullivan, Jane. (1998). "The Electronic Journal: Combining Literacy and Technology." *The Reading Teacher.* September, 52(1): 90–93.

Film

The Island on Bird Street. 106 minutes, color. Available from The American Friends of the Ghetto Fighters' House, 181 The Plaza, Teaneck, NJ 07666.

APPENDIX A

Additional journal prompts:

1. What was your first reaction to this book? How did your reaction change as you read? After you finished?
2. What was the most important fact about the Holocaust that you learned from this book? What did you learn about yourself?
3. What questions do you have as a result of reading this book?
4. What age should students be when they read this book? Should it be their introduction to the study of the Holocaust? Why? Would you recommend this book to your parents? Why?
5. What surprised you most about what you read? What passages most clearly challenged your ideas, beliefs, or attitudes about the Shoah? Were you surprised by any of your reactions to what you read?
6. In what ways did this book remind you of other books, poems, or stories you have read, or TV shows or films you have seen?
7. Why do you think the author wrote this book?
8. What is your opinion of the novel's title? Do you have suggestions for alternatives?

Journal prompts or enrichment questions specific to *The Island on Bird Street:*

1. Discuss the differences among the concepts of miracle, fate, and luck. As you examine them, discuss what part they played in Alex's survival.
2. Discuss the concept of "choiceless choices." Identify such choices in the novel, examining the implications of each possible choice. Discuss the importance of refraining from using hindsight to judge the actions of Jews in the Shoah.
3. Alex recreates scenes from his life with his parents to help him make decisions and to keep from being unbearably lonely. How do these recreated conversations help the reader to understand his life before the war? His actions during his time in hiding?
4. Examine Alex's feelings throughout the book. They include, but are not limited to, fear, disappointment, relief, hope, loneliness, despair, and, ultimately, joy. To illustrate his range of emotions, graph them (or otherwise visually represent them) as you trace the plot of the story.
5. How do the minor characters strengthen the story? What is the role of the mouse? What is its importance to the story? What role do the partisans play? The doctor? Which of the minor characters made the strongest impression on you? Why?
6. How are we to judge those who turned Jews in to the Nazis? Are collaborators different from the Nazis themselves? How are we to think about such Jews as the Gryn family? Do we have a right to judge their actions?
7. In the upside-down world of the Holocaust, even ordinary possessions took on unusual value. In what ways do Alex's circumstances cause him to evaluate every object he finds in the ghetto? By what measures does he judge the value of things?
8. For many young people, the time of the Shoah was the end of the innocent world of childhood. What events signaled, for Alex, an end to his innocence?
9. What is a hero? What do you admire most about Alex? Do these traits make him heroic? Are there any (other) heroes in this book? Explain.
10. When this book was made into a film, the filmmakers experimented with two different endings. In one, it is unclear if the father has really returned, or whether Alex is just dreaming that he sees him. In the other, there is no doubt of the father's return. In your opinion, which is a stronger and/or more satisfying ending to this story?
11. Some people have criticized this book because it has a "happy ending" of sorts. They say that the majority of real Holocaust stories did not end this way. If this is the only book about the Holocaust that students will read in class this year, should they read, instead, one more representative of the majority?

APPENDIX B

The following six elements form the core project:

- The formation of cooperative learning groups in each participating classroom, pairing groups of Americans with groups of Israelis.
- The exchange of monthly letters (October—May) between cooperative learning groups.
- Lessons designed to introduce students to the study of the Shoah in general and/or the ghetto experience in particular, providing a historical context for the literature.

- The reading of *The Island on Bird Street* and / or *The Sandgame*.
- The use of personal response journals.
- A computer-generated literary response journal based on the readings and jointly designed by students working cooperatively through e-mail.

A P P E N D I X   C

What might a typical class involved in the project look like? Assuming that students know and accept their responsibilities for each day, they might be:

- responding to a passage from the novel
- illustrating the cover
- designing the layout for the title page
- writing the journal dedication and introduction
- writing an "About the Authors" page
- examining and selecting archival photographs and documents
- choosing and exploring a limited research topic
- finding relevant testimony and sharing it via e-mail
- taking and scanning photos
- making decisions about fonts, colors, borders, graphics, placement of research findings and photos, testimonies, and artwork
- translating a letter or a response
- proofreading and editing
- writing interview questions for Uri Orlev
- designing a culminating in-school activity
- writing letters or an article about the project

CHAPTER

6

Analyzing Short Stories about the Holocaust via a Multiple Intelligences and Reader-Response Approach

SAMUEL TOTTEN

Just as the characters in Holocaust stories find their expectations violated by the situations that assault them, so readers entering this imagined world must adjust to the strenuous demands it makes on their *power to imagine.*

—Langer, 1995b, p. 238

As a rule, when I have my students read short stories about the Holocaust it is to help illuminate some aspect of the history I am teaching (e.g., the incremental and sustained deprivation of civil and human rights of the Jews by the Nazis in the early years of the latter's rule, the pervasive fear induced by Nazi policies and actions, the choiceless choices foisted upon the Jews by the Nazis, the abject brutality of the Nazis, life and death in the ghettos, the horrific nature of the deportations, or the horror of the death camps). It is a way, along with the inclusion of personal accounts, to assist the students to begin to understand the various, and often horrific, trials and tribulations to which both individuals and groups of people were subjected. Put another way, the inclusion of short stories can supplement a study of genocide by moving it "from a welter of statistics, remote places and events, to one that is immersed in the 'personal' and 'particular'" (Totten, 1987, p. 63).

One of the more thought-provoking ways in which I've engaged secondary and university students in an examination of Holocaust literature is through the use of an exercise using "multiple intelligences" (Armstrong, 1994; Gardner, 1983, 1993). It is a strategy that allows for open and creative responses by students to a piece of literature and reveals insights that might not be gleaned via a more traditional pedagogical approach.

Simply stated, "multiple intelligences" constitutes what Harvard educational theorist Howard Gardner (1983 and 1993) defines as "the broad range of abilities that humans possess" (Armstrong, 1994, p. 2). As to why he chose to use the term "intelligences" as opposed to another descriptor, Gardner has explained: "I'm deliberately being somewhat provocative. If I'd said that there's seven kinds of competencies, people would yawn and say 'Yeah, yeah.' But by calling them 'intelligences,' I'm saying that we've tended to put on a pedestal one variety called intelligence, and there's actually a plurality of them, and some are things we've never thought about as being an 'intelligence' at all" (cited in Weinreich-Haste, 1985, p. 48).

Expounding on his discussion and description of multiple intelligences, Gardner (1997) observed:

> The standard view of intelligence is that intelligence is something you are born with; you have only a certain amount of it; you cannot do much about how much of that intelligence you have; and tests exist that can tell you how smart you are. The theory of multiple intelligences challenges that view. It asks, instead, "Given what we know about the brain, evolution, and the differences in cultures, what are the sets of human abilities we all share?"
>
> My analysis suggested that rather than one or two intelligences, all human beings have several intelligences. What makes life interesting, however, is that we don't have the same strength in each intelligence area, and we don't have the same amalgam of intelligences. Just as we look different from one another and have different kinds of personalities, we also have different kinds of minds. (p. 9)

In order to meet the needs of all students and to capitalize on their ways of learning, "it is of the utmost importance that we recognize and nurture all of the varied human intelligences, and all of the combinations of intelligences" (Gardner, 1987, p. 1).

The seven intelligences Gardner initially identified were: linguistic (e.g., "the capacity to use words effectively whether orally or in writing"), logical-mathematical (e.g., "the capacity to use numbers effectively and to reason well"), spatial (e.g., "the ability to perceive the visual-spatial world accurately and to perform transformations upon those perceptions such as an artist or inventor would"), bodily-kinesthetic (e.g., "the expertise in using one's whole body to express ideas and feelings and facility in using one's hands to produce or transform things"), musical (e.g., "the capacity to perceive, discriminate, transform, and express musical forms"), interpersonal ("the ability to perceive and make distinctions in the moods, intentions, motivations, and feelings of other people"), and intrapersonal (e.g., "self-knowledge and the ability to act adaptively on the basis of that knowledge") (Armstrong, 1994, pp. 2–3). In the 1990s Gardner added an eighth intelligence, "the naturalist intelligence" (Checkley, 1997, p. 8). The naturalist intelligence focuses on the ability to recognize patterns in nature and classify objects such as flora, fauna, and rocks, as well as cultural artifacts such as logos and cars. Biologists and naturalists provide classic examples of the latter because biologists, for example, have a mastery of certain taxonomies and a deep understanding of different species. In 1999 Gardner mentioned in an interview that he was now considering the addition of yet another intelligence to his list—an "existentialist intelligence," or one that is concerned with issues of human existence and meaning.

Introducing Students to the Concept of Multiple Intelligences

Prior to engaging the students in an activity around a Holocaust short story requiring the use of multiple intelligences, it is imperative to provide them with a sound sense as to the following: the concept of multiple intelligences, the actual intelligences and examples of each, and the way in which the various intelligences may be employed by the individual in everyday life.

How teachers provide such an overview is only limited by their creativity and time constraints. Ideally, the introduction should be lively, engaging, and thought-provoking, and provide clear examples that are illustrative of the beauty and power of the concept of multiple intelligences. If a teacher plans to incorporate multiple intelligences throughout the rest of the academic year, then a relatively lengthy and in-depth introduction to the concept is called for—and as a result, it will be anything but a waste of precious time. That said, as Armstrong (1994) notes, "One of the most useful features of MI theory is that it can be explained to a group of children as young as 1st grade in as little as five minutes in such a way that they can then use MI vocabulary to talk about what they learn" (p. 37). (For unique ways to introduce students to the theory of multiple intelligences, see Chapter 4, "Teaching Students about MI Theory," in Thomas Armstrong's *Multiple Intelligences in the Classroom* [1994].)

Using Multiple Intelligences at Various Points in a Study of a Piece of Holocaust Literature

Virtually any literary work—be it a novel, novella, short story, poem, or play—can be interpreted or examined via a multiple intelligences approach, and it can be accomplished at virtually any point in a study. When and where it is incorporated, obviously, is contingent on a teacher's goals and objectives.

In an initial approach—before any discussion about the piece of Holocaust literature is conducted—students could read a short story or poem and then work individually, in pairs, or in triads and interpret the poem using one or more of the eight aforementioned multiple intelligences. Following such an activity, a more detailed discussion of the literary work could be held, including the historical context and significance of the story, novel, poem, or play. Those teachers who wish to do so, of course, could provide the historical context for the literary work prior to the students' engagement with the story, novel, poem, or play.

When reading a long short story, students could be required to interpret a particular situation, conflict, or character via a multiple intelligences approach. Again, depending on the goals and objectives, students may have already discussed the historical context of the literary work and examined a host of literary and historical issues germane to the piece of literature.

Then again, during the conclusion of a study, a summative approach could be used. In this situation, the students could—as a concluding activity—use a multiple intelligences approach to respond to the entire piece of literature.

One Approach for Using Multiple Intelligences to Interpret a Piece of Holocaust Literature

What is shared here is an activity that the author developed and has used approximately a half-dozen times in various settings (a semester-long high school course on the Holocaust, an undergraduate course on middle level education, an undergraduate literature course, and a Holocaust workshop with high school sophomores, juniors, and seniors). In each setting the activity has resulted in powerful insights into the piece of Holocaust literature.

After providing a succinct overview of multiple intelligences, I inform the students that they are about to listen to a Holocaust story and that following the story they will interpret the story via a multiple intelligences approach. More specifically, I tell them that when interpreting the story they can do so in any way they wish as long as they go about it in a serious manner and attempt to create a genuine and original response to the work. Next, I have them write down the title and author of the work and then I either read the story aloud or ask for a volunteer to do so. When I use a poem, I generally place it on the overhead, read it to the class, and then leave the overhead up during the remainder of the class session. The students are encouraged to listen *very carefully* to the story in order later to recall the story line, setting, and conflict, and the personalities, words, and actions of the various characters, and so on. Immediately after the story has been read, the students—either individually, in pairs or in triads—are required to respond to and interpret the story.

Over the past several years I have used a number of different stories for this activity, including but not limited to Ida Fink's "The Key Game," "Crazy," and "Zygmunt"; Tadeusz Borowski's "The Man With the Package"; Jozef Zelkowicz's "25 Live Hens and One Dead Document"; and Sara Nomberg-Przytyk's "The Verdict." Each of these stories is used for a different reason and to highlight and illuminate different aspects of the history and problems faced by the Jews during the Holocaust years. Fink's "The Key Game" is used to highlight such issues as the Nazi dragnet to capture and incarcerate all Jews, the life-and-death situations faced by Jews during the Nazis' reign of terror, the desperation faced by individuals when they chose to go "in hiding," the "choiceless choices"[1] people were forced to make, the overwhelming complications faced by Jews with young children, etc. I use Fink's "Crazy" to illuminate such issues as the roundups and deportations of the Jews by the Nazis, the choiceless choices the Jews had forced upon them, the myriad ramifications of the choices the victims had forced upon them, and life in the aftermath of the Holocaust. Fink's "Zygmunt" is useful for discussing such issues as the fear induced by the Nazis, the brutality of the Nazis, choiceless choices, the mass murder perpetrated by the Nazis, and the way in which different victims faced their fate. Tadeusz Borowski's "The Man With the Package" is useful for exploring such issues as the "selections" of the Jews to be gassed, the mass killings, the concept of "Muslims" or "mussul-men," the fact that coming down with a sickness often destined one for the gas chambers, the differences—in many cases—between how the Jews and other prisoners were treated, and the sense of "hope against hope" that many clung to even under the most dire circumstances. Jozef Zelkowicz's "25 Live Hens and One Dead Document" is capable of highlighting issues regarding life and death in the Lodz Ghetto, collaborators and collaboration, the extortion committed by certain Gentiles against the Jews, the role of the Jewish police in the ghetto, and, above all, the savagery faced by the Jews. Sara Nomberg-Przytyk's "The Verdict" reveals important aspects of life and death in Auschwitz, the deceit of the Nazis, the role of Dr. Josef Mengele in the killing process, the horrific brutality the Jews were subjected to at Auschwitz, and the choiceless choices faced by the prisoners.

There are both general and specific concerns and criteria that should be addressed when Holocaust stories are used in such an activity. First, in regard to general issues, the stories must be historically accurate. That is true of both the facts (e.g., dates and geographical locations) as well as the historical context of the story (e.g., accounts of such events as Kristallnacht). To include historically inaccurate stories is senseless and miseducative. This is particularly true if a goal of the instructor is, as it was in my case, to deepen the students' understanding of various aspects of the Holocaust. Second, and this should be a given, the stories should be well written, and engaging or thought-provoking. Third, in most cases the stories should be rather short (e.g., certainly no more than four to five pages in length). The rationale for this is simple: (1) stories longer than five pages take a fair amount of time to read; (2) students are likely to have a hard time remembering the details of a story that is much longer than five pages; and (3) time is at a premium in classrooms, and an inordinate amount of time should not be taken up with the reading of the stories, for that will cut into the ensuing multiple intelligences activity. Fortunately, there are many very fine short stories about the Holocaust available, thus this part of the criteria will have no averse effect in regard to presenting the students with high quality pieces of literature for this activity.

An alternative, of course, to reading the story aloud to the students is for the teacher to select four to six short stories related to the topic or theme to be focused on, succinctly inform the students about the focus of each story, and then allow the students to select a story, read it on their own, and interpret the story. While this method certainly requires more time—for some students invariably decide that the story they have chosen to read is not to their liking and thus they end up selecting another story and starting all over again—it is one that allows for the reading of both more and longer stories, which, in turn, adds a certain diversity to the offerings to which the students are introduced.

Once the story is read, the students need to decide whether they wish to work individually, in pairs, or in triads. If a group has a strong rationale for including more than three students in its effort, such a rationale is given serious consideration. Different students approach the work ahead in different ways. Many discuss the work they've chosen, attempting to establish a meeting of the minds in regard both to what the story is about and what it means to each of them. Some, though, immediately begin talking about how they wish to interpret the story; that is, the intelligence(s) they wish to use to interpret it. In more cases than not, the students who take the second approach often find that they have put the proverbial cart before the horse and often scrap their initial intentions and go back and discuss the story itself, ultimately focusing on both their individual and collective understanding of it. (For those teachers who prefer to provide their students with very specific directions, and have them work in a more structured manner, see the Appendix to this chapter, "Directions for the Multiple Intelligences [MI] Activity.")

No matter what approach is used, at some point the students need to decide which intelligence(s) they are going to use to interpret the story as well as how they are going to present their interpretation to the rest of the class. As mentioned earlier, their interpretation may involve one or more of the eight intelligences. Thus, an interpretation may involve, for example, composing and singing a song, creating and doing a mime, creating and performing a dance, creating a piece of art or music, writing a sequel to the story, conducting a panel discussion, etc. The students are encouraged to be as creative as possible, and informed that if they choose to do something in the linguistic intelligence then it should not be a staid lecture. *At one and the same time, they are told that their creativity should be driven by a serious attempt to interpret the story in as thorough a manner as possible, and that just because this activity is "free-flowing" it should not result in something frivolous or silly, or be comprised of mindless "fun and games."* This is an important caveat to issue, and I have discovered this the hard way—for early in my use of this approach, a group of my university students did approach this activity in such a way that it degenerated into something that was pointless and jejune.

In order to facilitate the students' work, I always bring in a variety of materials, including old magazines with lots of colored pictures, large pieces of poster board, a large roll of butcher paper, magic markers, crayons, pencils, pens, scissors, construction paper of various colors, tacks, a ball of string, scotch tape, masking tape, paper clips of different sizes, a stapler, lined paper, white paper, bells, drum sticks, drinking glasses, forks, spoons, wood blocks, a combination radio/tape recorder, and blank cassette tapes, and sometimes clay and watercolors.

Students are informed that upon completion of their interpretation (which generally takes a class session), each individual, pair, or triad is required to conduct, perform, or display their interpretation for the rest of the class members. Following each presentation, the rest of the class is required to discuss the meaning behind the individual's, pair's, or triad's interpretation.

During the next class session, individuals, pairs, or triads present their interpretations. For example, if they've choreographed a dance, they perform it; or if they've created a collage, they hang it on the wall, without commenting on it. Then the rest of the class, as a group and out loud, analyzes the interpretations. Playing off of each other's ideas, there is considerable interaction as students question, comment, or provide interpretive suggestions. During this class exchange, the individual or pair or triad that designed the response remains silent, observes, and carefully listens to what is being said. At the conclusion of the group interpretation, the individual, pair, or triad is required to tell the class how and why they decided to approach the story in the manner in which they did. Here they are expected to discuss why they chose to use the intelligence(s) they did, explain how they actually designed and developed their interpretation, and delineate their own interpretation in a good amount of detail. At this time, they are also expected to comment on the larger group's interpretation (e.g., whether it was accurate or inaccurate and why that is so, and whether they—the original interpreters—gained new insights into the piece and/or their own interpretation).

This particular multiple intelligences approach also constitutes a "reader-response theory-like" approach. More specifically, it is one that is student-centered and predicated on the idea that each reader comes to a piece of literature with a rich background of worldly experience and a broad knowledge base in many different subjects. Thus, for a reader to get the most out of a work of literature, he or she must bring his or her own insights, knowledge base, and past experiences to bear on his or her reading of the literary work.

Reader response theory also perceives reading as a "social act" (Sheridan, 1991, p. 805). Reader response theorists argue convincingly that the reading experience is often more powerful and revelatory when it involves discussion and debate with others. In this way, a community of readers comes together in which each member's ideas, questions, likes and dislikes, and concerns converge in a way that helps to illuminate the work under study.

As O'Neill (1994) has written in "Rewriting the Book on Literature: Changes Sought in How Literature is Taught, What Students Read," "Basically, reader response theory differs most radically from previous theories about teaching literature in the degree of emphasis placed on the reader's response to an interpretation of the text. . . . In reader response theory, the text's meaning is considered to reside in the "transaction" between the reader and the text, not from the text alone" (p. 7).

Interpreting Holocaust Short Stories:
The Unique and Multiple Interpretations
of Students Using Multiple Intelligences

The ways in which my students respond to the pieces of Holocaust literature via a multiple intelligences approach never cease to amaze me. This is largely due, of course, to the flexibility inherent in the concept of multiple intelligences as well as the creativity that ensues when students are given *real* latitude in how they go about tackling a problem or project.

While my students have used numerous and widely different approaches in interpreting Holocaust short stories via a multiple intelligences and reader response lens, I shall only describe four approaches herein. One of the more thought-provoking approaches was an interpretation that focused on Ida Fink's "The Key Game" and involved the design of a box, about the shape and size of a shoe box, which was decorated with provocative graphics that were germane to various aspects of the story. In addition to the graphics, most of which were cut out of magazines, the students slit a hole in the top of the box and created two additional pieces that could be inserted and removed, which, in turn, revealed additional aspects of their interpretation of the story.

More specifically, on the front of the box was a hinged door and on this door was a graphic that included an ornate setting that was comprised of a series of doors that reached tunnel-like ever deeper into a room. In the inner sanctum were two figures engaged in serious discussion. On the opposite side of the door, a vivid framed picture of the grim reaper appeared. Glancing inside of the box itself, one's eye was immediately drawn toward the body of a young boy that was hanging from a gigantic chain. He was framed on both sides by walls of bars that suggested a jail cell. On the outside of the box, one noticed that on the cardboard piece from which the boy was hanging by the chain was the direction: "Pull up." Directly behind it, in the same slot cut into the top of the box, was another cardboard piece with the directions: "Push down in middle slot." When the first piece was pulled up and the second piece was pushed down it revealed a coffin. As the cardboard piece with the coffin on it was pushed downward, one noticed that there was something at the inside rear of the box. Removing the piece with the coffin on it revealed a picture of a man and women staring skyward, their bodies being grabbed by a gigantic, frightening-looking pair of talons.

Also focusing on Fink's "The Key Game," six students working together developed a discussion activity designed around a modified version of a method called *fishbowl*. A typical fishbowl exercise is a discussion technique used with large groups where participants take turns being in the "fishbowl," or a small discussion group in front of the class. Several chairs are arranged in front of the class for the students who will discuss the topic at hand with a leader while the rest of the group observes. The discussion continues as long as it is fruitful and then it is opened up for a large class discussion. In the modified version designed by my students, the students working together divided themselves into three pairs. Each pair took on the persona of *one* of the characters in the story, for example, the father, the mother, or the child. The task they gave themselves was as follows: It was 20 years after the incident in the story and each member of the respective pairs needed to reflect back on what had occurred in the story and discuss with his or her partner the thoughts and feelings they were experiencing at the time of the incident and how they now perceived the "role" they and the others played. As a whole group, they decided that during the fishbowl discussion only one member of the pair could speak at a time, and if the member who was not speaking wanted to speak, then he or she needed to tap his or her partner on the shoulder and take his or her place in the fishbowl (in other words, they played the same role, but could speak only one at a time). The purpose of having two pairs of students play the same role was that it contributed to (1) more students being involved in the discussion, and (2) played off the theory that two heads are better than one. This modified fishbowl activity resulted in a heated but thorough and insightful discussion regarding the choiceless choices that the parents were forced to make; the climate of the times in which the choices were foisted upon them; the resentment of the child, but also a certain appreciation for what the parents were faced with; the parents' observations of the long-term ramifications of being hunted down like animals and having to place a small child in a life-and-death situation, and so on.

The development of collages are particularly popular with students and evidence of this is that a vast majority of the students, often in pairs and triads, choose to interpret a story through this medium. The popularity may be due to one or more reasons, including the unique opportunity to create a piece of art, and the opportunity to interpret a story using a method other than the linguistic approach.

In one combination collage/drawing, two students, working together, interpreted Fink's "Crazy." In the collage, a tiny, hunchbacked man, with a shriveled face and huge forlorn eyes stared out of a building with bars over the windows. Surrounding him, as if he were in a nightmare, swirled wild and disparate images: a sweet scene of innocent children on a swing in a glorious field of daises over which was juxtaposed a gaping skull, and a broom sweeping what looks like the inside of a head. On the outside edges of each of the four sides of the collage were ugly snarling faces of men each with little swastikas in place of their eyes. Sprinkled all over the collage, in loud colors and all sizes of type, was the phrase, "choices haunt." In ragged letters at the bottom of the collage is the title: "It is said that 'cowards die a thousand deaths.' But, do they really? For who were the real cowards? And what have they experienced over the years?"

Another student chose to create a series of charcoal drawings in which she interpreted Jozef Zelkowicz's "25 Live Hens and One Dead Document." Interestingly, she created four drawings using realism and four drawings in which she used surrealism and abstract art. The two most memorable drawings, both using realism, depicted the following. First, there was a document with the phrases: "13 hens were returned, 6 were sent to Drewnowska Street, 1 hen—Rozenblat, 5 hens, i.e., 20 meals—Hilfs-Ordunngsdienst." On the outer lefthand side of the edge of the document were 25 chickens actively moving about, pecking the ground for food, fluffing their feathers, while on the outer righthand side of the edge of the document were 24 people, all identified as Jews by their stars, on the ground and piled in a rickety wagon, dead. The second drawing was of a Gentile youth (as denoted by not having a star) turning his coat inside out (signifying his choosing to become a collaborator with the Nazis), his hands holding wads of money, dripping some type of liquid (seemingly blood), with a smirk on his dog-like face.

The most powerful surreal/abstract drawing depicted a gigantic hand with a swastika tattoo on it squeezing the barbed wire ghetto and its inhabitants to death. Crawling around on the outside of the hand, beating back those Jews who attempted to escape the hand, were Jewish policemen.

All in all, what this young lady created constituted a powerful tour de force that captured our imaginations and encapsulated the power and various levels of the story. One student in the class commented, "It's too bad that Janine's drawings couldn't be inserted into the fabric of the story. I know it would've helped me to gain a deeper understanding of it."

Over and above the aforementioned efforts to interpret various Holocaust stories, in the past other students have created skits, created songs and sung them, created and recited poetry, developed and carried out a serious (versus a sideshow or carnival-like) talk show/panel discussion, and written a series of letters as part of an ongoing correspondence between themselves and the major characters in the short story.

Large Class Discussion of an Interpretation: A Vignette

What follows is a vignette from one of the classroom discussions that centered around an interpretation of Ida Fink's "The Key Game" by a pair of students who created the previously mentioned "shoe box"-like affair. In order to interpret the interpretation, all of the students in the class got out of their seats and went to the section of the room where the box was on the floor, and then, in no particular order, students began commenting and positing questions regarding the interpretation/decorated box. Anyone, except the individuals who created the original interpretation, was encouraged to play off of each comment and/or question and/or to offer a new insight or question. (At the outset, the class comes to a consensus on which story they are discussing.) The individuals who created the original interpretation were not allowed to say *anything* until the discussion had concluded; and then, at that time, they were to discuss their own interpretation as well as the class's analysis of their interpretation. In doing so, they understood that they were welcome to comment on whether the class's analysis was an accurate view of their interpretation and why or why not that was so; what, if anything, the class had overlooked; whether the class had "overinterpreted" something or, conversely, whether the class actually provided the original interpreters with new insights into their own interpretation and/or the short story.

MARK: To start off, the box is like the room or apartment that the parents and child are in, and, to me, the bars suggest, that, ironically, what is usually a haven—that is, one's home—has become a place of fear, one where they are, kind of, imprisoned, due to outside forces.

KATIE: Yeah, not really a prison per se, but something that has become prisonlike . . . a place where you're not really free, where you feel your options are . . . limited . . .

JODIE: Is it just the room or is the room a metaphor for the larger society which, under the Nazis, has become one giant prison?

MARK: Yeah, yeah, that's good.

CHANTELLE: But is the home really a prison? It's not like they are locked up in it. They are able to open the door and unlike a prison the father is using the apartment as a hiding place.

MARK: That's a good point, too. But I think it is like a prison, in a sense. A prison, like Katie said, limits your choice, your movement, your freedom and the apartment has definitely become that but it's because of the larger prison atmosphere outside.

CHANTELLE: Hmmm, I'm not so sure. . . .

RACHEL: What caught my attention right away was the little boy hanging by the chain. It reminded me of that saying about the weakest link in the chain . . . That a chain is only as strong as its weakest link and . . .

BOBBY: Yeah, and if the little boy fails, the whole family will face disaster.

RACHEL: Exactly.

THOMAS: And that's exactly what the coffin behind the chain and the little boy suggests, that if the chain breaks then the result might be death.

RACHEL: Yeah, and so what we have here, of course, is that there may or may not be a disaster but it's like the fate of the whole . . . the entire family hangs on the actions of the child.

LUCY: Which is just the opposite of what is normal; that is, in most families the baby is not . . . that is, the parents are the ones who are in control of the situation but here it's the child.

BRAD: While it's rather obvious that the claws around the adults stand for the Nazis, I think the picture is powerful because it suggests that the Nazis have the parents in their clutches and the talons are sharp and wicked-looking and deadly.

NICK: I also think it's important that while the claws are on them, they are not totally wrapped around them, so they do have a chance of getting away, even if the chance is only narrow.

REBECCA: To me, it looks like they are looking to heaven for help.

JASON: I think so, too, but the only help they are going to get in the story is from the child and we don't know if that is going to work out or not.

HENRY: It's like the whole family is in chains, coming back to the kid hanging from the chain, which, again, is prisonlike.

JEFF: Which makes the title of the story so . . . so . . .

REBECCA: Weird, because it's anything but a game. It's a life-and-death situation, which is what the inside of the door suggests, the grim reaper . . .

TOM: But why is the grim reaper on the inside of the door? Why not on the outside, which is where the Nazis are?

REBECCA: Maybe because the inside is where the death will occur if the father is caught, or . . .

RACHEL: Or a certain death already is inside . . . like the death of childhood. The baby, the little boy, is miserable and his childhood has been stolen by the Nazis because he is in a situation no child should be in.

KELLY: That no person should be in.

RACHEL: Right, but especially a child.

The discussion went on and on with the students playing off one another, probing the interpretation, and adding their own insights as they went. Each and every class interpretation moves along at a good pace and is generally revelatory in its own way. Such sessions provide the fodder for an ensuing discussion that incorporates the history of the Holocaust, character analysis, and key literary concerns such as conflict and symbolism.

Incorporating the Historical Context into the Activity

If a social studies or history teacher is already teaching about the Holocaust and chooses to use a short story to complement and/or illuminate a particular aspect of the history (e.g., the abject fear induced by the Nazis, the roundups, deportation, the choiceless choices forced upon the victims, going into hiding, resistance, the savagery of the Nazis), then, more than likely, he or she has already provided a historical context for the short story.

Teachers of English and other subjects are not as likely as social studies and history teachers to automatically provide a historical context for the short stories they use with their students. If they wish to do so—and this author believes that it is imperative to do so if the students are going to gain a deep understanding of the Holocaust period—there are numerous ways in which to provide such a context. Three methods that this author has used will be delineated herein. First, an English teacher could team up with a social studies or history teacher in order to conduct an interdisciplinary study of the Holocaust. In designing the curriculum, both teachers could decide which aspects of the history they wish to illuminate via the use of Holocaust short stories. Thus, either during and/or after the social studies or history teacher has taught about a specific aspect of the history, the English teacher could teach a short story that reveals and/or probes that particular component of the history.

Another option for teachers outside the discipline of social studies/history is to have their students read one or more essays about the specific aspect of the history that the short story addresses. A particularly useful source for obtaining such information is Israel Gutman's (Ed.) *Encyclopedia of the Holocaust,* for it comprises relatively short and easy to understand (at least for high school students who are capable readers) entries on a wide array of topics. While most high school libraries will not have the Gutman text in their collections, all major university libraries and many smaller colleges will own it. If one does not live close to an institution that has the encyclopedia, then one may be able to obtain it through interlibrary loan. Other useful and possibly more accessible sources are: Raul Hilberg's *The Destruction of European Jewry,* Leni Yahil's *The Holocaust: The Fate of European Jewry,* Lucy S. Dawidowicz's *The War Against the Jews, 1933–1945,* and Michael Berenbaum's *The World Must Know: The History of the Holocaust as Told in the United States Holocaust Memorial Museum.*

Third, a teacher could show a film that highlights the topic/issue addressed in the short story. While this is a relatively easy way to provide the historical context, teachers need to be very careful in selecting the film to be used. This is true because while there are many excellent films available on various facets of the Holocaust, there are also many available that are historically inaccurate, bereft of adequate depth, and/or focus on the "whats" of the history but neglect to address the "whys" behind it. Still others contain a barrage of violent scenes that may pander to the puerile interests of young people or altogether overwhelm the viewers to the point where they become so numb that they learn nothing from the film. As the authors of the United States Holocaust Memorial Museum's *Guidelines for Teaching about the Holocaust* note:

> Graphic material should be used in a judicious manner and only to the extent necessary to achieve the objective of the lesson. Teachers should remind themselves that each student and each class is different, and that what seems appropriate for one may not be for all.
>
> Students are essentially a "captive audience." When we assault them with images of horror for which they are unprepared, we violate a basic trust: the obligation of a teacher to provide a "safe" learning environment. The assumption that all students will seek to understand human behavior after being exposed to horrible images is fallacious. Some students may be so appalled by images of brutality and mass murder that they are discouraged from studying the subject further; others may become fascinated in a more voyeuristic fashion, subordinating

further critical analysis of the history to the superficial titillation of looking at images of starvation, disfigurement, and death. Many events and deeds that occurred within the context of the Holocaust do not rely for their depiction directly on the graphic horror of mass killings or other barbarisms. It is recommended that images and texts that do not exploit either the victims' memories or the students' emotional vulnerability form the center piece of Holocaust curricula. (Parsons & Totten, 1993, p. 6)

In order to be assured that one is selecting a historically accurate, well made, and pedagogically sound film, it is recommended that teachers refer to highly respected videographies of the Holocaust. One of the best videographies currently available was specifically designed by the United States Holocaust Memorial Museum for teachers; it is simply entitled *Annotated Videography*. (For a copy of this videography, write to the Education Department, c/o United States Holocaust Memorial Museum, 100 Raoul Wallenberg Place, SW, Washington, D.C. 20024.)

Caveats

Contingent upon one's goals, each teacher must decide whether there is a need to provide a historical context prior to or following the multiple intelligences activity. Providing or not providing a historical context will dramatically affect the students' interpretation of the short story. Many, if not most, purists of reader response theory may argue that students *should not* be provided with the historical context prior to their own interpretation of a work because that would "limit" or "sway" their interpretation. Yet purists of Holocaust education would likely argue that in order for students to gain the greatest insights into a literary work about the Holocaust, they need to understand the historical context of the story *prior* to attempting to interpret it.

Ultimately, whether at the beginning of the study or later in the study, in order to gain a better and deeper understanding of the Holocaust, as well as of the story itself, students need to be assisted in placing the events of the story in a historical context. Such a context will, hopefully, provide students with critical insights into the period of the piece, the larger events taking place around the more telescoped events in the story, the conflict faced by the characters, the "choiceless choices" facing the characters, the setting, etc. All good literature can be understood on various and increasingly complex levels; and thus, establishing the historical context may enable students to more readily access and explore additional levels of a literary work.

Another major caveat in regard to using such multiple intelligence type activities in the classroom is the need to avoid a situation in which the activity degenerates into a fun-and-games sort of atmosphere. Oftentimes when students experience something entirely new and unique, they have a tendency (and this is true even at the collegiate level) to respond in a less than serious manner and/or in an altogether foolish way. In doing so, students may attempt to try to outdo one another in being outlandish in their responses, responding in puerile and/or superficial ways, and/or develop a project that is dashed off in a way that is bereft of much thought or care. Thus, when incorporating such a method or activity into one's curricular program, it is imperative that an instructor set the right tone. This needs to be direct and to the point. When all is said and done, for a teacher to use such an approach simply because it is "catchy" and/or to allow a "fun-and-games" atmosphere to prevail is unprofessional and unconscionable—and this is especially the case when dealing with such a profoundly serious subject as the Holocaust.

Part and parcel of avoiding a frivolous situation is the need to provide students with key guidelines for all aspects of the activity, including how the larger group should go about responding to another student's (or group of students') interpretation of a story. When carried out in a systematic and pedagogically sound fashion, the large group interpretation is capable of generating deep thinking by most students. In light of that, it is a good idea for teachers to model how—and explain why—students need to delve below the surface in their interpretations and work in concert to attempt to develop deeper understandings. Students need to understand that this involves playing off of one another's ideas, challenging one another, and asking for clarification of a student's interpretive point if is not clearly understood.

Conclusion

When first introduced to this activity, many students are wary about it because they are not accustomed to doing something of this nature. However, once they begin the process of interpreting the short story, and realize that they have the freedom to do so in any way they wish, most become thoroughly engaged in the process.

When directly questioned about their involvement in the activity, many students—whether junior high, high school, or university undergraduates—comment on how revelatory (not their word) the process turned out to be. Almost everyone (including the instructor—which is true no how matter how many times this activity is conducted) comments on how amazed they are at the varied, imaginative and powerful interpretations of the different individuals and groups. Many students also comment on how the activity and the varied responses to it have prompted them to look at the piece of literature with "new eyes." Frequently, some comment on the high levels of thinking that resulted in both the development of the responses to the stories as well as the subsequent whole class discussion and interpretation of the stories. In fact, students often comment on how astounded they are that such an ostensibly simple activity could result in such creative and critical thinking. Finally, some invariably comment—and this is generally offered by undergraduates—that a major reason certain interpretations were so interesting was due to the fact that presenters tapped some of the intelligences less commonly used in classrooms and/or used the more commonly used intelligences (e.g., linguistic) in creative ways.

When all is said and done, any examination of Holocaust literature should involve students in an active confrontation with at least two different stories: the characters' stories and the story of the Holocaust. When conducted with care, the above activity is capable of reaching both goals, and doing so in a remarkably powerful way.

N O T E

1. The term *choiceless choice* refers to "crucial decisions [foisted upon the Jews by the Nazis] that did not reflect options between life and death, but between one form of abnormal response and another, both imposed by a situation that was in no way of the victims' own choosing." (Langer, 1982, p. 72) Put another way, choiceless choices are those that "whatever you choose, somebody loses." (Langer, 1995a, p. 46)

R E F E R E N C E S

Armstrong, Thomas. (1994). *Multiple Intelligences in the Classroom.* Alexandria, VA: Association for Supervision and Curriculum Development.

Beach, Richard. (1993). *A Teacher's Introduction to Reader-Response Theories.* Urbana, IL: National Council of Teachers of English.

Borowski, Tadeusz. (1980). "The Man with the Package." In Tadeusz Borowski (Ed.), *This Way to the Gas, Ladies and Gentleman* (pp. 147–151). New York: Penguin Books.

Checkley, Kathy. (September 1997). "The First Seven . . . and the Eighth: A Conversation with Howard Gardner." *Educational Leadership 55*(1): 8–13.

Dawidowicz, Lucy S. (1987). *The War Against the Jews, 1933–1945.* New York: Bantam Books.

Fink, Ida. (1989). "Crazy." In Ida Fink, (Ed.), *A Scrap of Time* (pp. 107–109). New York: Schocken.

Fink, Ida. (1989). "The Key Game." In Ida Fink (Ed.), *A Scrap of Time* (pp. 35–38). New York: Schocken.

Fink, Ida. (1989). *A Scrap of Time.* New York: Schocken.

Fink, Ida. (1997). "Zygmunt." In Ida Fink (Ed.), *Traces: Stories* (pp. 25–29). New York: Henry Holt.

Gardner, Howard. (1983). *Frames of Mind: The Theory of Multiple Intelligences.* New York: Basic Books.

Gardner, Howard. (1987). "Beyond IQ: Education and Human Development." *Harvard Educational Review, 57*(2): 187–193.

Gardner, Howard. (1993). *Multiple Intelligences: The Theory in Practice.* New York: Basic Books.

Gutman, Israel. (1990). *Encyclopedia of the Holocaust.* 4 Volumes. New York: Macmillan.

Hilberg, Raul. (1985). *The Destruction of the European Jews.* 3 volumes. New York: Holmes and Meier.

Langer, Lawrence. (1982). *Versions of Survival: The Holocaust and the Human Spirit.* Albany: State University of New York Press.

Langer, Lawrence. (1995a). *Admitting the Holocaust: Collected Essays.* New York: Oxford University Press.

Langer, Lawrence. (1995b). "Fiction." In Lawrence Langer (Ed.), *Art from the Ashes: A Holocaust Anthology* (pp. 235–239). New York: Oxford University Press.

Nomberg-Przytyk, Sara. (1995). "The Verdict." In Lawrence Langer (Ed.), *Art from the Ashes: A Holocaust Anthology* (pp. 264–267). New York: Oxford University Press.

O'Neill, John. (June 1994). "Rewriting the Book on Literature: Changes Sought in How Literature is Taught, What Students Read." *ASCD Curriculum Update,* 1–4, 6–8.

Parsons, William S., and Samuel Totten. (1993). *Guidelines for Teaching About the Holocaust.* Washington, DC: United States Holocaust Memorial Museum.

Probst, Robert. (1988). *Response and Analysis: Teaching Literature in Junior and Senior High School.* Upper Montclair, NJ: Boynton/Cook.

Purves, Alan; Theresa Rogers, & Anna O. Soter. (1995). *How Porcupines Make Love III: Readers, Texts, Cultures in the Response-Based Literature Classroom.* White Plains, NY: Longman Publishers.

Rosenblatt, Louise. (1978). *The Reader, the Text, the Poem: The Transactional Theory of the Literary Work.* Carbondale: Southern Illinois University Press.

Rosenblatt, Louise. (1983). *Literature as Exploration.* New York: Modern Language Association.

Sheridan, Daniel. (November 1991). "Changing Business as Usual: Reader Response in the Classroom." *College English, 53*(7): 804–814.

Totten, Samuel (1987). "The Personal Face of Genocide: Words of Witnesses in the Classroom." Samuel Totten (Ed.), Special issue of the *Social Science Record* ("Genocide: Issues, Approaches, Resources"), *24*(2): 63–67.

Weinreich-Haste, H. (1985). "The Varieties of Intelligence: An Interview with Howard Gardner." *New Ideas in Psychology, 3*(4): 47–65.

Yahil, Leni. (1990). *The Holocaust: The Fate of European Jewry.* New York: Oxford University Press.

Zatzman, Belarie (2001). "Using Drama in a Study of the Holocaust." In Samuel Totten and Stephen Feinberg (Eds.), *Teaching and Studying the Holocaust.* Boston: Allyn and Bacon.

Zelkowicz, Jozef (1994). "25 Live Hens and One Dead Document." In Milton Teichman and Sharon Leder (Eds.), *Truth and Lamentation: Stories and Poems on the Holocaust* (pp. 45–51). Urbana and Chicago: University of Illinois Press.

APPENDIX: DIRECTIONS FOR THE MULTIPLE INTELLIGENCES (MI) APPROACH

Following the reading of three different stories about the Holocaust, each student will decide independently which story he or she wishes to interpret via one or more of the multiple intelligences. After selecting the story he or she wishes to interpret, the student will team up with a group of no more than one to two other students who wish to interpret the same story. Once formed into a team, they will:

1. Discuss the story (its plot, theme, symbols, deeper meanings);
2. Come to a group consensus in regard to what they deem to be the most interesting and significant aspects of the story in regard to its theme, etc.;
3. Make a group decision in regard to those aspects of the story they wish to convey in their interpretation;
4. Discuss, as a group, which intelligence or intelligences would be most useful and interesting in conveying their interpretation of the story;
5. Develop/design a method/way to convey their interpretation. *Again, the interpretation must make use of one or more of the MIs that Gardner has delineated.* The interpretation should be creative, thought-provoking, and in-depth. In other words, it should not be simplistic or perfunctory.
6. Once every group has developed a means to convey its MI interpretation of the story, the class will do the following:
   a. Analyze the presentation/creation of each group;
   b. Without *any* participation from the group that created the interpretation, the whole class will discuss the presentation/creation/interpretation and, in

doing so, attempt to interpret the presentation/creation/interpretation under review. During this part of the activity, each member of the larger group should take an active part and really try to play off of his or her fellow students' ideas in an attempt to come to a thorough understanding regarding what the presentation/creation/interpretation stands for;

c. Once the whole class has completed its analysis and discussion of the presentation/creation/interpretation, the group that designed the work will comment on

(i).   The interpretations offered by its peers (whether they were on target or not and why; whether the creators gained new insights from the group's interpretation and why that is so, etc.);

(ii). Its own interpretation of the work (that is, what it was the group intended to convey); and

(iii). The process (the hows and whys) that the group used to create what it did.

POETRY

CHAPTER

7   "Written in Pencil in the Sealed Railway-Car"

Incorporating Poetry into a Study of the Holocaust via a Reader Response Theory Activity

SAMUEL TOTTEN

In this chapter I discuss how I use reader response theory (which will be described shortly) to engage the students in a study of Dan Pagis's poem entitled "Written in Pencil in the Sealed Railway-Car." The poem is short but extremely thought-provoking; indeed, it is one that never fails to captivate the students' interest. Ultimately, this exercise—which is ideal for use during a single period— illustrates the unusual power that a thought-provoking poem in conjunction with reader response theory (Beach, 1993; Karolides, 1997; Probst, 1988; and Rosenblatt, 1978) can have in assisting students to gain a deeper understanding about various facets of the Holocaust.

My goals in using this strategy are to (1) assist students in gleaning unique insights into the history of the Holocaust; (2) introduce students to a haunting poem on the Holocaust; (3) provide students with the means to examine a piece of Holocaust literature in a unique manner; and (4) leave the students with something to ponder long and hard about. The latter is important, for this history is not simply another piece of history; it has, I believe, immense ramifications in regard to who we are as individual human beings and members of a particular society (the United States), as well as larger society (global) and what it means to live in a world where genocide has become rather commonplace.

At first, many students are puzzled by the "odd" poem; and indeed, some are put off by it. The students' initial responses, though, frequently contribute to the revelatory insights that they eventually glean from both the poem and the activity itself.

This poem and this activity are ideal for use in the social studies, history, or English classroom. They are also ideal for use in an interdisciplinary study of the Holocaust, one in which English and social studies teachers, for example, team up to teach a lesson or unit on the Holocaust. *Before* conducting an activity such as the one described herein, a teacher must decide whether there is a need to provide a historical context for the poem. To a large extent, this will be contingent, of course, on his or her goals and objectives. Providing or not providing a historical context will dramatically affect the students' interpretation of the poem. Some purists of reader response theory may, in fact, argue that students should not be provided with the historical context in that it would inhibit, limit, or sway a student's interpretation. On the other side, purists of Holocaust education may argue—and understandably so—that in order for students to gain the deepest insights possible into a literary work about the Holocaust, they need to understand the historical context of the period *prior* to attempting to interpret the literary piece.

It is the opinion of this author that, ultimately, in order to gain a better and deeper understanding of the Holocaust, as well as of the literary work itself, students need, *at some point*, to be assisted in placing the situation described in the poem within a historical context. This may well be after the students have completed the reader response activity, and that is fine. The point, though, is that such a context will likely provide students with critical insights into the period of the piece, the larger events taking place around the more telescoped events in the literary work, the conflict faced by the characters (including the "choiceless choices"), the setting, etc.

Pagis's poem can be used to reach various goals and objectives and it can be used in various ways. For example, it could be used within a study of the Holocaust to enhance student understanding of certain facets of the history such as the issue of the plight of the victims, the culpability of perpetrators and bystanders, issues of personal responsibility, and the impact the Holocaust has on humanity. Or, it can simply be taught in an English classroom on its own merit as an outstanding piece of poetry. If the poem is taught within the context of a unit on the Holocaust then an ideal place to teach it would be during a discussion of the deportations of the Jews or during an examination of the "relationship" of perpetrators, victims, collaborators, and bystanders.

If a social studies or history teacher is not teaching a lesson or unit on the Holocaust but wishes to provide a historical context for this poem, an efficient way of doing so is to have the students read scholarly essays on the Holocaust (e.g., Niewyk's [1995] "Holocaust: The Genocide of the Jews") or a complete text on the history of the Holocaust (e.g., Michael Berenbaum's *The World Must Know: The History of the Holocaust as Told in the United States Holocaust Memorial Museum.* Boston: Little, Brown, 1993). An alternative to using a book—and this is especially useful for those teachers with limited funds and time—is to show the film entitled *Genocide 1941–1945*, which is part of the World at War Series. The latter relates the story of the destruction of European Jewry through the use of archival footage and the testimony of victims, perpetrators, and bystanders. Ideally, teachers should use a key essay or two to supplement the information about the film. As for English teachers, they may wish to use the poem in conjunction with a novel, memoir (e.g., Elie Wiesel's *Night*), and/or an essay on the history of the Holocaust.

Reader response theory activities such as the one described herein can be used with virtually any poem, short story, novel, or play. Ultimately, the key is to provide a forum for the students to personally react to a work via their own unique perspective, and to provide them with the opportunity to engage in an in-depth and thought-provoking dialogue with their peers and teacher regarding both the aesthetic (literary and personal) and efferent (informational) issues at work in the literary work, to use reader response theorist's terminology (Karolides, 1997, pp. 28; Rosenblatt, 1978).[1] It is a process in which readers construct meaning, drawing on their prior learning and experience (Cox, 1997, p. 32). What is delineated here, then, is just one of innumerable ways to involve students in an engaging and hopefully revelatory discussion about a powerful piece of literature using reader response theory.

Reader Response Theory

Reader response theory is predicated on the idea that each reader comes to a piece of literature with a rich background of worldly experience and a broad knowledge base in many different subjects. Thus, it is assumed that most, if not all, readers will likely have unique insights into a piece of literature; and that by sharing, wrestling with, and reflecting on their own insights as well as on those of others, they will eventually be able to make meaning of a piece of literature—that is, "create their own unique meaning" (Beach, 1993; Rosenblatt, 1978). Of course, this is counter to those who perceive literary works as having a single "correct" meaning or believe that the only "true" way to understand a literary work is by solely studying its symbolic structure, motifs, language, etc. As Louise Rosenblatt notes, reader response theorists believe the reader *should not be perceived* as "a blank tape registering a ready-made message" (quoted in Sheridan, 1991, p. 804).[2] Rather, he or she should be integrally and actively involved in wrestling with all aspects of the literary work in order to construct an understanding of it.

Further, in this regard, reader response theorists posit, and urge teachers to appreciate the fact that in authentic situations "readers respond for a range of different purposes. Readers may respond to express their emotional reactions, to explore difficulties in understanding, to corroborate or verify their opinions with others, to build a social relationship through sharing responses, or to clarify their attitudes" (Beach, 1993, p. 50).

Thus, in part, for a reader to get the most out of a work of literature, he or she must bring his or her own knowledge, insights, and past experiences to bear on his or her reading of the literary work. Put another way, readers must "invest themselves in the experience." (This, of course, does not preclude the examination of symbolic structure, motifs, and other literary concerns. Indeed, many of the latter are likely to arise in the reader's initial and ongoing reaction to the story.) In this way, a reader is constructing meaning as he or she wrestles with the poem, story, or novel.

Ultimately, individual readers take their unique insights and understanding and engage in discussion with others that results in a community of learning. As Sheridan (1991) argues, reader response constitutes a "social act" (p. 805). The reading experience is often more powerful and revelatory when it involves discussion and debate with others. Thus, ideally, when a community of readers comes together, each member's ideas, questions, likes and dislikes, and concerns should converge in a way that helps to illuminate the work under study.

As O'Neill (1994) has written in "Rewriting the Book on Literature: Changes Sought in How Literature is Taught, What Students Read":

> Basically, reader response theory differs most radically from previous theories about teaching literature in the degree of emphasis placed on the reader's response to an interpretation of the text. . . . In reader response theory, the text's meaning is considered to reside in the "transaction" between the reader and the text, not from the text alone.
>
> In practice, reader response theory considers very carefully how students respond intellectually and emotionally to the text . . . By validating students' responses, teachers can spark a lively discussion from which a careful literary analysis will flow. . . . Rather than beginning with a discussion of symbolism or metaphor, for example, teachers should allow an exploration of these aspects to develop from students' own observations about the work.
>
> *The emphasis on getting students to respond to the literature doesn't mean that any response is as good as another. Students are continuously urged to return to the text to find validation for their views.* [italics added] (pp. 7, 8)

The key, then, is to provide students with an opportunity to begin to examine literature from their own unique perspective, without imposing either the teacher's or a critic's interpretation on them. What is at work here is the purposeful avoidance of expecting the students to "please the teacher" by coming up with the "single correct answer." As anyone who appreciates the beauty and power of literature knows, good literature is multilayered and, concomitantly, the meaning inherent in a literary work is also multilayered. Thus, when students are prodded—as they often are in the so-called traditional classroom—to come up with the "correct answer" in regard to the meaning of a poem or novel, the result is often a perfunctory study bereft of real thinking and engagement by the student; not to mention a minimization, if not distortion, of the multiple interpretations inherent in any solid literary work.

As Karolides (1997) notes: "In [a reader response approach], it is understood that no person can read/experience a literary text for another. A friend or teacher telling you about a book is not an act of reading—engagement—for you, nor is reading a summary an act of experiencing the text. [Likewise, a teacher telling a student what a text means does not allow for student engagement with a text.] Others can no more read or experience a text for you than they can relieve your hunger pangs by eating your dinner" (p. 9).

[handwritten: ONE RESPONSE NOT AS GOOD AS ANOTHER]

Finally, as noted earlier, "The emphasis on getting students to respond to the literature doesn't mean that any response is as good as another" (O'Neill, 1994, p. 8). Indeed, not only will certain students' points be more perspicacious, but the teacher also has a significant role to play in "orchestrating" the class discussion. It is during the latter that he or she should urge the students to play off of one another's ideas, challenge the students to dig deeper, and play the devil's advocate. It is also during this time that the teacher is able to assist students to explore issues that they may be only alluding to in the most peripheral of ways or may not be addressing at all. In this way the teacher is able to introduce historical and literary issues and concerns and provide a context for a more penetrating discussion of the literary work. As Karolides (1997) notes, "Readers' responses may be enhanced and deepened with selected strategies to evoke the impact of language—word play, structural and stylistic effects . . . as well as historical-cultural insights. These are usually most appropriate after the reader has [responded on his or her own to the work]" (p. 18). Further, Karolides (1997) observes that "[h]elping students to consider the relationship of their experiences to the text and to suggest routes of connection and understanding is consequential in process reading" (p. 6).

Directions for the Activity

Initially, one should simply project the poem on an overhead. Alternatively, the teacher could photocopy the poem and provide each student with his or her own copy:

Written in Pencil in the Sealed Railway-Car
by Dan Pagis[3]

Here in this carload
I am Eve
With Abel my son
If you see my other son
Cain son of man
Tell him that I . . .

From *Points of Departure*. Published 1982 by the Jewish Publication Society. Used by permission.

The exact directions given the students are as follows: "In your letter to Dan Pagis, the poet, you may write anything you wish about the poem. You may tell the poet what you like or dislike about the poem, what you don't understand about it, that you don't like it, and/or you may ask probing questions about the poem or even offer your own interpretation and insights. The point is, you may approach it in any way you wish. It is your perspective, your point of view that is important. Don't write this for me, the teacher, write it for yourself in which you present your most honest response to the poem."

Once any questions the students may have about the directions for the assignment are addressed, it is a good idea to ask, What does every letter begin with? (The students will generally answer "the date" and "a salutation or greeting.") The students should also be asked: "And what do letters generally conclude with?" (Here the students usually answer with "a closing" and "your name.") If the teacher does not ask such questions, many students will neglect to set the assignment up in letter format.

Next, the students should be given 15 to 20 minutes to write their letters. Initially, many students will moan and groan and complain that they cannot think of what to say. Allow the groaning but warn them not to say anything aloud *at all* about why they feel they do not have anything to say. That, and anything else they wish to comment on, should be included in their letters. As with any assignment, some students will finish in a matter of minutes, while others will still be writing once the 15 to 20 minutes is up.

At the conclusion of the writing activity, students should be placed in groups of three or four and given the following directions: "Initially, each person should simply read his or her letter while the rest of the group listens. Once everyone has read his or her piece, each person should read his or her letter again. This time, however, after each person reads his or her letter, a discussion should ensue. During the course of the discussion, the other members of the group are free to ask questions and make comments about the other person's letter; and in doing so, one may corroborate certain points by drawing on thoughts and feelings reflected in one's own letter and/or play the devil's advocate by questioning and probing. As you discuss the ideas in the various letters, be sure to keep returning to the poem in order to substantiate and clarify your ideas. As soon as the discussion of one person's letter wanes, the next person in line should read his or her letter and the process of discussion should begin anew."

I further explain that in order for the class to conduct a large-group (e.g., class) follow-up discussion, it will be necessary for each group to have a recorder who jots down the most pertinent points made during the course of the small group discussion. That being the case, I ask each group to quickly decide who the recorder is going to be, and I ask for that individual to raise his or her hand. The latter ensures that each group has a recorder. After all of the recorders have been duly noted, I tell the students that during the general discussion the onus *will not be on the recorder* to carry the discussion for his or her group, but rather it will be the responsibility of the entire group to expound on their collective ideas. Thus, while the recorder will initially share the key points that have been made in his or her group, any subsequent discussion of the group's points should be a group effort.

As the small groups engage in the aforementioned work, I circulate from group to group, and, as a rule, I simply listen to the discussion and refrain from making any comments. However, if an individual or an entire group is stuck at a point where they are simply saying "The poem doesn't make any sense," I offer the following advice and encouragement: "OK, that's a good starting point. Now you need to discuss *why* it doesn't make any sense. What aspects/components of the poem lead you to make that judgment. Start with that, and I assure you that your discussion will lead into some very interesting and fruitful areas." Once students broach their points, they should be encouraged to try to relate them to what that may tell us about the poem. With some groups it takes more encouragement and prodding than others, but by gently prodding and urging them to go with their initial reactions and then to examine and wrestle with those, the students inevitably come up with some very interesting, and often perspicacious, insights. As Allen and Reed (1997) note, it is often the "discussions in a small group, as opposed to talk in the larger, whole-class context, [that] provide opportunities for [students] to fully share, examine, and clarify their responses to literature" (p. 55).

It is during the small group and large group discussions (which will be delineated below) that the real work of the teacher begins. By listening in on the small groups and jotting notes down about what the students are discussing and wrestling with, the instructor is able, during the large group discussion, to help students make connections between various students' comments. Furthermore, in the large group discussion, the instructor is able to broach issues that were discussed in small groups that might not, for whatever reason, be brought up in the large discussion group. Both of these strategies assist in maintaining the flow of the discussion, deepening the discussion, and challenging the students to play off of one another's ideas and to consider various and sometimes radically different points of view. I have found that during those few class sessions where I neglected to take notes and/or did not broach issues that generated heated discussion in the small groups that many times the large group discussions were not as dynamic, interesting, or thought-provoking as they could or should have been.

As for the value of the large group discussion, another instructor who uses reader response in her class has made the following observation:

> I think that another thing [that working] in a group [does for students is that it allows them to] build on other people's comments; it seems to open doors [for them], doors of understanding, and [they] are able to reach into stories more deeply. It's like an oh! and then [they] pick up on something and take it a step further, and I think that's something that an in-depth group [discussion] can provide for [them]. (Allen and Reed, 1997, p. 61)

Discussion of the Activity

Herein I shall highlight the various responses a group of 10th-, 11th-, and 12th-grade students came up with in a special college preparatory summer course held at the University of Arkansas, Fayetteville, for young people whose family members have never attended college. In doing so, I shall provide direct quotes from their letters and comment on the gist of the discussion that ensued in the small and/or large groups. What follows constitutes only a fraction of the number of issues that was addressed in the period-long discussion.

It is worth noting that the students who wrote these responses were engaged in a study of the Holocaust. It is not surprising, then, that some of the students directly related this poem to certain aspects of the Holocaust. That said, this poem generates a fascinating and worthwhile discussion whether or not students are studying the Holocaust. If the students are not studying the Holocaust, it is interesting to see how they relate the poem to various historical periods. For example, in certain cases in the past students have related the poem to the slaves fleeing bondage via the Underground Railroad and the deprivation of human rights in South America. Interestingly, other students in the same classes have also related the poem to the Holocaust.

> Dear Dan,
>   What can I say? I don't understand poetry much so this just blows my mind. It doesn't rhyme, it doesn't make sense. It is a fragment. What does it mean?

This is an honest and heartfelt response. Interestingly, it goes beyond the lack of comprehension that the student suggests he or she is experiencing. Indeed, it addresses the structure of the poem (bereft of rhyme, which could lead to an interesting discussion as to why the topic Pagis is writing about might not lend itself to rhyming), and the fragmentary sense of the poem (which actually generated a whole class discussion about the situation Eve is in and what that has to do with fragmentation—of the spoken word, of emotions, and the fragmentation caused in the world by hate, prejudice, and violence).

> Dear Mr. Pagis,
>   I don't get what you mean in your poem. Did you not finish it? I see you have two sons, but why do you use Cain and Able [*sic*]? I did not get your poem because of the words not meaning anything and the words not fitting together in my mind.

In a traditional discussion of literature a teacher may be quite discouraged by such a response, but when using reader response theory such a response provides a series of excellent entry points to the poem. Again, the teacher and the rest of the students in the group will need to probe what the writer of the letter does not seem to understand. As they work together to unknot that lack of understanding, ideas will begin to flow. In actuality, this student provides plenty of food for thought. First, there is the issue of whether or not the poet completed the poem. Second, the very fact that the student broaches the issue of the names of Cain and Abel provides everyone with the opportunity to discuss the meaning of the names, how they are related (pun intended), possibly the historical and biblical significance of the names, and the role they play in this poem.

Even when students' letters appear flippant in tone, there is often ample food for thought and discussion. For example:

> Dan,
>   I don't see how a man could be Eve. I will do you a favor by telling Cain that "I . . ." So, how is Abel. Has he and Cain gotten on better

terms? I hope so. My thoughts of this poem are, you didn't eat anything with hallucinaginics [*sic*], did you? If you didn't then I will pray for you. So, how is the railway-car? You only mentioned Cain being the son of man. Does this mean he is not the son of woman, too?

While the tone of the letter is distasteful and juvenile, the issues broached here branched out into a worthwhile discussion concerning many aspects of the poem. A key aspect is: Who is the speaker of the poem—the poet or the persona of Eve? The student also realizes and broaches the point, even if a bit sarcastically, that Eve is calling on the reader to convey her message for her. As a result, the reader is drawn into the situation that is taking place in the poem. The "oddity" of the poem is broached through the allusion to hallucinogenics, and this issue provoked the students to examine exactly why and what makes the poem seem so odd. In doing so, they discussed the abrupt and inconclusive "ending." Even the nonchalant and distasteful question about the railway car led to a discussion about the fact that it is sealed, and the immense ramifications of that. Finally, the whole issue of what "son of man" means here can lead to a discussion of humanity's place (e.g., responsibility) in regard to the situation highlighted in the poem. If the students do not broach such issues as this, the teacher certainly can do so; and from there, he or she can lead the students in an open discussion in which they air their opinions and insights.

> Dear Mr. Pagis,
>   I have read your poem and I'm not sure that I understand the meaning. What exactly did you want the readers to get out of it? It seems to be incomplete, almost as if you stopped in the middle of a thought. I'm definitely not a poet but I think this poem needs something to make the point a little clearer. Maybe this has something to do with Cain killing Abel. That could be why you called him the son of man. Maybe referring [*sic*] that man is evil. That is the only thing that comes to mind upon reading this poem.

Even though this student claims she is confused by the poem, her comments and questions raise a host of important issues. First, she addresses the abrupt ending of the poem, and—notwithstanding the fact that she assumes incorrectly that Pagis is the persona speaking in the poem—she even suggests a reason for the abrupt ending. She also considers the biblical allusion and carries that thought over to the evil in the world. While her thoughts appear in fits and starts, they provide fascinating clues to the meaning of the poem. Indeed, her comments generated ample discussion among her fellow group members.

> Dear Eve,
>   Where are you going? Why have you lost your son Cain? What am I to tell him? Are you safe with your son Abel?
>   Why is Cain the son of man? I will hope you find him—even if he had done something wrong. But, I really don't know what you want.

gendered approach —
~~letter~~ *to Eve*

While this student did not follow the exact directions of the assignment (i.e., write a letter to the poet), her letter to Eve is thought-provoking. She was one of the few students to ask Eve where she was going and whether she was safe or not. This, in turn, prompted the students to ask: What are the exact circumstances here? and Why is the railway car sealed? Like others, this student also raises the issue of the phrase *son of man,* and more specifically, she wonders why Cain (as opposed to Abel) is referred to as the *son of man.* (The student's "mistake" in writing to Eve is an interesting one, and suggests that an alternative assignment could require the students to write the letter to Eve rather than Pagis. In fact, the more I think about this alternative, the more sense it makes.)

> Dear Mr. Pagis,
> The poem you have written titled "Written in Pencil in the Sealed Railway-Car" is very unique. I would like to know what Eve was going to say before she died. If she were to finish, I'm sure we could tell her son what she wanted us to say. I am very concerned about what she wanted us to tell him.

This student has obviously connected with the poem, and feels the need to convey Eve's message to the rest of the world. The fact that she (the student) is concerned about Eve's admonition to the reader to carry her message to Cain resulted in a discussion that centered around the connection between the speaker and the reader of the poem. It also prompted students to focus on what Eve was about to say as well as why Eve never completed her message.

> Dear Dan Pagis,
> Was it that you couldn't say the words? Maybe you felt that if you said them they would become true. That what you were actually trying to do was say good bye forever.
> Somehow I know that the last two words to your poem are "love him." I bet that he knew that.
> Where is the railway car taking you and did you ever get to say those two little words to Cain?
> What is the biblical significance? I'm clueless! Best wishes and I admire your strength.

While this student is confused as to what is the true voice in the poem, the student is anything but "clueless." Indirectly, the student questions why Eve did not complete her thoughts. The student's guess is that Eve did not want to risk bringing about the reality of what she feared. During the whole class discussion the former point generated a series of thought-provoking ideas such as the possibility that Eve's pencil broke, that she had abruptly arrived at her destination and was being forced out of the railway car, that someone was possibly preventing her from completing her thought, and that she may have died or been killed.

This student also raises the issue as to why Eve is even in a railway car; and at one and the same time, she raises the issue of Eve's fate. Finally, by raising the biblical implications of the names, this student prompted other students to delve into the poet's rationale in using such names. Indeed, during the students' general discussion of this point, they undertook an enlightening discussion of Genesis and the concomitant issues of good and evil (including the significance of the apple and the snake in the garden, the transgression of Adam and Eve, and what the forbidden knowledge eventually wrought).

> Dear Mr. Pagis,
>
> I must say that I am having some difficulty understanding your poem. Weren't you able to finish it? Maybe there is a meaning to the work which only you comprehend. I know that I cannot interpret your exact thoughts at the time you wrote your poem because I was not there. Was Eve scared? Was she being watched? Perhaps you or Eve wanted your readers to try to finish the poem and take it into their own hearts. I will keep wondering.

In addition to various other points, this student broaches the issue of the responsibility of the reader to complete the poem, or, at the very least, to continue to contemplate its meaning. In that way, she suggests that the incomplete nature of the poem serves the purpose of prodding the reader to dig deeper into the poem and, indirectly, the need for continued vigilance and remembrance vis-à-vis the various issues raised by the Holocaust—both of which are directly tied to the survivors' admonition to future generations to "Never Forget!" and "Remember!"

The next three letters are all indicative of the emotive nature that the letters can take. Each of the students seems to identify with Eve's situation; and thus, instead of approaching this assignment as just one more assignment to get out of the way, each of the students effectively combines the cognitive and affective in a unique and powerful way:

> Dear Mr. Pagis,
>
> Your poem started to bring tears to my eyes. I could imagine you with one of your sons, perhaps the son who'd always been good and kind. But, as you realized that perhaps you'd never see your other son again, you realized all the things you wanted to say before you died, but never got to say. . . . Your poem made me think about the mortality we all have, and how we should be at peace with our fellow neighbors.

> Dear Dan,
>
> After reading your poem, I immediately wondered what your intent was. Is everything in life insignificant except for forgiveness and love? Is that what you wanted to tell Cain, the murderer? Or is it that you wanted to chastise Cain, blaming him for starting the string of murders throughout the generations? I must admit I like the poem, perhaps mostly because it can have such a double meaning. I am beginning to feel that the maternal view suggests love and forgiveness, but

even mothers can be cold and unforgiving—especially if other loved ones are hurt.

> Dear Dan Pagis,
>   I do not like your poem. I took the meaning to be a mother with her son who is on the train on her way to die. I don't think that she can find her other son, but she wants someone to tell him where she is going, but she doesn't want to say that she is about to die. I don't like this poem because I think that it is extremely sad and depressing, and I cannot even begin to imagine all of the horrible thoughts that must be going through her head.

In addition to emoting over the piece, the author of the last letter offers the insight that Eve can't bring herself to tell her other son the truth. The student obviously identifies with Eve's acute pain, and though she doesn't like the poem, it is equally obvious that the poem has deeply affected her.

As previously mentioned, numerous students made a connection to the Holocaust, or at least alluded to it. Among the letters that reflect such a connection are as follows:

> Dear Mr. Pagis,
>   Your poem does not make sense to me. It is unclear when you [*sic*] read it and the poem is confusing. The more I read it, though, the clearer it gets. You are trying to say that you lost a son but you still have one left. You use names of people from the Bible to emphasize your point. You know what you are writing. You are saying that the son of man, referred to as Cain, symbolizes the Germans who are killing people such as Cain did Abel, and that the mother, Eve, or the Jewish people, is very sorrowful over all the murders. That is all I understand of it.

> Dear Dan Pagis,
>   I am thinking that Eve and her son Abel are curious to know why Cain did what he did—which was murdering an innocent victim. I am wondering if this was in the back of the Jews, Gypsies and some of the German's minds. It seems to be very obvious as to why they would ask such a question. I think the Jews and the other victims—in a similar but somewhat different vein from Eve's—would wonder why and how they (the Nazis) or he (Cain) would and could do this. I think it is a sense of confusion in their eyes.

> Dear Dan Pagis:
>   The mental picture that I received from your poem was of a young Jewish woman being stripped of her rights as she boarded a railway car to one of the death camps. I imagined her holding a small child. I believe it reaches much deeper because Cain, the son of man, is used as

a symbol of the Nazis. Cain, in the Bible, killed his own brother Abel, just like the Nazis killed their fellow brothers, the Jews.

Dear Dan,

Your poem is very emotional. I can see your point clearly. The ending gave it a sense of reality. How it never ended, just like the Holocaust has never really ended.

Dear Dan:

I liked your poem alot [*sic*] because it described human beings during the period of the Holocaust. To me, Eve symbolized the human race and its goodness. Abel symbolized the Jews and others who were being persecuted. Cain symbolized the Nazis and the people who can't see past the material world and who symbolize all that is wrong with our society today.

The Actual Class Discussion: A Vignette

What follows is a minute segment of the actual large class discussion that ensued around Pagis's poem. Pseudonyms are used throughout.

GREG: I've never seen, that is read, anything like it [the poem]. It's just so different. . . . Like, well, first of all, it just stops. . . . There's no . . .

GEOFF: Yeah, it's abrupt!

SHELLY: I think Eve was so overwhelmed with her situation, so distraught, that it was as if something were caught in her throat; that is, that she was so grief-stricken, she just couldn't get the words out.

CINDY: Yeah, our small group discussed that possibility as well. But we also considered the possibility that all of a sudden the doors of the train opened and all chaos broke out as they were assaulted by—

GEOFF: Yeah, they arrived at a concentration or death camp and she didn't have time to complete her thought and—

FRANCISCO: And she either died or was murdered there.

GEOFF: Or that she died in the boxcar . . . was suffocated.

DAVID: Possibly, but there are all sorts of other possibilities as well. It was written in pencil so maybe the lead broke. Or maybe she was pushed and shoved in such a way that she couldn't move her arm. Or, yeah, maybe she was suffocated and died in the boxcar, or—

CINDY: I still think she was overwhelmed . . . it is just . . . so horrible that she runs out of words. Here is a mother who is caught up in this inferno and she doesn't know where she is heading with her one son—and then, again, maybe she does—and she doesn't know the whereabouts of her other son.

KELLY: And look who the mother is: Eve, the mother of us all.

GEOFF: Yeah . . . yeah . . . but where is Adam, her husband.

CINDY: We don't know that but we do know that she is with her one good son, Abel, and she doesn't know where her bad son, Cain, who slew Abel, is. . . .

DAVID: Let's go back for a second to who Eve is. Over and above the fact that she is, as Kelly says, "the mother of us all," isn't she also the one who was responsible for evil in the world?

GREG: Whoa, you guys are good.

SAEED: We talked about that in our group, too, but in this case, during the Holocaust, it was the Nazis who were and are responsible. In fact, we discussed how Cain may represent the Nazis and Abel and his mother the Jews. So, on the one hand, when it comes right down to it, while we are all different, we are also all the same, humans, one another's brothers and sisters *but, then again,* that doesn't seem to matter for the differences, to some, outweigh the similarities and that often results in prejudice, racism, discrimination and at its most extreme, murder and mass murder.

GREG: Man, yeah!

DAVID: So what we have are the victims and the perpetrators and what's that make us, the read—

MARK: Collaborators?

DAVID: No, I don't think so. I think it makes us kind of like witnesses.

MARK: You mean, bystanders?

DAVID: No, witnesses! I see them as being different. We're witnesses today, not then.

SHELLY: Well, that kind of plays into another way of seeing the end of the poem, which, I think, is not so much the end as . . . well, it does just seem to just end but if you read the last line and the first line together, it's like the poem starts all over again: "tell him that i, here in this carload."

REGGIE: Hey, yeah! So it's like it never ends . . . like the hatred and the fighting and the killing?

SHELLY: Maybe, or that evil is always with us and that the situation that was played out at the beginning of time, in the Garden of Eden—this evil of brother against brother—is with us like . . . like a stain . . . like . . .

CINDY: Like the mark of Cain. . . .

SHELLY: Right!

TOTTEN: In one small group discussion it was suggested that the poem is fragmented. Is that germane to what you are saying here? Also, if it is fragmented is that somehow significant?

NATHAN: Yeah, we said that! It's like the Jewish people, in a sense, after the Holocaust. Only a fragment is left. I mean, look, six million people were murdered, died, at the hands of the Nazis.

RICHARD: I don't know if this makes sense or not, but the world seems fragmented, broken. You know what I mean?

NATHAN: Yeah, it is. It's like, how can the world remain the same or whole or not broken after something as . . . as horrible . . . as devastating as the Holocaust.

SAL: We, my group, thought that the title "sealed railway car" referred to the gas chambers, you know, how they were, what's the word, her . . . hermet . . .

SHELLY: Yeah, hermetically sealed.

SAL: Right, hermetically sealed.

As one readily ascertains, the resultant discussion was free-flowing, with the students playing off of one another's ideas. And while the discussion seems to be switching from one topic to another, two things actually happen during such a discussion: First, the students always end up addressing a host of pertinent issues; and second, sooner or later, sometimes at the urging of the instructor but often under their own volition, the students return to many key issues and ultimately discuss them in a good amount of depth.

During the course of the discussion, the teacher ought to feel free to challenge the students to move from their initial observations and insights into an even deeper probing of the poem. For example, at some point—but certainly not until *after* the subject of Cain and Abel is first broached by a student (as the brothers almost always will be) and their significance is amply discussed by the class—the teacher should probe, if the students do not do so, how the "historical" Cain and Abel differ, if in fact they do, from the "contemporary" (in this case, the "Holocaustal") Cain and Abel. That is, it is worth having the students ponder what literary critic Lawrence Langer (1998) asserts is the "the shift from fratricide to genocide" (p. 61). Some advocates of reader response may feel that this is "leading" the students to a particular interpretation, but my sense is that if it is done carefully and with the right intention, it will broaden and deepen the discussion in a positive manner.

Conclusion

While most of the students initially asserted that Pagis's poem made little or no sense to them, all of them ended up positing critical questions and issues that were worthy of ample discussion. It was through such questioning and discussion that they eventually came to a clearer and deeper understanding and appreciation of the poem. Indeed, it is through the combination of in-depth discussion with their peers and the teacher's guiding and probing questions that students are able to mine a wealth of meaning from a poem that, at the outset, seemed somewhat confusing, if not meaningless to them. As Cox (1997) has stated:

> [It is] the tension and discomfort that seem to produce the rich, meaningful, and diverse responses students produce when they question or challenge a text. The

children I have observed are most engaged with literature when something irritates them, like a grain of sand in the oyster that eventually produces a pearl. Encouraging children to respond authentically and aesthetically, to address the things they find anomalous, and accepting diversity of responses could provide a rich medium of growth for reading and language development as well as literary understanding, critical interpretation, and self-knowledge through transactions with literary works. (p. 47)

Concomitantly, in this case, it is through such discussions—in which the students wrestle with the meaning of the poem—that the students can, ultimately, with some guidance from their teacher—come to a deeper and more profound understanding of various aspects of the Holocaust.

Students are generally anxious for the teacher to tell them what the "meaning" of the poem is, or at least what the poet had in mind. In fact, during the small group discussions many students asked me what Pagis meant by the poem. I answered that I did not have *the* answer to that question, and that, together, we had to do our utmost to come up with our understanding of the poem.

What I do share with the students *at the conclusion of the exercise* is that Pagis was a Holocaust survivor. More specifically, I tell them that Dan Pagis was born in Bukovina (formerly part of Austria, then Romania, and finally Russia) in 1930, and that he spent his early years in a concentration camp in the Ukraine from which he escaped in 1944. I also share with them that eventually he settled in Israel where he became a well-known poet, and that he died in 1986.

NOTES

1. In regard to the efferent and aesthetical stances, Cox (1997) states that: "Any text can be read efferently or aesthetically, and readers move back and forth on a continuum from efferent to aesthetic. . . . During a more efferent reading, the reader's focus of attention is on the information the reader will take away from the text. . . . During a more aesthetic reading, the reader's focus of attention is on the lived-through experience of the reading event, or the more private aspects; for example, reading a novel and picturing yourself as one of the characters. A more efferent reading focuses on what is in the text and a more aesthetic reading focuses on the associations, feelings, attitudes, and ideas that the text aroused in the reader. Most readings are a mix of both stances, and any text can be read more efferently or more aesthetically and readers may adopt a different stance toward the same text at different times and in different situations. Rosenblatt maintains that for most experiences with literature, our primary responsibility is to encourage the aesthetic stance" (pp. 30–31).

2. In 1978, with the publication of *The Reader, The Text, The Poem,* Louise Rosenblatt focused more specifically on a pedagogical program for the classroom. She was highly critical of the narrow focus of much literature instruction in inferring "correct answers." This led to her distinction between two opposing modes of experiencing a text—the "efferent" and the "aesthetic." In responding in an efferent mode, readers are driven by specific pragmatic needs to acquire information; they simply want to comprehend what the text is saying. . . . In contrast, in responding in the aesthetic mode, readers are responding according to their own unique lived "through experience or engagement with a text . . .

"Rosenblatt recognizes that readers may shift back and forth along a continuum between efferent and aesthetic modes of reading. ". . . Unfortunately, teachers often use activities that entail only efferent responses: short-answer or multiple-choice questions that presuppose a 'correct answer,' discussion questions that are limited to 'literal recall,' questions about 'known information,' or discussions that are 'recitations' in which 'procedural display' of 'mock participation' undermines any genuine, mutual sharing or experience. Thus, in reading a text in preparation for a class, students anticipate responding in an efferent mode, limiting their experience to getting the facts . . . by setting an interpretive agenda in advance of a class, which leads the student toward a particular meaning, a teacher undermines the potential for the surprising, unusual response" (Beach, 1993, pp. 50–51).

3. Certain anthologies reprint Pagis's poem in all lower case letters. Hebrew, which is the language in which the poem was originally written, is not comprised of upper or lowercase letters. That is, all letters are the same font or size. Thus, when the poem appears in English and the print is all lowercase, readers should not assume that the proper nouns (Eve, Cain, Abel) that appear in lowercase have a special or symbolic significance.

It is worth noting that some variations of the poem also include ellipses at the very end of the poem, following the line "tell him that I. . . . ," while others do not. The ellipses mean to some that the poem is circular and thus suggest the "need" to return to the first line of the poem, "Here in this carload." Ultimately, teachers will have to decide which version of the poem makes the most sense to use.

REFERENCES

Books

Allen, Shelley H., & Reed, Peg. (1997). "Talking About Literature 'In Depth': Teacher-Supported Group Discussion in a Fifth-Grade Classroom." In Nicholas J. Karolides (Ed.), *Reader Response in Elementary Classrooms: Quest and Discovery* (pp. 53–68). Mahwah, NJ: Lawrence Erlbaum Associates.

Beach, Richard. (1993). *A Teacher's Introduction to Reader-Response Theories.* Urbana, IL: National Council of Teachers of English.

Berenbaum, Michael. (1993). *The World Must Know: The History of the Holocaust as Told in the United States Holocaust Memorial Museum.* Boston, MA: Little, Brown.

Cox, Carole. (1997). "Literature-Based Teaching: A Student Response-Centered Classroom." In Nicholas J. Karolides (Ed.), *Reader Response in Elementary Classrooms: Quest and Discovery* (pp. 29–49). Mahwah, NJ: Lawrence Erlbaum Associates.

Karolides, Nicholas J. (Ed.) (1997). *Reader Response in Elementary Classrooms: Quest and Discovery.* Mahwah, NJ: Lawrence Erlbaum Associates.

Karolides, Nicholas J. (1997). "The Reading Process: Transactional Theory in Action." In Nicholas J. Karolides (Ed.), *Reader Response in Elementary Classrooms: Quest and Discovery* (pp. 3–28). Mahwah, NJ: Lawrence Erlbaum Associates.

Langer, Lawrence L. (1998). "The Alarmed Vision: Social Suffering and Holocaust Atrocity." In Lawrence Langer (Ed.), *Preempting the Holocaust* (pp. 59–79). New Haven, CT: Yale University Press.

Niewyk, Donald L. (1995). "Holocaust: The Genocide of the Jews." In Samuel Totten, William S. Parsons, and Israel W. Charny (Eds.), *Genocide in the Twentieth Century: Critical Essays and Eyewitness Accounts* (pp. 167–207). New York: Garland Publishing.

O'Neill, John. (1994, June). "Rewriting the Book on Literature: Changes Sought in How Literature is Taught, What Students Read." *ASCD Curriculum Update,* 1–4, 6–8.

Pagis, Dan. (1989). "Written in Pencil in the Sealed Railway-Car." In *Variable Directions: The Selected Poetry of Dan Pagis.* San Francisco: North Point Press.

Poe, Elizabeth A., & Hicks, Nyanne J. (1997). "Journey through the Eastern Hemisphere: Listening and Responding to Many Voices." In Nicholas J. Karolides (Ed.), *Reader Response in Elementary Classrooms: Quest and Discovery* (pp. 261–277). Mahwah, NJ: Lawrence Erlbaum Associates.

Probst, Robert. (1988). *Response and Analysis: Teaching Literature in Junior and Senior High School.* Upper Montclair, NJ: Boynton/Cook.

Purves, Alan, Rogers, Theresa, & Soter, Anna O. (1995). *How Porcupines Make Love III: Readers, Texts, Cultures in the Response-Based Literature Classroom.* White Plains, NY: Longman Publishers.

Rosenblatt, Louise. (1978). *The Reader, The Text, The Poem: The Transactional Theory of the Literary Work.* Carbondale, IL: Southern Illinois University Press.

Rosenblatt, Louise. (1983). *Literature as Exploration.* New York: Modern Language Association.

Sheridan, Daniel. (1991, November). "Changing Business as Usual: Reader Response in the Classroom." *College English, 53*(7): 804–814.

Film

Genocide 1941–1945. World at War Series. Available from Arts and Entertainment Home Video, P.O. Box 2284, South Burlington, VT 05407.

SELECT BIBLIOGRAPHY OF BOOKS ON READER RESPONSE THEORY

Richard Beach, *A Teacher's Introduction to Reader-Response Theories* (Urbana, IL: National Council of Teachers of English, 1993). 209 pp. Paperback. Beach provides a comprehensive overview of the wide range of reader-response theories that have dramatically impacted the field of literary theory, criticism, and pedagogy. In doing so, he highlights the work of such theorists as Louise Rosenblatt, M.S. Abrams, and Terry Eagleton.

Nicholas J. Karolides. (Ed.), *Reader Response in Elementary Classrooms: Quest and Discovery.* (Mahwah, NJ: Lawrence Erlbaum Associates, 1997). 368 pp. Paperback. This volume comprises 17 essays that address a variety of key issues and approaches vis-à-vis the incorporation of reader response theory into the elementary classroom. Many of the essays—"The Reading Process: Transactional Theory in Action," "Literature-Based Teaching: A Student Response-Centered Classroom," "Talking About Literature 'In-Depth': Teacher-Supported Group Discussion in a Fifth-Grade Classroom," and "Journeying Through the Eastern Hemisphere: Listening and Responding to Many Voices"—address ideas and issues that teachers at all levels (elementary through the college level) are likely to find enlightening.

Robert Probst. *Response and Analysis: Teaching Literature in Junior and Senior High School.* (Upper Montclair, NJ: Boynton/Cook, 1988). 272 pp. Paperback. In this highly readable book, Probst draws on the work of Rosenblatt to argue that the meaning of a literary work does not simply reside in the text but in the transaction between the reader and the text.

Alan C. Purves, Theresa Rogers, & Anna O. Soter. *How Porcupines Make Love III: Readers, Texts, Cultures in the Response-Based Literature Classroom.* (White Plains, NY: Longman Publishers, 1995). 215 pp. Paperback. Extremely engaging and teacher friendly, this book provides valuable insights into how teachers from the middle level through the high school level can incorporate reader response theory into the classroom.

Louise Rosenblatt. *Literature as Exploration* (New York: Modern Language Association, 1983). 304 pp. Paperback. In this influential work, Rosenblatt discusses the importance of the interaction of the text and reader, and includes numerous suggestions for tying various analytical approaches to the affective domain of learning. In part, Rosenblatt discusses the social concepts that impact the study of literature and examines what the student brings to the process.

Louise Rosenblatt. *The Reader, The Text, The Poem: The Transactional Theory of the Literary Work* (Carbondale, IL: Southern Illinois University Press, 1978). 210 pp. Paperback. In this highly acclaimed work, Rosenblatt provides a solid theoretical basis for the reader response approach.

CHAPTER

8

The Babi Yar Massacre

Seeking Understanding Using a Multimedia Approach

WILLIAM R. FERNEKES

Studying the Holocaust poses many curricular and pedagogical challenges to the classroom teacher. Among the most difficult is helping students establish connections between three core topics in Holocaust education: the historical foundations of antisemitism, the actual policies and practices of Nazi Germany, and the legacy of the Holocaust for contemporary society. Each of these topics has multiple dimensions and could constitute separate courses in their own right. But within the limited time available for classroom instruction at the precollegiate level, curriculum units can be developed that pose questions inviting students to consider critical relationships among such core topics.

This chapter presents a curricular unit successfully employed in multiple classes at Hunterdon Central Regional High School in Flemington, New Jersey. Within the social studies course "The Holocaust and Human Behavior," and after having learned about the historical foundations of antisemitism in Western society, particularly during the nineteenth and early twentieth centuries, 11th- and 12th-grade students examine the Babi Yar massacre as a case study of Nazi policy in the Soviet Union. The Babi Yar massacre was chosen as the focus of this study for several distinct reasons. First, given the time constraints faced by classroom teachers, selecting one case study emblematic of Nazi Germany's genocidal processes in this phase of the Holocaust is an appropriate strategy to enhance the depth of the study. As the largest single case of mass executions conducted by the Einsatzgruppen in the U.S.S.R. during World War II, the Babi Yar massacre demonstrates, in exacting detail, the determined efforts of Nazi Germany to annihilate Jews set in the context of its (Nazi Germany's) war of racial extermination against the Soviet Union. Second, the availability of perpetrator and survivor testimony, as well as historical documents outlining the aims and actions of the Einsatzgruppen, make the Babi Yar massacre an ideal case for student inquiry regarding the close relationship between Nazi Germany's military aims and its genocidal project against the Jews. Third, there is substantial evidence available on both the historical events themselves and the controversy surrounding the efforts to suppress commemoration of this brutal tragedy in the Soviet Union following the end of World War II. Finally, the poem "Babi Yar" by Yevgeny Yevtushenko is a powerful indictment of antisemitism, which makes its significance for study of the Holocaust and its legacy even more compelling.

Complementing the focus on the development of historical understanding, the unit employs literary and multimedia sources—primarily Yevtushenko's poem "Babi Yar," selected eyewitness accounts, German government documents, documentary photographs, and music (Shostakovich's Symphony no. 13)—to render a complex picture of the Babi Yar massacre and its legacy for classroom study. As constructed within the Powerpoint computer presentation software, the goal is to have students consider the legacy of the Holocaust for contemporary society, using the controversy in the Soviet Union about the contents of the poem "Babi Yar" and Shostakovich's Symphony no. 13 as the catalyst for issues-based inquiry. Integrating the study of documentary, literary, photographic, and audio-visual sources facilitates the engagement of a broad range of learning styles while helping students recognize that study of the Holocaust, although rooted in historical understanding, retains significance in how current generations construct meaning about the past and navigate the relationship between memory and history. (See the Appendix to this chapter for specific unit goals and a listing of resources employed.) The chapter concludes with suggestions for future research about curricular and instructional issues in Holocaust education emerging from this case study.

Historical Context

On June 22, 1941, Germany invaded the Soviet Union. Integral to the design of the German invasion was the mass killing of civilians by specially trained SS units, known as Einsatzgruppen, or "special killing squads." The four Einsatzgruppen units, each consisting of approximately 900 officers and men, entered the occupied Soviet Union following the advancing troops of the Wehrmacht, and perpetrated systematic massacres, overwhelmingly of Jews, but also including some Roma and Sinti (i.e., Gypsies) and Soviet partisans. Between June 22, 1941 and mid-December 1941, the personnel of these four units murdered over 300,000 people in a reign of terror extending from the Baltic Sea to the Southern Ukraine (Hilberg, 1985, pp. 295–296).

The largest single instance of mass killing occurred in Kiev, capital of the Ukrainian S. S. R., between September 28 and 30, 1941. Over this three-day period, members of Einsatzgruppe C murdered 33,771 Jews from Kiev in the Babi Yar ravine outside of the city. Evidence from captured German documents, as well as eyewitness accounts by Soviet citizens who witnessed the deportations from Kiev, indicate the systematic, brutal nature of this "operation" (Arad and Krakowski, 1989, pp. 173–174). On the morning of September 28, 1941, some 2,000 notices were posted in Kiev calling upon "all Jews of the City of Kiev and its environs" to appear at 8 a.m. on September 29 at a location near the city's cemetery (Korey, 1993, p. 62). Anyone who failed to appear would be executed; this threat was supplemented by a false rumor deliberately spread by the Germans that Jews who assembled were going to be evacuated and resettled. When Jews gathered on the morning of September 29, 1941, there were mostly mothers with children, the elderly, the sick, and the disabled. Most Jewish males in Kiev had already departed with the retreating Red Army. The assembled thousands were marched along Lvovskaya Street, in the words of Soviet Jewish writer Ilya Ehrenburg, representing "a procession of the doomed . . . the mothers carrying their babies, the paralyzed pulled along on hand carts" (Ehrenburg, quoted in Korey, 1993, pp. 62–63). Ukrainian police collaborated with Sonderkommando in making certain the slow procession moved toward the cemetery. Once they arrived at the cemetery, victims were ordered to remove their clothing and proceed through a narrow pathway that was bounded by barbed wire and antitank obstructions, all the while being beaten by rubber truncheons and sticks. The now naked victims, whose clothing had been piled in neat bundles before entering the narrow passageway, were divided into groups of 100 each and marched into the Babi Yar ravine. Once in the ravine, they encountered squads of Sonderkommando C consisting of 30 men each, whose task had been precisely defined by their commander, Paul Blobel. Testifying at his own trial in 1951, Blobel recounted how he had instructed the men to shoot the Jews from the crest of the ravine for an hour; then they would be replaced by a second squad which continued the process. The killing lasted into the night. Upon complete darkness, the remaining Jews were placed in garages to await their execution the following day. On September 30, the Sonderkommando resumed the mass killing, eventually dynamiting the ravine "so as to cover the dead and those still alive" (Korey, 1993, p. 63). The official Einsatzgruppe report summarized the three days' work in this manner: "The transaction was carried out without friction. No incidents occurred" (Einsatzgruppe report, as quoted in Korey, 1993, p. 63).

Not satisfied that all Jews had been killed, the Sonderkommando scoured the city to locate Jews who might be hiding, or who had otherwise escaped their clutches. Dina Pronicheva, a survivor of the massacre, related some years after the war that: "After a massacre of the Jews, the Germans combed apartments and houses. If they found children of a Jewish mother they killed them, even when, as in our case, the father was a Russian" (Pronicheva, quoted in Korey, 1993, pp. 63–64).

The scale and brutality of the Babi Yar massacre was recorded in local residents' eyewitness accounts of the German occupation, a number of which have already been cited. Despite eyewitness evidence of the massacre, particularly the overriding emphasis on the extermination of Jews, official Soviet policy downplayed the massacre of the Jewish victims in favor of the claim of a generic onslaught against "Soviet citizens." Subsequent efforts between 1944 and the mid-1950s by Jewish writers such as Ilya Ehrenburg, Savva Golovanivsky, and Leonid Pervomaisky to raise the issues of why the massacre of Jews was not recognized at

Babi Yar and how Ukrainians had collaborated with Germans in the massacre were denounced by the Soviet government, which labeled such efforts as "nationalist slander" and "defamation of the Soviet nation" (Korey, 1993, p. 64). Clearly, the blatantly antisemitic policies of the postwar Stalin regime, which resulted in the persecution and death of many leading Soviet Jewish intellectuals, were reflected in the official denial of Babi Yar as the most heinous crime committed by Nazi Germany against Jews in the Soviet Union. While other sites of massacres had memorials erected to commemorate efforts of the Soviet people to overcome the atrocities of the "Hitlerite" forces, no memorial was erected at Babi Yar.

Following Stalin's death in 1953, the gradual "thaw" within Soviet society engendered a greater openness of debate and discussion about issues which for decades had been suppressed by the state. Among these issues was the pervasive antisemitism in Soviet society, which despite the attempt by the Soviet state to create a "new man" in the image of Marxist-Leninist ideology, had persisted and indeed been reinforced in policy and practice by Stalin's own virulent antisemitism. It is in this context that Yevgeny Yevtushenko's 1961 poem "Babi Yar" emerged, along with the storm of praise and criticism it generated. Confronting the long heritage of antisemitism in Russia, Yevtushenko's piece brought to the surface issues of prejudice and discrimination against Jews, along with the Soviet policy of blatant indifference to the Holocaust, which was disguised under the umbrella of the "Great Patriotic War" against fascism.

Soon after the poem appeared, leading Soviet composer Dmitri Shostakovich contacted Yevtushenko and requested permission to employ it as the choral text in the first movement of his Symphony no. 13, to which Yevtushenko consented enthusiastically. Despite efforts by the Soviet government to censor the opening performance in Moscow, the symphony was premiered to a very positive response by the concert hall audience, while *Pravda's* (the official Soviet newspaper, the title of which means "truth") statement on the concert was restricted to one line. Government officials then pressured Yevtushenko to revise two lines of the poem to broaden the message and generate empathy for all Russians killed by German policies, and Yevtushenko relented, although Shostakovich was opposed and refused to change any of the symphony's lyrics (Wilson, 1994, 361–362). Until the symphony emerged in the West with the original text, performances in the Soviet Union were restricted to those using the altered version. Today, some 36 years following its premiere, it is recognized as one of the composer's supreme masterpieces.

Designing the Unit

The Holocaust and Human Behavior (HHB) is a social studies elective course taught to 11th- and 12th-grade students within Hunterdon Central's block schedule. Students electing the course receive 45 consecutive days of daily instruction, each day consisting of one 80-minute block schedule period. Inaugurated in the 1996–97 school year, HHB has become a popular elective in the school, expanding from two to three sections.

Intensive block scheduling, particularly when courses are taught every day rather than on alternating days, requires careful planning to facilitate in depth inquiry by students into course topics. At any given time, students in HHB are engaged in two to four ongoing activities, some of short duration and others of extended duration. For example, students can simultaneously analyze evidence from primary documents during a class discussion while working at home on reader response journal entries concerning in-class activities or outside readings, and using the library to build the research bibliography for their quarter-length project. Students who take the course recognize its demanding requirements and learn quickly that multitask expectations are integral to its design.

Engaging students with complex, illustrative case studies in Holocaust education requires that foundational knowledge (i.e., the historical basis of anti-semitism in European societies) and core concepts for application to new situations and content (examples include genocide, prejudice, stereotyping, and discrimination) be taught prior to introducing the Babi Yar massacre. As previously mentioned, these criteria were employed to determine which case studies would most effectively address the three course goals. First, there are substantial sources available about the Babi Yar massacre from multiple contemporary perspectives (perpetrator, bystander, and victim) and its significance as a touchstone in addressing the legacy of the Holocaust for later generations (see the Units Resource list in the Appendix to this chapter). Second, ongoing controversies about the persistence of antisemitism in the former Soviet Union and the relationship between history and memory as revealed in conflicts about Holocaust memorials is strikingly evident in the Babi Yar case study, when viewed through the lens of the Yevtushenko poem and the Shostakovich symphony. Third, the ongoing debate regarding the uniqueness and/or universality of the Holocaust and its legacy for contemporary society is embedded in the Babi Yar case study, not only in the analysis of Soviet responses to the Holocaust but in how artistic representations of controversial historical issues pose important questions about the responsibility of people and governments to remember and learn from historical tragedies such as Babi Yar.

Given the available literary, audiovisual, and documentary sources available about Babi Yar, the teacher has a rich array of learning materials for use. Following instructional units on the historical foundations of antisemitism and the development of student understanding about core sociological and psychological concepts regarding behavior (prejudice, stereotyping, discrimination, distancing, and compensation), HHB students examine the development of Nazi policies against targeted groups chronologically. At the point where the invasion of the Soviet Union is examined, students are primed to undertake the Babi Yar case study. Taking advantage of audiovisual and computer-based technology, a computer software program was constructed using the Microsoft Powerpoint program, which permits integration of text and visual sources into a slide show presentation format. Copies of photographs from the U.S. Holocaust Memorial Museum Research Institute were purchased and scanned into Powerpoint, then combined with captions developed by the author. The resulting presentation, entitled "The Legacy of Babi Yar," contains two sections. Section 1 provides an overview of the key details about the Babi Yar massacre, integrating excerpts from primary documents (German and Soviet eyewitness accounts) with documentary photographs of Kiev during the 3 days of the massacre, and photos of the Babi Yar ravine itself. Section 2 addresses the postmassacre controversy about the Soviet response to Babi Yar, with emphasis placed on the furor caused by the publication of Yevtushenko's poem "Babi Yar" and the efforts to censor performances of Shostakovich's Symphony no. 13. The full text of the poem is contained in Part 2 of the Powerpoint presentation, accompanied in real time by a performance of the Shostakovich Symphony no. 13, as played on a CD player. As students view the words of the poem and listen to the symphony, documentary photographs of the victims of Babi Yar are interspersed with the text slides of the poem.

Before encountering the multimedia/Powerpoint presentation, students read about the Einsatzgruppen's activities in the Soviet Union, using a narrative text (Michael Berenbaum's *The World Must Know: The History of the Holocaust as Told in the United State Holocaust Memorial Museum*) and selected documents from the class anthology (*A Holocaust Reader*). Specifically, these documents include the "Secret Order by Field Marshal Keitel, March 13, 1941"; "Crushing the 'Jewish-Bolshevist System': Field Marshal Von Reichenau's Orders of October 10, 1941"; and "Field Reports from Chiefs of Einsatzgruppen," including Einsatzgruppen C's report on the Babi Yar massacre and related events in Kiev from early October 1941. (All of the aforementioned documents are from Lucy Dawidowicz's *A Holocaust Reader*. [West Orange, NJ: Behrman House, 1976.])

Comprehension of the scale of the mass killings is aided by use of the CD-ROM *Historical Atlas of the Holocaust* (available from Macmillan), which students can access easily on the school's computer network. Maps and related print resources on the CD-ROM offer a thorough visual and text-based background to what took place in Kiev from September 28 to 30, 1941. Maps and photos on the CD-ROM permit in-depth visual examination of the city environs of Kiev, as well as the site of the Babi Yar massacre itself.

Following this introductory component, students are primed to examine the unit's core question: How should societies interpret the legacy of the Holocaust for future generations? One might question why introduction of such a "legacy" question is posed when the course is not ready to conclude, and since instruction about this event usually takes place at approximately day 30 of the 45-day class. In response, it is important to recognize the necessity of engaging students throughout this course about issues of contemporary or long-term significance, not just as a concluding activity. Embedding study of legacy issues in case studies is integral to course design because it (1) facilitates the constant examination of historical patterns of human behavior and their implications for contemporary life, and (2) facilitates the raising of questions about how social institutions should confront issues of guilt and responsibility, particularly where distortion and suppression of the truth has taken place. When students continually examine the relationship between past, present, and future, they are better able to make concrete connections between course content and daily life. When such activities are only done at the end of a course, they are often deemed unimportant by students and become peripheral undertakings.

Placing students in an investigative posture is critical at this juncture. Because artistic works can and should be subject to multiple interpretations, emphasizing divergent thought is appropriate and serves as a springboard for consideration of alternative views. Students receive the poem "Babi Yar" by Yevtushenko, and after a brief verbal introduction about the author, are asked to read it, highlighting any references in the text to antisemitism and the Holocaust. The poem is then read aloud, with different students in the class taking responsibility for different verses. This component can be done either in small groups or as a full class activity.

Following the oral reading, students are asked to identify words or phrases that puzzle them or about which they desire more information. Clarifications are provided by other students and the instructor. The instructor then asks students to discuss their interpretation of text passages which they believe are relevant to antisemitism and/or the Holocaust. Among the many examples in the poem are the following, which illustrate both the historical foundations of antisemitism and connections to the Holocaust, respectively.

[Historical Foundations of Antisemitism]
Here I plod through ancient Egypt.
Here I perish crucified, on the cross,
and to this day I bear the scars of nails.
I seem to be

       Dreyfus

[Holocaust History]
I seem to be
       Anne Frank
transparent
       as a branch in April.
And I love.
       And have no need of phrases.
My need
       Is that we gaze into each other.
How little we can see
       or smell!

Students have little difficulty in recognizing the historical allusions to Western antisemitism (i.e., Jews as the killers of Christ, Jews being persecuted in Egypt), and the problems faced by Anne Frank are well known by most students, given the popularity of her diary in school curricula. At the same time, students have more difficulty addressing the overtly Russian references in the poem. The instructor's role in facilitating analysis of connections between diverse themes in the poem is magnified here, since students may not be familiar with the persistence of antisemitism in Soviet society. This example from the poem highlights the continuity of antisemitism in Europe, in this case as it relates to Russia and the Soviet Union.

I seem to be then
                    a young boy in Byelostok.
Blood runs, spilling over the floors.
The barroom rabble-rousers
give off a stench of vodka and onion.
A boot kicks me aside, helpless.
In vain I plead with these pogrom bullies.
While they jeer and shout,
                    "Beat the Yids. Save Russia."

At the end of the poem, Yevtushenko makes a very overt criticism of Soviet antisemitism, illustrated in the closing verse.

The "Internationale," let it
                    thunder
when the last anti-Semite on earth
is buried for ever.
In my blood there is no Jewish blood.
In their callous rage, all anti-Semites
must hate me now as a Jew.
For that reason
                    I am a true Russian!

The apparent contradiction in the final verse, highlighting the impotence of Marxist-Leninist ideology (the "Internationale") to eradicate antisemitism ("For that reason I am a true Russian") stands as a stark contrast to the penultimate section of the poem, where Yevtushenko underlines the tragedy of having no monument at Babi Yar, and by implication, the failure of the Soviet people and the state to confront historical truth.

The wild grasses rustle over Babi Yar.
The trees look ominous,
                    like judges.
Here all things scream silently,
                    and, baring my head,
slowly I feel myself
                    turning grey.
And I myself
                    am one massive, soundless scream
above the thousand thousand buried here.
I am
      each old man
                    here shot dead.
I am
      every child
                    here shot dead.
Nothing in me
                    shall ever forget.

After students share their individual interpretations of specific verses concerning the historic references to antisemitism and Holocaust history, they are asked to discuss verses which stand out as memorable on the basis of their ability to (1) convey powerful images and/or (2) express key messages about the Holocaust and its legacy. Reading specific verses aloud, students share their interpretations and clarify diverse interpretations. One example occurs in the first verse. Some students interpreted "Today I am as old in years as all the Jewish people. Now I seem to be a Jew" as a message unique to Europeans, one focusing solely on Russians and their legacy of antisemitism. Others hear that verse as a universalizing message, inviting the reader to see the world from the position of a persecuted group, in the process generating empathy for the Jews and setting the stage for understanding the Holocaust and antisemitism as transcendent moral crises.

Through discussion, students also construct interpretations of the entire poem once they have clarified their understanding of the many historical references in the work. For example, some students view the work as time-bound, with its significance focused primarily on the continuity of antisemitism in the Soviet Union and the poet's effort to raise consciousness about it. These students see the references to the Holocaust and historic antisemitism as a necessary foundation for the powerful appeal in the final verse, where Yevtushenko's ironic verse, "The Internationale, let it thunder when the last anti-Semite on earth is buried for ever," shames the Soviet system and calls for self-examination about the U.S.S.R.'s failure to overcome antisemitism as a societal problem. In contrast, other students interpret the poem's overall meaning more universally. They note the diversity of references to antisemitism (i.e., ancient Egypt, Christ's crucifixion, the Dreyfus Affair, pogroms in Eastern Europe, and Anne Frank) and cite the frequent uses of universalizing language as critical for seeing this work as a call for commemoration and social responsibility that speaks to audiences beyond the Soviet Union and to generations beyond the survivors of World War II and the Holocaust. In particular, one verse—"And I myself am one massive, soundless scream above the thousand thousand buried here. I am each old man here shot dead"—is cited by these students as emblematic of the poem's far-reaching message, one that has no geographic, cultural, or chronological limitations. For the teacher, it is important to recognize that students will develop quite different interpretations of the text. These interpretations should be carefully analyzed, citing actual references to the verses. The teacher's role should be to help students clarify their individual interpretations, and where possible, determine if a common meaning is possible. Once a thorough analysis has been completed, consensus may not have been reached on one overall interpretation of the work, and that is one legitimate result of the process. Students can return to their interpretation of the poem's overall meaning later in the unit, notably when they engage the issues of social responsibility and memory concerning the legacy of the Holocaust for contemporary society.

Following text analysis of the poem, students are ready for the multimedia/ Powerpoint presentation. Prior to beginning the presentation, which should ideally be given in a setting where the computer image can be displayed on a large screen (it can also be shown on a small, 13-inch computer monitor, but the impact is lessened somewhat due to the smaller screen image) and the music can be amplified to recreate a concert hall setting, the following question is posed for student investigation: How would you interpret the legacy of Babi Yar? Students will gather information from the multimedia/Powerpoint presentation, and then discuss their findings, using evidence from the presentation and other sources studied earlier. A full-class discussion with the computer slide show available for reference is recommended, as students should be expected to make concrete connections to the presentation slides in defending their positions. Additionally, students often inquire as to how the evidence from the victim's perspective was gathered, in light of the efforts by Germans to find and kill every Jew in Kiev. Kuznetzov's *Babi Yar: A Document in the Form of a Novel* is very helpful here, as it contains Dina Pronicheva's eyewitness account of her survival of the massacre and subsequent hiding in Kiev until its liberation by the Red Army later in the war (Kuznetzov, 1970, pp. 99–120).

Alternatives for summative assessment of the unit can take multiple forms. Entries in the HHB reader response journal have been the dominant format, but others are certainly feasible. Journal prompts have included these questions: How should societies affected by the Holocaust address issues of remembrance and responsibility? and What responsibility do societies have to address the memory of genocidal acts? Samples of the student responses to these questions is provided later in this essay. Alternative work products could include written essays on themes of remembrance and responsibility, creation of student multimedia presentations where designs of memorials or monuments can be represented along with textual descriptions of their significance in dealing with issues of societal responsibility for remembrance, and student-led discussions emphasizing public policies in societies that have, to varied degrees, addressed historical controversies where issues of justice and fairness are intertwined with conflicting power relationships (examples include the Truth Commission in South Africa; efforts to expose human rights violations in Latin America; and controversies regarding the creation of museum exhibits in the United States about problematic issues such as the use of atomic weapons in Japan, Native American history, slavery, and Japanese internment). Irrespective of the type of final student work product, the instructor needs to emphasize adherence to standards of clarity, cogency, and careful use of evidence to support assertions and arguments.

Student Response to the Unit

During the 1996–97 and 1997–98 school years, the curriculum unit on the Babi Yar massacre was taught to approximately 65 students electing HHB. Documentation of student journal responses was gathered and analyzed in light of stated unit goals, with emphasis placed on how students constructed meaning about issues related to the legacy of the Holocaust for contemporary society. Specifically, journal responses were prompted by these two questions:

1. What responsibilities do societies have to address the memory of genocidal acts? (1996–97)
2. How should societies affected by the Holocaust address issues of remembrance and responsibility? (1997–98)

The changed emphasis in the 1997–98 question resulted from a desire on the instructor's part to more specifically focus the question on societies affected by the Holocaust, so that the linkage between the events and sources in the case study could be more precisely defined by students.

Patterns of Student Response

Overwhelmingly, students argued that issues of remembrance and responsibility were critical concerns for contemporary generations and for the future. Students often noted that the power of remembrance was a compelling rationale for action by societies to both commemorate and educate so that such tragedies could be prevented in the future. Below are illustrative journal excerpts, with the year of their creation noted in parentheses:

> I sit and think of the millions of invisible graves. Forgotten and unknown faces fill my mind as I wonder—to hold responsibility is to hold power. This certain type of power will not allow us to prevent the past, but relive the memories to ensure our future. This is not a burden, it is our duty. I hold this in my hands. (1996–97)

> The biggest responsibility each society must take on is to make sure that these genocides never happen again. The fact that for years no monument was ever erected on the site of Babi Yar robs the people of the required emotions necessary to take action against these genocides. What I'm trying to say is that if a monument is constructed where thousands upon thousands of innocent men, women and children were murdered, and you stand at the foot of that monument, overwhelming emotions are going to surge through your veins. At least it would for me. . . . The world must work together to try and stop these cowardly and prejudiced acts. (1996–97)

> I was shocked to know that throughout all of the learning that I have had in middle school and high school I had never heard about this [Babi Yar] until now. A massacre spanning a few days, killing over 30,000 people and I didn't hear about it until now? I think that just shows that a lot of the education that is received in school in the U.S. about that time period is focused around the war, not the Holocaust, because how could one not learn about Babi Yar when discussing the genocide that is the Holocaust. . . . The biggest, and, by far, the most important responsibility that societies have in addressing the memory of genocidal memories is to educate the minds of the people who don't know what has taken place. (1996–97)

> We all could see the faces of family members in the photos of the Babi Yar presentation. Death is something that everyone can understand. It is that power that should not ever allow us to forget . . . the people who the Holocaust affected the most, the families that it destroyed, and the people it killed need to be remembered. They are no longer here to remind us of their suffering. The people who died at Babi Yar

can't ask us to remember those three days. But their story lives on in everyone who educates themselves about the Holocaust. As a service to those that died, in their honor, we should remember. (1997–98)

I feel that even if only one person died at Babi Yar, they deserve to have a monument erected to celebrate their memory and life. Every time a life was taken without the consent of the person it was taken from, that person earned the right to have a monument erected for them. It doesn't matter if it was one or 33,771 lives that were taken at Babi Yar, it shouldn't have taken until 1976 for a small, shabbily erected monument to be put in its rightful place. (1997-98)

Students also made concrete references to Yevtushenko's poem, demonstrating their ability to integrate previously learned information and concepts in their learning about the case study. Course themes and concepts applied in each excerpt are shown in parentheses.

I think the worst thing a community can do is ignore the issue altogether. This was the case in Babi Yar. The poem starts out with negativity. It says "No monument stands over Babi Yar." This immediately gives the reader the impression that something is left undone, which was exactly the case. . . . So while the Russian government may have been protecting itself from criticism, it created a whole new issue of antisemitism and anger. Even in the poem, there is a line about antisemitism and Russians. It says, ". . . let it thunder when the last anti-Semite on earth is buried forever." (Historic antisemitism, prejudice) (1997–98)

Societies, too, are often eager to forget their dead. This is particularly true when they are somewhat responsible for the tragedy. This is not to say that a society necessarily became a murderer, but perhaps through their silence, they became the eternal footman. Genocides illustrate this idea very clearly. While the societies of victims may not be the perpetrators, their indifference helps those responsible. In the case of Babi Yar, the poet Yevtushenko suggests this in his poem by the same name. "They're coming here? Be not afraid. Those are the booming sounds of spring . . . Are they smashing down the door? No it's the ice breaking. . . " (Bystander behavior, prejudice) (1997–98)

For twenty-five years after the war, the Soviet Union barely acknowledged Babi Yar, and no memorial stood there until 1974. Even then, the word *Jew* was not used on the monument. Soviet poet Yevgeny Yevtushenko wrote about Babi Yar as a symbol of national shame, reminding the Soviet Union of the persistence of Jewish persecution and antisemitism in the lines, "The 'Internationale,' let it /thunder/ when the last anti-Semite on earth/ is buried forever." (Antisemitism, prejudice) (1996–97)

Students also commented about the ongoing debate concerning the uniqueness or universality of the Holocaust:

"I am each old man, here shot dead. I am every child here shot dead." This is both universal and unique. It is unique to every person who had been shot and killed. The universality comes in because so many people suffer from the claws of hate; when groups are persecuted we are affected in some way. (1996–97)

In the poem, it said, "I am each old man here shot dead." There were thousands of innocent people killed. If that's not reason for a memorial, I don't know what is. Each community involved holds the responsibility to erect some sort of site to honor and remember the individuals who were persecuted there. As it was said in the poem, "We are denied the leaves; we are denied the sky." They were denied their lives, and future generations should not be denied the right to learn and remember. (1997–98)

Everybody in school should be taught about Babi Yar and the whole Holocaust in general. Pretty soon the survivors won't be able to tell their stories, and then it will be up to us to pass it down. The survivors have had to remember this horror for the rest of their lives: the families they watched die and the people they had to see die right in front of them. "I am each old man here shot dead. I am every child here shot dead. Nothing in me shall ever forget." So why should our generation and generations to come "ever forget"? (1997–98)

Students also discussed the power of the poem and its integration within the overall multimedia presentation, emphasizing the need to address diverse learning styles. Note that none of the journal prompts specifically focused on this issue.

When I watched the Babi Yar presentation I really felt like they did a good job writing the piece to music. It was amazing and so powerful to see how the words changed with the tempo. (1997–98)

I think that visual works such as poems, artwork, or videos or movies and music, are also ways for societies to address remembrance and responsibilities, because with today's generation, these are the ways in which messages get across . . . I really like the poem Babi Yar because it sends a message across and really makes you think. Especially when we were in the auditorium with the music. (1997–98)

But it should be the responsibility of society to make sure that everyone has the chance to learn about events like Babi Yar, not just those who live close to the place. Babi Yar took place in the Ukraine; many Americans will never see the monument at the site. There[fore] it is imperative that people like Yevgeny Yevtushenko write poetry about it, and people like Dmitri Shostakovich put that poetry to music, so that the legacy of Babi Yar can be felt around the world. Also, by remembering it through different forms like poetry and music, it enables people of all levels to understand and personalize it. Some people wouldn't be struck by a stanza of a poem, yet when hearing music, [that] could make it [more] meaningful. . . . Poetry, music, art, theatre, even dance are all ways to acknowledge and honor an event such as Babi Yar. (1996–97)

Conclusions and Suggestions for Further Investigation

The evidence delineated in student responses demonstrates that the combination of poetry, historical documents, historical photographs, and music has a powerful impact on learning. Using an issues-based approach, teachers of the Holocaust can provide learning opportunities where students can develop clear links between historic events such as the Babi Yar massacre and efforts to construct collective memory about genocidal acts. More often than not, students exhibit cognitive dissonance when confronted with the overwhelming evidence of genocidal policies and practices, and the unwillingness of a society to acknowledge and honor the memory of the victims. Because the central question for their investigation was posed in an open-ended manner (How should societies address the legacy of the Holocaust for future generations?), this encouraged my students to engage the content as pregnant with possibilities for social action and policy development, rather than as a "closed issue." Educational programs, construction of memorials, and development of artistic representations all emerged in student journal responses to the prompts about remembrance and responsibility, demonstrating the value of inviting students to examine possible courses of action based upon encountering a rich blend of resources via instruction.

The variety of resources used in the unit spurred students to comment on the effectiveness of multimedia instructional strategies, which are enhanced when delivered with technology that facilitates their integration, such as in the Powerpoint presentation software. A next step in the process is the creation of units and instructional activities where students themselves establish conceptual links between various types of sources and construct their own multimedia presentations about topics in Holocaust studies. Events such as Kristallnacht and the Warsaw Ghetto uprising lend themselves to such technologies, given the wide availability of literature, poetry, historical documents, photos, and music that can be blended to construct historical interpretations and pose questions about the legacies of these events for contemporary society.

The success of this unit in helping students develop historical understanding of genocidal policies while examining the legacy of the Holocaust and patterns of antisemitism for the modern world suggests that educators can develop thematic units that help students construct meaning about complex historical issues while simultaneously applying core concepts to contemporary experience. Using poetry as the artistic medium for entry into the controversy about remembrance and responsibility assists the learner in gaining ownership of interpretation, and serves as an important gateway for understanding that the legacy of the Holocaust still affects our ability to ground social policy on historical truth rather than distortion and propaganda.

ACKNOWLEDGMENT

The insights and contributions of Jennifer Peck and her students in the Holocaust and Human Behavior class at Hunterdon Central Regional High School are gratefully acknowledged.

REFERENCES

Arad, Yitshak, & Shmuel Krakowski. (Eds.) (1989). *The Einsatzgruppen Reports.* New York: The Holocaust Library.

Hilberg, Raul. (1985). *The Destruction of the European Jew.* New York: Holmes and Meier.

Korey, William. (1993). "A Monument over Babi Yar?" In Lucjan Dobroszycki and Jeffery S. Gurock (Eds.), *The Holocaust in the Soviet Union: Studies and Sources on the Destruction of the Jews in the Nazi-Occupied Territories of the USSR, 1941–1945* (pp. 61–74). New York: M. E. Sharpe.

Wilson, Elizabeth. (1994). *Shostakovich Remembered.* Princeton, NJ: Princeton University Press.

APPENDIX

The unit goals listed here are taken from the course of study entitled The Holocaust and Human Behavior, an elective social studies class at Hunterdon Central Regional High School in Flemington, New Jersey.

Unit Goals

Using the case study of the Babi Yar massacre, students will:

- Analyze and evaluate the impact of Nazi policies of discrimination, persecution, and genocide on targeted groups in occupied Europe during the period 1933–1945, with special emphasis placed on the culture of European Jewry.
- Analyze the aims, processes, and results of Nazi policies designed to isolate, dehumanize, and destroy targeted victim groups during the Holocaust, with special emphasis on European Jewry.
- Examine diverse interpretations concerning the role of the Holocaust as a genocide of the 20th century, with particular emphasis on the debate concerning the uniqueness or universality of the Holocaust.

Unit Resources

Arad, Yitshak, & Shmuel Krakowski. (Eds.). (1989). *The Einsatzgruppen Reports.* New York: The Holocaust Library. Pages 164–165, 172–174, and 217–220 contain field reports regarding the provocation for the massacre and the report of the results of the massacre itself, along with a status report on the collaboration of the German Wehrmacht (army) and the Security Police with the Einsatzgruppen.

Berenbaum, Michael. (1993). *The World Must Know: The History of the Holocaust as Told in the United States Holocaust Memorial Museum.* Boston, MA: Little, Brown. Pages 94–101 deal specifically with the Einsatzgruppen and the Babi Yar massacre.

Dawidowicz, Lucy S. (Ed.). (1976). *A Holocaust Reader.* West Orange, NJ: Behrman House. This anthology contains a useful selection of primary source documents on the preparation and implementation of mass killing policies in the USSR.

Fernekes, William R. Powerpoint software presentation on "The Legacy of Babi Yar" incorporating photographs from the U. S. Holocaust Memorial Museum Research Institute, and music from Dmitri Shostakovich's Symphony no. 13.

Hilberg, Raul. (1985). *The Destruction of the European Jews.* Three Volumes. New York: Holmes and Meier, 1985. Excerpts from Volume I are very useful as a teacher resource about the planning and implementation of the Einsatzgruppen massacres.

Korey, William. (1993). "A Monument over Babi Yar?" In Lucjan Dobroszycki and Jeffery S. Gurock (Eds.), *The Holocaust in the Soviet Union: Studies and Sources on the Destruction of the Jews in the Nazi-Occupied Territories of the USSR, 1941–1945* (pp. 61–74). New York: M. E. Sharpe. This well-documented study of the Babi Yar controversy combines historical analysis of the massacre with an account of the controversy in the post-World War II Soviet Union regarding commemoration of the event and recognition of Jews as the primary victims of Nazi policies of genocide.

Kuznetzov, A. Anatoli. (1970). *Babi Yar: A Document in the Form of a Novel.* New York: Farrar, Straus and Giroux. This version of the famous "documentary novel" is the complete, uncensored text containing Dina Pronicheva's eyewitness account of her escape from Babi Yar, recounted to Kuznetsov some 2 decades after the Babi Yar massacre.

Shostakovich, Dmitri. *Symphony No. 13, "Babi Yar."* Russian Disc RD CD 11 191. This is the live Soviet recording of the opening night performance, which contains the original text of the Yevtushenko poem, as employed by Shostakovich in the symphony's first movement.

United States Holocaust Memorial Museum. (1996). *Historical Atlas of the Holocaust CD-ROM.* New York: Macmillan Publishing. This Windows format CD-ROM has excellent maps that provide opportunities for students to examine the range of Einsatzgruppen activities in Eastern Europe, as well as detailed maps and related print sources on the Babi Yar massacre itself.

United States Holocaust Memorial Museum Research Institute. *Photographs of the Holocaust in the Soviet Union* (selected items). Copies of photographs in the USHMM Photographic Archive were purchased for classroom instructional use by the author and later incorporated into the Powerpoint presentation.

Yevtushenko, Yevgeny. (1995). "Babi Yar." In Hilda Schiff (Ed.), *Holocaust Poetry.* New York: St. Martin's Press.

Wilson, Elizabeth. (1994). *Shostakovich Remembered.* Princeton, NJ: Princeton University Press. This compilation of firsthand accounts about Shostakovich's life and career contains important recollections of the genesis of the Symphony no. 13 by the poet Yevgeny Yevtushenko; Kiril Kondrashin, the conductor of the first performances of the work; and other Soviet artists such as Mtislav Rostropovich and Isaak Schwartz, who address the difficulties of artistic expression in the Soviet Union.

CHAPTER

9 Tapping the Sensibilities of Teens

BETH DUTTON

Ms. Dutton, this is like positively the very worst day of my whole entire life. My life might as well be over!"

"You're much too important to all of us to say that, Amy. How is this the worst day of your life? What happened?"

"Vivian wrote Joel a note telling him a wicked humungous lie about me, and now he's going to take her to the game tonight and not me. And I thought she was my best friend. I just wanna die."

"I'm so sorry about that. Isn't there someone else you can go to the game with? Can you go with other girls? Could you go by yourself?"

"Oh, sure, like I'm going to the game with *girls!* Like I'm going to tell the whole world I don't have a date and so I have to like go by myself! That's going to help me a lot! I told you: this is the worst day of my whole entire life."

"Ms. Dutton, when my Dad sees this grade on this report, I'm dead meat! I might as well be really dead!"

"Come on, Jason, we'll talk to your Dad together about this, and we'll get him to work out with us how you can redo the paper to bring your grade up. I'll tell him I'll work with you after school."

"Okay, but you know he's going to ground me for like a hundred million years until I do bring the grade up. I'll be too old to do anything with anybody! I told you, I might as well be dead!"

"Ms. Dutton, my whole life is like ruined, just ruined. I'm never going to get into college! All my hard work might as well just be thrown in the dump!"

"For heaven's sake, Becky, what has happened? You've been doing so well. You're on your way to early admission."

"The CP exam in chemistry I was supposed to take today at Dartmouth? I called and called all day Saturday and couldn't find anyone to tell me what time to be there today. How am I supposed to know what time to be there? How am I supposed to know where to go? If I don't take that exam, I'm dead!"

"I understand why you're upset, Becky, I know how much you've studied for this. Let's go to the guidance office, have them call the college, find out the time and the place, and I'll personally get someone to take you there."

"Oh, God!" says Becky, as she accompanies me down the stairs to the guidance office (where her problem was solved in 10 minutes), "Is nothing in my life ever going to work?"

And so it goes. These are factual scenarios of some of the everyday dramatic events and crises in the lives of my students, with only the names changed to protect the wounded. Teachers of teens everywhere have similar dramatic stories of their own. And there is never any question but that the pain is real; the fear, the hurt, the certainty that all is lost, are terribly real; and woe to the teacher—or the parent or friend—who takes the problem less than seriously.

But, as parents and teachers know, these same students can also care deeply about the plight of others. Recognizing this 10 years ago when I began to teach Holocaust Studies on a regular basis—10 weeks per semester each to two separate groups of students—10 weeks to ninth grade Civics students and 10 weeks to juniors and seniors in my Asian Studies course—I was determined to assist them to come to care deeply enough about the tragedy of the Holocaust to want to do all they could possibly do to see that its ramifications become a reality in their lives and possibly to act on that in the larger world.

I have learned that what may make it easier for me to teach Holocaust studies than for some other teachers I know is the students' civics course. More specifically, prior to the study of the Holocaust, my students gain a solid grounding in the Constitution of the United States, especially in the Bill of Rights and the Fourteenth Amendment. They have memorized the amendments, have studied the historic circumstances under which they came about, and have studied the court cases related to the amendments. They have even held mock trials in which they argue the case histories of violations of one or another of the amendments. In other words, they come to appreciate what it means to live in a democracy.

I begin the study of the Holocaust with the 2,000-year history of Christian antisemitism. It is worth mentioning that when we reach the place where I begin to teach about Christian antisemitism, my students are able to accept that my teaching is fully objective, not only because by this time they know what my moral and ethical stance is on issues of discrimination and persecution, but also because they know I am by birth and upbringing a Christian, albeit, as I explain, a "post-Auschwitz Christian." Also, they and their parents see me in church. I don't have to soften language for fear that students or their parents or the school administration (which, by the way, is fully supportive of my Holocaust studies course) will think I am "operating" from the standpoint of a personal religious agenda. They know, too, I have behind me years of study and writing on the subject.

When we study the indoctrination of populaces all over Europe by Christian religious leaders, from the fifth century onward, to the effect that Jews were God killers, incurably vile, and a danger to the moral order of the world (Berenbaum, 1993, p. 13; Gilbert, 1987, pp. 19–20; Hilberg, 1985, pp. 13–17), students are able to form opinions about what was the real danger to the moral order of the European world, having already learned what such a moral order can be and should be in a just world.

Indeed, they are astounded when we read in Berenbaum (1993) that:

> Enmity toward the Jews was expressed most acutely in the church's teaching of contempt. From Augustine in the fifth century to Luther in the sixteenth, some of the most eloquent and persuasive Christian theologians excoriated the Jews as rebels against God and murderers of the Lord. They were described as companions of the devil, a race of vipers. During the Middle Ages, Jews were accused of the blood libel: Jews supposedly murdered Christian children as an act of ritual worship or to prepare unleavened bread for the Passover seder." (p. 13)

When we reach that part of history where "the Jews of England, France, Germany, Spain, Bohemia and Italy, from the thirteenth to the sixteenth century" (Hilberg, 1985, pp. 6–7) were not allowed to live among Christians unless they converted to Christianity (Hilberg, 1985, pp. 6–7), the students are enormously moved.

When we reach the nineteenth century and the growing ideology, already preached by Martin Luther, that the Jews are incapable of being converted and saved, are a subhuman species and a virus spreading its pernicious evil hindering Christian Europe from being saved (Hilberg, 1985, pp. 13–15), the students clearly see and begin to understand the antecedents of the antisemitism that poisoned the atmosphere of early twentieth century Europe—the antisemitism to which the Nazis would add their virulent racial ideology.

When we reach the twentieth century it becomes necessary to teach a considerable amount of Germany history, particularly as it pertains to the rise of the Nazis, in order to enable the students to grasp the steps that were taken toward the Final Solution.

"How could it happen?" is a question young people ask. How to explain that all this could take place in the middle of modern Europe with the whole of the civilized world looking on? That is among the most enormous tasks that confront us as teachers of the Holocaust.

The way it could happen is gradually to subvert a government, a fledgling democracy that was riddled with a shaky history and a people who had suffered an acutely embarrassing and painful loss in World War I and were now suffering economic hardship. That is, subvert the type of government such as the students had studied. Especially helpful to me and to the students were Leni Yahil's (1990) *The Fate of European Jewry, 1932–1945,* and Raul Hilberg's (1985) *The Destruction of the European Jews.* Each helped us to formulate, however loosely in the time we had, the steps that were taken which made the Final Solution possible.

In studying this history, we examined the Enabling Law, passed by the Reichstag in early 1933 and used by Hitler to help establish his dictatorship. We also studied about the one-day national boycott of Jewish businesses that was carried out in Germany on April 1, 1933; the 1933 quotas that were applied in Germany limiting the number of Jewish students allowed in institutions of higher learning; and laws prohibiting Jews from working in government offices. We learned about the Nuremberg Laws, which defined who may be a citizen of Germany, codified future legal exclusion of Jews from German life, and influenced subsequent anti-Jewish policy. Overshadowing all of this were the racial theories of the Nazis, which dehumanized a people and asserted that Jews, Gypsies, and certain categories of Slavs were *untermensch,* or something less than human.

And, of course, we continued to learn about and discuss other restrictions and cases of isolation faced by the Jews—including their removal to ghettoes, which totally disrupted their lives and forced them live in insufferably over-crowded, filthy, and disease-ridden conditions.

We studied about the decimation of the Jews—how their caloric intake was drastically restricted, with starvation and death soon following for many. And we learned about the decimation in vast numbers of people when they were shipped to labor camps, which was brutal, often pointless, and humiliating. And finally, we came to the "Final Solution," which resulted in the extermination of millions of the rest of the hated.

And still we were faced with the impossibility of dealing with such vast depersonalized numbers with which the students are confronted. It becomes necessary somehow to personalize those numbers, make them tangible, help students new to all this horror to care that the Holocaust happened, care that people like themselves and their families and their friends were murdered—murdered due to obsessive hate born of a racist ideology.

The books the students have used in the study of all this history include the following: *Smoke and Ashes* (1988), by Barbara Rogasky; *Night* (1960), by Elie Wiesel; *On Both Sides of the Wall* (1977), by Vladka Meed; *Auschwitz and After* (1995), by Charlotte Delbo; *The Atlas of Jewish History* (1993), and *The Atlas of the Holocaust* (1991), by Martin Gilbert; *The Diary of a Young Girl* (1991), by Anne Frank; and *In Kindling Flame: The Story of Hanna Senesh 1921–1944* (1985), by Linda Atkinson. (For a complete citation of these and other works, please see the bibliography at the end of this chapter.)

There is fortunately a vast body of literature (fact and fiction), prose, and poetry that helps teachers put faces and images to those impossible numbers. I use a great deal of it. Oddly enough, some of the most effective literature for my students turns out to be poetry—the stuff at which most young people shudder! There are a number of fine poems that students are able to dramatize—poems that help them grasp a little of what the Holocaust was all about.

But first, a year ago, before we reached the stage of dramatizing all the poems with which we were to deal in that class, an event arose which helped this teacher see that the material already presented had so sensitized the students to discrimination that they were willing to take a hard public stand.

We have in Windsor County, Vermont, a wonderful senator named Ben Ptashnik, who cares about schools, education, teachers, and students; and who cares about issues of justice and equity. His parents are survivors of Auschwitz-Birkenau. I have had the pleasure of hearing both of them speak at the annual International Holocaust Institute for Youth which is held at two Vermont colleges and for which I teach a course on Holocaust history. They were among last year's guest speakers at the Institute at the University of Vermont, and moved us all with their stories—as did Senator Ptashnik's proud introduction of his parents.

Senator Ptashnik had, with other legislators, been discussing campaign financing in the Vermont legislature, and an opponent of his had been writing letters to the editors in opposition to Ptashnik. In his letters, the writer repeatedly used terms bordering on ethnic slurs. He suggested improprieties by the senator and repeatedly referred to Senator Ptashnik as "Ben Zion Ptashnik."

My students, who have to bring to class a news item to discuss each day, brought in copies of the letter to our local newspaper. They asked to use the class period to write a letter of their own to the editor of *The Windsor Chronicle*. Following is the text of the letter they wrote and which appeared in the newspaper on Thursday, June 12, 1997.

Seeds of Intolerance Sown Among Us

As part of our Civics course of studies involving discrimination, hatred, and civil and human rights, during April and May of this year, we have been studying the Holocaust of Jews in Europe perpetrated by the Germans and their allies before and during World War II. We have studied, too, the betrayal of the Jews and other victims of the Holocaust by the United States, Great Britain, France, and the Soviet Union in their role as passive bystanders to what was happening at those times when their help was terribly needed.

We do not want to be passive bystanders to any form of hatred and discrimination.

We have also studied the Civil Rights movement in our country and what amendments and Supreme Court decisions have strengthened the rights, we hope, of all people in our country.

One of the things we have most hoped as we study the Holocaust is that its consequences would have meaning to the countries of the world, and most particularly to the United States, where, we have come to believe, the greatest document ever put together to outline what a democratic system of government ought to be, painfully and with many compromises, was given birth, our Constitution.

It is painful to us who are new to the study of human and civil rights to realize that racism still exists in our country. We hope to do our part to help to remedy that.

It is painful to us, too, to see so many evidences that in this century of history's darkest night of hatred and discrimination in the deliberate extermination of the Jews, just because they were Jews, that anti-Semitism continues to exist, and not just in Europe, but here, and not just abroad in the United States, but right here in Windsor and in towns neighboring ours.

One of the things we learned was that one way to isolate the Jews and to make it easier to round them up and to send them to their deaths—whether at forced labor or in death camps—was to label them, to mark them with Stars of David so they could be identified by all the people around them. Those people would then, presumably, cooperate in the isolation and discrimination against

Jews, and in the implementation of the "final solution" to what was called the Jewish problem. (It was a racist, antisemitic problem, not a Jewish one.)

To label them and to mark them. It is hard to describe how we feel when we
read letters in the newspapers about campaign spending from people who label by
innuendo one of our senators, Ben Ptashnik, as a Jew (something he has never hidden
and something to be proud of) for the sake of all those bigots out there who might not
know he is a Jew and who can now be rallied against him. Not a one of the other
office holders mentioned with regard to campaign spending was tagged with an
ethnic or a religious label. We don't really wonder why that is so. We know from
our studies now what an old and evil practice such labeling is and why it is used.

We'd like to say right away that the labeling knife cuts both ways. We may
now know what some of us might not have known before, that Senator Ptashnik is
a Jew. But we also now know what those other people are, those labelers, and that is
not something they should be proud of. We admire Senator Ptashnik. Contempt
would be more like our sentiments regarding the others.

*Signed by Sherry Call, Krystal Chase, Matthew Cutts, Robin Denison, Gary Gar-
row, Hannah Hammond, Ryan Hebert, Kelly Honsinger, Caitlyn Hood, Laura Hundeman,
Jessica Jones, Luke Lemery, Martin Mastic, Katy Mower, Mark Nowlan, Shannon Roberts,
Raelene Robinson, Bethany Scheffer, Nathan Shute, Sara Sinclair, Stephanie Small,
Michael Walker, Kristy White.*

One of the first poems students come to love and to dramatize, both in class
and before a wider public (at commemorative services we have been invited to
give in local churches and in Montpelier, Vermont's Universal Unitarian Church),
is a poem by Moses Schulstein entitled "I Saw a Mountain." The complete poem,
which was translated by Mindele Wajsman and Bea Stadtler, is cited in Michael
Berenbaum's *The World Must Know: The History of the Holocaust as Told in the United
States Holocaust Memorial Museum* (Boston, MA: Little, Brown, 1993, pp. 145 and
147). It is usually performed by three students who alternate their voices every
three or four lines and who then come together to speak the most powerful and
telling of the lines. These students decided among themselves how it should be
presented, usually in the following format:

I Saw a Mountain

ONE VOICE: I saw a mountain
               higher than Mount Blanc
               and more holy than the mountain of Sinai.
               Not in a dream.

THREE VOICES: It was real.

ONE VOICE: On this world it stood.
               Such a mountain I saw
               Of shoes in Majdanek.
               Such a mountain!

THREE VOICES: Such a mountain I saw.

ONE VOICE: And suddenly
               a strange thing happened.

THREE VOICES:	The mountain moved!
ONE VOICE:	Moved! And the thousands of shoes arranged themselves
ONE VOICE:	by size
ONE VOICE:	by pairs
ONE VOICE:	and in rows
THREE VOICES:	and moved.
ONE VOICE:	Hear! Hear the march. Hear the shuffle of shoes left behind, that which remained from each and every one. Make way for the rows,
ONE VOICE:	for the pairs,
ONE VOICE:	for the generations,
ONE VOICE:	for the years and years.
THREE VOICES:	The shoe army: It moves and moves!
ONE VOICE:	We are the shoes. We are the last witnesses. We are the shoes from children;
ONE VOICE:	from fathers and mothers;
ONE VOICE:	from grandparents;
ONE VOICE:	from grandchildren;
ONE VOICE:	from Prague;
ONE VOICE:	Paris;
ONE VOICE:	Amsterdam
ONE VOICE:	And because we are only made of stuff and leather and not of blood and flesh, each one of us avoided the hell-fire, We shoes that used to go strolling
THREE VOICES:	in the marketplace or with the bride and groom to the chuppa.
ONE VOICE:	We shoes from simple Jews,
ONE VOICE:	from butchers and carpenters;
ONE VOICE:	from crocheted booties of babies just beginning to walk and go on happy occasions.

ONE VOICE:	Weddings and even until the time of giving birth;
THREE VOICES:	To a dance;
ONE VOICE:	To exciting places;
THREE VOICES:	TO LIFE!
ONE VOICE:	To a funeral.
ONE VOICE:	Unceasingly we go. We tramp.
ONE VOICE:	The hangman never had a chance
ONE VOICE:	to snatch us into his sack of loot.
ONE VOICE:	Now we get to him.
ONE VOICE,	Let everyone hear the steps
SLOWLY:	which flow as tears, the steps that measure out the judgment.
THREE VOICES,	I saw a mountain
FORCEFULLY:	higher than Mount Blanc,
REVERENTLY:	And more holy than the Mountain of Sinai.

Moses Shulstein, "I Saw a Mountain." Trans. Mindele Wajsman and Bea Stadtler, in Michael Berenbaum (ed.), *The World Must Know* (Boston: Little Brown, 1993). Reprinted by permission of the United States Holocaust Memorial Museum.

Sometimes the performers are moved to remove their shoes and stack them in a pile, leading the others in the class, or others in a small audience, to do the same. This has encouraged many of the students to engage in discussions about how it feels to imagine that this is all that is left of their lives, of their endeavors, their dreams, their parents' dreams for them, their hopes for the future—this pile of shoes. It is a sobering demonstration both for them and for me.

I have told them about seeing a real mountain of shoes at Majdanek and another at Auschwitz, and I have a poster hanging in the classroom from the United States Holocaust Memorial Museum; of a part of that shoe mountain in Auschwitz. (To obtain a complete set of posters and the set of lesson plans, contact the United States Holocaust Memorial Museum, 100 Raoul Wallenberg Place, SW, Washington, D.C. 20024-2126.) We talk about the shoes in the poster, the shoes that were found in a barracks after the death camp was liberated; and we take as much time as the students need to go over the lesson, which accompanies the poster set in which the "shoes" poster, developed by educators associated with the United States Holocaust Memorial Museum, is included. In doing so, we pay particular attention to the complete "loss of self" that occurred in the camps.

This poem, the poster, and our discussions bring home to the young people in my classes the enormity of what happened to people just like themselves: the dignity of the lives of masses of human beings stripped down to moldering mountains of shoes.

An excellent way to begin a discussion of the poster is simply to ask the students what they see. Some of the many observations students have made in the past are: a huge pile of shoes, scuffed shoes, shoes of all sizes and styles, women's shoes, fancy shoes, a shoe with buckles, children's shoes, work shoes, dress shoes, men's shoes, baby's shoes, etc. As the students call out what they see, the teacher should list the items on the board. Once the list has been compiled, the following question can be asked by the teacher: What do these images on the board tell us about the Holocaust? The latter question often generates an insightful and moving discussion, in which the following issues are dealt with: the huge spectrum of victims; the age of the victims (including the fact that babies who had hardly begun to live were victims of the Nazis, too); and the fact that gender, age, wealth, and lack thereof did not preclude an individual from becoming a victim of the Nazis.

One student named Sarah was moved to write the following:

> It is so hard for me to comprehend what it must have been like to be so completely stripped of all a person's belongings, of a person's very name, instead of which one was given a cold, hard number, of one's entire past, and then of one's future as that person is led to the gas chamber. Or even led to the kind of labor like the women had to do in Charlotte Delbo's book that would eventually lead to death, maybe even a worse one than gas.
>
> I try to imagine stepping out of my shoes onto a cold floor and then walking that awful way to the "showers." Little kids, how they must have shivered and been scared. Old people, how they must have found it hard to walk on their old feet. Those women in the fields, how they must have suffered in those awful wooden clogs, leaving bloody footprints behind them.
>
> Do you know what has happened to me since I've been reading that poem and staring at that poster and learning what those people went through? I've been learning how to walk all over again. I've been feeling my comfortable shoes. I've been thinking how good it feels to step on a bath mat and the bedroom carpet. Then, I've been thinking how I would feel if I were in the places of those people who left their shoes behind, or who were torn from their shoes. I've been learning to walk in six million pairs of shoes. I know there weren't six million pairs in that mountain of shoes, but six million people left shoes somewhere, and I'm learning to walk in the shoes they left behind.

Another topic we discuss with the study and the dramatization of this poem is the distances the captors made so many millions of people travel to meet death. The idea for doing this came from a student—Sarah again—after she viewed such videos as *Escape from Sobibor* and *Schindler's List*. These movies include scenes of Jewish prisoners on trains, and portray the cramped conditions, lack of water and food, the evident fear, the wrenching experience of traveling from the known to the unknown. Sarah asked the questions: "How long did they have to suffer like that? From where to where and during how many days? So we can try to understand a little of the pain and terror they knew."

Using Martin Gilbert's (1991) *Atlas of the Holocaust*, we follow the train lines, first from the cities named in the poem—Prague, Amsterdam, Paris—to the concentration camps and the killing centers we have already learned about: Auschwitz-Birkenau, Sobibor, Mauthausen, Buchenwald, Sachsenhausen, Bergen-Belsen, Dachau, Treblinka, Majdanek, etc. Then, we study train schedules and routes—here we are able to use Hilberg's (1985) studies on the subject and, again, Gilbert's (1991, pp. 157–217) *Atlas of the Holocaust*—from all the other countries of Europe from which Jews and other victims were transported to the camps. We were hardly scientific about this, but after reading Hilberg (1985) and Gilbert (1991), students plotted the distances from Holland to Sobibor, from Drancy in France to Auschwitz, from Warsaw to Treblinka, and so on. This exercise made much more vivid the experiences of the people of the shoes.

Other things to be learned from and around the poem are something of the culture, the customs, and the history of the people who were torn from their shoes. As much as time allows us, we uncover the long-time culture of the Jews in such places as Vienna, Budapest, Hamburg, Amsterdam, Venice, Rome, Prague, Warsaw, Kiev, and so many other places.

What has been extremely helpful to us here is a several week-long research project the civic students have already done on ethnic Americans in the United States. Where have they come from? What was life like in the "old country"? When and why did they emigrate? Where did they settle when they reached this country? What have their contributions been to our culture and history?

Whenever possible, students have used their own family histories: they design time lines; examine family trees, letters, and photos; and do interviews with parents, grandparents, aunts, and uncles. They interview friends and neighbors about their family histories. When possible, they bring in a relative who knows something about the family history. We study all the ethnic American groups at one time or another, but when we reach the Holocaust, the most helpful have been the histories of those whose families have come from Russia, Germany, Italy, France, the Netherlands, Denmark, Sweden, and all the countries of central and eastern Europe. Some among them have been Jews, and their stories are particularly poignant.

We can ask: What have they left us? What have they brought to the United States to enrich our lives here? What were *shtetls*? What was Eastern European Jewry like, that culture that has been lost to the world with the destruction of 6,000 Jewish communities? What is a *chuppa*? What is a Hebrew wedding ceremony like? Through what kinds of dances did those shoes carry the people? Other than the butchers and carpenters mentioned, what were some of the age-old crafts and professions of the Jews throughout Europe?

Our guests, both survivors and rescuers, are able to help us with a number of these questions. Harry Bialor, born Chaim Lebel Bialosukinski (about whom I have written the book, *Night People, A Story of the Holocaust*) is a survivor of the Holocaust in Poland. He lived as a child in the shtetl of Rutki, near Bialystok, Poland. His father was a tailor who had friends in many trades and crafts, and all his family but one sister were massacred there. He comes to us and talks not only of his experiences as a child in the Holocaust but of shtetl and Jewish family life. He has a great relationship with young people and holds them enthralled. They all read the book about him before he comes to visit our class from Brooklyn, and they ask scores of questions. He is a singer, pianist, and composer, and sings Yiddish songs and teaches us Yiddish and other Jewish dances.

"Harry makes it all so real to us," wrote Amos in his journal. In an unique afterthought, Amos mused: "I can see the streets, almost taste his mother's cooking—I wish I knew what *tsimis* tastes like, I can feel the music; and when he talked about when the Germans came, and all his family being killed and about the mass grave, and the synagogue that was burned, and all the people that were beaten and killed, it made me think they were killing God. I wonder if God cries?"

The story of Stephan Lewy, a child growing up in Berlin when the Nazis came to power, is one of his parents' frantic and years-long effort to get him out of Germany, through France, into and out of Vichy France, to North Africa, and finally to America. He tells us about Berlin and Jewish life there, a life that included his father's serving in the German military during World War I, for which he earned a medal for valor.

Marion Pritchard, a rescuer from the Netherlands who now lives in Vermont and whose story is in the book *The Courage to Care* and the video by the same name, tells us not only of her experiences and those of other rescuers trying to hide and save Jewish children but of the Jewish community in Holland and the rich culture they made there.

After one of Marion's visits, a student wrote: "She's so tiny and so gentle. It's hard to believe all she did, all the risks she took. What she really did, or what it boils down to, I think, is that she took on the whole German occupying army to save those children and other families, and she won. I wanted to hug her."

Another student wrote: "I realized that cultural conditioning is no excuse for cowardice. This woman, Marion Pritchard, this hero, did things that I have difficulty seeing woman [sic] do in today's society . . . Marion Pritchard has earned more than my respect, she has earned my undying admiration."

A poem that helps us both ask and answer questions about the Holocaust and the experience of those millions who suffered in it is in Charlotte Delbo's *Auschwitz and After* (1995). The poem, which is untitled, is once again read either in small groups that have had a chance to practice it, or by an individual girl who has rehearsed. A girl is chosen because the book is about women's experiences in Auschwitz.

> This dot on the map
> this black spot at the core of Europe
> this red spot
> this spot of fire this spot of soot
> this spot of blood this spot of ashes
> for millions
> a nameless place.
> From all the countries of Europe
> from all the points on the horizon
> trains converged
> toward the nameless place

loaded with millions of humans
poured out there unknowing of where
poured out with their lives
memories
small aches
huge astonishment
eyes questioning
bamboozled
underfire
burned
without knowing
where they were.
Today people know
have known for several years
that this dot on the map
is Auschwitz

This much they know
as for the rest
they think they know.

Charlotte Delbo, "This Black Dot," from *Auschwitz and After* (1995). Reprinted by permission of Yale University Press.

This poem has a powerful effect on my students, as powerful as any poem they study. Here again they ask the questions: Who were the people? Where did they come from? What did they leave behind? How far did they have to travel? What were the conditions aboard those trains that came "from all points on the horizon"? What must they have felt coming to this nameless place?

Similar discussions and journal writings as we'd had after "A Mountain of Shoes" followed upon the reading of this poem. Melissa, one of the "coolest" and least easily moved of my students, sat in deep thought after the first reading of this poem. Then she asked for the opportunity to read it aloud alone, which she did, quietly. Finally, she took up her pen and wrote in her journal, in part:

> I get nervous sometimes just going on a field trip to Boston to see the museums. I can't imagine—I try, but I can't imagine what it would be like to be pushed on that train, maybe alone with my family all gone somewhere, and to be sent hundreds of miles to a strange place where there is fire and where there is [*sic*] ashes falling, and I can only guess what they mean; and the dogs are barking, and I'm shoved into a line of other scared people, and I wonder if I'll ever again see those things I'm familiar with . . . It makes me want to cry because I feel so bad for those people, and it makes me want to cry because I can't put myself in their shoes, and it just makes me want to cry. I hate that dot on the map!"

Melissa and her neighbor, Jeff, one of our best athletes and a boy in love with the game of chess, talked for a while, and then Jeff, after writing something similar to Melissa's response, added to his journal:

I think I maybe know what Charlotte Delbo meant when she wrote that today people know about Auschwitz the place, but "as for the rest, they think they know." She knew no one could know what it was like there. I don't think that I can ever understand what it was like for those people on the trains going from all over Europe to that spot on the map and never leaving it again. What I do think is that it changes the way I think about other people and about the bad things that happened to people—I mean I wouldn't ever want to be responsible for being powerful enough to move people around like pieces on a chessboard.

Another of the favorite pieces of literature of my students is *In Kindling Flame,* the factual story of martyred Hannah Senesh, the young Jewish poet who left the safety of Palestine to return with the British Air Force to her homeland, Hungary, to fight with and for her people. Her apprehension by the Arrow Cross and her months of torture, under which she never broke to reveal the names of partisans and the radio code, and then her execution on the very eve of the arrival of the Russian troops into Budapest, capture the imagination of my students every year. They always ask themselves, "What would I have done under those awful circumstances?" None of us knows what we would have done of course, but the students involve themselves in discussions about our responsibilities as human beings to other human beings. Are our lives worth living if we continue life at the expense of others, at the cost of the lives of others whom we might help or save?

The students' favorite poem by Hannah Senesh is the following:

Blessed is the Match
by Hannah Senesh

Blessed is the match
that is consumed
in kindling flame.

Blessed is the flame that burns
in the secret fastness
of the heart.

Blessed is the heart
with its strength to stop
its beating for honor's sake.

Blessed is the match
that is consumed
in kindling flame.

Quoted in *In Kindling Flame* by Linda Atkinson. Copyright © 1985 by Linda Atkinson. Used by permission of HarperCollins Publishing.

The images called up in such a poem are many, poignant, and always thought-provoking. They provoke amazing discussions among students as young as the ones in the class, 14 and 15 years of age.

First they explore among themselves what Hannah's imagery is in the poem and suggest to one another how the burning match can be compared to a heart, especially Hannah's heart; or to their heart, if they care deeply enough about something or someone.

"Do I care enough about anything or anyone to die for it or him or her?" pondered Amy, a young woman who is already working hard to save money for the college she knows her parents can't pay for, but who has the softest heart around, though she wouldn't admit to it.

"Maybe it's hard for us to be sure, because we have never really been faced with anything that threatens anyone close to us, or that threatens me personally," said Joey, a handsome young man from a comfortably situated family, who will probably never have to work very hard to accomplish all he wishes to and who is a fine student and a creative graphic artist.

"I have been faced with something that threatened someone close to me," said Jennifer, a tiny blonde and a real renaissance woman, expert at all she does, who loves to read and perform in the drama group, and who brings down the house when she's in a play or musical. "My cousin who grew up next door to me had cancer, and I remember our families talking about how it was going to be necessary to have bone marrow transplants. Some of the family in both houses were having tests made to see if they could donate. It scared me, because I heard them talk about how uncomfortable, even painful, that kind of donation was going to be—you know, not like just giving blood. Her brother, who is only a couple of years older than I am, volunteered; and I couldn't sleep for wondering what I would say if someone asked me to go ahead and try to donate."

"What did you decide?" I asked.

"I didn't have to decide anything, because it was decided he could donate. My cousin is not cured yet, but she is somewhat better. But I don't think I'll ever get over being a little ashamed that I had about decided I couldn't do it. I still don't know what I would say if it came down to me. And it's such a little thing compared with what Hannah Senesh did."

"I have sometimes not come forward to tell the truth about something that happened in school—when I maybe could have kept a student out of trouble," commented Dorinne, a lovely, gentle child and a favorite of all her classmates. She's a student with learning disabilities, but one who works harder than anyone else in any class. "I don't like to think about that. It makes me wonder how I would act in really awful circumstances."

Last year at the institute in a student journal, the following was written:

With us here is a girl who came from Bosnia and who is staying with relatives in New Hampshire. What she described that had happened to her and her family was terrible. Just like they did to the Jews during the Holocaust, she said they were rounding up all the people in her town and throwing them on trucks and driving them to camps—I think she said the Serbs were rounding up her people, but I'm not sure. And her family and friends were put on trucks and taken to camps. She couldn't tell us all that happened to her and our teacher told us not to put pressure on her to answer.

Anyhow, I remember that one evening in our talks, she suddenly said she was going to try to go back to Bosnia, and she is only 17, and she told us she was going to do everything she could so nobody would have to go through what she and her family had gone through, so that other kids could have their childhood better than she had hers. She said she just wanted people to live in peace and to have enough food to eat.

I would be scared to go back, but I have a feeling that she'll get there if she can and that she'll do exactly what she said she would do. She reminds me of Hanna Senesh in the book and video [*Hanna's War*] Ms. Dutton had us study.

I wonder, and a lot of us talked about it, if I could go back to something like that where I might be tortured or put in a camp or die. I think that is what Hanna meant in her poem about a heart having enough strength to stop beating for something honorable. I really think that for me my head would have to stop itself from thinking first, so I wouldn't be afraid and could just go ahead and do what I have to do. But then, maybe that isn't courage. Courage, I guess, would be to be afraid and to act anyhow.

The students talked about the various things they had been studying and what some of the causes were that people had suffered and died for. They also discussed exactly what Hanna could have meant by honor and what honor meant to them. One student, Dorinne, wrote:

I think honor must mean knowing what is the right thing to do and not letting anything at all stop you from doing that, even if that means you are in a certain kind of danger. I think another person who knew what was right and who was willing to stop his heart from beating for honor's sake was that writer and teacher Ms. Dutton read to us about, Janusz Korczak, when he went with the children in the orphanage he was taking care of to the train and then to the death camp. He could have stayed alive, but then the kids would be scared, and it wasn't right to let them go off all alone on the train being scared; so he went with them to die. That's honor.

They asked questions of one another, sometimes without trying to answer the questions, just having their own kind of courage phrasing the questions: What does honor mean to me personally? Could I die for it? What kind of courage does it take to die for a cause? What kind of strength? What kind of belief? Do I have it? Where did the Jews and so many others find the courage and the strength to die for what they believed in, whatever it was?

In response to these questions, another journal writer, Tim, a giant of a boy, dark, muscled, already a football star on the Junior Varsity, and sweet of nature, wrote:

What kind of courage did it take for Harry Bialor to lie hidden in that tiny bunker under a barn for two years, to sneak out at night and face wolves and people who wanted to kill him, to steal food so the peasant's wife would let them stay hidden? He wanted to die and be away from the hunger and the cold and the lice and the rats and the fear, but he remembered his father before he was murdered telling him he had to survive because he was the only one left. They didn't know about Masha [the sister] then. He did things I can't imagine anyone being able to do, and I think he found the courage because of the honor of keeping something of his family alive. I'm so glad he did, but I don't know how he did it when he was just my age.

Another student, Susan, who already knows that what she wants out of life is to have five children as her parents did; to live in a big, rambling house; to have yard enough and barns enough to have pets of every description; and to sit on the front porch and paint pictures of Vermont mountains and forests, wrote:

> I guess I've just come to believe that our living a kind of life, our really being spoiled, is no excuse for not doing the right thing. The hard part would be to be courageous and to be strong and to do something for honor if I thought no one would ever know about it. Hanna didn't know anyone would know what she had done for honor, but she did it anyhow. That makes me want to cry when I think about it.

There is one more poem we use which I wish to share. I was fortunate enough to be one of those who participated in the annual summer seminar sponsored by the American Gathering of Jewish Labor Committee and the American Federation of Teachers. Led by the wonderful Vladka Meed, who as a young woman was a member of the Warsaw Ghetto resistance, we traveled to and studied in Poland, where we visited the death camps. At Yad Vashem, the Holocaust Martyrs' and Heroes' Remembrance Authority, where we studied under noted scholars, writers, and survivors, we were given batches of literature that we could add to our courses of studies on the Holocaust. The following poem, which was published there and which has no named author, was among the literature:

Ein Leben

In the month of her death, she is standing by the windowframe,
a young woman with stylish permanent wave.
She seems to be in a contemplative mood
as she stands there looking out the window.

Through the glass an afternoon cloud of 1938
looks in at her, blurred, slightly out of focus,
but her faithful servant. On the inside
I'm the one looking at her, four years old almost,

holding back my ball, quietly
going out of the photo and growing old,
growing old carefully, quietly
so as not to frighten her.

Anonymous.

This is a poem we do not immediately discuss, but rather we read it several times over. This is a poem that could break your heart, and young hearts are already too easily broken. But this is an important image and one that may prompt us all to care very deeply. We all write in our journals what we think and feel about the poem, and then we are able "quietly/so as not to frighten her" to discuss what it may be about. We ask questions to which there can be no answers, only painful conjectures.

Nineteen thirty-eight is a significant year, the year of "the month of her death." Whose death? Apparently someone's mother—at least, we believe that is so. How did she die? In 1938, German Jews were beginning to die at the hands of their countrymen and women, at the hands of Nazi officials, in that awful year of Kristallnacht (a planned action of violence carried out by the Nazis on November 9 and 10, 1938, throughout the Reich, which then included Germany, Austria, and the Sudetenland, when over 1,000 synagogues were burned, 7,000 Jewish businesses were vandalized, and over 90 Jews were killed). Was this "young woman"—we assume she was Jewish from the way the poem came to us—murdered along with the 90 or so others?

And what of the child, either a girl or a boy who is playing with a ball? The child was saved, somehow, from the fate of her mother, the "young woman." What saved her? Who saved her? What rescuer was there, like Marion Pritchard, with "the courage to care" enough about a Jewish child to hide her, save her, allow the child to grow old? To grow old as the mother in the photo never had the chance to do.

There are many stories, many histories, many conclusions in the journal accounts that have centered around this poem over the past few years, but every one of them agrees that this poem is the image that can make one care deeply about what happened. It is the image necessary to personalize all those millions who died in the Holocaust.

One student last year wrote the following, which I confess made me cry when I read it:

"This poem I think is what will burn 'in the secret fastness of my heart' for as long as I live."

Another student, Katie, with long brown curls, five foot nine inches tall, with a slim athletic form which she puts to star use as a field hockey player, and the child of a physician (mother) and teacher (father), wrote:

> I've thought and thought and thought about that woman in the picture, and it made me think of all the times I've fought with my own mother when she wouldn't let me do something I wanted to do. I've looked at some photos of my mother with the rest of us and wonder how I would feel if, like the person with the ball in the picture, I had to leave my mother, alone, in that picture, to grow old without her. I try to imagine things like we have learned happening to me and my little brother and my parents—and I can't! It hurts. I want to be better to my mother. I just want all the hating and hurting to stop.
>
> But what must have been the very hardest for the girl leaving the picture is that she probably never knew as she grew older what had happened to her mother. She must have imagined what happened and had terrible thoughts and dreams about it, because she would hear what awful things had happened to other people like her mother. So more than just the mother suffered. The girl must have suffered all her life wondering how her mother had died.
>
> How many millions of people who [survived] have wondered the same sad things about their lost families?

Do any of these lessons we have learned together last? Do they become a permanent part of the consciousness of the students? Do they help to determine how students will act in later years? Do they remember beyond graduation?

I should mention that 7 years ago a wonderful woman in Waltham, Massachusetts, having heard about our Holocaust Studies program from newspaper accounts, granted Windsor High School an annual scholarship fund for the best

Holocaust essay produced each year. I was to select the best essay, and the funds were to be administered by me and the school administration. So each year we have the essay contest, and each year the essays that come across my desk are wonderful to read. Some have been entered in the annual essay contest sponsored by the United States Holocaust Memorial Museum in Washington, D.C. One of the winners of that contest, Hallie Davis, wrote her essay when she was a junior. She was one of the frequent performers of the poem "A Mountain of Shoes," and went on to college at Boston College. In her first year there, she wrote me the following letter, which *The Windsor Chronicle* published:

Dear Ms Dutton,

My friends and I frequently gather around talking about various ethnic groups among us. These friends consist of a tall black man, a nineteen-year-old Hispanic girl, and three or four Caucasian women such as myself.

Xenia, the Hispanic girl, mentions that she has been called a 'spic.' Nigel, our black friend, says that he has had racial slurs directed towards him. I am frustrated to hear two of my friends talk so calmly about the injustice they have faced. I cannot tolerate ignorance. I grow emotional as I remember all the feelings evoked in me when I was at Windsor High in the Holocaust Studies Course.

The Holocaust occurred in Europe but affected the entire world. It was a time when people were killed because of the same kind of racial labeling and hatred, though more intense, which my friends have faced. In Europe the target of the hatred was mostly the Jewish populations of various countries. The so-called Aryan people rejected anyone who did not fit into their ethnic and religious mold. They depicted those "outsiders" by looks, names, slurs. With their own set of guidelines, the Aryans disposed of Jews, Gypsies, the physically challenged, political dissidents, and others, while the world watched.

The United States and its allies fought a war against Hitler and the Nazis for territorial and political reasons, but no effort was made to end the killing of so many millions of minorities, mostly the Jews. Most of the countries of Europe were even glad to extend the concentration camps, and collection centers beyond Germany to within their own borders.

Millions upon millions of people were rendered powerless and then were exterminated for their differences. Just that—for being different. What have we learned from that black night in history? Fifty years after those mass killings, people are still judging, still segregating others because they are different. My friends are labeled, just as the Jews and others were. They are made to feel inferior, as those who suffered in the Holocaust were made to feel inferior.

The hatred that brought about the Holocaust is still everywhere in our world. In Bosnia. In Rwanda. In Indonesia. In Myanmar. In the United States. No one should tolerate such hatred and discrimination. I would not want to see my friends walking into gas chambers for the insane reason that they are different. Too many have already died for that reason.

Obviously, Hallie has carried what she learned with her and will go on being the best possible role model for her friends and classmates. I am confident she will carry what she learned, what she came to care deeply about, into all the experiences of her life, as other students have. Is there any reward for a teacher greater than that?

In addition to studying about what the Jews and others suffered in the Holocaust, we have spent considerable time concentrating on all aspects of the resistance of the Jews to what was being done to them, both armed and spiritual resistance. We study the Warsaw Ghetto uprising, the escape from Sobibor, the Bielski Partisans in the forests of Poland, the revolts in Treblinka and in Auschwitz, and we learn as much as we can of all the many ways Jews throughout Europe defied the edicts of the Nazi masters against educating their children and against holding religious services. We can only touch upon a few of the thousands of acts of resistance, but those few make a difference to the students learning about them.

One journal writer, our "cool" Melissa, about whom we've already written, put it this way:

> Now that we are about through, I don't know what stays with me the most, but I do know I believe the Jews in all the ways they resisted what was happening to them were the bravest people I have ever heard about. No one should have to die to teach the rest of us how to live in peace with one another, but I can't think anymore about the Jews and the others being just victims. They are our teachers. And that's cool. I just hope that we can learn enough from them to turn our world around and stop hating.

Another student, Kimberly, who is very quick, bright, and talented in a variety of ways; conscious of her weight; and with a history of being argumentative and even verbally assaultive, eloquently said:

> I don't know how I can ever again call someone a name because they are different from me. I don't know how I can ever hate anyone again—except maybe the people who hate others. No, not even them. The thing about Harry Bialor I'll always remember is that he is so kind, that he can't hate anyone, that he and his sister wouldn't even let the Russians find his father's murderers and punish them. "I was through with hate," he said. So am I.

REFERENCES

Atkinson, Linda. (1985). *In Kindling Flame: The Story of Hanna Senesh 1921–1944*. New York: Beech Tree Books.

Berenbaum, Michael. (1993). *The World Must Know: The History of the Holocaust as Told in the United States Holocaust Memorial Museum*. Boston, MA: Little, Brown.

Delbo, Charlotte. (1995). *Auschwitz and After*. New Haven, CT: Yale University Press.

Dutton, Beth. (1995). *Night People, a Story of the Holocaust*. New York: Hanna Publications.

Frank, Anne. (1991). *The Diary of a Young Girl.* New York: Doubleday.

Gamm, Hans Jochen. (1984). "Anti-Semitism from Christian Roots." In Shalom Leven (Ed.), *International Anthology on Racism and Anti-Semitism* (pp. 17–21). Germany, France, Israel, Netherlands, U.S.A.: International Committee of Educators to Combat Racism, Anti-Semitism and Apartheid.

Gilbert, Martin. (1987). *The Holocaust: A History of the Jews of Europe During the Second World War.* New York: Henry Holt.

Gilbert, Martin. (1991). *Atlas of the Holocaust.* New York: Pergamon Press.

Gilbert, Martin. (1993). *Atlas of Jewish History.* New York: William Morrow.

Hilberg, Raul. (1985). *The Destruction of the European Jews.* Student Edition. New York: Holmes and Meier.

Landau, Elaine. (1992). *The Warsaw Ghetto Uprising.* New York: New Discovery Books.

Levin, Nora. (1973). *The Holocaust: The Destruction of European Jewry 1933–1945.* New York: Schocken Books.

Meed, Vladka. (1977). *On Both Sides of the Wall.* Beit Lohamei Haghettaot/Ghetto Fighters House Kibbutz: Hakibbutz Hameuchad Publishing House.

Rittner, Carol, & Meyers, Sondra. (Eds.) (1989). *The Courage to Care: Rescuers of Jews During the Holocaust.* New York: New York University Press.

Rogasky, Barbara. (1988). *Smoke and Ashes: The Story of the Holocaust.* New York: Holiday House.

Senesh, Hanna. (1985). "Blessed Is the Match." In Linda Atkinson, *In Kindling Flame: The Story of Hanna Senesh 1921–1944.* New York: Beech Tree Books.

Shulstein, Moses. (1993). "I Saw a Mountain." Mindele Wajsman and Bea Stadtler, trans. In Michael Berenbaum (Ed.), *The World Must Know: The History of the Holocaust as Told in the United States Holocaust Memorial Museum* (pp. 145, 147). Boston, MA: Little, Brown.

Wiesel, Elie. (1960). *Night.* New York: Bantam Books.

Yahil, Leni. (1990). *The Holocaust: The Fate of European Jewry, 1932–1945.* New York: Oxford University Press.

CHAPTER

10 Choiceless Choices and Illusions of Power

A Study of *Throne of Straw in the Lodz Ghetto* in an Advanced Placement English Class

CAROL DANKS

How much darkness must we acknowledge before we will be able to confess that the Holocaust story cannot be told in terms of heroic dignity, moral courage, and the triumph of the human spirit in adversity?

—Langer, 1995, p. 158.

Nothing is more corrupting than the illusion of power. Your plumage casts no shadow and your throne is made of straw.

—Lieberman and Lieberman, 1982, p. 134.

A common thread in Holocaust literature focuses on how and why people behaved in situations of extremity. This is certainly true of Harold and Edith Lieberman's *Throne of Straw,* a play about the Lodz Ghetto in Poland and, in particular, the motives and actions of Mordechai Chaim Rumkowski, the head of the *Judenrat* or Jewish Council.

Among the many questions that served as focus points for my Advanced Placement (AP) English seniors as we studied *Throne of Straw* were the following: What real options do people have when only negative choices are offered? What does it mean to act morally in a world pervaded by immorality? How can a reader or audience member be drawn into a world filled with forced choices that probably have no ultimate positive impact on a character's life? What is an appropriate response from an audience watching the unfolding of such dilemmas on stage?

Lodz, an important textile center and the second largest city in the country, is located in the southwest section of Poland; it was home to the second largest number of Jews in Poland at the beginning of World War II. After the city's occupation by the Germans on September 8, 1939, Lodz Jews were almost immediately subjected to brutal persecution in all facets of their lives. On October 13–14, 1939, the Germans appointed a *Judenrat,* or council of Jewish elders, who were responsible for carrying out German orders, with Rumkowski as its chair. Hans Biebow headed the ghetto administration and oversaw the creation of 120 factories in which Jews worked as slave laborers through the summer of 1944.

Rumkowski wielded much power, but his measure of choice in performing his duties was found only within the German orders; not to obey those orders was not a viable alternative in the face of retributive German actions. In general, Rumkowski displayed "great zeal and organizational ability in running the factories and the internal life of the ghetto. He exploited to the full the wide powers given to him and did not give veteran leaders and Jewish public figures any role to play in the affairs of the ghetto. In addition, he manifested domineering and self-promoting tendencies" (Krakowski, 1990, p. 1313). As a result, his great authority "earned him the hatred of most of the ghetto population" (Krakowski, 1990, p. 1313).

In 1941 he had "warned [the ghetto population] of the potential consequences of idleness" (Dobroszycki, 1984, p. 195). In a long speech delivered on January 4, 1942, Rumkowski was specific about the idleness that he observed:

> From the beginning I have been striving to achieve one basic goal. That goal is to be able to demonstrate to the [German] authorities that the ghetto is composed exclusively of working people . . . Unfortunately, a large portion of ghetto society has not wished to understand this. . . . Representatives of the new population, I appeal to you again to finally adapt to the conditions of life in the ghetto. Aren't you ashamed that I have had to use policemen to force you to work? That I had to resort to confining you to your work crews? (Dobroszycki, 1984, pp. 113–115)

Then, in a speech to about 5,000 people on May 31, 1942, he "emphasized that considerable blame is to be borne here by the populace itself for having been reluctant to work" (Dobroszycki, 1984, p. 195). With tactics such as these, Rumkowski managed to keep Lodz the longest-functioning ghetto and save the largest number of inhabitants relative to other ghettos.

Opinions about the morality of his actions vary considerably. Rumkowski himself believed that he was doing the best he could to save as many Jews as possible. However, some people see him as "a traitor and a collaborator. Others believe that his policies—toward both the Jews and the Germans—helped extend the life span of the Lodz ghetto" (Krakowski, 1990, p. 1314).

Throne of Straw presents situations based on historical scenarios in which both Rumkowski and other Jewish characters are confronted with decisions for which no choice seems entirely laudable. Among such issues are: Is it better to force people to work in an attempt to save their lives or to allow them to do as they wish knowing full well that they will likely face deportation if they do not work?

Is it better to work for the Jewish police and perhaps save one's life, or refuse on principle to join a force one sees as antagonistic, knowing full well that should you refuse you and your family face potential deportation?

All of the students at Roosevelt High School in Kent, Ohio, a mid-sized university town in middle America, study literature of the Holocaust for 3 to 6 weeks during their freshman English class. That unit provides extensive historical background and focuses on a variety of Holocaust literature, especially first-person accounts, primary documents such as Nazi laws and speeches, and poetry. Students write poems and short stories that have their origin in some aspect of the Holocaust unit. During their sophomore and junior years, students have little or no opportunity to study anything about the Holocaust. Given the flexibility of the Advanced Placement English 12 curriculum that I teach, I have the liberty to include a unit on Holocaust literature. However, because of the need to prepare students for the Advanced Placement test in May, I do not feel that we can devote a long unit to the subject.

I am privileged to have had many of the current seniors in my freshman English classes and thus was curious to see how much information about the Holocaust they retained. A key is to have my seniors revisit some of the moral questions and dilemmas arising from their earlier study of the Holocaust.

The major goals of my 5-day unit on *Throne of Straw* are: to extend the students' knowledge of the Lodz Ghetto, to address the emotional responses raised by the play, and to confront moral questions. Since the students study a variety of drama during the year, from Sophocles to Shakespeare and from Miller to Beckett, they already have a grounding about drama itself which allows them to grapple with the problems of how to depict Holocaust issues on the stage. Because of the latter and the strong analytical focus of the AP course, another major goal is to address issues of dramatic technique and presentation, especially aspects of presenting historical events like the Holocaust through fictional means.

I begin the unit by asking the students to write for 5 minutes about what they know about the Holocaust and, if they know a lot, to focus on what they remember about the ghettos. Because of their freshman unit, I expect them to have a reasonable amount of knowledge. Nearly all of them comment on specific information they remember—historical events, a poem, a book. Some echo Caitlin Winnen's statement that one of [her] most vivid memories from the ninth-grade Holocaust unit is reading *Night* (the powerful memoir of survivor by noted author Elie Wiesel). She also comments on the tremendous personal impact of a visit to the Holocaust Museum in Washington, D.C. Another student, Heather Lipinski, has similar strong memories of that school trip to the museum:

> I really don't remember much from 9th grade English class, but in April of that year I went to D.C. and we went through the Holocaust Museum and I just remember the enormous piles of shoes. I remember the wall that went all the way to the top of the building filled with pictures of those that died and that my person [on the identity card that museum patrons carry with them throughout the main exhibit] survived through the first two-thirds of the tour but died as we entered the third.

Hayley Halter wrote that she didn't "remember specifics just the overall of what happened," and then continued with numerous specifics such as the existence of ghettos, the wearing of the star, the imposition of curfews, near starvation, deportation, concentration camps, and mass killings.

Given the students' knowledge base, I feel comfortable with a short unit focusing on a single play; but teachers must be careful to tailor their classroom units to their specific students. It would be irresponsible for a teacher to simply insert any unit on the Holocaust willy-nilly. Students must understand the historical background of the Holocaust when they experience the literature. They must realize that there are no easy answers to questions of why and how civilized people committed genocide.

In his introduction to *The Theatre of the Holocaust: Four Plays,* editor Robert Skloot (1982) points out that playwrights of the theater of the Holocaust are motivated by five objectives: (1) to pay homage to the victims, if not as individuals, then as a group; (2) to educate audiences to the facts of history; (3) to produce an emotional response to those facts; (4) to raise certain moral questions for audiences to discuss and reflect upon; and (5) to draw a lesson for the events recreated (p. 14).

Throne of Straw admirably addresses all of these objectives. As previously mentioned, the play's point of departure is the existence of the ghetto in Lodz and the leading role played by the *Judenrat* leader Mordechai Chaim Rumkowski. It combines four historically accurate individuals with a fictional Jewish family and focuses primarily on conflicts among the Jewish victims rather than conflicts between the Jews and the Nazi perpetrators. Because of the near absolute Nazi power over the Jews, there was little actual "conflict" between those two groups. For Jews, punishment and/or death at the hands of the Nazis was the most common resolution of conflicts. The Nazi-imposed power structure to implement orders within the ghetto, namely a *Judenrat,* meant that points of conflict were more likely to occur between the Jews who were forced to carry out those orders and the Jews who were impacted by them.

Literature about the Holocaust is proliferating at such an astonishing rate that the choices for teachers are abundant. That said, over and above the quality of the play itself, two factors guided my selection of *Throne of Straw*: time and focus. Because we only had one week for this unit, the work had to be one that could be dealt with adequately in that span of time. A novel seemed too long and short stories and poems too fragmented for a sharp focus. Thus, I looked for a play. Because I wanted the students to focus on moral dilemmas, a topic we discussed in our study of other literature throughout the year, I felt that the character of Rumkowski was most appropriate. While any play dealing with the Holocaust may address issues of moral choice, *Throne of Straw* does so in a very direct, focused, and effective way.

The freshman unit includes a focus on the Warsaw Ghetto, and students learn little or nothing about the Lodz Ghetto. Thus, we begin the unit with three background pieces. I show a 20-minute segment from the beginning of an excellent video entitled *Lodz Ghetto* (1992), which provides background on the creation and early days of the ghetto. I also give students a copy of the Rumkowski entry from the *Encyclopedia of the Holocaust* (Krakowski, 1990, pp. 1312–1314), plus the following chronology of historical events which I compiled from the *Encyclopedia of the Holocaust's* "Lodz" entry (Krakowski, 1990, pp. 900–909):

9/1/39:	German invasion of Poland
	Lodz—665,000 population: 34% Jews, 55% Poles, 10% Germans
9/8/39:	Germans occupied Lodz
9/18/39:	Decrees by Germans:

	Economic:	Jewish bank accounts frozen.
		Jews restricted to $377 cash (in zlotys).
		Jews forbidden to be in the textile business.
	Transportation:	Jews forbidden to use public transportation.
		Jews could leave Lodz only with permission from the Germans. Jews were also forbidden to have cars.
	Religious:	Synagogue services outlawed.
		Jews were forced to keep shops open on Jewish holidays.

10/13-14/39:	Germans appointed a *Judenrat* with Mordechai Chaim Rumkowski as chairman.
11/9/39:	Lodz annexed by Germany.
11/11/39:	All *Judenrat* members except Rumkowski arrested. Eight finally released; 23 killed. Rumkowski ordered to set up new *Judenrat*.
11/12/39:	Decision made to launch mass deportations.
11/15–17/39:	All synagogues in Lodz destroyed.
11/17/39:	Jews forced to wear yellow badges in the form of a Star of David.
12/10/39:	Germans issued a secret order for the creation of a ghetto in Lodz in Jewish Baluty slum quarter.
2/8/40:	Public announcement of the establishment of the ghetto.
4/11/40:	Germans renamed Lodz as Litzmannstadt (for German general who had conquered Lodz in WWI).
4/30/40:	Ghetto blocked off (1.54 sq. miles; 164,000 Lodz Jews forced in).
5/25/40:	Hans Biebow, head of ghetto administration, ordered factories to be set up in ghetto (forced Jewish labor yielded about $14 million profit for Germans—350 million reichsmarks).
Late 1940–1942:	*Judenrat* involved with housing, sanitation, and food distribution.
Until 10/41:	*Judenrat* ran a school system.
12/40–6/42:	Deportations to forced-labor camps and then to extermination camps.
1/16/42 through 5/42:	Deportations directly to Chelmno extermination camp.
Until summer of 1942:	*Judenrat* continued to operate five hospitals.
By 8/42:	*Judenrat* staff numbered 13,000. Chief problems: starvation and deportations.

9/4/42:	Rumkowski gave "Give me your children" speech.
9/5–12/42:	Second wave of deportations to Chelmno.
9/13/42 to	
5/44:	No deportations to extermination camps.
	Relative quiet in ghetto; 90% of Jews working in factories; few children and old people in ghetto.
Spring 1944:	Nazis decide to liquidate Lodz Ghetto.
	Nazis reactivate Chelmno extermination camp.
6/23/44:	Deportations to Chelmno resumed (on pretext of forced-labor transports).
8/7/44:	Deportations to Auschwitz begun.
8/30/44:	Last transport left Lodz Ghetto for Auschwitz.
Fall of 1944:	40–60 freight cars a day took Lodz Ghetto Jews' possessions and factory equipment to Germany (600 Jews had been left to collect these possessions and prepare them for shipment). They were also joined by 230 more, who were seized in hiding.
1/19/45:	Remaining Jews liberated by Soviet army.

To extend the use of the chronology, I ask students to look for patterns and connections among the events and to think about the significance of any discrepancies they discover between historical facts and the text. In this and other ways, the students are alerted to the importance of accuracy and authenticity of historical persons and events in fiction about the Holocaust and asked to ponder this issue as they read the play and relate the chronology's historical data and the facts about Rumkowski to the play itself.

In addition to noting points of both historical accuracy and inaccuracy, I ask students to write down moments of moral choice faced by the characters. Each character has at least one moment (and some have many) in which they must make a moral decision. Within the context of the Holocaust, many of these decisions can be termed what Lawrence Langer (1982) calls "choiceless choice[s], where crucial decisions did not reflect options between life and death, but between one form of abnormal response and another, both imposed by a situation that was in no way of the victim's own choosing" (p. 72).

The four historical characters in *Throne of Straw* are: Rumkowski; Miriam, the woman who becomes his wife; Artur Greiser, the commander of Warthegau, the region of German-occupied Poland where Lodz is located; and Hans Biebow, a Nazi whose job was to turn Lodz into a great war production center. The other characters are fictional and include the Wolf family and Yankele, a rather mad (otherworldly) religious Jew who sings songs, does odd jobs, and acts as the play's witness and narrator. Although Yankele's failed attempts to find a master have made him behave oddly, his perceptive and insightful comments about both characters and actions make him a reliable narrator.

Throne of Straw raises questions about the morality—or lack thereof—of the behaviors and choices made by Rumkowski and other characters. Rumkowski is the play's protagonist and readers/viewers follow him as he must make choices to try and increase the survival possibilities of his people. Other characters must make choices regarding their own safety and/or that of their family. As Edward Feld (1994) points out, in the circumstances endured by the Jews in the Holocaust,

> the will to live, to survive, demands a certain selfishness. You must know how to fight for your life. How to steal from the dying, if need be, if that is what will keep you alive; how to use guile, how to trust few people. The will to live demands the ability to make terrible and difficult decisions; it means that you will act in a way others may understand to be immoral because you know that is what you need to do to survive. Delicate souls will not make it. And life must overcome death. . . . Yet if one simply allows toughness to rule, if one in fact becomes completely ruthless, then all is lost. The secret of surviving is knowing how to maintain the balance; it is a delicate and dangerous act, but it is all we are left with. (p. 131)

The comments of student Emma Kreyche, an insightful and thoughtful young woman, make it clear that she understands that those decisions are neither easy nor one-dimensional:

> To me, the "moments of moral choice" in *Throne of Straw* seem to be the essence of what the play is about, despite the fact that many of these "choices" are what we have labeled as "choiceless choices." In other words, the choices appear to be between bad and worse, sometimes between survival and moral compromise. I say that these "choices" are the essence of the play because there is not a single character who is not forced [to confront one of those] moments at some point during the play. Even Yankele, who serves as the play's witness and narrator, makes the choice to divide the bread with Moshe and David. I interpret that moments of moral choice are choices that *every* person faces at some point or another during his/her life. I also interpret that the choices made during those moments cannot possibly be judged by other people who have not been put in exactly the same position. This brings to mind Rumkowski's decision to ask his people to hand over their elderly, their children, and their ill. This kind of situation is *unfathomable* by the rest of the human race, and therefore goes far beyond our ability to judge.

In a writing assignment that is given on the first day but due on the last day of the unit, I also ask students to write about their definition or conception of a moment of moral choice. In "The Americanization of the Holocaust on stage and screen," Langer (1995) talks about "how thoroughly the Nazi system of terror and genocide poisoned that vital source of human dignity that made man an instrument in his fate: the phenomenon of choice" (p. 162). One of the more independent thinkers in the class, student Dyani Scheuerman, sensed this kind of poisoning when she wrote:

> I think that a moment of moral choice is better, or at least more accurately, described by its other name, "a choiceless choice." Everytime we discuss such

moments in class it is that which I think of. A choice in which one outcome is definitely favored but the other decision is the only possible route could be one example. There is also the type in which both outcomes are so undesired that it would be virtually impossible to choose one as favored. Most of the choices made in *Throne of Straw* by Harold and Edith Lieberman fall into the first category. In the choice he [Rumkowski] had to make about initially giving up the sick and elderly (later with the children, then everyone), it is obvious that ideally none of the people [should] be sent away. [His] one option, to completely disobey orders, was essentially nonexistent, because if he would have taken it, most likely Nazis would have had him killed or sent off and then seized the people in the ghetto anyway. Either choice led to the same outcome; it was just a matter of who directly made the final choice. In my opinion, [presenting] someone with such a choiceless choice is one of the most cruel things that can be done. Either way the blame will fall on them, and the only effect that might be slightly variable is the amount of guilt they felt over what their choice led to. In the second type of choiceless choice, choosing between two equally horrible outcomes, the burden of guilt would most likely be heavy in either case.

Steve Gano, a quiet, sensitive student and wrestler, focused on whether or not one should judge these choices:

In the play there are many so called "moments of moral choice" that involve decisions about what is right for survival and what is right as a human being. Although some of these choices may not be the most beneficial to everyone, we cannot judge whether or not the decisions they made were right or wrong. They have been [so] deprived of their humanity that they have nothing to rely upon except the basic animal instinct of survival. They were put in a position where helping someone else would mean to hurt themselves [or someone else], thus they must now abide by Darwin's theory of "survival of the fittest." To understand this, the reader needs to look at why they are in their position in the first place, which is the Nazis [i.e., the Nazis forced the Jews into this position]. By blaming the Jews for their actions we are blaming the victim and not looking at the big picture.

The second day of the unit I asked students to write for 5 minutes on the following question: Is it imperative/desirable/irrelevant that fictional literature written about the Holocaust be historically accurate? Most students felt that it is imperative that it be accurate. Sarah Arrington, a thoughtful student, wrote:

Through literature, people learn about the Holocaust and even though fictional literature may have made up characters, the events should be accurate. You can't change history, and why would you want to. It is owed to the people who died in the Holocaust and their families who survived to report the events accurately.

Effective literature by its very nature transforms events of history and imagination into emotionally charged visions. As these students suggest, the literature should maintain historical accuracy regarding events and personalities while creating new and perhaps fictional frameworks for understanding that history.

Skloot (1982) says that a critical problem with Holocaust drama "centers on the use of realism" (p. 16). The dilemma, which he points out, is "how to give stage images their full burden of meaning without making them unrecognizable through abstraction or untruthful through replication" (Skloot, 1982, p. 17). Given the enormity of events in the Lodz Ghetto, how does a playwright appropriately and authentically depict events, characters, and dilemmas?

Langer (1995) says that "one test of [a work's] authenticity as Holocaust literature" is the presence of a "view of the apocalypse" (p. 161). He means that any literary work that fails to disclose the enormity of evil and shattering consequences of the Holocaust is skewed, if not false.

Another necessary element that must be introduced to make the representation of the Holocaust complete is "the realm of the unthinkable" (Langer, 1995, p. 162). A world in which a mother comforts her child on the way to death for both of them in a gas chamber defies normal thought. A world in which a people's leader, like Rumkowski, is forced to choose which of his people will be put to death goes beyond rational comprehension. Yet that is the world of the Holocaust. Authentic Holocaust literature must not shy away from entering these painful regions.

Langer (1995) also warns about the sin of moral oversimplification when writing about the Holocaust:

> [Too often,] we find comfort in schemes of cause and effect: villains destroy; victims submit or resist. [However,] we will never understand the behavior of the victims until we gain greater insight into the motives of their murderers . . . [It is imperative to understand that the] Jews were killed by men and women like themselves, not by automatons. . . . [Thus, literature that is authentic] must confront the challenge of characterizing those instruments of doom who, through a combination of ruthlessness and manipulation, deprived their victims of moral space to maneuver with dignity. (p. 166)

For Langer (1995), "Holocaust writing itself serves two masters: a clear intellectual perception of how Nazism shrank the area of dignified choice and reduced the options for human gestures; and the instinct to have victims survive heroically even within these less-than-human alternatives" (p. 169).

The Liebermans chose to weave historical characters with fictional ones and create a plot that hinges on historically accurate facts but involves fictional scenarios. The authenticity of the historical characters is maintained and the historical events are chronologically accurate. One has a clear sense of a realm of the unthinkable where choices with no personal control are forced upon Jews. Existing in Lodz on a daily basis is presented as anything but simple, a place where one must decide which choice is the lesser of two evils. And yet, throughout the play, the Jewish characters exhibit a yearning for life and a desire to become the masters of their fate. Langer might find fault with *Throne of Straw* because of its focus on the Jews rather than on the Nazi perpetrators. Nazi motives *are* glossed over, *but* there is no question that their primary motive is the humiliation and ultimate death of the Jews. Be that as it may, to focus on the Jews' reactions and responses in an untenable situation only tends to emphasize the unthinkable nature of the Nazi plans.

I make a point of showing another brief segment from the *Lodz Ghetto* video, Rumkowski's "Give me your children" speech, which he made on September 4, 1942. In this speech he begged the parents of children under ten to give them up in order to save other, older ghetto inhabitants. This "choiceless choice," which the Nazis forced upon Rumkowski, is included in the play and actual portions of the speech are interwoven with the action. We discuss the circumstances under which he was even put in a position to consider such a request and what, if any, other options Rumkowski had. Seeing footage of Rumkowski and hearing the voice of now deceased author/survivor Jerzy Kosinski speak the text helps students confront the reality of such a choiceless choice.

Students need to realize that moments of moral choice during the Holocaust were dealt with differently by different individuals. Although the focal character in *Throne of Straw* is Rumkowski, I give a minilesson on Adam Czerniakow and Janusz Korczak, both of the Warsaw Ghetto, in order to broaden the students' understanding of the various ways in which Jewish leaders confronted their situations. As heads of their respective *Judenrats,* both Rumkowski and Czerniakow were forced to implement Nazi directives which resulted in the deaths of thousands of people, and each man dealt with his choiceless choices differently. On July 23, 1942, when Czerniakow, chief elder of the Jewish Council in the Warsaw Ghetto, was told to deliver a large number of Jews, including many children, for deportation, he committed suicide rather than make such a choiceless choice. This decision could be criticized as more of an act of cowardice than courage because Czerniakow was no longer able to help his fellow ghetto inhabitants deal with the challenges created by the Nazis. Conversely, it could be viewed as the ultimate protest. Rumkowski, on the other hand, tried to work within the system and argue his positions, always believing that in doing so he was ultimately saving more Jews than the Nazis intended. This decision has been criticized as an example of collusion with the Nazis because Rumkowski did implement many of their directives.

Another example of individuals faced with similar dilemmas but making different choices involves Janusz Korczak and Rumkowski. Korczak, the physician and director of children's homes in the Warsaw Ghetto and also called the "Father of Orphans," chose to walk calmly at the head of the line of his children as they were being deported. He and all of the children were murdered in Treblinka. He made the choice to remain with the children rather than accept the clemency that was offered by the Nazis. Rumkowski secured money to build an orphanage in Helenowek, outside of Lodz, and was its director between World War I and World War II. Even so, believing he had no options, in September 1942, he begged parents to follow Nazi orders to give up their children in order to save older Jews. He chose to risk complicity with the Nazis in the hope of saving more Jews. When the final deportations from Lodz occurred in August 1944, Rumkowski was deported with the rest of the adults of Lodz to Auschwitz and murdered.

The purpose of calling attention to these different responses is not to ask students to compare or judge the individuals; each person did what he believed he had to do at that moment in time. However, it does provide a variety of examples of responses to "choiceless choices." During class discussion students noted the virtual impossibility of Czerniakow, Korczak, and Rumkowski making decisions that truly involved any personal choice or that had any positive consequences. They were also quite quick to comment that they felt no one should judge these men because of their decisions; judgment should fall on the Nazis who had put them in those situations in the first place.

Throughout the play, Rumkowski talks to God and is very protective of the children in the ghetto. When Biebow tries to humiliate him and forces him to expose his penis, Rumkowski, in return, manages to get Biebow to increase food rations for the children. Later, when Biebow demands 11,000 deportees and says, "There is one place left to fill out that shipment," Rumkowski retorts, "*Them!* You'll never get them [the orphanage children] from me" (Lieberman and Lieberman, 1982, p. 173). Forced to carry out this order, he makes his "Give me your children" speech and soon thereafter pleads with the audience to "put yourself in my position. Put yourself in my position. Put yourself in my position" (Lieberman and Lieberman, 1982, p. 181). In an effort to protect the Jews, Rumkowski refused to allow strikes and dissident activities, often calling for the arrest of participants. Rumkowski's third wife, Miriam, becomes disillusioned with his approach and urges that he no longer go along with the Nazi demands. To this, Rumkowski replies:

> First ask yourself where are the other ghettos? Why is it that only one survives? Because I understood that when the end is good, everything is good. I won't deny that I had to do terrible things. To give away my poor pigeons. But for every hundred I saved a hundred. I stood as a watchman before the door of death and snatched them from the furnace one by one. *And I am not ashamed.* (Lieberman and Lieberman, 1982, p. 187)

Rumkowski was correct; the Lodz Ghetto had the longest existence and the most survivors of any ghetto. It is often said that if the Russians had crossed the Vistula River in Poland in a timely manner and liberated Lodz sooner, Rumkowski would be seen as a hero. But the lack of Russian movement meant the total destruction of the ghetto and most of its inhabitants.

Yankele further raises the focal point of the dilemma of choiceless choices in a song entitled "Maimonides." Referring to the eminent 12th-century philosopher and theologian Moses Maimonides, the song includes a section in which a group of men asks Maimonides to guide them because the enemy has ordered them to pick one of their own to be killed. Maimonides replies, "Since you judged him innocent / In no way must he die for you . . . Join him. Nothing less will do!" (Lieberman and Lieberman, 1982, p. 148). Yankele's song epitomizes Rumkowski's dilemma: the German enemy demands that he select innocent Jews for death or they will select even more. A revered man of six centuries earlier provides a solution: Rumkowski should refuse to select innocent men and should join them in death.

However, Yankele's response to Maimonides shows that the world has changed, that direct, easy answers no longer apply:

> Rabbi Maimonides, if we do as you suggest
> How will a remnant be saved?
> But on the other hand
> If we don't do as you say
> What kind of remnant will it be?
> (Lieberman and Lieberman, 1982, p. 148)

A footnote indicates that the applicability of Maimonides' Code is a central philosophical concern in the play. Maimonides' *Thirteen Principles of the Faith* focuses on people's relationship with God and on how people can attain full connection between the human and the divine. Rumkowski must choose between following Maimonides (and losing everyone, including himself, but retaining his humanity) and following the Germans (and losing only some people but also his own humanity). In Maimonides' system "contemplation and understanding are given pride of place and become the central value, the essential goal of life. The acquisition of knowledge and understanding is considered to be the essence of our humanity" (Feld, 1994, p. 74). How, in the morass of the Holocaust, could humans attain such a life? How could humans make decisions based on an understanding of what was going on around them? During class discussions these questions help students grapple with the terrible dilemma of the Jews being forced into situations where they had to make such choices. Through the play's plot and characters they begin to understand that the Nazi tactics were geared to attack the very essence of the Jews' humanity.

As Rumkowski tries to negotiate the path of least harm to his fellow Jews, the other characters verbalize both positive and negative attitudes toward him and his decisions. Israel, the patriarch of the Wolf family, speaks in a derogatory manner about him, calling him at one point "a nobody" (Lieberman and Lieberman, 1982, p. 132). Rosa Wolf, a strike organizer, sees Rumkowski as working against the people's rights. The idea of workers striking in the ghetto may seem far-fetched, but it helps point out that some people felt that by demanding high production from the ghetto textile workers, Rumkowski was helping the Nazis too much. To fight against the Nazis, Rosa asserts, the Jews could stop creating so much material for them.

Yankele, the play's commentator, is the most outspoken. Early on in the play he tells Rumkowski: "Nothing is more corrupting than the illusion of power. Your plumage casts no shadow and your throne is made of straw" (Lieberman and Lieberman, 1982, p. 134). "Pharaoh" and "Kaiser" are also Yankele's names for Rumkowski (Lieberman and Lieberman, 1982, pp. 159, 164). These direct comments about Rumkowski provoke excellent student discussion. They understand Yankele's view that Rumkowski is nothing more than an empty mouthpiece who comes across as a proud peacock sitting on a worthless seat. The idea that the illusion of power is worse than power itself prodded students into discussions of what it means to have real power. Students examined the historical figures of Pharaoh and Kaiser and explored how Yankele's allusion to them deepened the sense of Rumkowski's evil deeds. The Pharaoh physically enslaved the Jews of Egypt and the Kaiser emotionally enslaved the people of Germany. However, even with these negative comments, Yankele indicates an understanding that nothing Rumkowski did could ultimately save them, and echoes the song of "Maimonides":

> Court Jew, Council Jew, shall I tell why you didn't pull us through this time? Your hand was always open, so how could you make a fist? But, even if you had, could a fist have saved us from them? (Lieberman and Lieberman, 1982, p. 192)

Some characters are more generous toward Rumkowski. David Abramowitz, an orphan adopted by the Wolf family, says to Rumkowski: "Everyone misses you a lot, me most of all. Do you still care about us?" Rumkowski responds: "What a question, I love you all more than ever" (Lieberman and Lieberman, 1982, pp. 135–136). Ada Wolf also speaks positively of the *Judenrat* leader and tries to ensure her family's longer survival by offering to sleep with Rumkowski. Gabriel Wolf, Ada's son who initially adamantly refuses to become a ghetto policeman but ultimately serves in that capacity with some gusto, also tends to support Rumkowski.

The latter two characters were responding in part to the realization that Rumkowski held the key to potential survival. As Gabriel says to his grandfather Israel: "Do you think I enjoy doing this [being a ghetto policeman]? My life has been a nightmare since I put on this uniform. But without it, you'd be deported" (Lieberman and Lieberman, 1982, p. 177). Then Israel raises a crucial dilemma in the play: "Dying is natural. Complicity is not" (Lieberman and Lieberman, 1982, p. 177). How much does one do to try and ensure safety for his family and himself? The students recognize the difficulty of Gabriel's dilemma. In class discussion they pointed out that only by complying with the Nazis and thus working against his own people could Gabriel save his own family. Many students said that if that were the only way they could save their family, they would do what Gabriel did.

The question of when going along with the enemy is solely an act of complicity and when it is a way to make the best of a bad situation is exemplified in this exchange between Rumkowski and Dr. Ari Cohen:

RUMKOWSKI: So let's resist. Take a stand. Plant our feet. Such fine phrases. Such bad advice. To go on breathing, *that* is the rebellion at this time.

COHEN: There is a step which once taken, locks in all the other steps to come. We must not do that voluntarily.

RUMKOWSKI: If we don't organize the move with decency and humanity, they'll do it by terror. (Lieberman and Lieberman, 1982, p. 150)

A major Nazi tactic involved the use of terror. Physical, emotional, and psychological terror all kept the Jews in a position of uncertainty, of submission to the Nazis. Some students said that Rumkowski's recognition of this technique and his subsequent actions of trying to lessen the negative impact of Nazi directives on his people could be seen as positive and Cohen's call for resistance futile.

Yankele begins both act 1 and act 2 and ends the play with speeches addressed to the audience. In the prologue, he asks a question and gives a warning:

So, if a Jewish community
Like the one you will see tonight
Is confronted with physical destruction
Should its leaders rescue what is possible
Or should all perish together as at Masada?
No idle question, then or now,
And please before you sit in judgment
Sit *shiva* first.
(Lieberman and Lieberman, 1982, p. 124)

This direct warning to the audience not to be quick to judge the characters and their choices is repeated in the final speech of the play. The house lights go up, exposing the audience and bringing them visually together with the character on the stage. One student commented in class that raising the house lights serves to put pressure on the audience; no one can hide in the dark of the theater. In his speech Yankele says:

> I take this passion play from place to place
> And please while it's with you
> Don't feed me your dinner table morals about how
> They should have behaved;
> Only say what you would have done.
> (Lieberman and Lieberman, 1982, p. 196)

By this point in the play the audience understands that there is no way anyone can say what they would have done; the directive only serves to emphasize the many moments of moral or choiceless choice encountered in the play.

We discuss the play during three class periods. In addition to keeping a list of moments of choice for the characters, as their final written evaluation students are asked to write a focused reflection on three points. As has been previously addressed, they are to discuss what they mean by a "moment of choice." In addition, they are to carefully reread Yankele's speech at the end of the play and discuss what he is saying and provide their response to it.

Eric Burroughs, a student who has solid analytical skills and hopes to become an engineer, commented as follows on Yankele's speech:

> I think this speech shows the hopelessness and despair felt by the Jews *after* the Holocaust. The lines, "Don't feed me your dinner table morals about how/they should have behaved," express the best view one can have looking back on the Holocaust. Oftentimes we read about the Holocaust and wonder why the Jews let it happen, why they did not leave initially, why they did not resist. Of course, I'm sure if the Jews could['ve] predict[ed] the future they would have acted differently. But they had no way of knowing that a country who created so many good things in art, music, technology, etc. could become so evil. I believe this is Yankele's point. Do not judge, but listen and don't let it happen again. These views are brought out in the play as people try to judge Rumkowski. Rumkowski only pleads, "Put yourself in my position."

Nate Stine, a bright, articulate student whose comments often helped clarify his peers' thinking, saw the passage

> as an invitation to judge impartially, a chance to empathize without imposing our society's morals and cultural biases. . . . The human race gains nothing from learning a bunch of horrifying statistics and never learning the human angle. . . . Our generations are learning what decisions were made, how they were forced into making those situations, but there is a void to be filled when dealing in the "why." Putting ourselves in the Jewish plight will aid us in our understanding of the great "why" and may help us should we ever have to choose ourselves. Sure, it is almost a cliché in history that the modern world should learn from the "mistake" of the Holocaust. What else can it be then? We learn from them and they will not be forgotten.

Yankele leaves the audience with one final query:

> Since shrouds have no pockets
> And ashes no permanent home
> Where will you keep them?
> (Lieberman and Lieberman, 1982, p. 196)

Student Scott Wilson, a coeditor of the student newspaper and a published playwright, sees this ending of the play as "asking the audience to make a moral choice: Where will I keep the memory of the Holocaust? Or should I ignore my emotions involving the Holocaust?"

This section of Yankele's speech "deals with the importance of remembrance," according to student Dyani Scheuerman. This quiet, thoughtful, and very insightful young woman wrote:

> It is a huge issue in virtually all Holocaust-related literature, and one which I agree is vital. I don't think the ashes he speaks of are meant to be taken literally at all, but instead like a person's soul or memory. There were so many people that it would be so easy to forget individuals, yet of course, they were. It also must refer to the memory of the entire event, as it is very important to keep such disasters in mind to assure that they will be avoided at all costs in the future. I agree with this entirely. I think that the memories of all these lives *need* to live on somehow. The main element from the rest of the play which seems to support this is Israel's diary. Everytime he is seen he is writing in it, which greatly stresses its importance. He meant to show things as they were, perhaps for himself later if he should live, and more likely for whoever finds it to make use of and learn from. The fact that Zosia immediately begins to write in it when Israel is taken away merely stresses its importance and shows that it has already passed on at least a little bit into a different mind and a different set of hands.

Student Melissa Brobeck agrees that Yankele "is directly asking the audience how they are going to remember the victims of the Holocaust." For Melissa, also a coeditor of the student newspaper and a sensitive reader and writer, this creates

> a very powerful ending to this play. I think that the capping off of the beginning and ending with speeches by Yankele is very effective. But I think that the final speech is effective because it catches the reader/audience off guard. I don't think that people realize that the first thing that they probably want to say is, 'Well, I would have done . . .' By ending with this speech, the reader/audience is more apt to really look at the decisions of the characters and to understand that those characters were put in a situation that the reader/audience will probably never experience. I feel that this end speech really helps to clarify the play and to give better understanding to the reader/audience.

Perhaps the highlight of this unit of study was the oral testimony of a Lodz Ghetto survivor, Mr. Jack Baigelman of Beachwood, Ohio. Mr. Baigelman spent nearly the entire war in the ghetto and was deported to Auschwitz in the summer of 1944, shortly before Rumkowski himself was deported. We sent Mr. Baigelman a copy of the play so he was familiar with what the students had studied, along with the following questions generated by the students.

- What personal goals did you have before the Holocaust? How did the Holocaust affect your reaching those goals?
- Describe a day of trying to live in the ghetto.
- Was there any specific point when you realized what was happening to you? To the Jews in general?
- Did you think things would get as bad as they did? What made you feel as you did?
- What happened to your family? Your friends?
- Did people in the ghettos know what went on in the camps? What were they told?
- Were you in the ghetto when Rumkowski gave his "give me your children" speech? If so, what was your reaction?
- What were your feelings about Rumkowski both during and after your experiences in the ghetto?
- How have you managed to cope with all that happened to you?

Because Mr. Baigelman had not spoken publicly of his experience in a number of years, he was nervous about both his presentation and his reception. His concerns proved groundless as he mesmerized nearly 50 AP English students with his story. We were in my classroom because I wanted a smaller, more personal venue. Despite the high temperature in the room, the students sat motionless for over an hour as he spoke of his life before, during, and after the war. Nothing can compare with the impact of personally meeting someone who was part of the history. In the students' thank-you letters, they verbalized how important this opportunity was for them; it made the history and historical characters come alive. We made a donation in Mr. Baigelman's honor to an organization of his choice and sent him a copy of the videotape of his presentation.

A valuable resource which should be incorporated into a study of *Throne of Straw* is *The Chronicle of the Lodz Ghetto 1941–1944* edited by Lucjan Dobroszycki (1984). The chronicle exists because of Rumkowski's decision on November 17, 1940, to form a department of population records. Ghetto inhabitants worked in the section, compiling a record of daily events in the ghetto. The compilers had to be extremely careful to avoid discovery. Thus, the tone is "very cautious" and there is an

> absence of evaluation whenever the Germans are mentioned . . . The chroniclers seemed to have adopted the following principle: since it is not possible to write about those who commit the crimes, we will speak of their victims and in some detail. . . . The text is full of euphemisms and impersonal descriptions. (Dobroszycki, 1984, p. xviii)

Because the work was at the behest of Rumkowski, there are few or no negative comments about him. "The image of Rumkowski presented by the chroniclers does not at all correspond to what people in the ghetto actually thought of him" (Dobroszycki, 1984, p. xxvii). *The Chronicle,* which provides information about the ghetto almost up until the final deportation on August 28, 1944, can be used to teach what was occurring on certain days in the ghetto, to discuss why certain facts may have been selected or not selected for inclusion, and to analyze and discuss the tone of the writing. It includes a large number of photographs of the ghetto and of Rumkowski. All in all, *The Chronicle* provides a rich resource of primary documents for classroom use.

Another valuable resource is a book of photographs entitled *With a Camera in the Ghetto* by Mendel Grossman (1970). As a photographer of the Lodz Ghetto, Grossman visually recorded the ghetto's daily scenes of privation, misery, and horror. Before his death at age 32 he had taken more than 10,000 photos in 4½ years. Brief pieces of text accompany some of the photos and the book concludes with a biography of Grossman written by Arieh Ben-Menahem. Students commented that seeing photographs, in addition to the video, helped to make the situations in the ghetto more real. To see actual still shots of the places and people and to realize the great personal risks that Grossman took to produce the photos made the horrific circumstances more concrete.

Given the rather unique population of Roosevelt students who studied the Holocaust extensively as freshmen, focusing on one drama about one ghetto provided opportunities for review and extension of their knowledge of the Holocaust. However, this dramatic work could be incorporated into virtually any study of the literature of the Holocaust for any group of secondary students. It is an excellent vehicle for providing the students with an opportunity to examine some of the real moral dilemmas faced by Holocaust victims as well as to determine the effectiveness of this dramatic portrayal of those events and dilemmas.

REFERENCES

Dobroszycki, Lucjan. (Ed.). (1984). *The Chronicle of the Lodz Ghetto 1941–1944.* New Haven, CT: Yale University Press.

Feld, Edward. (1994). *The Spirit of Renewal: Finding Faith after the Holocaust.* Woodstock, VT: Jewish Lights Publishing.

Grossman, Mendel. (1970). *With a Camera in the Ghetto.* Israel: Ghetto Fighters' House and Hakibbutz Hameuchad Publishing House.

Krakowski, Shmuel. (1990). "Lodz," pp. 900–909. In Israel Gutman (Ed.), *Encyclopedia of the Holocaust, Vol. 3.* New York: Macmillan Publishing.

Krakowski, Shmuel. (1990). "Rumkowski, Mordechai Chaim," pp. 1312–1314. In Israel Gutman (Ed.), *Encyclopedia of the Holocaust, Vol. 3.* New York: Macmillan Publishing.

Langer, Lawrence L. (1982) *Versions of Survival: The Holocaust and the Human Spirit.* Albany: State University of New York Press.

Langer, Lawrence L. (1995). "The Americanization of the Holocaust on Stage and Screen." In Lawrence L. Langer, *Admitting the Holocaust: Collected essays* (pp. 157–177). New York: Oxford University Press.

Lieberman, Harold, & Edith Lieberman. (1982). "Throne of Straw." In Robert Skloot (Ed.), *The Theatre of the Holocaust: Four Plays* (pp. 114–196). Madison: The University of Wisconsin Press.

Lodz Ghetto. National Public Broadcasting Service. (1992). (Available from The Anti-Defamation League, Department JW, 823 United Nation's Plaza, New York, NY 10017.) A teacher's guide is included.

Skloot, Robert. (Ed.). (1982). *The Theatre of the Holocaust: Four Plays.* Madison, WI: The University of Wisconsin Press.

CHAPTER

11 Entering the "Night" of the Holocaust

Studying Elie Wiesel's *Night*

SAMUEL TOTTEN

> *Never shall I forget that night, the first night in camp, which has turned my life into one long night, seven times cursed and seven times sealed. Never shall I forget that smoke. Never shall I forget the faces of the little children, whose bodies I saw turned into wreaths of smoke beneath a blue sky.*
>
> *Never shall I forget those flames which consumed my faith forever.*
>
> *Never shall I forget that nocturnal silence which deprived me, for all eternity, of the desire to live . . . Never shall I forget these things, even if I am condemned to live as long as God himself. Never.*
>
> —Wiesel, 1969, *Night,* p. 44.

Many powerful and thought-provoking works—diaries, memoirs, historical studies, novels, short stories—have been written about the Holocaust, but few seem to so thoroughly engage secondary-level students as Elie Wiesel's *Night*. It is a memoir about a young boy's horrific experiences as he, his family, his community, and people are ripped from their homes, transported to Auschwitz, and brutalized and murdered in ways that are difficult for the "average" person to fathom. For many, it seems to be a story that penetrates to the core of one's being, never to leave, never to dissipate.

As with any work of literature—be it a diary, a memoir, a short story, a novel, or a play—there are innumerable ways to teach *Night*. What is delineated here comprises a combined literary and historical approach. Prior to discussing the aforementioned approach, a summary of Elie Wiesel the person, the activist, and the author is provided.

Elie Wiesel: "A Messenger to Humanity"

Born in 1928, Elie Wiesel grew up in a remote area of Transylvania—in the small town of Sighet in Rumania, a Hungarian-speaking town in the Carpathian mountains—in a highly Orthodox Jewish family. Sighet was part of the Northern Transylvania region of Romania that became part of Hungary in 1940 as a reward to the Hungarians for their alliance with Germany. Immersed in the religious life, he began the study of the Torah and the Talmud at a tender age. At the age of 12 he also began to immerse himself in the study of the Zohar, cabbalistic books, and Jewish mysticism. All of that ended abruptly in 1944, during Passover week, when he, his immediate family, and approximately 15,000 fellow townspeople, were herded onto boxcars and transported to Auschwitz.[1] His mother and youngest sister were immediately murdered in a gas chamber. Following a series of harrowing experiences, he and his father, along with many other prisoners, were forced on a death march to Buchenwald, shortly after which his father perished in Elie's arms. In Auschwitz, Elie Wiesel not only lost his youth but came out doubting both God and life. In regard to the loss of his youth, he has said: "When I was 18 . . . I was not 18. I was an old man. What I knew then, the teachers of my teachers [of the Talmud and other religious works] never knew. What I lived in an hour people don't live in a generation." (quoted in Freedman, 1983, p. 35). As for his relationship with God, he has observed that "Usually, we [Jews] say, 'God is right,' or 'God is just'—even during the Crusades we said that. But how can you say that now, with one million children dead [as a result of the Holocaust]?" (quoted in Freedman, 1983, p. 68). Elsewhere, and mirroring his assertion in *Night,* he has stated that "I [never] denied God's existence, but I doubted His absolute justice" (quoted in Eckardt, 1979, p. 18).

Following his liberation, Elie refused to be repatriated, and was sent to France. There, he was eventually reunited with an older sister. Stateless, he chose to remain in France.

He has observed that, "So heavy was my anguish that in the spring of 1945 I made a vow: not to speak, not to touch upon the essential for at least ten years. Long enough to unite the language of humanity with the silence of the dead" (Kanfer, 1985, p. 78). Here one is reminded of Goethe's statement that when one is in pain one becomes mute because of that pain.

From 1948 to 1951 he studied philosophy at the Sorbonne, where he read and was influenced by the writings of the French existentialists Albert Camus and Jean Paul Sartre. In 1949, he became chief foreign correspondent for the Israeli daily *Yedioth Ahronot* and then in 1957 he also began writing for the New York-based *Jewish Daily Forward.*

Eventually, Wiesel began to write of his ordeal. He published *Night,* his first book, in French, in 1958. In addition to *Night* and numerous novels (including *Dawn, The Accident, The Town Beyond theWall, The Gates of the Forest, A Beggar in Jerusalem, The Oath, The Fifth Son*), he has written numerous collections of essays, a cantata (*Ani Maamin*), two plays (*Zalmen, or The Madness of God* and *The Trial of God*) and books on a wide range of topics, from *The Jews of Silence: A Personal Report on Soviet Jewry* to *Souls on Fire: Portraits and Legends of Hasidic Masters.* In all, he has written over 30 books. "I really believe I have to write," he has said. "There's a certain compulsion. I owe it to everybody but myself. I owe it to the dead. I owe it to the living" (quoted in Freedman, 1983, p. 36). In a similar vein, he has said that, "I feel that having survived, I owed something to the dead. That was their obsession to be remembered. Anyone who does not remember betrays them again" (Berger, 1986, p. 4).

Wiesel eventually moved to the United States, where he became a U.S. citizen in 1963. A long-time resident of New York City, he first began teaching at the City University of New York and now teaches at Boston University. For many years Wiesel was also the chairman of the United States Holocaust Memorial Council, the body that created the United States Holocaust Memorial Museum in Washington, D.C.

An indefatigable human rights activist, Wiesel has traveled to and spoken out about human rights violations and tragedies in Biafra, Lebanon, Vietnam, Cambodia, South Africa, Central America, Bosnia, Rwanda, and Kosovo. Writing about what drives Wiesel to speak on the behalf of the oppressed around the globe, Christian theologian Robert McAfee Brown (1979) has observed that:

> [T]he opposite of participation and mutuality is not only isolation; it is also the spectator role, so chillingly embodied in the observer at the window in [Wiesel's novel] *The Town Beyond the Wall*, the man who feels nothing as Jews are taken to the camps, the one who does nothing, but actually by his doing nothing sides with the executioners rather than the victims. He is the most complicit of all human beings, worse even than the executioner. His is a voluntary withdrawal from participation and abdication of personhood. (p. 23)

In recognition of his life-long work on the behalf of others around the globe, Wiesel was awarded the Nobel Prize for Peace in 1986. In awarding Wiesel the Nobel Prize, the Nobel committee statement observed that "Wiesel's commitment, which originated in the suffering of the Jewish people, has been widened to embrace all oppressed peoples and races" (Markham, 1986, p. 4).

A man of remarkable eloquence and a prolific writer who is driven to tell the story of the Holocaust, Wiesel has been referred to over the years as "a messenger to all humanity," "the conscience of a people's anguish and a people's hope," and "chronicler of the Holocaust." Ultimately, Wiesel is a witness and a teacher. In regard to his role—and that of other survivors—as a writer and a witness, he has said: "If the role of the writer may once have been to entertain, that of the witness is to disturb, alert, to awaken, to warn against indifference to injustice—any injustice—and above all against complacency about any need and any people" (Wiesel, 1979, p. 36). As for his role as a teacher, he has said of himself and other survivors who tell their stories and write about the Holocaust, "[T]he survivors chose to teach; and what is their writing, their testimony, if not teaching?" (Wiesel, 1978, p. 267).[2]

Developing a Cluster around the Term "Holocaust": A Preassessment Activity

Prior to having the students read *Night*, I have each student develop a cluster (also frequently referred to as a mind-map or conceptual map) around the "target word" Holocaust. A cluster has been defined as "a nonlinear brainstorming process that generates ideas, images, and feeling around a stimulus word until a pattern becomes discernible" (Rico, 1987, p. 17). More graphically, teacher Michael O'Brien (1987) has defined clustering in the following manner: "Think of them as flowers. Clusters do, after all, resemble flowers whose petals burst forth from the central corolla. Note that clusters do beautifully in both remedial and advanced classes . . ." (p. 25).

To develop a cluster, I inform my students, they need to place the term *Holocaust* in the center of a piece of paper (at least as large as 8½" × 11"), circle it, and then draw spokes out from the circle on which they attach related terms or ideas. Each time a term is added, they need to circle the term and connect it, with a simple line, to those other terms and/or concepts that are related to it. Each new or related idea should lead to a new clustering of ideas. As Rico (1987) points out: "A cluster is an expanding universe, and each word is a potential galaxy; each galaxy, in turn, may throw out its own universes. As students cluster around a stimulus word, the encircled words rapidly radiate outward until a sudden shift takes place, a sort of 'Aha!' that signals a sudden awareness of that tentative whole . . ." (p. 17). Furthermore, "Since a cluster draws on primary impressions—yet simultaneously on a sense of the overall design—clustering actually generates structure, shaping one thought into a starburst of other thoughts, each somehow related to the whole" (Rico, 1987, p. 18).

Clustering (or mind-mapping or webbing) is a more graphic and, generally, easier and more engaging method to use to delineate what one knows about a topic than, say, outlining a topic.[3]

In order to make sure that my students know exactly what I mean by clustering, and as a way to illustrate that which constitutes a more complex cluster versus one that is simplistic, I demonstrate the development of, first, a very simple cluster of a topic (on one other than the Holocaust, e.g., the school's sports program), and then take that simple cluster and turn it into a more complex one. I use the two clusters to model; first, a nonexemplar (e.g., the simplistic cluster) and then, second, an exemplar (the more complex cluster). The reason it is important for the teacher to *avoid* developing a cluster on the Holocaust is that many students may be tempted simply to copy what the teacher has done; that is, use the exact same information and make the same sort of connections that the teacher has made in his or her cluster.

In giving directions for the development of the cluster, I encourage my students to develop the most detailed, comprehensive and accurate cluster they possibly can. At the same time, I encourage them to make a Herculean effort to carefully delineate the connections, when appropriate, between and amongst the various and separate items/concepts/events/ideas.

Once each student has completed his or her cluster, I place the students in groups of three and four and have them share and discuss their individual clusters. I tell them that it is an imperative that each and every student be allotted time to succinctly explain his or her cluster (1 to 3 minutes should be ample). Each student should address the following: a quick overview of key points, a rationale as to why he or she included certain ideas, and a brief explanation of the connections between and amongst various ideas. At this time I also note that after every student has presented his or her cluster, each person in the group should add, if he or she so wishes, items from other members' clusters to his or her own cluster. *In adding the new information, he or she should use a color other than the one he or she used in his or her original cluster.* This will simply indicate the type and number of ideas borrowed from others.

Finally, at the end of this session, I ask them to sign their own cluster. Finally, we tape the clusters to the walls around the classroom. The purpose of the latter is to allow us to revisit the clusters, if the need arises, during the course of our study of *Night.*

Having the students develop clusters serves a number of purposes: first, students actually depict for themselves what they know and don't know about the subject; second, as a teacher, I gain a concrete illustration of both the students' depth of knowledge as well as the sophistication of their conceptual framework of a subject; and third, I am able to ascertain the accuracy of students' knowledge as well as any inaccuracies, misconceptions, and/or myths they may hold about a topic. Basically, then, such an exercise serves as a powerful preassessment exercise. Over and above that, clustering provides the students with a unique method to express their ideas; and in doing so, it allows them to tap into an "intelligence" (e.g., spatial) other than the typical one of writing ("linguistic"), to borrow a concept from Howard Gardner (1983; 1993).[4]

As will be discussed below, I have my students read *Night* twice during our unit: the first time allows them to become familiar with the work and to engage in a reader response activity; while the second time around, we analyze the work from both a historical and literary perspective. At the conclusion of our *first reading* of *Night,* I have the students complete a second cluster. Doing so provides us with a vivid sense as to the students' new insights, the new connections they make between and amongst key topics, and/or whether their newfound knowledge is couched in a more sophisticated understanding of the topic of the Holocaust. Finally, after the students have read *Night* for the second time and we've conducted the historical/literary study of the work, the students develop a third and final cluster, which they then compare and contrast with both their initial and second clusters. After developing their second and third clusters, the students are required to address one or more key points. For example, What is the most pronounced difference between the two clusters, and what does this tell you about your knowledge base in regard to the Holocaust? and/or, Are there any items on your last cluster that you feel are absolutely imperative for someone to include on such a cluster, and why?

After the development of each and every cluster, I have my students develop a working definition of the Holocaust based on their most current knowledge base.

Using the Cluster/Mind-Map to Develop a Working Definition of the Holocaust

Next, using the information (facts, concepts, connections) the students have included in their initial cluster, each student develops a working definition of the Holocaust. In doing so, they are advised to examine carefully all of the components of their cluster and then make every effort to develop the most comprehensive and accurate definition they possibly can. I also tell them that as they go about developing their definition, if they discover they have left out key facts or concepts or have failed to make certain connections, they are free to add those to their clusters, but that they should use a different color than they have previously used. Likewise, I tell them that they need to add the new color and its purpose to the legend of their cluster.

Once everyone has developed his or her definition, the students are placed in small groups (a maximum of three to four people) where they share their definitions. The groups can be comprised either of the same students as or different ones than the last small group exercise; it doesn't really matter. Again, I tell them that every member of the group should share his or her cluster, that once a person has shared his or her cluster with the group a short discussion should ensue in regard to any questions or concerns that other group members have, and that someone should take down the most salient points during the course of the discussion of the various definitions.

At the conclusion of the small group discussions, we hold a general discussion in regard to what the students learned during this activity, and we also place any questions or points they are unsure about on sheets of butcher paper with the heading, "Holocaust: Issues to Examine in More Detail." I explain that as we proceed with our study of *Night* we will return to these questions/concerns and attempt to answer them. In doing so, I explain, we will attempt to clarify our understanding of what the Holocaust was (and/or wasn't) as well as come to a more comprehensive and accurate definition of the historical event now referred to as the Holocaust.

Simply to provide the students with an accepted definition of the Holocaust (e.g., the one used by the United States Holocaust Memorial Museum) would be much easier and faster but it would not be the most pedagogically sound approach. In using the method I've described, the students are able to construct their new insights and knowledge of the Holocaust by reexamining their previous ideas against the new information and insights they are gleaning during the course of the study. In that way, they are more likely to come to a more in-depth and lasting understanding of how and why scholars wrestle over definitions and why such definitions are so important in framing an understanding of complex issues and events.

This process, of course, does not preclude, at some point, the examination of different scholars' definitions of the Holocaust. On the contrary, comparing their definition to those of scholars deepens the students' thinking about the historical process as well as their understanding of the Holocaust.

From the outset, the development of definitions by the students provides me with unique insights into their understanding of the Holocaust as well as their misunderstanding, misconceptions, inaccurate information, and so on. This, of course, serves as another powerful preassessment exercise.

What follows is a sample of some of the many initial definitions that a class of high school students came up with at the outset of a study of *Night*. The examples are purposely grouped according to the types of information found in them.

The initial grouping includes those definitions that were the *least* inaccurate among the definitions developed by the students. The wording "least accurate" is deliberately used here for the express purpose of highlighting the fact that *all* of the following definitions are bereft of key information in regard to *why* the Holocaust was perpetrated.

> Holocaust: When the Nazis decided the Jews were the cause of Germany's problems. In WW II the Nazis tortured and killed Jews. The Nazis wanted a genocide of the Jews.

> Holocaust: To gain political power, Hitler blamed the Jews for Germany's hardships after WWI. This created much of the negative sentiment necessary for Hitler to come to rule Germany. He began imprisoning Jewish people in concentration camps. Eventually millions were murdered and treated like animals.

> Holocaust: The persecution and/or extermination of people of primarily Jewish background by the Nazis during WW II, involving the creation of Jewish ghettos, forced labor forces and concentration camps.

> Holocaust: Persecution of Jews during 1940s in Germany and near areas of Europe; led by Adolf Hitler a Nazi dictator; took place during WWII; many Jews died in concentration camps due to crowded housing and gas chambers. They were cremated.

> Holocaust: A time during WWII when Hitler's Nazi party punished the Jews for "causing all of Germany's problems." The Jews were forced to wear the yellow star of David and had virtually no rights. Many were sent to concentration camps, and many died.

> Holocaust: Hitler forced Jews into hiding and killed 6 million Jews in concentration camps. Jews were forced to wear the Star of David, and be segregated from others because Hitler believed that the Germans were the supreme race.

When comparing the above definitions with the one used by the U.S. Holocaust Memorial Museum (1994), one can readily ascertain the gaps in the students' definitions: "The Holocaust refers to a specific event in 20th-century history: the state-sponsored, systematic persecution and annihilation of European Jewry by Nazi Germany and its collaborators between 1933 and 1945. Jews were the primary victims—six million were murdered; Gypsies, the handicapped, and Poles were also targeted for destruction or decimation for racial, ethnic, or national reasons. Millions more, including homosexuals, Jehovah's Witnesses, Soviet prisoners of war, and political dissidents, also suffered grievous oppression and death under Nazi tyranny" (p. 3). In addition to leaving out a good number of the aforementioned concerns, very few of the students' definitions take into consideration the major historical trends that contributed to the Holocaust. As scholar Donald Niewyk (1995) has pointed out: "A number of historical trends combined to make the Holocaust possible: anti-Semitism, racism, social Darwinism, extreme nationalism, totalitarianism, industrialism, and the nature of modern war. The absence of any one of these trends would have made the genocide of the Jews unlikely" (p. 175). Also obvious is the fact that some students confused "concentration camps" with "death camps," or at least didn't seem to differentiate the major differences between the two. That said, the students who developed the above definitions were at least on the right track in regard to what Nazi Germany was about and who was victimized. Still, obviously, the students had a tremendous amount to learn in regard to why and how the Holocaust was perpetrated.

The next set of definitions not only are bereft of key information but are flawed in various and major ways. More specifically, many include major inaccuracies and misconceptions:

> Holocaust: The destruction of an entire race by a pathological maniac who felt he was in his right as playing God destroying one race and creating a better one.

> Holocaust: The Germans boycotted the Jews and Adolf Hitler had his army ship them off to concentration camps where they were starved to death.

> Holocaust: Discrimination against Jews by Germans in which they were forced into concentration camps, tortured, murdered, gassed, and it caused a world war. Hitler ran the Nazis [sic] party.

> Holocaust: A time in history many of us wish we could forget. The Nazi German type of people were beaten, raped, murdered, put in concentration camps and shot just because they look [sic] different or other things.

> Holocaust: The Holocaust was between 1939–1945. It was when Hitler gathered people (mostly Jews) and put them into death camps, or just killed them. Jews were educated people, and when they started taking most of the jobs, that's when the trouble started. Millions of people died and families were torn apart.

> Holocaust: During WWII Nazi Germany had a problem with Jews. The Holocaust was when the Nazis killed 45 million Jews during that time period.

As one can ascertain, the inaccuracies and misconceptions of some of the students are, to say the least, glaring. More specifically, in some instances, the students referred to the Jews as a race (which they are not, though the Nazis referred to them as such; for a discussion of the fallacious concept of race, see Montagu, 1964 and Gates, 1997); insinuated that the Holocaust was the result of one man's efforts (when, in fact, it involved the Nazi hierarchy, the SS which ran the camps, and tens of thousands of others who contributed in various ways); that the destruction of the Jews was *the* cause for the world to go to war (it wasn't the persecution of the Jews, but rather the bellicosity of the Germans and Japanese); and that the Jews were prospering in Germany while no one else was and/or at everyone else's expense (both of which are simply flat-out wrong). Another student was under the impression that the Nazis killed 45 million Jews (when in fact, they killed approximately six million Jews and millions of other people). One student was under the misconception that the sole mistreatment of the Jews was their starvation by the Nazis (when the fact is that they were killed in numerous ways, including being shot, hanged, starved to death, beaten to death and, of course, gassed). The most glaring misconception is the student who totally misconstrues who the victims and perpetrators were (e.g., "the Nazi German type of people were beaten, raped, murdered, put in concentration camps and shot just because they look [*sic*] different or other things"). Again, it is worth noting that not a single student mentioned the issue of antisemitism, let alone the rabid and deadly form of antisemitism practiced by the Nazis. Nor did any mention the racism of the Nazis.

After the development of each cluster, the students are required to develop a new definition of the Holocaust and to compare and contrast, in writing, their latest definition with their earlier definition(s).

The First Reading:
A Reader Response Approach

As previously mentioned, when I teach *Night* to high school students—and I have done so numerous times—I generally have them read it twice. The first time they are told simply to read it through in the course of one or two sittings. This is to introduce them to the memoir in such a way that they become immersed in it without interruption, to allow them to respond to it in their own personal way without the superstructure of a deeper historical or literary analysis, and to provide them with an opportunity to soak the story in on their own and without any "interference" on my part or the part of their fellow students. The second reading involves, for lack of a better term, a more *historical/literary* approach, where the students gain an overview of the history of the Holocaust period and are encouraged to delve into the story in a more analytical fashion; that is, one in which they consider Wiesel's experiences in light of the history of the period along with an examination of such literary concerns as biblical allusions and inverted symbolism.

Initially, I assign *Night* to my students on a Thursday and ask them to complete it by Sunday evening, or at least prior to class the following Monday. It is a relatively short book of 127 pages, and so engaging that even those who generally do not like to read find it extremely engaging and hard to put down.

Prior to making the assignment, I provide what should be a "refresher" mini-lesson on the differences between fiction and nonfiction (including the distinctions between a diary, an interview, a memoir, and a novel). Unfortunately, many teachers teach *Night* as a novel, when in fact it is a memoir. Concerned about this issue himself, Wiesel (1995) emphatically states, in *All Rivers Run to the Sea: Memoirs*, that "*Night* is not a novel" (p. 271). It is at this juncture that I broach and teach them about the use of heightened language (including metaphorical language), and "invented dialogue" for later discussions. The latter is particularly significant to address since *Night*, which includes a large amount of dialogue, was written a good number of years after the incidents took place.

The assignment that accompanies the reading of *Night* is as follows:

> During this unit of study you will read Elie Wiesel's *Night* twice; once simply to become familiar with it and to react to it in the most personal of ways. The second time, you shall be reading it more closely; and in doing so, you shall take into account the history of the period and also examine it from a more literary point of view.
>
> Thus, for this first reading, you should simply do the following: Read *Night* through quickly, noting when applicable, those images, incidents, words, sentences, thoughts that most move you and/or provide you with telling insights into what the Jews, and particularly Elie and his family, experienced during the Holocaust. Once you have concluded the book, take your notes and write a letter to Elie. In your letter, which should be a very personal letter from you, write exactly what you wish about the book. More specifically, you may write anything you wish about the memoir. You may tell the author how his story made you feel, offer your own insights into any aspect of his story, posit any questions you may have about his story or any of the various situations he faced, inquire about anything you still don't understand, or comment on whether you would recommend the book to others or not. The point is, you may approach it in any way you wish. It is your perspective, your point of view that is important. Do not write this for me, the teacher, write it for yourself in which you present your most honest response to the memoir.

Once all of the questions students may have about the directions for the assignment are addressed, I have found that it is a good idea to ask, What does every letter begin with (the students will generally answer "the date" and "a salutation or greeting"). The students should also be asked, And what do letters generally conclude with? Here the students usually answer with "a closing" and "your name." If the teacher does not ask such questions, many students will neglect to set up the assignment in letter format.

During the first class session after the students have read *Night*, I place them in groups of three and provide them with the following directions: "Initially, each person should simply read his or her letter while the rest of the group listens. Once everyone has read his or her piece, each person should read his or her letter again. This time, however, after each person reads his or her letter, a discussion should ensue. During the course of the discussion, the other members of the group are free to ask questions and make comments about the other person's letter; and in doing so, one may corroborate certain points by drawing on thoughts and feelings reflected in one's own letter and/or play the devil's advocate by questioning and probing. As you discuss the ideas in the various letters, be sure to keep returning to the memoir in order to substantiate and clarify your ideas. As soon as the discussion of one person's letter wanes, the next person in line should read his or her letter and the process of discussion should begin anew." While this exercise would work with groups of four, I have found that three in each group is really the optimal number. That is due primarily to the fact that many of the students' letters to Wiesel are rather lengthy, and with four or more students in a group, the activity consumes an inordinate amount of time and some students tend to lose focus.

I further explain that in order for the class to conduct a large-group (e.g., class) follow-up discussion, it will be necessary for each group to have a recorder who jots down the most pertinent points made during the course of the small-group discussion. Since that is the case, I ask each group to decide quickly who the recorder is going to be, and I ask for that individual to raise his or her hand. The latter ensures that each group has a recorder. After all of the recorders have been duly noted, I tell the students that during the general discussion the onus will not be on the recorder to carry the discussion for his or her group, but rather it will be the responsibility of the entire group to expound on their collective ideas. Thus, while the recorder will initially relate the key points that have been made in his or her group, any subsequent discussion of the group's points should be a group effort.

As the small groups engage in the aforementioned work, I circulate from group to group, and as a rule, I listen to the discussion and refrain from making any comments. However, if an individual or an entire group is at a standstill and asserts something along the lines of "We've covered everything. We're through," I generally ask them if they have any lingering questions about the book, and if so, what they are. Then I encourage them to probe those. If there are none, then I may ask them to consider why Wiesel entitled his book *Night,* and what is the significance of such a title. Initially, I will listen to the outset of their discussion and then come back to see where the discussion has gone. If the discussion has waned again, I may ask the individual members of the group each to come up with a title of their own for the memoir and a rationale as to why they would attach such a title to the work. And once again, I would encourage them to discuss their different ideas.

If, however, a group is stuck on a point—for example, in one group a student was arguing that in Auschwitz Wiesel had forsaken his God, while another argued that God had forsaken the Jews, and yet still another remarked that Elie reminded him of Job—I offer the following advice and encouragement: "OK, that's a good starting point. Now each of you needs to go to the text and provide evidence for your case, and then there needs to be a group discussion around those points. And go to Job in the Bible and read that out loud in order to compare and contrast Job's revolt with that of Wiesel as spelled out in *Night.* See where that discussion goes."

Also, as I move from group to group, I prod the students to *really* wrestle with each student's point and, in doing so, to tie it directly to the memoir and/or to refer to the text in order to corroborate, contest, or expand on the point. With some groups it takes more encouragement and prodding than others, but by gently prodding and urging them to go with their initial reactions and then examine and wrestle with those, the students inevitably come up with remarkably interesting, if not perspicacious, insights.

It is during this initial assignment and during the course of the small group discussions that the students raise a host of questions and issues vis-à-vis various aspects of the Holocaust (e.g., What are Fascists?; What is Passover?; Why did the Jews have to wear a star?; Over and above what the citizens of Sighet heard about the mass killings from Moché the Beadle, which they didn't believe, what did the Hungarian Jews really know about the death camps in 1944?; What did nations outside the Nazis' sphere know about the mass killings and what did they do to help or warn the Jews?; When the Jews were rounded up to be deported, why didn't they resist?; How could anyone live through something like that or even want to live through it?), and questions about Wiesel's style of writing (When was *Night* written and how could he [Wiesel] remember all of those conversations?; There is an eerie cadence to the words when he says "Never shall I forget . . ." over and over again, but at the same time it reminds me of certain passages in the Bible). Many of the issues broached and discussed in the small groups were subsequently discussed in the large group discussions. Furthermore, the issues and students' comments were duly noted by me for the express purpose of revisiting and expanding upon them during the class discussion following the second reading of *Night*.

It is both during the small group and large group discussions that the real work of the teacher begins. If handled with care and skill, the large group discussion becomes extremely rich, informative, and enlightening. By having visited and listened in on the small groups and having jotted down notes about what the students were discussing and wrestling with, the instructor is able to help make connections between various students' comments during the large group discussion. Furthermore, the instructor is able to broach issues that were discussed in small groups that might not, for whatever reason, be brought back up in the large discussion group. Both of these strategies assist in maintaining the flow of the discussion, deepening the discussion, and challenging the students to play off of one another's ideas and to consider various and, sometimes radically different, points of view. I have found that during those few class sessions that I neglected to take notes and/or did not broach issues that generated heated discussion in the small groups, the large group discussions were often not as dynamic, interesting, or thought-provoking as they could or should have been.

Included below are a few excerpts from the students' initial response to *Night* (the letters to Elie Wiesel):

Dear Elie,

Last night I prayed for you, your mother, sisters and father *and for* the world that was silent while you suffered so horribly. I prayed, too, for myself, asking for the strength to not be callous and cold when people are desperate and in need of help.

What I cannot understand is how people—other nationalities, other religions, other races, other backgrounds—can be so cruel to other people. I just cannot understand how a human can hurt another human in the way the Nazis did little babies, children, old people, or anyone for that matter. That's what I feel I need to try to understand. How can such hate be developed in a whole people? How can people be so thoughtless, cruel, horrible to one another? Right now I feel as if I will never be able to understand that. Never! But I will try. (Karen)

Dear Elie,

My heart goes out to you in a way it has never gone out to anyone before. I do not know how you made it through everything that the Nazis put you through and your family through. I could have not made it through.

I thought I knew alot [*sic*] about the holocuast [*sic*] before I read *Night*, your story. Many years ago I had read *The Diary of Anne Frank*, and more recently I had watched some things on the Discovery Channel, and I even saw Schindler List [*sic*] twice, but what you experienced and what you wrote about and how you wrote about it left me feeling that I had no real idea what the holocaust [*sic*] was about.

I don't know what got me most about your story, your experiences—the brutality of the Nazis (which was horrorific [*sic*]) or the fact that no one really tried to help you and your family and community members. (Mike)

Dear Mr. Weisel [sic],

Over and over again I keep thinking about the first line in your book in chapter 3 that says, "The cherished objects we had brought with us thus far were left behind in the train, and with them, at least, our illusions." As you and your parents and sisters saw the horrer [*sic*] of Auschwtz [*sic*] it suddenly hit you what the Nazis were up to. To kill! To wipe out! To torture and murder a hole [*sic*] people. To turn living people into ash and smoke. To wipe every trace of a persons [*sic*] life, all Jew's lifes [*sic*], into nothing. No one could even imigine [*sic*] that before because it was to [*sic*] far-featched [*sic*], to [*sic*] unbeleiveable [*sic*], to [*sic*] crazy to even think about, but not any more. Not anymore. As you also say, "Today anything is allowed. Anything is possible, even these crematories. . . ." (Adam)

Dear Elie,

. . . I am a very religious person and when you said that "I ceased to pray" (p. 55), tears came to my eyes. You, too, were very religious but what you went through made you Job-like. You say, "I did not deny God's existence, but I doubted His absolute justice" (p. 56). Selfishly, I guess, I am glad you did not deny God's existence, but I do understand, at least to a certain extent, why you doubted His justice. And I can also understand, again, at least to a certain extent, why the men who were forced to watch the hanging of the little boy asked "Where is God? Where is He?" (p. 76). I guess my questions are: Where was the humanity in the Nazis? Where was the humanity in the individual men who ran Auschwitz? And where was humanity, period! [*sic*] while all of this was going on? And where is humanity today when so many atrocities are being perpetrated across the globe? (Kelly)

As one can ascertain from these few short excerpts, the letters written by the students were thought-filled, compassionate, and thought-provoking. Indeed, collectively, they generated many significant topics that were ultimately examined, analyzed, and debated—initially in small group discussions and then in a large class discussion.

Among the many questions and issues generated by the above excerpts were: What drives people to commit mass murder? This question spurred a discussion about the Nazis' propaganda machine and its race policies that perceived Jews as vermin and bacillus that reputedly posed a danger to the "Aryan race"; the silence of the world as the mass murder was committed as well as what the world knew and when; the sheer impossibility, at the time, to imagine that one group of people would actually plan and implement the "manufacture of death" of another group of people; the illusions and false hope that many Jews harbored as the Nazis closed in on and "had their way" with the Jews; and a debate over theodicy (defense of God's goodness and omnipotence in view of the existence of evil).

This initial approach—the writing of the personal letters and the subsequent discussions—is based on reader response theory. As John O'Neill (1994) has written in "Rewriting the Book on Literature: Changes Sought in How Literature Is Taught, What Students Read":

> Basically, reader response theory differs most radically from previous theories about teaching literature in the degree of emphasis placed on the reader's response to an interpretation of the text . . . In reader response theory, the text's meaning is considered to reside in the "transaction" between the reader and the text, not from the text alone. . . .
>
> In practice, reader response theory considers very carefully how students respond intellectually and emotionally to the text . . . By validating students' responses, teachers can spark a lively discussion from which a careful literary analysis will flow. . . . Rather than beginning with a discussion of symbolism or metaphor, for example, teachers should allow an exploration of these aspects to develop from students' own observations about the work. . . .
>
> The emphasis on getting students to respond to the literature doesn't mean that any response is as good as another. Students are continuously urged to return to the text to find validation for their views. (pp. 7, 8)

The key is to provide the students with an opportunity to examine literature from their own unique perspective, without imposing either the teacher's or a critic's interpretation on them. It is also a way to avoid having the students attempt to "please the teacher" by coming up with the "single correct answer." As anyone who appreciates the beauty and power of literature knows, good literature is multilayered; and as a result of that, the meaning inherent in a literary work is also multilayered. Thus, when students are prodded—as they often are in the so-called traditional classroom—to come up with the "correct answer" vis-à-vis the meaning of a literary work, the result is, more often than not, a perfunctory study that is bereft of real thinking and engagement by the student, not to mention lacking true insight into the literary work.

This is not to say that the teacher does not have a role in the process. In fact, the role of the teacher, as indicated by the above quote, is critical to the entire endeavor. The teacher's role is to serve as a facilitator of the discussion and to challenge the students to play off of one another's ideas and to plumb the work as deeply as possible by using their personal experiences and background knowledge to elucidate and expand on various points. It is also the teacher's job to introduce new ideas, thoughts, and angles in order to deepen everyone's thinking.

As previously mentioned, following the first reading of *Night*, I required each student to develop a second cluster and definition and that is followed by both small and large group discussions of various facets of the Holocaust and its definition. With very few exceptions, most of the second and third clusters by the students are more detailed, more accurate, and more sophisticated in their depiction of various facets and connections regarding various issues vis-à-vis the Holocaust.

Once the initial session is concluded, the students are required to read *Night* a second time, but instead of doing so in one fell swoop, they are assigned one chapter per evening and asked to examine the chapter more carefully in regard to both historical and literary concerns.

The Second Reading:
A Historical/Literary Approach

Based on the inaccurate information and misconceptions (and, in certain cases, myths) evident in many of the students' first clusters (and in the second, to a lesser extent), I have come to the firm conclusion that there is a critical need to provide students with an accurate and fairly thorough historical overview of the history of the Holocaust *at some point during the study of a piece of Holocaust literature*. Without such knowledge, many, if not most, students are liable to read a piece of literature and walk away ignorant about the historical context of the piece. The latter situation, of course, also impedes a more complete understanding of the piece of literature.

There are, of course, numerous ways to provide students with key historical background information about the Holocaust and the historical period specifically addressed in the piece of literature. Herein I shall delineate the various ways I have accomplished this task. Since I have generally had ample time (unlike many teachers who face extreme time constraints) to engage my students in such a study—either because I was teaching a semester-long course or engaged in an interdisciplinary unit that spanned 3 to 4 weeks—I have had the opportunity to use a multiple approach during each of my units of study. Those teachers who are facing extremely tight time constraints may choose to implement a truncated version of what I describe herein. That is fine, as long as the approach used is well thought out, thorough, and includes (1) a general overview of the Holocaust and (2) historical information that is germane to the specific literary work under study. In regard to the latter, for example, the teacher could focus on the Nazi policies and actions in the country or countries where the story is set and the reaction(s) of the local populace. Thus, in the case of *Night*, the students would examine the situation in Hungary and Poland in 1944. They might also examine issues that are central to the larger story, such as the difference between concentration and death camps or the purpose and horrific reality of the death marches.

I should note that when I first began teaching *Night* to high school students, which was in 1978, I did very little in the way of preparing the students to understand or appreciate the historical context germane to the period. Rather, during the course of our class discussions I added bits and pieces of information as the need arose. Rather quickly, though, I came to the conclusion that I needed to be more systematic and thorough in providing such a context.

In more recent years, the initial activity my students engage in during this section of the study is an examination of an accurate and comprehensive chronology of the Holocaust period. Useful chronologies for this activity can be found in the *Encyclopedia of the Holocaust,* edited by Israel Gutman (New York: Macmillan, 1990, pp. 1759–1782); *Teaching about the Holocaust: A Resource Book for Educators* (Washington, D.C.: United States Holocaust Memorial Museum, 1994, pp. 111–115); and *Teaching and Studying the Holocaust,* edited by Samuel Totten and Stephen Feinberg (Boston: Allyn and Bacon, 2001). I begin by providing each student with a copy of a chronology (and personally, I prefer the more concise but still fairly comprehensive chronologies such as those found in the latter two works), and ask each student to read carefully over the chronology, noting any *significant patterns* they come across. They are directed to jot down their observations in order to share and discuss them both in small and large groups. After 10 minutes or so, I organize the class into small groups (a minimum of three students, and generally no more than four) and ask each group to share and discuss its insights. Prior to initiating the discussion, I have an individual in each group volunteer to serve as a recorder whose task is to write down the most salient points the group makes and to note agreements, disagreements, and whether the group members come to a consensus or not in regard to whether there are, in fact, any notable patterns. They are also required to discuss the significance of such patterns. Once the small groups have concluded their discussions, we meet again as an entire class and discuss the various groups' findings. Generally, this is done by having one group's recorder report on his or her group's discussion, and as he or she reports, the rest of the class members are free to concur or disagree with a point, posit questions, play the devil's advocate, ask for clarification, and so forth. It is always understood that the recorder is not solely responsible for answering the questions or addressing any challenges but rather that all of the members of his or her group are expected to share the responsibility of engaging in the larger discussion. Once one group has shared its findings and the class discussion is exhausted, we move on to the next group. Invariably, a major finding and discussion point revolves around the incremental nature of the Nazi assault against the Jews, beginning in 1933 and moving inexorably toward ever more drastic measures. We also discuss what such a pattern meant for individual Jews, the community of Jews, non-Jews, and the larger world. In regard to the latter, students begin to discuss the fact that if someone—particularly the leaders and citizens of free nations—had spoken out early on in an urgent and persistent fashion, then possibly something could have been done to have prevented the most drastic actions of all by the Nazis—the mass extermination of millions. This exercise is absolutely essential in setting the stage for what Wiesel, his family and community, and the Jewish people faced in 1944 at the hands of the Nazis. Indeed, it prevents the students from studying the abject horror of the Holocaust in a vacuum in which they may mistakenly be led to believe that the genocide of the Jews by the Nazis simply erupted out of nowhere.

As the students read and discuss the historical essays (see below) and then read *Night* for a second time, they take part in the development of "their own" chronology of the Holocaust period. More specifically, a long piece of butcher paper is stretched along one wall. On the lefthand side of the paper the date 1933 is written (it is important to leave ample space between the edge of the paper and the date, for that way much earlier events, such as the Versailles Treaty of 1919, can be placed on the chart), and on the righthand side is placed the date 1945 (again, it is important to leave space between the date and the very edge of the paper). As various key incidents, events, decisions, promulgations, and dates come up in our discussion (e.g., the Enabling Law, the Nuremberg Laws, Kristallnacht, the Wannsee Conference), the entire class adds them to the chronology, always noting the exact day(s) and year(s). Such a strategy provides the students with a visual aid that assists them to place the events in *Night* and various aspects of the history in a meaningful context. It also provides them with an opportunity to revisit certain key issues throughout the study.[5]

It is during the reading of the historical essays and the second reading of *Night* that the students are required to maintain a "learning log." Succinctly stated, a learning log is a formal running record of the student's thoughts, insights, comments, feelings, and questions vis-à-vis the readings, class discussions, and class activities. Each student is given a copy of the following directions to follow in developing his or her learning log:

As the co-directors of a noted Holocaust education program, Facing History and Ourselves, observe: "Daily . . . writings can chart for each student the process and progress of the course [and] illuminate his or her response to it...The journal becomes a means for each student . . . to record ongoing encounters with the many issues that emerge from the course. As students make their way into this history, they will in effect be bearing witness to their own living history, responding to their own growth and change during the course.

"Every individual perceives the world through his or her own experiences and understanding. A student's insights, questions, and memories have an internal reality that is both unique and valuable. If the student can record these perceptions with honesty he or she will have taken an important step toward self-understanding. What the students choose to confront in their journals can tell them much about who they are." (Strom and Parsons, 1982, p. 25)

1. Be sure to place the date and a heading at the top of each response/entry. The heading may simply be a single word that signifies what the entry is about, along with the title of the essay or chapter to which you are responding.

2. Keep a daily learning log/journal. In doing so, you may include virtually anything you wish about your study of the Holocaust, in general, and *Night*, in particular. That is, you may focus on anything from what you are learning to your thoughts and feelings about what you are learning. For example, you may wish to: write about something new you learned in class or in a reading; (b) comment on something that took place in class or something you came across in your reading that was particularly thought-provoking or "eye-opening"; (c) remark on new insights you gleaned from a class session or reading; (d) comment on something you do not understand or want to understand in more depth; (e) address something you disagree with that cropped up in your reading, or took place or was commented on in class by the instructor or a fellow student; (f) provide insights as to how a certain class session could have been altered in such a way to have made it more engaging or thought-provoking for you; and (g) reflect on the value of what you are learning. In other words, it is your journal and you are welcome and encouraged to address any issue you wish that is germane to this course and the study of *Night* and the Holocaust.

3. Periodically, Dr. Totten may posit a question regarding some aspect of *Night* or the Holocaust and ask each student to respond to it in his learning log. Likewise, he may write a quote on the board from *Night*—which may stand by itself or be accompanied by a question—and ask each student to respond to the quote and/or the quote and the question. When responding to the quotes, be sure to copy the quote into your learning log and then respond to it. You are free to respond to the quotations or questions in any way you wish, and this may include relating it to other aspects of the memoir or another piece of Holocaust literature, relating it to some aspect of the history we've studied, positing your own questions, etc.

Please note that during the course of reading *Night* for a second time, you will be given six (6) questions per chapter to address in some detail in your log. One question will deal with the history or literary aspects of the memoir and one will require you to respond in a personal way to the information in the chapter.

4. Dr. Totten will read the journals. In doing so, he will write comments in response to your various entries. In certain cases, he may raise a question(s). Once you get your learning log back, you should make a point of answering/addressing the question(s) he raises in a fair amount of detail.

5. Since it is hoped that the learning log will become a reflective experience for you and serve as a means of dialogue between you and Dr. Totten, you should also feel free to raise questions for Dr. Totten to address as well.

6. The emphasis in the learning log should be on quality versus quantity. That is, a shorter entry that reflects high quality of thought and a genuine effort to wrestle with key issues and feelings is more highly valued than a longer entry that is bereft of much thought.

As mentioned above, during the course of reading *Night*, the students are given six questions per chapter to respond to in their log—four of the questions are in the cognitive domain (e.g., posited at the highest levels of the domain—analysis, synthesis, and/or evaluation) and two in the affective domain (e.g., dealing with emotions, feelings, beliefs). Each year, certain questions are culled out and new questions are added; so the set of questions students address from year to year are generally different.

The questions are also used as "discussion starters" during subsequent class sessions. Some of the questions deal with incidents in the story, while others may deal with certain literary conventions such as the previously mentioned issue of heightened language, biblical allusions, inverted symbolism, invented dialogue, etc.

Early on in developing this unit, I decided that it would be both expeditious and valuable to set the stage by giving a short lecture on the whos, whats, wheres, whens, and whys of the Holocaust and the specific situation faced by Hungary and Hungarian Jews during the Holocaust. In general, I avoid lecturing, for I favor a more interactive approach; but since the rest of the unit of study is highly interactive I have no problem giving a lecture in this situation. To prepare the lecture, I generally obtain information from a variety of scholarly books by some of the most noted Holocaust scholars. These include, but are not limited to, Lucy S. Dawidowicz's *The War Against the Jews 1933–1945* (New York: Bantam Books, 1986); *A History of the Holocaust* by Yehuda Bauer (Danbury, CT: Franklin Watts, 1982); and Raul Hilberg's *The Destruction of the European Jews* (New York: Holmes & Meier, 1985). While this approach brought about a more informed discussion of *Night,* I still felt that more could and should be done to provide a solid historical context. Thus, during the teaching of subsequent units on *Night,* I combined the aforementioned lecture with the viewing of *Genocide, 1941–1945.* The film addresses the destruction of the European Jewry through the use of archival footage and the testimonies of victims, perpetrators, and bystanders. *Genocide 1941–1945*, which is part of the World at War series, is currently one of the best films available for providing a general overview of the Holocaust. Not only is it readily available, but it is a film that is historically accurate, highly engaging, and readily understood by upper-level secondary-school students. *I should note that I would never be satisfied simply showing this film and skipping the above-mentioned lecture or the readings to which the students read and respond.* That is due to the fact that not only do I wish to provide the students with an overview of the Holocaust (which the film *Genocide* does fairly well), but I also find it crucial to provide the students with specific information regarding the fate of the Hungarian Jews, which Elie Wiesel's family and community were a part of, as well as, for example, specifics regarding the deportations, life and death in Auschwitz, and the death marches. In order to provide the latter information, both the lecture and the readings are a necessity.[6]

Finally, in addition to the aforementioned lecture and the film, I have added another component that requires the students to read and respond to a series of key essays, chapters, and/or articles. Generally, I have the students read and respond to one or two general pieces on the Holocaust and two pieces on the fate of the Jews in Hungary during the Holocaust. These readings are to be completed *prior to* my lecture and the viewing of *Genocide.* Over the years, the exact articles and essays have changed, which is due to the fact that as new books, essays, and articles have appeared, I have made an attempt to locate and use ever more readable pieces that provide a fairly succinct but still thorough overview of major issues vis-à-vis the Holocaust and/or the fate of the Hungarian Jews. Over the years I have used, in various combinations and at different points in time, the following pieces, all of which, "in their own way," have proved useful and informative: Chapter 1, "Precedents" in *The Destruction of the European Jews* by Raul Hilberg (which examines the long, sordid history of antisemitism through time, and the three successive goals of anti-Jewish administrators through the ages: "You have no right to live among us as Jews; You have no right to live among us; You have no right to live" [Hilberg, 1985, p. 8]); "The Evolution of Nazi Jewish Policy, 1933–1938" and "The Final Solution" in *A History of the Holocaust* by Yehuda Bauer; Donald Niewyk's "Holocaust: Genocide of the Jews" (which provides a short but solid overview of key aspects of the Holocaust, including key historical trends that combined to make the Holocaust possible); Randolph L. Braham's "Hungary—Jews During the Holocaust"; György Ranki's "Hungary—General Survey"; and various sections in *The World Must Know: The History of the Holocaust as Told in the United States Holocaust Memorial Museum* by Michael Berenbaum.

In order to allow ample time for the students to read such pieces, I assign them for homework over a 4-day period—Thursday, Friday, Saturday, and Sunday. I inform the students that they are expected to use part of each day, or at least what is comparable time to using a part of all 4 days, to complete the reading assignment.

Teachers who are limited by time need to examine the aforementioned essays as well as others in order to ascertain those that are most ideal for their own situation. That said, if a teacher has a fair amount of time to dedicate to such a study— as well as the financial support to purchase a set of books for the purpose of providing a historical overview—then I strongly recommend that they consider using Michael Berenbaum's *The World Must Know: The History of the Holocaust as Told in the United States Holocaust Memorial Museum* (Boston: Little, Brown, 1993). This book, which was written by the former director of research at the United States Holocaust Memorial Museum, was developed for the general reader and is ideal for use with a secondary level student audience. Not only is it accurate in its portrayal of the history, but it is highly readable, packed with photographs that complement the text, and includes fascinating and informative excerpts from first-person accounts.

Once the students have read the articles, listened to the lecture, and viewed the film, we begin to read and discuss *Night* a second time. As we discuss it, we use the history the students recently learned in order to deepen their understanding of Wiesel's experiences. At one and the same time, we also revisit many of the issues raised during our initial reading of the book. Throughout our discussion, a host of issues, topics, and questions posited by the students provoked deep thought and passionate response. Among some of the many issues and topics that were addressed during one such discussion were the following:

(1) The fact that Wiesel repeatedly mentions that following extremely traumatic incidents, everything in Sighet eventually went back to "normal" (e.g., "Then one day they expelled all the foreign Jews from Sighet . . . Several days passed. Several weeks. Several months. Life had returned to normal" [Wiesel, 1969, p. 15]; Moché, a foreign Jew who had been deported, returned to Sighet and reported that "The Jews [who were deported] were made to dig huge graves. And when they had finished their work, the Gestapo began theirs. Without passion, without haste, they slighted their prisoners. . . . Babies were thrown into the air and the machine gunners used them as targets . . . People refused not only to believe his stories, but even to listen to them. . . . That was toward the end of 1942. Afterward life returned to normal") ([pp. 15, 16, 17]). These and other examples of "returning to normality" moved the students to talk about a host of related issues, including the fact that (a) even in abnormal times, many people feel compelled to lead as normal lives as possible; (b) that leading a "normal" life under such circumstances constituted a classic case of denial of the facts; (c) that as long as individuals were not

personally attacked, they found a way to inch back to "normalcy"; (d) that seeking "normalcy" was, in part, the downfall of the Sighet Jews; and (e) that the Nazis symbolized "abnormalcy" but few in the world seemed to appreciate just how abnormal their abnormalcy was.

(2) Tied directly to the latter point, almost all of the students were shaken by the following statement in Chapter 1 of *Night:* "Was he [Hitler] going to wipe out a whole people? Could he exterminate a population scattered throughout so many countries? So many millions! What methods could he use? And in the middle of the twentieth century?" (p. 17). Here the students talked about how, at one time in the history of humanity, in fact just under 60 years ago, people could not even imagine something like the mass murder of millions, that of an entire people. What particularly disturbed the students is that today such a horror is "accepted as a given," not even questioned, at least in regard to whether it is possible or not. As one student said, quietly and with sadness, "We live in a very different world today." Here, we also talked about the methods of the mass killing and I gave a mini-lecture on the Nazis' experimentation with mass murder, from the shooting of hundreds of thousands of Jews by the Einsatzgruppen in the Soviet Union beginning on June 22, 1941 to the killing of 600 Soviet prisoners of war on September 3, 1941, in a hermetically sealed cell into which crystals of Zyklon B gas were thrown, to the development and use of gas vans, and finally the refinement of the killing process with the development of the gas chambers and crematoria (Arad, 1990, pp. 461–463). Here, too, we branched off into a discussion of the concepts of "progress" and "civilized," and what the two mean in a world where weapons of mass destruction are a given and are within an arm's reach of many who distrust, if not detest, "the other."

(3) Speaking about the fate of the Jews at the hands of the Nazis, Wiesel observes early on that "There was no longer any questions of wealth, of social distinction, and importance, only people all condemned to the same fate" (p. 31). This provoked ample discussion about the Nazis' philosophy, goals, and treatment of the Jews. Here I incorporated information about the racial philosophy of the Nazis and the Nuremberg Laws. (For an excellent overview of the racial policies of the Nazis, see "Racism" by George Mosse in the *Encyclopedia of the Holocaust,* and for a succinct but solid overview of the Nuremberg Race Laws, see "Nuremberg Laws" by David Bankier in the *Encyclopedia of the Holocaust.)* During this same discussion, I brought in Wiesel's (1979b) assertion, which he made years after he wrote *Night,* that "While not all victims [of the Nazis] were Jews, all Jews were victims, destined for annihilation solely because they were born Jewish. They were doomed not because of something they had done or proclaimed or acquired but because of who they were: sons and daughters of the Jewish people" (p. iii). I also shared this similar but somewhat different observation of Wiesel's with the students: "Their [the Jews] being was the target to be destroyed. All Jews everywhere shared the same fate, old and young, rich and poor, beggars and princes, children and their grandparents, all had to disappear" (Wiesel, 1977, p. 6).

(4) The issue of the Nazis holding an entire group of people or an entire community responsible for the single action of an individual also resulted in a lengthy

discussion. This was prompted by Wiesel's statement regarding the deportations, during which a German officer warned those being crammed into a railway car: "There are eighty of you in the wagon . . . If anyone is missing, you'll all be shot, like dogs" (p. 34). This issue of "collective responsibility" and the fear it must have induced in people segued into a discussion about resistance and just how difficult it would be to decide to resist in light of the fact that one's actions could result in the deaths of so many others. Here I introduce the fate of Lidice, a village in Czechoslovakia, 10 miles from Prague, that was completely annihilated by the Germans during World War II. In retaliation for the assassination of Reinhard Heydrich, a high-ranking Nazi, by Czech resistance fighters, "early in the morning of June 10, 1942, all the inhabitants of the village of Lidice were taken out of their homes, and all the men in the village—192 in all—were killed, as were 71 women. The remaining women, numbering 198, were imprisoned in the Ravensbrück concentration camp. . . . Of the 98 children who had been 'put into educational institutions,' no more than 16 survived. . . . Lidice was [then] razed to the ground, the official reason being that the villagers had helped the assassins—an allegation that had no basis in fact—and that two men from Lidice serving with the Czech forces in Britain had assured the parachutists that they could trust the villagers" (Goshen, 1990, pp. 870, 871, 872).

Here, too, I draw the students' attention to the issue of choiceless choices. In speaking of the Holocaust and those options that the victims were given by the Nazis, Langer (1995) describes *choiceless choices* as being one where "whatever you choose somebody loses" (p. 46). Elsewhere Langer (1982) describes *choiceless choices* as those "where crucial decisions did not reflect options between life and death, but between one form of abnormal response and another, both imposed by a situation that was in no way of the victim's own choosing" (p. 72). Such discussions as these serve to complicate, in the best sense of the word, the students' thinking about this history and what it meant to be caught up in the maw of the Nazis.

(5) Throughout the discussion of *Night,* the students, prompted by Wiesel's comments and their own questioning, returned time and again to the issue of "silence"—the silence of the world and the silence of God. Two of the passages that provoked heated discussion were as follows:

> Not far from us, flames were leaping up from a ditch, gigantic flames. They were burning something. A lorry drew up at the pit and delivered its load—little children. Babies! Yes, I saw it—saw it with my own eyes...those children in the flames. . . . I pinched my face. Was I still alive? Was I awake? I could not believe it. How could it be possible for them to burn people, children, and for the world to keep silent? (Wiesel, 1969, p. 42)

And:

> For the first time, I felt revolt rise up in me. Why should I bless His name? The Eternal, Lord of the Universe, the All-Powerful and Terrible, was silent. (Wiesel, 1969, p. 43)

[handwritten note in top margin: shoes at auschwitz — what do you see?]

(6)   After entering Auschwitz, Wiesel states that "I became A–7713. After that I had no other name" (Wiesel, 1969, p. 53). After we discuss what it means to lose one's name and to be referred to as a number, I introduce a poster that is comprised solely of the shoes of hundreds of victims of the Holocaust. It is one poster in a set developed by the United States Holocaust Memorial Museum. I hold the poster in front of the class and ask the students to simply describe what they see. Slowly but then with more confidence as different students share their observations, the students call out such comments as: "All types of shoes!"; "Mounds of shoes"; "Battered shoes, fancy shoes, tiny shoes"; "Men's and women's and baby's shoes"; "Twisted shoes"; "Pairs of shoes and shoes without the other pair"; "Shoes with no feet, no bodies"; "Shoes of rich people and possibly poor people"; "Shoes with buckles." Next, I ask, "What is the importance of shoes in a person's life?" Here the students respond with comments like: "They tell whether you're 'with it' or not'"; "Whether you're a man, woman, teenager, baby or . . ."; "Not always," responds another student, "'cause look at how many old people wear tennis shoes today"; "They tell something about your personality"; "They're individual, like you, as a person"; and so on and so forth. Next, I posit this question: "What do these shoes make you think about when you think about the Holocaust?" Here the students answer with statements like: "The piles of dead in photographs you often see"; "They're discarded, just like the victims were"; "They're all shoes but different types and different ages and different styles, just like the people who were murdered"; "They're without names"; "Just as those murdered in the death camps never received a proper burial, the shoes have just been discarded helter-skelter." This discussion generally spans at least half a period or more, and probes into a host of issues regarding identity and the ramifications of being denied one's identity and why the Nazis set out to accomplish such a goal in the camps.

(7)   Ultimately, we confronted the concept of theodicy (e.g., the issue of God's goodness and omnipotence in view of the existence of evil in the world), not a word the students knew but one they broached in their own words, and which at least one student had broached in her letter to Wiesel. An explosion of discussion erupted around this concept when the students read about the hanging of a young boy by the Nazis:

> One day when we came back from work, we saw three gallows rearing up in the assembly place . . . Roll call. SS all round us, machine guns trained: the traditional ceremony. Three victims in chains—and one of the them [a little boy]. The head of the camp read the verdict. All eyes were on the child . . . The three necks were placed at the same moment within the noose . . . "Where is God? Where is He?" Someone behind me asked. . . . I heard a voice within me answer him: "Where is He? Here He is. He is hanging here on this gallows. . . ." (Wiesel, 1969, pp. 75, 76).

The issues mentioned above are just a few of the many issues we addressed as we read and discussed *Night*. To provide a description of the complete discussion would consume a small book. Still, what has been delineated here provides key insights into the issues the students raised and how I made a constant attempt to introduce key aspects of the history in order to deepen the students' understanding of the Holocaust and what the targeted people faced at the hands of the Nazis.

As mentioned earlier, there are, obviously, innumerable ways teachers and their students could approach the study of *Night,* but one method that is particularly intriguing has been developed by Grace Caporino, a long-time Holocaust educator and English teacher at Carmel High School in Carmel, New York. More specifically, she notes that "in searching for a way to help students reach beyond their own immediate worlds and relate to Holocaust readings [not necessarily *Night*], I have delineated five thematic categories that can frame readings and can help them understand the interactions of the different categories. I outline these categories as victim, perpetrator, bystander, collaborator, and rescuer. . . . Different works lend themselves to the exploration of the categories" (Caporino, 1999, p. 227). For a discussion as to how Caporino (1999) uses this approach with a poem about the Holocaust, see her essay "Teaching the Holocaust in the English Classroom." Obviously, teachers will have to adapt such an approach in various ways to make it useful for teaching a memoir.

Dr. William Fernekes, a social studies supervisor and teacher at Hunterdon Central Regional High School in Flemington, New Jersey has his students, in part, examine works of literature via the history of antisemitism and the four stages of destruction of the Jews that historian Raul Hilberg (1985) delineates in his *The Destruction of European Jewry:* definition, expropriation, concentration, and annihilation. Writing about the issues of definition, expropriation, concentration, and annihilation in his book *The World Most Know: The History of the Holocaust as Told in the United States Holocaust Memorial Museum,* Michael Berenbaum notes that:

> First Jews were categorized; then civil liberties were restricted and property confiscated. Next, Jews were dismissed from universities and civil service jobs, which often included school teaching, and were barred from the professions. Jewish businesses were taken over and Aryanized. Jews were then isolated, forced to wear the Jewish star and forbidden to use public facilities.
>
> Finally, Jews were assembled, first, in large cities and then in transit camps. From 1942 on, they were deported from these transit camps to the death camp in the east. (p. 68)

To deepen one's understanding and key insights into the four stages, teachers should obtain copies of the student edition of Hilberg's *The Destruction of European Jewry* or the complete three-volume set by the same name. Again, Michael Berenbaum's *The World Must Know: The History of the Holocaust as Told in the United States Holocaust Memorial Museum* is worth consulting as well, particularly in light of the fact that it delineates the four stages in a highly readable manner and in a way that is understandable to most upper-level secondary-level students.

Concluding Activities

For those teachers and students who have the time and inclination, there are numerous concluding and/or extension activities that can further the students' understanding both of Elie Wiesel's work and of the Holocaust. What is highlighted here are two activities that the author has used with a great deal of success.

A final essay examination could require students to respond to one of the following quotes by Elie Wiesel:

> The Nazis' aim was to make the Jewish universe shrink—from town to neighborhood to street, from street to house, from house to room, from room to garret, from garret to cattle car, from cattle car to gas chamber.
> And they did the same to the individual—separated from his or her community, then from his or her family, then from his or identity, eventually becoming a work permit, then a number, until the number itself was turned into ashes. (Wiesel, 1984, p. 1)

> It was easier for a camp inmate then to imagine himself or herself free than for a free man or a free woman to imagine himself or herself today in the victim's predicament. Imagination fails us. Usually in literature imagination precedes reality, but this time reality preceded imagination." (Wiesel, 1978, p. 270)

> I've got more faith in Hitler than in anyone else. He's the only one who's kept his promises, all his promises, to the Jewish people. (Wiesel, 1969, p. 92, *Night*)

> Let us remember that what Nazism did to its Jewish victims was considered to be legal. It was legal to imprison political adversaries, it was legal to practice euthanasia on mentally retarded patients, it was legal to hunt down and execute resistance-fighters, it was legal—and commendable—to push Jews into ghettos to torment them, to torture them, to gas them, to burn them: everything was done with so-called due process, according to German law. That means: the Nazis had corrupted the law itself. They made it into a weapon against humanity. Remember that it can be done—for they did it. The law itself became immoral. Inhuman. (Wiesel, 1982, p. 9)

In responding to one of the quotes, the students could address the validity and significance of the idea expressed in the quote and use specific examples and additional quotes from Wiesel's *Night* to support their position and arguments.

As an extra-credit extension activity, students could be provided with the opportunity to respond to *Night* in an artistic manner. They should be informed that their response could take any form they wish, including but not limited to the following: a musical composition, a painting, a drawing, a choreographed dance, a collage, a piece of sculpture, a mobile, a bulletin board display, or a mural.[7]

Conclusion

It is a cliché that each time a reader returns to a good piece of literature he or she discovers new and different insights; but I must say that—at least for me—in the case of *Night*, it is the truth. Indeed, each and every time I reread *Night* and assist my students in grappling with Wiesel's story and the ramifications that the Holocaust has for humanity today, I leave with a greater appreciation of the work.

Both during and following each reading I am left pondering a whole host of issues, my mind swimming with thoughts about that which makes us human and inhuman, that which constitutes a truly civilized society, and what it means to live in a world where genocide is a "fact of life." The latter invariably finds me pondering Wiesel's comment, not made in *Night* but elsewhere: "The opposite of goodness is not evil; it is indifference to evil." Ultimately, it is my ardent hope that my students also leave the study pondering—hard and long—their own musings.

NOTES

1. Though Hungarian Jews faced discrimination and persecution, Hungarian Jews escaped the "final solution" (e.g., systematic killing) until the Germans invaded in March of 1944. In April the Jews were ghettoized and between May 15th and July 8th, 1944—a full eighteen months after the destruction of Polish Jewry—437,402 Jews were deported on 148 trains to Auschwitz. Wiesel and his family were among the deportees.

2. Readers interested in learning more about Wiesel's life should read his *All Rivers Run to the Sea: Memoirs.* New York: Schocken Books, 1995. Another book that provides valuable insights into Wiesel as a person and a writer is *Harry James Cargas in Conversation with Elie Wiesel.* New York: Paulist Press, 1976.

3. For some excellent and thought-provoking discussions by classroom teachers concerning the clustering method, see Carol Booth Olson's *Practical Ideas for Teaching Writing as a Process.* Sacramento, CA: California State Department of Education, 1987.

4. For an interesting discussion of how to incorporate multiple intelligences into the classroom, also see Thomas Armstrong's *Multiple Intelligences in the Classroom.* Alexandria, VA: Association for Supervision and Curriculum Development, 1994.

5. This idea was originated by Stephen Feinberg, a long-time history teacher at Wayland Middle School, who now works at the United States Holocaust Memorial Museum.

6. *Genocide, 1941–1945* is available from Arts and Entertainment, 800–423–1212 or write A & E Home Video, P. O. Box 2284, South Burlington, VT 05407. An excellent annotated bibliography for locating historically accurate films on a wide range of issues germane to the Holocaust is the United States Holocaust Memorial Museum's (USHMM) *Annotated Videography.* For a copy, contact the USHMM's Education Department at 100 Raoul Wallenberg Place SW, Washington, D.C. 20024.

7. For additional ideas for extension activities, see Samuel Totten's "Teaching Holocaust Literature" in Samuel Totten and Stephen Feinberg (Eds.), *Teaching and Studying the Holocaust* (Boston: Allyn and Bacon, 2001.)

REFERENCES

Arad, Yitzhak. (1990). "Extermination Camps." In Israel Gutman (Ed.), *Encyclopedia of the Holocaust* (pp. 461–463). New York: Macmillan Publishing.

Armstrong, Thomas. (1994). *Multiple Intelligences in the Classroom.* Alexandria, VA: Association for Supervision and Curriculum Development.

Bankier, David. (1990). "Nuremberg Laws." In Israel Gutman (Ed.), *Encyclopedia of the Holocaust* (pp. 1076–1077). New York: Macmillan Publishing.

Bauer, Yehuda. (1982). *A History of the Holocaust.* Danbury, CT: Franklin Watts.

Berger, Joseph. (1986, October 15). "A Witness to Evil: Eliezer Wiesel." *The New York Times*, p. 4.

Braham, Randolph. L. (1990). "Hungary—Jews During the Holocaust." In Israel Gutman (Ed.), *Encyclopedia of the Holocaust* (pp. 698–703). New York: Macmillan Publishing Company.

Braham, Randolph L. (1981). "What Did They Know and When?" In Yehuda Bauer and Nathan Rotenstreich (Eds.), *The Holocaust as Historical Experience: Essays and a Discussion* (pp. 109–131). New York: Holmes & Meier Publishers. [A more detailed version of this essay appears in Braham's *The Politics of Genocide.* New York: Columbia University Press, 1981.]

Brown, Robert McAfee. (1979, Spring). "The Moral Society and the Work of Elie Wiesel." *Face to Face: An Interreligious Bulletin* [Special Issue: "Building a Moral Society: Aspects of Elie Wiesel's Work"]. Volume 6, pp. 22–27.

Cargas, Harry James. (1976). *Harry James Cargas in Conversation with Elie Wiesel.* New York: Paulist Press.

Caporino, Grace. (1999). "Teaching the Holocaust in the English Classroom: Hearing the Voices, Touching the History," In Carol Danks and Leatrice B. Rabinsky (Eds.), *Teaching for a Tolerant World: Grades 9–12: Essays and Resources* (pp. 218–234). Urbana, IL: National Council of Teachers of English.

Dawidowicz, Lucy S. (1986). *The War Against the Jews 1933–1945.* New York: Bantam Books.

Eckardt, Alice L. (1979, Spring). "Rebel Against God." *Face to Face: An Interreligious Bulletin* [Special Issue: "Building a Moral Society: Aspects of Elie Wiesel's Work"]. Volume 6, pp. 18–20.

Ezrahi, Sidra DeKoven. (1982). *By Words Alone: The Holocaust in Literature.* Chicago, IL: The University of Chicago Press.

Freedman, Samuel. (1983, October 23). "Bearing Witness: The Life and Work of Elie Wiesel." *The New York Times Magazine,* pp. 32–36, 40, 65–69.

Gardner, Howard. (1983). *Frames of Mind: The Theory of Multiple Intelligences.* New York: Basic Books.

Gardner, Howard. (1993). *Multiple Intelligences: The Theory in Practice.* New York: Basic Books.

Gates, E. Nathaniel. (Ed.) (1994). *The Concept of "Race" in Natural and Social Science.* New York: Garland Publishing.

Goshen, Seev. (1990). "Lidice." In Israel Gutman (Ed.), *Encyclopedia of the Holocaust* (pp. 870–872). New York: Macmillan Publishing.

Hilberg, Raul. (1985). *The Destruction of European Jewry.* "Revised and Definitive Edition." Three Volumes. New York: Holmes & Meier.

Hilberg, Raul. (1985). *The Destruction of the European Jews—Student Edition.* New York: Holmes & Meier.

Kanfer, Stefan. (1985). "Author, Teacher, Witness: Holocaust Survivor Elie Wiesel Speaks for the Silent." *Time,* March 18, pp. 79, 90.

Langer, Lawrence L. (1982). *Versions of Survival: The Holocaust and the Human Spirit.* Albany: State University of New York Press.

Langer, Lawrence L. (1995). *Admitting the Holocaust: Collected Essays.* New York: Oxford University Press.

Markham, James M. (1986, October 15). "Elie Wiesel Gets Nobel for Peace as 'Messenger'." *The New York Times,* pp. 1, 4.

Montagu, Ashley. (1964). *Man's Most Dangerous Myth: The Fallacy of Race.* Cleveland and New York: The World Publishing Company.

Mosse, George. (1990). "Racism." In Israel Gutman (Ed.), *Encyclopedia of the Holocaust* (pp. 1206–1217). New York: Macmillan Publishing.

Niewyk, Donald. (1995). "Holocaust: Genocide of the Jews." In Samuel Totten, William S. Parsons, and Israel W. Charny (Eds.), *Genocide in the Twentieth Century: Critical Essays and Eyewitness Accounts* (pp. 167–207). New York: Garland Publishing, Inc.

O'Brien, Michael. (1987). "Propagating Clusters." In Carol Booth Olson (Ed.), *Practical Ideas for Teaching Writing as a Process* (p. 25). Sacramento, CA: California State Department of Education.

O'Neill, John. (1994). "Rewriting the Book on Literature: Changes Sought in How Literature Is Taught, What Students Read." *ASCD Curriculum Update* (June): 7, 8.

Parsons, William S., & Totten, Samuel. (1993). *Guidelines for Teaching About the Holocaust.* Washington, D.C.: United States Holocaust Memorial Museum.

Ranki, György. (1990). "Hungary—General Survey." In Israel Gutman (Ed.), *Encyclopedia of the Holocaust* (pp. 693–698). New York: Macmillan Publishing.

Rico, Gabrielle. (1987). "Clustering: A Prewriting Process." In Carol Booth Olson (Ed.), *Practical Ideas for Teaching Writing as a Process* (pp. 17–20). Sacramento, CA: California State Department of Education.

Rosenfeld, Alvin, and Greenberg, Irving. (Eds.). (1976). *Confronting the Holocaust: The Impact of Elie Wiesel.* Bloomington: Indiana University Press.

Strom, Margot Stern, & Parsons, William S. (1982). *Facing History and Ourselves: Holocaust and Human Behavior.* Watertown, MA: Intentional Educations, Inc.

United States Holocaust Memorial Museum. (1994). *Teaching About the Holocaust: A Resource Book for Educators.* Washington, D.C.: Author.

Wiesel, Elie. (1969). *Night.* New York: Avon Books.

Wiesel, Elie. (1977). "The Holocaust as Literary Expression." Speech. 15 pages.

Wiesel, Elie. (1978, April). "Then and Now: The Experiences of a Teacher." *Social Education,* Volume 42 Number 4, pp. 266–271.

Wiesel, Elie. (1979a, Spring). "A Personal Response." *Face to Face: An Interreligious Bulletin* [Special Issue: "Building a Moral Society: Aspects of Elie Wiesel's Work"]. Volume 6, pp. 35–37.

Wiesel, Elie. (1979b). "Preface." *Report to the President.* Washington, D.C.: President's Commission on the Holocaust.

Wiesel, Elie. (1982, May–June). "Address of the Chairman of the U.S. Holocaust Council." *Martyrdom and Resistance,* p. 9.

Wiesel, Elie. (1984, August 19). "All Was Lost, Yet Something Was Preserved. A Review of The Chronicle of the Lodz Ghetto, 1941–1944." *The New York Times Book Review,* p. 1.

Wiesel, Elie. (1990). *From the Kingdom of Memory: Reminiscences.* New York: Schocken Books.

Wiesel, Elie. (1995a). *All Rivers Run to the Sea: Memoirs.* New York: Schocken Books.

Wiesel, Elie. (1995b, August 27). "The Decision—An Excerpt from *All Rivers Run to the Sea*—From the New Autobiography by Elie Wiesel." *Parade Magazine,* pp. 4–6.

Diminishing the Complexity and Horror of the Holocaust

Using Simulations in an Attempt to Convey Historical Experiences

SAMUEL TOTTEN

In an effort to provide students with a "real sense" as to what Jews went through during the Holocaust, some teachers (including university professors) latch on to the use of simulations. Others, including many long-time Holocaust educators and concerned Holocaust survivors, look askance at the use of simulations, arguing that they provide an unrealistic view of tortuously complex and horrific situations and serve to minimize the significance of what victims experienced.

The focus of this essay is twofold: first, it delineates why and how some educators have used simulations to teach their students about various aspects of the Holocaust; second, it argues that the use of such simulations constitutes poor pedagogy as a result of its drastic over-simplification of Holocaust history.

Why and How Teachers Use Simulations of the Holocaust

"The truth of the matter is that we need to use anything we can find to allow students to make connections between their lessons and their life."[1] This sentiment expressed by one teacher with regard to Holocaust education is, unfortunately, shared by many others at the elementary through university levels.

Some teachers believe that simulations are desirable pedagogical devices for capturing student interest. First, they argue that simulations are a powerful way to provide students with a sense as to what people have experienced in different historical situations. Second, they insist that through simulations, students are able to glean insights into aspects of history that they would not necessarily gain via more traditional methods, such as reading the history of the period. Third, they argue that because simulations tap into the affective domain and are so radically different from other classroom activities, they thoroughly engage student interest and are capable of leaving lasting impressions on students.

None of these arguments stand up under close scrutiny when applied to teaching about the Holocaust. As for the first point, to suggest that one can approximate even a scintilla of what its victims went through is sheer folly. Addressing the second and third points, there are ample resources available—such as primary documents, first-person accounts of survivors and liberators, very readable secondary sources, and powerful and accurate documentaries—that are highly engaging, thought-provoking, and memorable. If none of these materials engage students then it is incumbent upon teachers to reevaluate whether their students are mature enough to study this history.

Stephen Feinberg, a noted Holocaust educator who taught history at the middle school level for eighteen years and is now employed at the United States Holocaust Memorial Museum, comments as follows about the use of simulations to attempt to convey to students what the victims lived through (e.g., in the ghettos, during the deportations, and in the concentration and death camps):

> I am very leery about using simulations to teach *any* aspect of the Holocaust. While it may be appealing to some educators to use simulations when addressing certain issues raised by the Holocaust, I believe the result would be more negative than positive. According to William A. Nesbitt, the author of *Simulation Games for the Social Studies Classroom*, "the reality represented [in a simulation] is reduced in size so that it is manageable. Only selected aspects of the real situation are included in a simulation. Developers of simulations reduce and simplify reality so students can focus on selected aspects of reality." This simplification of reality can, when applied to a study of the Holocaust, lead to a facile understanding of complex issues and, worse still, a trivialization of the Holocaust.[2]

This author is in total agreement with Feinberg's position.

The following are examples of simulations that some teachers use to "recreate" aspects of Holocaust history in order to "place students in the shoes of the victims." They were gleaned from various sources: Holocaust curricula, articles in which teachers describe their use of simulations, descriptions of simulations that teachers have shared over the Internet on the Holocaust.listserve, and examples that teachers shared with my colleagues and me as we presented sessions at conferences on Holocaust education.

> Prior to class, a 7th grade social studies teacher clears all the desks from the middle of the room and draws a long, broad rectangle in chalk on the floor. After the students enter, she explains that today they are going to gain an understanding of what it was like for the Jews to be deported to concentration camps in cattle cars. After lining the kids up, she swiftly marches them into the imaginary boxcar. As the space becomes increasingly crowded, she urges them to squeeze tighter together; and as they do so, she keeps feeding more students into the space. When the last student is in, she pretends to slam the imaginary door closed. Then, as they stand there, giggling, com-

plaining about their feet being stepped on, gently pushing and shoving each other, she orders them quiet and then reads them a selection from a first-person account that describes the cattle cars. At the end of the simulation, she announces, "Now you have some idea as to what the Jews went through. You should never forget it."[3]

My students and I [Hilve Fierek] spent . . . two weeks exploring Hitler's war against the Jews and other "undesirables": the historical events, the facts and figures, the personal accounts. We watched videos and read poem after poem, story after story. I was certain my students were learning. I mean, I had brought in all this stuff; surely now my ninth graders recognized the importance of our study.

To test my theory, I once again asked my students to take out a sheet of paper. "Imagine this is Germany during World War II," I instructed. "Decide whether you'd rather be a Nazi soldier or a Jew and explain why." Most started writing, but one young man raised his hand. With sincere curiosity, he asked, "Now which ones got beaten up again?"

My first impulse was to run from the room crying . . . I had failed, and failed miserably. . . . Thinking quickly, I told students to clear their desks and give me their absolute, undivided attention. "This mobile unit is now Germany in 1943," I told them with every bit of total authority I could muster. "I am Adolf Eichmann, a chief administrator for the Final Solution. Decide now whether you are a Nazi or a Jew. If you choose to be a Nazi, line up along the right wall. If you choose to be a Jew, assemble in the left corner. You may not choose to be an 'innocent' bystander. And I want silence."

I was surprised at how quickly and easily I assumed the role of dictator. I was equally surprised at how quickly and easily my students assumed their chosen roles. . . . I instructed those students who had congregated in the corner to remain silent while I took the five students who had elected to be Nazis outside. I assigned each one rank, naming one young woman my second-in-command. They were to follow my orders to the letter, with no questions asked. They readily agreed.

Back in the room, I told one Nazi commander to select three Jews for immediate extermination. "But how . . ." he began. "Do it," I commanded. He chose three students randomly and took them to the other side of the room. I told the selected students they were now dead and could not participate in the rest of the activities. There were a few giggles, giggles that I immediately stifled with my newly found dictator glare.

For the next 15 minutes my mobile unit was, for us, World War II Germany. The tension became so thick that several times I considered stopping the activity. For instance, when I told one girl who had elected to be a Jew to select two of her classmates for medical experimentation, she at first refused. "Choose now, or I take six," I barked. The girl, a Jehovah's Witness, replied with tears in her eyes, "Take me."[4]

When I [Ginger Moore] was a sophomore in college, in a three-week Winter term course on the Holocaust, the professors wanted us to understand at least a little bit what trips in cattle cars were like (most of us never having been inside a cattle car in our lives). So they had us squeeze into the approximate space on the floor, try sitting (not possible), try moving (not possible), and then try to imagine having to go to the bathroom (horrifying). They also gave us other qualifiers; we were indoors, not out with the weather and temperature, it was light, we had had breakfast, and so forth. I know I came away from it with a much clearer idea than words or even pictures could have provided. While I'm sure it didn't even come close to what the victims experienced, it did make a connection with most of the students which we otherwise would not have had. It was a way to avoid numbing. So we came away not with the feeling that we really felt what the victims had felt, but with a much clearer idea than we had had before.[5]

The Auschwitz Platform: to allow students to consider the arbitrary decisions made at Auschwitz and the effects on the survivors who are aware that death has only been postponed. a. The teacher should prepare a supply of blue cards and white cards; b. As each student enters the class, give him/her a white card or a blue card; c. All students holding blue cards should sit on the teacher's left; all those holding white cards should sit on the teacher's right; d. After all of the students have been seated, inform those with blue cards that they are to be exterminated and their bodies burned in the gas chambers. Those holding white cards will be allowed to live one more day at least; e. Explain what happened on the notorious platform at Auschwitz when the railroad cars delivered the prisoners to the camp and life-and-death decisions were made, depending on sex, age, strength, and the intended use of the prisoners; f. Allow the students to express their feelings about the Auschwitz platform through classroom discussion and/or writing.[6]

You are a member of the *Judenrat* [Jewish Council] in the Warsaw Ghetto. With the other members of that Council, you must select five of our people in the ghetto to be removed from the transport to a death camp. The *Judenrat* has been called into session to discuss the people who are listed below as "possible candidates" for removal and eventual extermination. . . . In your Council, decide on five people who you as the *Judenrat* will remove from the ghetto and send to the extermination camp tomorrow morning.[7]

Simulations such as these are vastly different from the typical classroom fare that most students in the United States face in their courses on a daily basis.[8] That is, such simulations move students from passive to active, literally involve student movement, and are interactive. Yet, are such activities pedagogically sound? Do they truly involve students in a solid study of the history? Do they truly provide students with accurate and deep insights into what the victims experienced? Are students left with anything more than a sense that they had "fun" during the class period? And, do such simulations avoid adding insult to the horrific injury already suffered by the survivors of the Holocaust?

Some teachers would answer with a resounding "Yes!" Hilve Fierek, who implemented one of the aforementioned simulations and is currently a professor of education at the University of North Carolina at Charlotte, offers the following argument in favor of using simulations:

. . . in some small way, I had engaged my students in actual learning . . . For a brief second, [I] helped my ninth graders find relevance in historical material they considered as removed from them as the Trojan War. If nothing else, I had them search their souls to consider if, given a choice, they would rather kill than be killed . . . I have heard much too often that what we teachers do in the classroom is not worthwhile. Most teachers I know who address the issues surrounding the Holocaust are doing the best they can to help students discover more about themselves and about the nature of human existence itself. Without an understanding of humanity, the Holocaust becomes just another footnote in history to be memorized and regurgitated on some standardized test. I choose instead to explore, with my students, why we, as human beings, make the decisions we do.[9]

Such arguments are common but, in my view, naive. They set up straw men in their unspoken assumption that the only way to engage students in an exploration of what it means to be human, and personally and socially responsible, is through game-like activities. This is not only anti-intellectual but disingenuous. As Sidney Bolkosky, a historian and co-author of the Holocaust curriculum entitled *Life Unworthy of Life,* asserts: "Nothing about the Holocaust needs dramatization."[10]

The Problems in Using Holocaust Simulations

For many scholars, educators, and survivors, there are a host of problems inherent in the use of simulations to teach about the Holocaust. These include, but are not limited to, the following: they are invariably simplistic; they frequently convey both skewed and incorrect information vis-à-vis the Holocaust; and more often than not, they are ahistorical. The simple fact is, no matter what a teacher and his/her students do in a simulation, *they will never, ever, even begin to approximate or simulate the horror that the victims suffered at the hands of the Nazis.* What is of critical importance here is that the use of such simulations often results in students believing that—at least to some extent—they do.

As for the problematic nature of using simulations to study complex human behavior for the purpose of helping students to "experience" unfamiliar situations, Totten and Feinberg argue:

> It needs to be understood that helping students in the course of a discussion or in a writing activity to explore a different perspective or to "walk in someone else's shoes" is different from involving a class in a simulation game. Likewise, conducting a simulation in order to thoroughly engage in *the study of a concept* is vastly different from conducting a simulation in order to have students "experience" what it was like for a victim to be jammed into a boxcar en route to a concentration camp or killing center or to experience what it was like to live day-in and day-out under the threat of abject brutality and death.
>
> . . . Students who use simulations only end up being exposed to an [absurdly] watered-down version of the actual situation. When applied to a study of the Holocaust, this inevitably leads to a facile over-simplification. It presents a skewed view of the history, and often serves to reinforce negative stereotypes. Indeed, in more cases than not, such simulations lead to a trivialization of the Holocaust. Such situations can also degenerate into a time of "play" that is bereft of real thinking. In the end,

students often remember the excitement of the game to the exclusion of the intended meaning of the exercises or its relationship to the history under examination.[11]

In a related line of criticism abut the use of simulations in teaching about the Holocaust, the authors (including this writer) of the *Guidelines for Teaching About the Holocaust*, developed under the auspices of the United States Holocaust Memorial Museum, note:

> Holocaust survivors and eyewitnesses are among the first to indicate the grave difficulty of finding words to describe their experiences. Even more revealing, they argue the virtual impossibility of trying to simulate accurately what it was like to live on a daily basis with fear, hunger, disease, unfathomable loss, and the unrelenting threat of abject brutality and death.
> . . . Since there a numerous primary source accounts, both written and visual, as well as survivors and eyewitnesses who can describe actual choices faced and made by individuals, groups, and nations during this period, teachers should draw upon these resources and refrain from simulations that lead to a trivialization of the subject matter.[12]

In her discussion of the use of classroom simulations to teach about the Holocaust, historian and Holocaust scholar Lucy Dawidowicz asserts:

> Besides lectures, readings, films, and discussions, most of the curricula that I examined use simulation games or role-playing to teach their moral lessons. Students play Gestapo, Concentration Camp, and Nuremberg Trial. They act out the roles of murderers, victims, judges. . . . The Jews who lived under Hitler's rule were confronted with cruel dilemmas, forced to make difficult, even impossible, choices about matters of life and death for which conscience could offer no direction and the past could give no guidance. Yet many high-school curricula frivolously suggest role-playing exercises in which students imagine how they would behave if confronted with such dilemmas. What kind of answers can come from American children who think of the Gestapo as the name of a game?[13]

Curriculum developers and teachers at all levels need to face the simple but profound fact that there is absolutely no way anyone, let alone secondary level students, will ever be able to experience the catastrophic nature of what millions went through as they were humiliated and brutalized by the Nazis. Indeed, no one can even begin to approximate, through simulations or roleplays, what it was like to be forced from one's home, crammed into a ghetto where people were literally dying in the street from disease and starvation, or be forced to undress at the lip of a ditch full of dead and direly wounded people and stand and wait until they were shot. Likewise, no one can experience the horror of being crammed into a boxcar that was either suffocatingly hot or literally freezing cold for days on end, without food or water, in which people were defecating, dying, and going mad.

As horrible as these images are, they do not even begin to approximate what the victims experienced. To illustrate the stark fact of this point, it is worth going to the victims themselves for descriptions of what they and their loved ones were subjected to during the Holocaust period.

The Power of Letting Victims and Survivors Speak for Themselves

Yitskhok Rudashevski, a fourteen-year-old Lithuanian Jew who kept a diary while incarcerated in the Vilna Ghetto from June 1941 through April 1943, recorded the following on April 6, 1943:

> The situation is an oppressive one. We now know all the horrible details. Instead of Kovno, 5,000 Jews were taken to Ponar where they were shot to death. Like wild animals before dying, the people began in mortal despair to break the railroad cars, they broke the little windows reinforced by strong wire. Hundreds were shot to death while running away. The railroad line over a great distance is covered with corpses.[14]

In early October of 1943, Rudashevski and some family members were discovered by the Nazis in their hideout and taken to Ponar, where they were all murdered.

Survivor Elie Wiesel tells this heartrending story of a mother and her two children:

> And in the city, the grand, ancient city of Kiev, stand that mother and her two children in front of some German soldiers who are laughing . . . they take one child from her and kill it before her eyes . . . then, they seize the second and kill it too . . . She wants to die; the killers prefer her to remain alive but inhabited by death . . . Then, she takes the two little bodies, hugs them against their chest and begins to dance . . . how can one describe that mother? How can one tell of her dance? In this tragedy, there is something that hurts beyond hurting—and I do not know what it is.[15]

Speaking about the nature and impact of the deportations on people, Sonja Fritz, a survivor of Auschwitz, relates the following:

> I remember very well the transports that came from Greece. Some of the staff of Block 10 had to go to the ramp to shave the hair of the new arrivals. The poor Greek girls had spent a long time in cattle cars and their hair was full of lice and so infested that we got blisters on our hands.[16]

In this recollection of arrival at a camp, a young girl speaks of her shock, horror and dismay:

> A fat S.S. woman said, "Take off everything." I think of my mother and all these strange people naked, and the German soldiers watching, and I cry. I had long, black, beautiful hair and they cut it, not even. Then into the shower, many under

one shower, very little water, and so cold. Everything happened so fast, no dress, no hair, nothing, wet and cold like an animal.[17]

Upon his arrival at Auschwitz as a thirteen-year-old boy and prisoner, Elie Wiesel was confronted with this scene:

Not far from us, flames were leaping up from a ditch, gigantic flames. They were burning something. A lorry drew up at the pit and delivered its load—little children. Babies! Yes, I saw it—saw it with my own eyes . . . those children in the flames.[18]

Speaking about a death march, survivor Reska Weiss recalls:

Urine and excreta poured down the prisoners' legs, and by nightfall the excrement, which had frozen to our limbs, gave off its stench. We were really no longer human beings in the accepted sense. Not even animals, but putrefying corpses moving on two legs.[19]

To take something so profoundly disturbing, and so overwhelming to those who lived through it, and to turn it into something that becomes for many, though certainly not all, "fun and games," is to make a mockery of what the victims lived through. No matter what teachers say in regard to the supposed efficacy of such simulations, students know full well that the simulation is an activity that will last for one class period with no harm or danger to them.

For students to walk away thinking that they have either experienced what a victim went through or have a greater understanding of what the victims suffered is shocking in its naivete. Even more galling is for teachers to think that they have provided their students with a real sense of what the victims lived through, and/or to think they have *at least approximated* the sense of horror that the victims experienced.

When one really thinks about it, Holocaust simulations are a waste of precious classroom time. This is especially true since so little time is given over to this history in our nation's classrooms. In light of the fact that teachers at all levels are constantly battling the clock and calendar in order to "cover" an overpacked curriculum, it is imperative that they use their time as wisely as possible. Thus, to attempt to teach the Holocaust over several days (which is all the time most teachers dedicate to this history), and then to do so with such simplistic devices as simulations that leave students with a skewed view of this history, simply does not make sense.

Over and above the pedagogical inappropriateness of using simulations to teach this history, there is the issue of being respectful and sensitive to both the victims and survivors of the Holocaust. Although the following comments by Elie Wiesel are directed at certain films of the Holocaust, they are equally apropos vis-à-vis the use of simulations to teach about it:

How can one "stage" a convoy of uprooted deportees being sent into the unknown, or the liquidation of thousands of men, women, and children? How can one "produce" the machine-gunned, the gassed, the mutilated corpses, when the viewer knows that they are all actors, and that after the filming they will return to the hotel for a well-deserved bath and a meal? Sure, this is true of all subject and of all film but that is also the point: *the Holocaust is not a subject like all the others. It imposes certain limits . . . in order not to betray the dead and humiliate the living, this particular subject demands a special sensibility, a different approach, a rigor, strengthened by respect and reverence and, above all, faithfulness to memory* [italics added].[20]

Still addressing the production of films on the Holocaust, Wiesel asks, "How can one explain such obscenity? How can anyone justify such insensitivity?" He goes on to state: "Newcomers to this history appoint themselves experts . . . They give the impression of knowing better than the victims or the survivors how to name what Samuel Beckett called the unnameable . . . [T]he temptation is generally reductionist, shrinking personalities to stereotypes and dialogue to cliches. All is trivial and superficial, even death itself."[21]

He concludes by asserting:

But then, the "experts" will ask, how do we transmit the message? There are other ways to do it, better ways to keep the memory alive. Today the question is not what to transmit but how. Study the texts—such as the diaries of Emanuel Ringelblum and Chaim Kaplan; the works of the historians Raul Hilberg, Lucy Dawidowicz, Martin Gilbert, Michael Marrus. Watch the documentaries, such as . . . Claude Lanzmann's *Shoah* and Haim Gouri's *81st Blow.* Listen to the survivors and respect their wounded sensibility. Open yourselves to their scarred memories, and mingle your tears with theirs. And stop insulting the dead.[22]

In Conclusion

Whether teachers like to admit it or not, by using simulations to try to provide students with a sense of what the victims of the Nazis were subjected to, they are minimizing, simplifying, distorting, and, possibly even, "denying" the complexity and horror of the Holocaust. These are strong words and accusations, but they are carefully chosen. By leaving students with even a minimal notion that they possess some sense as to what the victims went through, teachers may be inadvertently playing into the hands of those Holocaust deniers who absurdly and falsely assert that "things were not as bad as the Jews and other victims purport them to have been."

The best advice in regard to simulations intended to provide students with a sense of Holocaust history, including what the victims lived through and/or the choices that both perpetrators and victims made, is to avoid them. Instead, teachers and students should focus on examining the primary documents, the first-person accounts, the accurate and well written histories, and the best films on this subject.

At this juncture in time, when survivors of the Holocaust and liberators of the concentration and death camps are still living, a teacher could hardly do better than to provide his/her students with an opportunity to listen to and engage in discussion with one of these people. The next best avenue is to view videotapes in which survivors and liberators tell about their experiences and/or to read their accounts available in print. Such accounts, if carefully chosen, *will* leave students with something they will never forget.

NOTES

1. Holocaust.listserve, July 26, 1995.
2. Stephen Feinberg, Personal Correspondence, July 17, 1991.
3. Shared by a teacher at a workshop on Holocaust education, Washington, D.C., July 1995.
4. Hilve Fierek, "By Fifth Bell, There Were No Nazis," *Inquiry in Social Studies: Curriculum, Research, and Instruction*. The Journal of the North Carolina Council for the Social Studies, 10–11.
5. Ginger K. More, Holocaust.listserve, July 26, 1995.
6. B. J. Brewer, P. A. Bijwaard, and L. P. Payne, *Teaching the Past Describes Today . . . Tomorrow, Human Rights Education, Focus: The Holocaust* (Richmond, VA: Virginia Department of Education, 1987), 46–47.
7. New Jersey Commission on Holocaust Education, Unit IV (Trenton, NJ: New Jersey Department of Education, 1995), 49.
8. John Goodlad, *A Place Called School: Prospects for the Future* (New York: McGraw Hill, 1984).
9. Fierek, 11–12.
10. Holocaust.listserve, July 27, 1995.
11. Samuel Totten and Stephen Feinberg, "Teaching About the Holocaust: Rationale, Content, Methodology and Resources," *Social Education* 59, no. 6 (October 1995), 331–332.
12. William S. Parsons and Samuel Totten, *Guidelines for Teaching about the Holocaust* (Washington, DC: United States Holocaust Memorial Museum, 1994).
13. Lucy Dawidowicz, "How They Teach the Holocaust" in *What Is the Use of Jewish History?* (New York: Schocken Books, 1992), 71, 80.
14. Laurel Holliday, ed., "Yitskhok Rudashevski" in *Children in the Holocaust and World War II: Their Secret Diaries*. (New York: Pocket Books, 1995), 183.
15. Elie Wiesel, "Trivializing Memory," in Elie Wiesel, ed., *From the Kingdom of Memory: Reminiscences* (New York: Schocken Books, 1990), 186.
16. Quoted in Lore Shelley, *Criminal Experiments on Human Beings in Auschwitz and War Research Laboratories: Twenty Women Prisoners' Accounts* (San Francisco: Mellen Research University Press, 1991).
17. Rhoda G. Lewin, ed., *Witnesses to the Holocaust: An Oral History* (Boston: Twayne Publishers, 1990), 46.
18. Elie Wiesel, *Night* (New York: Avon Books, 1969), 42.
19. Reska Weiss, *Journey Through Hell* (London: Vallentine, Mitchell, 1961), 211.
20. Wiesel, *From the Kingdom of Memory: Reminiscences*, 167–168.
21. *Ibid.*, 170–171.
22. *Ibid.*, 171–172..

INDEX